Transubstantiation

THEOLOGY, HISTORY,

AND CHRISTIAN UNITY

Brett Salkeld

Baker Academic

a division of Baker Publishing Group

Grand Rapids, Michigan

© 2019 by Brett Salkeld

Published by Baker Academic
a division of Baker Publishing Group
PO Box 6287, Grand Rapids, MI 49516-6287
www.bakeracademic.com

Printed and bound by CPI Group (UK) Ltd, Croydon, CR0 4YY

Library of Congress Cataloging-in-Publication Data

Names: Salkeld, Brett, author.
Title: Transubstantiation : theology, history, and Christian unity / Brett Salkeld.
Description: Grand Rapids : Baker Publishing Group, 2019. | Includes bibliographical references and indexes.
Identifiers: LCCN 2018059474 | ISBN 9781540960559 (pbk.)
Subjects: LCSH: Transubstantiation—History of doctrines. | Lord's Supper—Real presence—History. | Christian union.
Classification: LCC BX2220 .S245 2019 | DDC 234/.163—dc23
LC record available at https://lccn.loc.gov/2018059474

ISBN 978-1-5409-6218-8 (casebound)

19 20 21 22 23 24 25   7 6 5 4 3 2 1

To the memory of Margaret O'Gara,
beloved *Doktormutter*, mentor, and friend.

Requiescat in pace

Contents

Foreword

Writing about a theological topic from an ecumenical perspective can be a delicate enterprise. It often involves comparing theologies that not only take contrasting positions on some important question but also function in different ways, following different norms and obeying different logics. Oppositions are only infrequently head-on; they tend to be oblique, at odd angles. Figuring out just where an opposition really lies involves interpretation, and interpretation is usually open to question.

The ecumenical inquirer is also expected to say something about the agreement or disagreement, compatibility or incompatibility of the differing theologies. The right balance of honesty, empathy, and commitment to the ecumenical cause is not easy to achieve, and any particular blend is likely to be seen by some as overlooking real differences and by others as clinging to outmoded divisions.

The conditions for the contemporary ecumenical theologian are even more fraught. The stagnation of new ecumenical developments has led to talk of an "ecumenical winter." The groundbreaking achievements of the ecumenical dialogues of the 1970s and 1980s and of such theologians as Otto Hermann Pesch and George Lindbeck have been hard to extend. A "new normal" seems to have taken hold, the intellectual possibilities for rethinking basic issues exhausted. The temptation for the theologian is either to decide fruitful work in this field is now over and move on or to attempt to force a breakthrough that contradicts the theological and ecclesiastical realities.

The Eucharist presents a particular challenge. Bitter debates erupted during the Reformation over the way in which the elements of bread and wine are and are not the body and blood of Christ and over the way the Mass is and is not a sacrifice. Medieval theology discussed the nature of Christ's presence in or as or under the eucharistic elements, at length. A broad consensus on basic assertions developed, reflected in official Church teaching, but details (e.g., just how the appearances of bread and wine related to the reality of Christ's body and blood) remained matters of dispute.

The medieval discussions were conducted in the language of the complex and sophisticated metaphysics developed by the Scholastic theologians. The medieval appropriation and radical rethinking of Aristotle as mediated by centuries of commentary was a great intellectual achievement. In the understanding of Christ's presence in the Eucharist, however, the use of this metaphysics creates a problem for the modern ecumenist. Not only did the Scholastics use technical metaphysical terms to describe this presence, but formal doctrinal statements by councils adopted some of this language, most notably the term "transubstantiation." Already in 1215, the Fourth Lateran Council used the term to describe what happens to the bread and wine of the Mass.

The ecumenist and the Catholic theologian thus face a difficult question of the hermeneutics of doctrine. On the one hand, a distinction must be made between the essential and unchanging content of the faith itself, the deposit given once and for all to the saints, and the particular language in which a doctrine is taught. While the former constitutes a core to be preserved, the latter is open to reconsideration. What is needed to state the faith in one context may be optional or even problematic in another. The Catholic West does not insist that the Orthodox East adopt the West's technical theological language as a condition of communion. The faith can be expressed in various ways, even if some ways of talking about the reality of Christ in the Eucharist must be rejected.

The particular concepts used by official doctrinal statements to make their point cannot be simply ignored, however. When the Council of Trent stated the Catholic teaching that the substance of the bread and wine become the substance of the body and blood of Christ, it added: "The Holy Catholic Church has suitably and properly [*convenienter et proprie*] called this change 'transubstantiation.'" The related canon underlines this addition when it condemns those who deny this change of the elements, "a change which the Catholic Church most appropriately [*aptissime*] calls 'transubstantiation.'" The use of such terms as "properly," "suitably," and "appropriately" does not imply that such language must be used; other terms and concepts might also be suitable, proper, and appropriate. But the council insists, as a matter of binding teaching, that the term "transubstantiation" rightly represents the faith, even if there might be other ways, linked to other conceptual schemes or forms of theological discourse, that also get at the reality described. That the language of official Catholic teaching rightly represents what occurs is thus here explicitly made a matter of official Catholic teaching. Joining together in the Eucharist does not require that all adopt this language, but it does require that this language not be rejected as misrepresenting what is going on.

Beyond the close interweaving of metaphysics and doctrine in official Catholic teaching on the presence of Christ in the Eucharist, a second ecumenical challenge lies in the close connection of how we understand that presence and aspects of concrete practice. After all, ecumenism is ultimately not about the relation between abstract theologies but about the relation between actual churches, churches whose lives involve specific practices and rituals. Some doctrines, even quite important doctrines, may be important for the Christian life, but in indirect ways. For example, the doctrine of justification, central to the Reformation, does not directly dictate or forbid many particular actions. The doctrine of the Eucharist, however, is immediately about a specific concrete practice. What is said in abstract doctrine may be bound up with practices deeply embedded in the lives of many Christians. For example, how one understands the nature of Christ's presence in relation to the elements might have implications for whether worship can be oriented toward the elements, a matter not merely of theology but of piety. It is no accident that the Council of Trent, in both its decree and its canons on the Eucharist, quickly follows its statement on transubstantiation with statements about the appropriateness of "the worship of adoration" being offered to Christ in the sacrament.

Brett Salkeld's study is an exemplary contribution to the ecumenical discussion of these difficult matters. It is alive to the difficulties and the possibilities buried in the history of these issues. Some early ecumenical dialogues (for example, the 1981 Final Report of the Anglican–Roman Catholic International Commission) sought to avoid the stalemates of the past by avoiding the vocabulary that embodied those stalemates. Such a procedure may have been an important step along the ecumenical path, and it achieved significant results, but it can leave an important question unanswered: How do the new ecumenical formulations relate to the language of the doctrinal statements of dialogue partners, statements that are still authoritative, even if to varying degrees? That question must sooner or later be addressed. Churches need to be open to new ways of thinking, but they cannot simply abandon doctrinal commitments of the past with a "that was then, this is now" wave of the hand.

Just here is where Salkeld's work is so valuable. Ecumenical discussions with Catholics on the Eucharist cannot evade the term "transubstantiation" and all that the term brings with it. Salkeld faces the issues head-on, bringing to the discussion both historical learning and ecumenical creativity and sensitivity. His proposals are carefully considered, but still provocative. Not all will agree with every detail. A strength of good theological work is that it stimulates fruitful further discussion. I myself have grown suspicious of the standard narrative in which Scotus and late medieval theology become the usual suspects to be rounded up each time we look for theological bad guys. An ecumenical theology appropriate to the present situation, however, must follow the sort of path explored by Salkeld. The stumbling blocks must be examined; perhaps for some reason we can today just walk around them, but those who went before us did not think that was possible. Books like this one by Brett Salkeld are what is needed.

Michael Root
The Catholic University of America

Preface

I once wrote a book with a title that was much too long called *Can Catholics and Evangelicals Agree about Purgatory and the Last Judgment?* Many people have teased me that the answer to that title question, presumably "no," is shorter than the title itself. This work's title, *Transubstantiation*, is at least slightly shorter, though many would suspect that the subject is at least as difficult to agree about. Indeed, there may be no other issue about which Catholics and Protestants have been so assured that they must disagree, but about which the vast majority of the ostensible disputants know so little. This is the great conundrum of transubstantiation in ecumenical dialogue: we are quite certain we disagree about a word that almost no one, Catholic or Protestant, actually understands.

This is because one of the great difficulties with transubstantiation, long before one gets to its technical elaboration, is its function as an identity marker. Accepting it is part of Catholic identity, just as rejecting it is part of Protestant identity. As we shall see in detail in chapter 1, decisions by ecumenical dialogues to avoid the term for precisely this reason backfired. They often saw the term as too loaded to be engaged productively, but its absence or marginalization in agreed statements was felt keenly by those who needed to know if the statements accepted or rejected the term strongly enough to be acceptable.

Thus the remarkable progress made by ecumenical dialogues on the question of Christ's real eucharistic presence remains incomplete. As Walter Cardinal Kasper, president emeritus of the Pontifical Council for Promoting Christian Unity, asks, taking stock of the achievements of the ecumenical movement to date, "Can consensus be found about the meaning of the term *transubstantiation* repudiated by all the Reformers, or does the rejection of this term demonstrate that a deeper difference still remains in the understanding of the real presence of the Lord?"[1] This book seeks to answer that question.

As Kasper notes, transubstantiation was universally rejected at the time of the Reformation. The rejection began in 1520 with Luther's charter document, *The Babylonian Captivity of the Church*.[2] In it, Luther decried what he called the threefold Roman captivity of the Eucharist. Interestingly, Luther felt transubstantiation to be less egregious than the other two captivities he enumerates, the withholding of the cup from the laity, and the Eucharist understood as sacrifice. Nevertheless, his rejection of it was taken up by the whole Reformation movement. Ironically, the Reformation itself would end up dividing on the question of Christ's eucharistic presence, with Luther declaring at one point, "Sooner than have mere wine with the fanatics, I would agree with the pope that there is only blood."[3]

Because of this division, both Martin Luther and, later, John Calvin (whose own rejection of transubstantiation was the more vehement) were forced to develop their own articulations of Christ's eucharistic presence in the wake of transubstantiation's rejection. It is generally recognized that these two articulations are the major competitors with transubstantiation in Western Christianity's attempt to understand Christ's presence in the Eucharist.[4] In

---

1. Walter Kasper, *Harvesting the Fruits: Basic Aspects of Christian Faith in Ecumenical Dialogue* (London: Continuum, 2009), 192. See also 205–6.

2. *The Babylonian Captivity of the Church* (1520), in *LW* 36:27–57.

3. *Confession concerning Christ's Supper* (1528), in *LW* 37:317. By "fanatics," Luther was indicating the Swiss Reformers at Zurich under the leadership of Ulrich Zwingli.

4. Virtually every book on the history of eucharistic doctrine has chapters on Thomas, Luther, and Calvin, and many articles are written precisely to compare and contrast their three articulations. See, e.g., Pope Benedict XVI, "The Problem of Transubstantiation and the Question about the Meaning of the Eucharist," in *Collected Works of Joseph Ratzinger*, ed. Michael J. Miller, trans. John Saward, Kenneth Baker, Henry Taylor, et al. (San Francisco: Ignatius, 2013), 11:218–42; Peter J. Leithart, "What's Wrong with Transubstantiation? An Evaluation of Theological Models," *Westminster Theological Journal* 53 (1991): 295–324; Egil Grislis, "The Eucharistic Presence of Christ: Losses and Gains of the Insights of St. Thomas Aquinas in the Age of the Reformation," *Consensus* 18, no. 1 (1992): 9–31. Grislis includes a section on Zwingli as well. See also Richard Cross, "Catholic, Calvinist, and Lutheran Doctrines of Eucharistic Presence: A Brief Note towards a Rapprochement," *International Journal of Systematic Theology* 4, no. 3 (2003): 301–18; John Colwell, *Promise and Presence: An Exploration of Sacramental Theology* (Milton Keynes, UK: Paternoster, 2005), 155–78; Douglas Farrow, "Between the Rock and a Hard Place: In Support of (Something like) a Reformed View of the Eucharist," *International Journal of Systematic Theology* 3, no. 2 (July 2001): 167–86; Robert W. Jenson, "Tenth Locus: The Means of Grace, Part Two: The Sacraments," in *Christian Dogmatics*, ed. Robert W. Jenson and Carl E. Braaten (Philadelphia: Fortress, 1984), 2:337–61; Karl Lehmann and Wolfhart Pannenberg, eds., *The Condemnations of the Reformation Era: Do They Still Divide?* (Minneapolis: Fortress, 1990).

order to discern the ecumenical potential of transubstantiation, then, we will need to carefully engage not only with the classic articulation of transubstantiation in the work of Thomas Aquinas, but also with the eucharistic theologies of Luther and Calvin.

Our method of proceeding will be as follows: we will begin, in the first chapter, by looking briefly at the rejection of transubstantiation in the works of Luther and Calvin (to be revisited in more depth in chaps. 3 and 4), and of its reassertion over against their concerns at the Council of Trent. Next, we will review the achievement of the ecumenical movement thus far on the question of eucharistic presence, noticing that the well-intentioned decision to marginalize the loaded term "transubstantiation" in ecumenical discussions and agreed statements is an important factor for understanding why the ecumenical movement, which achieved so much so quickly, is now stalled on this question. Then we will look at the ways in which transubstantiation is commonly misunderstood in both popular and academic discourse, finishing by investigating a key philosophical development in the High Middle Ages contributing to that misunderstanding.

In the second chapter, we will trace the historical development of the idea of transubstantiation in the context of the eucharistic controversies of the ninth and eleventh centuries, before turning to the work of Thomas Aquinas (on which Trent was heavily dependent).[5] In order to clear the ground for this work, we will first need to carefully consider two vexed questions: the theological relationship between transubstantiation and real presence, and the role of Aristotelian philosophy in Thomas's articulation. Then, after a sustained engagement with the relevant questions in Thomas's *Summa Theologiae*, this chapter ends with a look at two test cases for understanding, one medieval and one modern. With a historically informed and ecumenically sensitive reading of Aquinas on transubstantiation in hand, we can proceed to an investigation of the articulations of real presence of Martin Luther, in chapter 3, and John Calvin, in chapter 4.

Chapter 3 begins by noting that Luther's own development on the question of Christ's eucharistic presence mirrors the broad span of the Church's own development in interesting and relevant ways. At first content to simply affirm Christ's real presence on the strength of the biblical witness and without any recourse to philosophy, Luther finds himself forced by his Swiss opponents to engage philosophically in order to show that belief in Christ's presence is not simply nonsense. This is not unlike the developments in the medieval Church

---

5. John Haldane, "A Thomist Metaphysics," in *Reasonable Faith* (London: Routledge, 2010), 23.

after Berengarius. After locating the origin of Luther's philosophical work in his debates with the Swiss, the chapter assesses that work, comparing and contrasting it with transubstantiation. The last two sections of this chapter look closely at a key issue that seems to separate Luther's own views from transubstantiation—namely, the persistence of the bread and wine after the consecration.

Chapter 4 also begins by noting a historical parallel. While Luther's own development mirrors the development in the medieval Church, Calvin's position more closely mirrors that of Thomas Aquinas himself. Like Thomas, Calvin was trying to find a way to speak of Christ's eucharistic presence that both assured its realism and maintained its sacramental character. Unlike Thomas, however, Calvin was writing in a time of fragmentation and polemic, which could not but impact his work. Nevertheless, the chapter goes on to detail the remarkable similarities that many scholars of many stripes have found between the articulations of Thomas and Calvin. It then takes a look at the important roles of both the ascension and the Holy Spirit in Calvin's theology of the Eucharist, relating Calvin's treatments to both his Lutheran interlocutors and to Thomas, before concluding with a brief study of how the medieval categories of *res tantum*, *res et sacramentum*, and *sacramentum tantum* can help overcome not just the differences between Catholic and Protestants, but even between Lutherans and Reformed Christians.

Abbreviations

ARCIC Anglican–Roman Catholic International Commission
BEM   World Council of Churches. *Baptism, Eucharist, and Ministry*. Geneva: World
       Council of Churches, 1982.
CDF   Congregation for the Doctrine of the Faith
DS   *Enchiridion symbolorum, definitionum, et declarationum de rebus fidei et
       morum*. Edited by H. Denzinger and A. Schönmetzer. 33rd ed. Rome: Herder,
       1965. Available in English as *Compendium of Creeds, Definitions, and Decla-
       rations on Matters of Faith and Morals*. Edited by Peter Hünermann. 43rd ed.
       San Francisco: Ignatius, 2012.
Inst.   Calvin, John. *Institutes of the Christian Religion*. Edited by John T. McNeill.
       Translated by Ford Lewis Battles. Library of Christian Classics. Philadelphia:
       Westminster, 1960.
LW   Luther, Martin. *Luther's Works* (American edition). Edited by Jaroslav Pelikan
       and Helmut T. Lehmann. 55 vols. Philadelphia: Fortress; St. Louis: Concordia,
       1955–86. New series, vols. 56–82. St. Louis: Concordia, 2009–.
NR   Neuner, Josef, and Heinrich Roos. *The Teaching of the Catholic Church as
       Contained in Her Documents*. Staten Island: Alba House, 1967.
PCPCU Pontifical Council for Promoting Christian Unity
SCG   Thomas Aquinas, *Summa contra Gentiles*
ST   Thomas Aquinas, *Summa Theologiae*

1

Introduction

Transubstantiation in Dispute and Dialogue

Rejection of Transubstantiation

Martin Luther

As noted in the preface, the first Reformation salvo against transubstantiation was launched by Martin Luther in 1520 in his landmark *The Babylonian
Captivity of the Church*.[1] In it he listed three "captivities" in which Rome
held the Eucharist, but termed the "second captivity"—namely, the doctrine
of transubstantiation—"less grievous"[2] than the other two. Because it supported the doctrine of real presence, of which Luther was a fierce advocate,
it did not get near the measure of Luther's ire that the third and greatest
captivity, the Mass understood as a sacrifice, did.[3] Nevertheless, Luther found
transubstantiation to be philosophically incoherent and resented its imposition by Church authority. In fact, by the late Middle Ages, several theologians
were following the lead of William of Ockham, one of the founders of the
nominalist school in which Luther was educated, who had concluded that

1. It is important to note, however, that the basic direction Luther was to take here was
already indicated in his work "A Treatise on the New Testament, That Is, the Holy Mass,"
written earlier that same year. See William R. Crockett, *Eucharist: Symbol of Transformation*
(New York: Pueblo, 1989), 130–33.

2. *The Babylonian Captivity of the Church* (1520), in LW 36:28.

3. The first captivity, the withholding of the cup from the laity, is no longer standard Catholic
practice and consequently not a major ecumenical question.

1

the theory known as consubstantiation was more philosophically coherent than transubstantiation and would be preferable had the Church not officially endorsed transubstantiation at the Fourth Lateran Council (1215).[4] Luther himself references "the learned Cardinal of Cambrai,"[5] one Pierre d'Ailly (1350–1420), a student of Ockham's, as convincing him that "to hold that real bread and real wine, and not merely their accidents, are present on the altar, would be much more probable and require fewer superfluous miracles—if only the church had not decreed otherwise."[6]

Luther was willing to let transubstantiation stand as a theological opinion— though he made it clear that he found it a poor one—but not as required doctrine, arguing that the Church does not have the authority to impose such a human opinion as an article of faith. Of Thomas, whom many scholars believe Luther knew only secondhand,[7] and his view of transubstantiation, Luther wrote,

> But this opinion of Thomas hangs so completely in the air without support of Scripture or reason that it seems to me he knows neither his philosophy nor his logic. For Aristotle speaks of subject and accidents so differently from St. Thomas that it seems to me this great man is to be pitied not only for attempting to draw his opinions in matters of faith from Aristotle, but also for attempting to base them upon a man whom he did not understand, thus building an unfortunate superstructure upon an unfortunate foundation.[8]

Luther's concerns about transubstantiation were twofold. First of all, Luther was convinced that, in the doctrine of transubstantiation, philosophy was allowed to override the biblical witness. The Bible does not speak of the accidents of bread, but of bread. Recourse to such Aristotelian categories is an unnecessary distraction from the witness of the Word of God. "Moreover," Luther asserts,

4. Roch A. Kereszty, OCist, *Wedding Feast of the Lamb: Eucharistic Theology from a Historical, Biblical, and Systematic Perspective* (Chicago: Hillenbrand, 2004), 137–38. Cf. Ian Christopher Levy, "The Eucharist in the Fourteenth and Fifteenth Centuries," in *The Oxford Handbook of Sacramental Theology*, ed. Hans Boersma and Matthew Levering (Oxford: Oxford University Press, 2015), 237–38; Reinhard Hütter, "Transubstantiation Revisited: Sacra Doctrina, Dogma, and Metaphysics," in *Ressourcement Thomism: Sacred Doctrine, the Sacraments, and the Moral Life*, ed. Reinhard Hütter and Matthew Levering (Washington, DC: Catholic University of America Press, 2010), 51–52.

5. *The Babylonian Captivity of the Church* (1520), in *LW* 36:28.

6. *The Babylonian Captivity of the Church* (1520), in *LW* 36:29.

7. Charles Morerod, *Ecumenism and Philosophy: Philosophical Questions for a Renewal of Dialogue* (Ann Arbor, MI: Sapientia Press of Ave Maria University, 2006), 54.

8. *The Babylonian Captivity of the Church* (1520), in *LW* 36:29.

the church kept the true faith for more than twelve hundred years, during which time the holy fathers never, at any time or place, mentioned this transubstantiation (a monstrous word and a monstrous idea), until the pseudo philosophy of Aristotle began to make its inroads into the church in these last three hundred years [i.e., since the Fourth Lateran Council officially established transubstantiation in 1215].[9]

Second, Luther was concerned that transubstantiation failed to respect the logic of the incarnation, on which the sacrament is based. He writes that

what is true in regard to Christ is also true in regard to the sacrament. In order for the divine nature to dwell in him bodily [Col. 2:9], it is not necessary for the human nature to be transubstantiated and the divine nature contained under the accidents of the human nature. Both natures are simply there in their entirety, and it is truly said: "This man is God; this God is man." Even though philosophy cannot grasp this, faith grasps it nonetheless. And the authority of God's word is greater than the capacity of our intellect to grasp it. In like manner, it is not necessary in the sacrament that the bread and wine be transubstantiated and that Christ be contained under their accidents in order that the real body and real blood may be present. But both remain there at the same time, and it is truly said: "This bread is my body; this wine is my blood," and vice versa.[10]

For Luther, both the biblical witness and the logic of the incarnation demand the same thing, namely, that one affirm the continued reality of the bread and wine. Transubstantiation fails for him precisely because it denies their reality.

Because the medieval theory of consubstantiation, preferred by Ockham and others, affirms the continued substance of the bread and wine after the consecration (transubstantiation, alternatively, teaches that the substance of the bread and wine is precisely what has *become* the substance of the body and blood of Christ), many have referred to Luther's own view as consubstantiation. However, despite the affinity between Luther's own view and the theory of consubstantiation, Luther himself did not use the term, nor do the Lutheran confessions; and many contemporary Lutherans reject it as an accurate description of their eucharistic doctrine, preferring, for example, the term "sacramental union."[11] Luther's concern that the Roman Church had abandoned the biblical witness for philosophy meant that he was not

---

9. *The Babylonian Captivity of the Church* (1520), in *LW* 36:31.
10. *The Babylonian Captivity of the Church* (1520), in *LW* 36:35.
11. See, e.g., John R. Stephenson, *The Lord's Supper*, Confessional Lutheran Dogmatics XII (St. Louis: Luther Academy, 2003), 109.

interested in replacing one philosophical explanation with another.[12] Nevertheless, as we shall see in chapter 3, Luther was willing to have recourse to
philosophy in his debate with the Swiss, led by Zwingli, who, in Luther's view
at least, reduced the Supper to a mere mnemonic device.

John Calvin

John Calvin, a second-generation Reformer, hoped to produce an articulation of eucharistic presence that would satisfy both the Lutherans and the
Swiss, thereby preserving the unity of the Reformation communities.[13] That
this hope was disappointed is a matter of historical fact, but despite his failure
in terms of unifying the Protestant movement, Calvin's eucharistic doctrine
remains immensely important. In fact, with Lutheran realists on the one hand,
and Swiss symbolists on the other, Calvin's attempt could be understood as
an early work of ecumenism. (Indeed, he encountered that perennial bane
of ecumenists: being rejected by both sides.) Unfortunately for us, Calvin's
ecumenical sympathies did not extend beyond the communities of the Reformation. And while he could write quite sensitively, seeking the truth in the
affirmations of the two disputing parties,[14] Roman Catholic articulations,
especially about transubstantiation and sacrifice, were not generally subject
to the same sympathetic treatment.[15]

Transubstantiation is, for Calvin, "this ingenious subtlety" through which
"bread came to be taken for God."[16] Like Luther, Calvin denounces the fact
that transubstantiation denies the presence of the bread and wine after the
consecration. The Church Fathers certainly talk of a "conversion" of the elements, admits Calvin, "but they all everywhere clearly proclaim that the Sacred
Supper consists of two parts, the earthly and the heavenly; and they interpret
the earthly part to be indisputably bread and wine."[17] And, also like Luther,

12. Crockett, *Eucharist*, 134.

13. Alasdair Heron, *Table and Tradition: Towards an Ecumenical Understanding of the Eucharist* (Edinburgh: Handsel Press, 1983), 122.

14. Cf. Heron, *Table and Tradition*, 124–26. See especially Calvin's "Short Treatise on the Supper of Our Lord," in *Tracts and Treatises on the Reformation of the Church*, trans. Henry Beveridge (Grand Rapids: Eerdmans, 1958), 2:163–98.

15. Reformed theologian George Hunsinger writes, specifically with respect to the theme of sacrifice, that "by comparison with his predecessors, [Calvin] also took greater notice of Roman Catholic rebuttals, though he rejected them out of hand." Hunsinger, *The Eucharist and Ecumenism: Let Us Keep the Feast* (Cambridge: Cambridge University Press, 2008), 105.

16. John Calvin, "Book IV, Chapter xvii: The Sacred Supper of Christ, and What It Brings to Us," in *Institutes of the Christian Religion*, ed. John T. McNeill, trans. Ford Lewis Battles, vol. 2, Library of Christian Classics 21 (Philadelphia: Westminster, 1960), 1374 (13).

17. Calvin, *Inst.* 4.17:1375; cf. Jaroslav Pelikan, *The Christian Tradition: A History of the Development of Doctrine*, vol. 4, *Reformation of Church and Dogma (1300–1700)* (Chicago:

Calvin points out the relatively recent vintage of the term: "For transubstantiation was devised not so long ago; indeed not only was it unknown to those better ages when the purer doctrine of religion still flourished, but even when that purity already was somewhat corrupted."[18] Furthermore, asserts Calvin, to deprive the bread and wine of their reality is to deprive the Supper of its sacramental nature and to make of it a deception rather than a revelation:

> Christ's purpose was to witness by the outward symbol that his flesh is food; if he had put forward only the empty appearance of bread and not true bread, where would be the analogy or comparison needed to lead us from the visible thing to the invisible? For, if we are to be perfectly consistent, the signification extends no farther than that we are fed by the form of Christ's flesh. For instance, if in baptism the figure of water were to deceive our eyes, we would have no sure pledge of our washing; indeed, that false show would give us reason to hesitate. The nature of the sacrament is therefore canceled, unless, in the mode of signifying, the earthly sign corresponds to the heavenly thing. And the truth of this mystery accordingly perishes for us unless true bread represents the true body of Christ.[19]

Rather than believing in a sacrament, wherein an earthly reality represents a heavenly one, the Catholic view is, according to Calvin, the product of a "crude imagination" that views the consecration as "virtually equivalent to magic incantation."[20] "That fictitious transubstantiation for which today they fight more bitterly than for all the other articles of their faith"[21] functions precisely to obscure the essence of the sacrament. Both the superstitious common folk and the leaders of the Catholic Church "are little concerned about true faith by which alone we attain fellowship with Christ and cleave to him. Provided they have a physical presence of him, which they have fabricated apart from God's Word, they think that they have presence enough."[22] Calvin, often caricatured as a mere memorialist on the question of eucharistic presence by those who have not read him, has turned the tables here. It is the

University of Chicago Press, 1984), 197–98. Pelikan notes that "Roman Catholics cited as 'clear testimony for transubstantiation' the ambiguous formula of Irenaeus that 'the Eucharist . . . consists of two realities, earthly and heavenly.'"

18. Calvin, *Inst.* 4.17:1375 (14). Calvin later adds, "Even in Bernard's time, although a blunter manner of speaking had been adopted, transubstantiation was not yet recognized. And in all ages before this comparison flitted about on everybody's lips, that the spiritual reality is joined to bread and wine in this mystery" (*Inst.* 4.17:1377).

19. Calvin, *Inst.* 4.17:1376 (14).

20. Calvin, *Inst.* 4.17:1377 (15).

21. Calvin, *Inst.* 4.17:1374 (14).

22. Calvin, *Inst.* 4.17:1374 (13).

Catholics with their transubstantiation who have the rather bare theology of eucharistic presence, not merely memorialist, but merely physicalist. According to William Crockett, Calvin "believed that in practice, the doctrine of transubstantiation had turned the real presence of Christ into an object on the altar that placed it at the disposal of human beings. This is simply blasphemy for Calvin. God is never at our disposal. We are always at God's disposal."[23]

The Council of Trent

To all of this, the Council of Trent responded with a staunch defense of contemporaneous Roman Catholic terminology and practice. Though the council did also offer clarification at places where what was being attacked by the Reformers did not accurately reflect the teaching of the Roman Catholic Church, the canons at the end of each decree anathematizing positions contrary to those of the council are what have historically stood out most strongly.[24]

The council's thirteenth session produced the "Decree on the Most Holy Sacrament of the Eucharist," which dealt with, among other things, the question of transubstantiation. In its first two canons we find a whole range of Reformation opinion on the matter refuted:

> 1. If anyone denies that in the most holy sacrament of the eucharist there are contained truly, really and substantially, the body and blood of our lord Jesus Christ together with the soul and divinity, and therefore the whole Christ, but says that he is present in it only as in a sign or figure or by his power: let him be anathema.

> 2. If anyone says that in the venerable sacrament of the eucharist the substance of the bread and wine remains together with the body and blood of our lord Jesus Christ, and denies that marvelous and unique change of the whole substance of the bread into the body, and of the whole substance of the wine into the blood, while only the appearance of bread and wine remains, a change which the catholic church most aptly calls transubstantiation: let him be anathema.[25]

And, following a series of canons concerned with defending practices of Catholic piety such as adoring the reserved host, canon 8, continuing in the

23. Crockett, *Eucharist*, 151.

24. David N. Power, OMI, *The Eucharistic Mystery: Revitalizing the Tradition* (New York: Crossroad, 1993), 254; see also Liam G. Walsh, OP, *Sacraments of Initiation: A Theology of Life, Word, and Rite*, 2nd ed. (Chicago: Hillenbrand, 2011), 335; Kereszty, *Wedding Feast of the Lamb*, 150.

25. *Decrees of the Ecumenical Councils*, ed. Norman P. Tanner (Washington, DC: Georgetown University Press, 1990), 2:697.

spirit of canons 1 and 2, anathematizes anyone who "says that Christ, when presented in the eucharist, is consumed only spiritually, and not also sacramentally and really."[26]

It is clear enough then, that, in the sixteenth century, both the Reformers and the Roman Catholic Church made statements categorically rejecting what they took to be the position of their opponents. Nevertheless, the perceptive reader might be asking whether there was more room for agreement than we have seen presented here. Indeed, it is hoped that this brief introduction indicates both the self-assuredness of the various parties and the rancor of the debate so as to help us better understand how the question of transubstantiation came to be so intractable for so many centuries. Furthermore, the emphatic role that transubstantiation played in the writings of Luther and Calvin, and in the canons of Trent, helps to explain how it has become so central to the ecclesial identity of both Catholics, in its acceptance, and Protestants, in its rejection.[27]

But, as important as it is to understand the depth of the disagreement in the sixteenth century and the emotional weight attached to these issues down the centuries, it is also essential to note that, at many key points, the combatants were talking past each other. In a less-heated ecclesial climate, it could become clear that what each party rejected was not always what the other party affirmed and that, underlying certain articulations that looked diametrically opposed, there lay common concerns and convictions. It is because of this that, once the Roman Catholic Church entered ecumenical dialogue in earnest following the Second Vatican Council in the 1960s, convergence on the Eucharist was able to proceed quite rapidly. A brief investigation of this phenomenon is our next task.

Agreement on Transubstantiation?

Given the centrality of disputes about the Eucharist in the division of the Western Church in the sixteenth century, it is not surprising that discussion about the Eucharist would play a prominent role in contemporary ecumenical dialogue. What *is* surprising is how quickly the descendants of Trent were able to come to wide-ranging eucharistic agreement with the descendants of Luther and Calvin, and even, to a lesser degree, those of Zwingli.

26. *Decrees of the Ecumenical Councils*, 2:698.
27. Cf. Hütter, "Transubstantiation Revisited," 22; Gerard Kelly, "The Eucharistic Doctrine of Transubstantiation," in *The Eucharist: Faith and Worship*, ed. Margaret Press (Homebush, Australia: St. Pauls, 2001), 56.

With the Second Vatican Council and its decree on ecumenism, *Unitatis Redintegratio*, promulgated November 21, 1964, the Catholic Church officially entered the modern ecumenical movement. By 1967, the Lutheran–Roman Catholic dialogue in the United States had produced the agreed statement *The Eucharist as Sacrifice*. By 1971, the Anglican–Roman Catholic International Commission (ARCIC), jointly launched in 1966 by Pope Paul VI and the archbishop of Canterbury, Michael Ramsey, had put forward *An Agreed Statement on Eucharistic Doctrine*. Also in 1971, the Faith and Order Commission of the World Council of Churches (WCC) released *The Eucharist in Ecumenical Thought*, a document that drew heavily on the unofficial Group of Les Dombes dialogue between Catholics and Reformed Protestants in France and its document *Towards a Common Eucharistic Faith?*[28] By 1973 these four documents were gathered into the slim volume *Modern Eucharistic Agreement*.[29]

What the WCC affirmed of its own document could easily be applied to the other agreements: "We believe that it reflects a degree of agreement that could not have been foreseen even five years ago and that our future is bright with hope."[30] (In 1992, the Vatican itself made a similar, if more measured, judgment about the ARCIC statement. The ARCIC report, it says, "witnesses to achievement of points of convergence and even of agreement which many would not have thought possible,"[31] and that "it is in respect of *Eucharistic Doctrine* [ARCIC I had also dealt with ministry and authority] that the members of the commission were able to achieve the most notable progress toward a consensus."[32]) In fact, by 1982, less than twenty years after the Roman Catholic Church's entry into the ecumenical movement, Roman Catholic theologians had joined signatories from Eastern Orthodox, Oriental Orthodox, Old Catholic, Lutheran, Anglican, Reformed, Methodist, United, Disciples, Baptist, Adventist, and Pentecostal communities

---

28. On the relationship between these two documents, see H. R. McAdoo, "Introduction: Documents on Modern Eucharistic Agreement," in *Modern Eucharistic Agreement* (London: SPCK, 1973), 8–13.

29. ARCIC, "An Agreed Statement on Eucharistic Doctrine," in *Modern Eucharistic Agreement* (London: SPCK, 1973), 23–31; A Lutheran–Roman Catholic Statement, "The Eucharist as Sacrifice," in *Modern Eucharistic Agreement* (London: SPCK, 1973), 33–49; Faith and Order Commission of the World Council of Churches, "The Eucharist in Ecumenical Thought," in *Modern Eucharistic Agreement* (London: SPCK, 1973), 79–89; Group of Les Dombes, "Towards a Common Eucharistic Faith?," in *Modern Eucharistic Agreement* (London: SPCK, 1973), 51–78.

30. Faith and Order Commission of the World Council of Churches, "The Eucharist in Ecumenical Thought," 84.

31. CDF/PCPCU, "The Official Response of the Roman Catholic Church to ARCIC I," *One in Christ* 28 (1992): 38.

32. CDF/PCPCU, "Official Response," 39.

in recommending the publication of the WCC agreed statement *Baptism, Eucharist, and Ministry (BEM)* for the consideration of Christians throughout the world.[33]

In response to such rapid progress and ecumenical productivity, at least two questions emerge: What is the actual content of these agreements? And how were they achieved so rapidly?

A Unique Presence

One of the most remarkable things about the agreements is that several dialogues were coming to roughly the same conclusions at roughly the same time.[34] That being the case, we need not wade through each document individually, but can rather highlight several themes that can be found in most or all of them.

Perhaps the most salient point, when considering all the agreements taken together, is the universal affirmation of Christ's real presence in the Eucharist. This should not be overly surprising when we consider that neither Luther nor Calvin ever rejected real presence, though it is worth noting how quickly the Zwinglian position became marginalized in ecumenical dialogue.[35] In the past, terms such as "bare memorialism" or "crude materialism" were used to denounce the views of one's opponents. In ecumenical dialogue such terms become, instead, boundary markers for orthodoxy.[36] Those affirming real presence assure us that they subscribe to neither of these two positions. The Group of Les Dombes statement, for example, speaks of "leaving aside both the spiritualistic subjectivism that makes Christ's presence depend on the faith of the communicants (and, taken to the extreme, reduces the sign to nothing) and the materialism which sees in the things themselves—the species—the more or less magical presence of Christ."[37] For its part, the Lutheran–Roman Catholic agreement affirms "in common a rejection of a spatial or natural manner of presence, and a rejection of an understanding of the sacrament as only commemorative or figurative."[38]

---

33. *BEM*, back cover.

34. McAdoo, "Introduction," 13.

35. Indeed, it is telling to note that defenses of Zwingli today rarely take the form of arguing for eucharistic absence, but rather of arguing that Zwingli is not such a professor of absence as is popularly presumed.

36. Cf. Bruce Marshall, "The Eucharistic Presence of Christ," in *What Does It Mean to "Do This"? Supper, Mass, Eucharist*, ed. Michael Root and James J. Buckley (Eugene, OR: Cascade, 2014), 47–48.

37. Group of Les Dombes, "Towards a Common Eucharistic Faith?," 74.

38. A Lutheran–Roman Catholic Statement, "The Eucharist as Sacrifice," 40. See also Lehmann and Pannenberg, *Condemnations of the Reformation Era*, 115.

Such clarifications in the bilateral dialogues opened the way for the WCC multilateral dialogue to declare in *BEM*, paragraph 13, that

> the words and acts of Christ at the institution of the eucharist stand at the heart of the celebration; the eucharistic meal is the sacrament of the body and blood of Christ, the sacrament of his real presence. Christ fulfills in a variety of ways his promise to be always with his own even to the end of the world. But Christ's mode of presence in the eucharist is unique. Jesus said over the bread and wine of the eucharist: "This is my body. . . . This is my blood . . ." What Christ declared is true, and this truth is fulfilled every time the eucharist is celebrated. The Church confesses Christ's real, living and active presence in the eucharist. While Christ's real presence in the eucharist does not depend on the faith of the individual, all agree that to discern the body and blood of Christ, faith is required.[39]

Sacrifice?

More surprising than agreement on presence, which had been explicitly affirmed by several prominent Reformers and the communities that followed them, was the concomitant agreement on sacrifice, which had been rejected by every Reformer and Protestant community. The agreement was "concomitant" because it was intimately linked with the idea that the Christ who becomes present in the Lord's Supper is none other than the crucified and risen—that is, *sacrificed*—Lord, who had instituted the Eucharist precisely as a memorial of his sacrifice. Christ's presence was the presence of his sacrifice. The key development here was the rediscovery of the depth of the biblical term for memorial, *anamnesis*. Whereas "memorial of sacrifice" and "sacrifice" had previously been understood as exclusive terms, biblical scholarship had demonstrated that *anamnesis* meant much more than simple remembrance.

The Protestant rejection of the Eucharist as sacrifice was largely based on concerns that it took away from the once-and-for-all (expressed by the Greek term *ephapax*) nature of Christ's sacrifice on the cross. Many Catholic articulations of eucharistic sacrifice seemed to Protestants to require a re-sacrificing of Christ in every Mass, something clearly rejected by Scripture. The deadlock was broken when it became clear that, as the great Catholic ecumenist Jean-Marie Tillard, OP, explains,

> *memorial*, in its biblical connotation, completely excludes any repetition of the event it is commemorating and any idea that the ritual celebration of the event is merely commemorative. To discern in the Eucharist the *memorial* of

---

39. *BEM*, 12.

the Passover demands, therefore, that we maintain and venerate the *ephapax*, in respect of time and formal content, of the sacrifice of Jesus, and at the same time affirm the presence *en musterio* (*in sacramento*) of this *ephapax* in the ritual of the liturgical banquet. The Eucharist is not something added on to the Passover and yet it is no hollow image or mere symbol of it. The category of *sacramental existence*, defined as a real mode of being but not pertaining to the natural order, entirely dependent on the power of the Spirit, takes full and precise account of this situation. Nevertheless, the notion of *memorial*, makes it clear that this "sacramental" presence is not simply to be restricted to the presence of the Body and Blood of the Lord. It includes all that is contained within the paschal mystery.[40]

With this recovery, the relationship between the cross and the Eucharist was able to be articulated in ways that satisfied both the Catholic concern for identity and the Protestant concern for distinction. It became clear from the scriptural sources themselves that the relationship was, in a word, sacramental. As the Lutheran theologian Robert Jenson writes, "The eucharist *is sacramentally* whatever it is; if it is a sacrifice, it is sacramentally and not otherwise a sacrifice, and its interpretation as sacrifice must be interior to its interpretation as sacrament."[41]

Thus, the members of ARCIC could declare together that

Christ's redeeming death and resurrection took place once and for all in history. Christ's death on the cross, the culmination of his whole life of obedience, was the one, perfect and sufficient sacrifice for the sins of the world. There can be no repetition of or addition to what was then accomplished once for all by Christ. Any attempt to express a nexus between the sacrifice of Christ and the eucharist must not obscure this fundamental fact of the Christian faith. Yet God has given the eucharist to his Church as a means through which the atoning work of Christ on the cross is proclaimed and made effective in the life of the Church. The notion of *memorial* as understood in the Passover celebration at the time of Christ—i.e., the making effective in the present of an event in the past—has opened the way to a clearer understanding of the relationship between Christ's sacrifice and the eucharist. The Eucharistic memorial is no mere calling to mind of a past event or

40. J. M. R. Tillard, OP, "Roman Catholics and Anglicans: The Eucharist," *One in Christ* 9, no. 2 (1973): 144.
41. Robert W. Jenson, *Unbaptized God: The Basic Flaw in Ecumenical Theology* (Minneapolis: Fortress, 1992), 35. Jenson points out in a footnote that this was "Thomas Aquinas's starting point, *Summa Theologiae* III, 79,7. 'This sacrament is not only a sacrament but also a sacrifice. For *in that* in this sacrament the passion of Christ is represented . . . it has *also* the character of sacrifice'" (emphasis added).

of its significance, but the Church's effectual proclamation of God's mighty acts.[42]

It is remarkable to compare this statement to what the wholly independent Group of Les Dombes concluded at almost exactly the same time:

> Christ instituted the eucharist as a memorial (*anamnesis*) of his whole life and above all of his cross and resurrection. Christ, with everything he has accomplished for us and for all creation, is present himself in this memorial, which is also a foretaste of his Kingdom. The memorial, in which Christ acts through the joyful celebration of his Church, implies this re-presentation and anticipation. Therefore it is not only a matter of recalling to mind a past event or even its significance. The memorial is the effective proclamation by the Church of the great work of God. By its communion with Christ, the Church participates in this reality from which it draws its life.[43]

Again, it was the success of the bilateral agreements that paved the way for *BEM* to be able to state, in paragraph 8,

> The eucharist is the sacrament of the unique sacrifice of Christ who ever lives to make intercession for us. It is the memorial of all that God has done for the salvation of the world. What it was God's will to accomplish in the incarnation, life, death and resurrection and ascension of Christ, God does not repeat. These events are unique and can neither be repeated nor prolonged. In the memorial of the eucharist, however, the Church offers its intercession in communion with Christ, our great High Priest.[44]

Two false dichotomies that were at the root of pre-ecumenical polemics were thus overcome. With regard to eucharistic presence it was now affirmed by all involved that Christ *really* is present—that is, his presence is objectively given *to* the Church and not simply represented symbolically *by* the Church. At the same time, all affirmed that such an objectively given presence was not at all natural, material, physical, or magical. It was precisely *sacramental*, and thus operated at a different, deeper level of reality than the one presupposed and implied by such terms. With regard to eucharistic sacrifice, Christians were now able to affirm together that Christ's sacrifice on the cross really was unique, unrepeatable, and once-for-all, while at the same time acknowledging that that unique sacrifice was made really present to the Christian community

42. ARCIC, "An Agreed Statement on Eucharistic Doctrine," 27.
43. Group of Les Dombes, "Towards a Common Eucharistic Faith?," 58.
44. *BEM*, 11.

in the celebration of the Eucharist. And both these dichotomies were overcome with the help of the biblical concept of *anamnesis*, which made clear that what Jesus intended at the Last Supper, where he would have used the Hebrew equivalent, *zikkaron*, was a memorial like the Jewish Passover, which made God's mighty acts present to the celebrating community without threatening the unique and unrepeatable status of those acts.[45]

Contextualizing Presence and Sacrifice

It is interesting to note that, despite their centrality in the division of the Church, presence and sacrifice don't even get their own sections in *BEM*. The Eucharist section of *BEM* has three parts: I. The Institution of the Eucharist; II. The Meaning of the Eucharist; and III. The Celebration of the Eucharist. The Meaning of the Eucharist is the longest part, and it has five subsections: A. The Eucharist as Thanksgiving to the Father; B. The Eucharist as Anamnesis or Memorial of Christ; C. The Eucharist as Invocation of the Spirit; D. The Eucharist as Communion of the Faithful; and E. The Eucharist as Meal of the Kingdom. As might be expected from the explanation given above, both presence and sacrifice are dealt with in subsection II.B, The Eucharist as Anamnesis or Memorial of Christ. Now it could certainly be argued that this was the most important section of the *Eucharist* document. And I think it is clear that this section generated the most response from the Churches in their official responses to *BEM*.[46] Nevertheless, it is important to note that, while controversy about the Eucharist has centered on these two issues, the meaning of the Eucharist itself is not confined to them (though all the meanings are, of course, interdependent).

By highlighting other essential aspects of eucharistic meaning, *BEM* was able to contextualize the debates about presence and sacrifice. First of all, it contextualized them by showing that, despite our vehement disputes about these issues, there is much about the Eucharist that continues to unite the various Christian communities. Second, the value of these two doctrines is certainly clearer when they are not artificially isolated and debated without reference to the rest of eucharistic theology. One example can serve to make this point. The role of the Holy Spirit, emphasized in section II.C, The

45. Tillard, "Roman Catholics and Anglicans," 143. See also Jorge A. Scampini, OP, "The Sacraments in Ecumenical Dialogue," in *The Oxford Handbook of Sacramental Theology*, ed. Hans Boersma and Matthew Levering (Oxford: Oxford University Press, 2015), 680.

46. *Churches Respond to BEM*, vols. 1–6 (Geneva: World Council of Churches, 1986–). *Churches Respond to BEM* is a six-volume series edited by Max Thurian and published by the World Council of Churches. It is common practice to refer to it by naming the responding Church, the volume in the series and the page number.

Eucharist as Invocation of the Spirit, helped many Churches to better appreciate what was and was not being affirmed by the articulation of real presence.[47] This passage, in paragraph 14, was especially helpful:

> The bond between the Eucharistic celebration and the mystery of the Triune God reveals the role of the Holy Spirit as that of the One who makes the historical words of Jesus present and alive. Being assured by Jesus' promise in the words of institution that it will be answered, the Church prays to the Father for the gift of the Holy Spirit in order that the Eucharistic event may be a reality: the real presence of the crucified and risen Christ giving his life for all humanity.[48]

The response from the Evangelical Church of the Augsburg Confession in the Socialist Republic of Romania demonstrates very clearly just how this section helped to undergird the agreement on presence:

> We welcome the emphasis on the activity of the Holy Spirit, since this makes it clear that the church has no control over the gifts of the sacrament but prays for the presence of God. In this connection, we are delighted with the emphasis on the real presence of Christ in the Lord's supper. We thereby affirm our repudiation of any magical or mechanical view of Christ's presence in the eucharist.[49]

The Anglican Church of Canada felt that "the emphasis on *epiclesis* not only restores the importance of the role of the Holy Spirit in the operation of the sacraments, but also makes it clear that the sacraments are prayer-actions and not mechanical means of grace."[50]

A Change of Attitude

In our brief survey of the content of ecumenical agreement on the Eucharist, we have already, unavoidably, started to answer our second question— namely, "What made such rapid convergence possible?" A recovery of the biblical notion of *anamnesis* and the situating of the critical issues of presence and sacrifice within a broader theological context were certainly proximate

---

47. William Tabbernee, "BEM and the Eucharist: A Case Study in Ecumenical Hermeneutics," in *Interpreting Together: Essays in Hermeneutics*, ed. Peter Bouteneff and Dagmar Heller (Geneva: WCC Publications, 2001), 36; Geoffrey Wainwright, "The Eucharist in the Churches' Responses to the Lima Text," *One in Christ* 25, no. 1 (1989): 59–60; Egil Grislis, "Eucharistic Convergence in Ecumenical Debate: An Intimation of the Future of Christianity?," *Toronto Journal of Theology* 6, no. 2 (1990): 256–57.

48. *BEM*, 13.

49. Quoted in Tabbernee, "BEM and the Eucharist," 36.

50. Quoted in Grislis, "Eucharistic Convergence," 256.

factors in this convergence. But other, less immediate, though no less important, factors were also at work.

The first thing worth noting is that the reason rapprochement seemed so impossible in the first place is that interconfessional polemics had made our differences look bigger than they actually were. Anglican bishop R. P. C. Hanson notes that rejections of "localized" presence or "physico-chemical" change "might by short-sighted persons be regarded as concessions by Roman Catholics, were it not that they are not difficult to reconcile with Roman Catholic doctrine."[51] Such a statement demonstrates that what we had spent much of five hundred years denouncing were not our opponents' actual positions, but caricatures of those positions. What was necessary to make that apparent was a change of attitude, not of doctrine.

This conclusion is backed up very forcefully by a careful study undertaken in Germany by Catholic, Lutheran, and Reformed theologians, which found that "the [sixteenth-century] condemnations which are directed at the theology of the Real Presence no longer apply to today's partner and have become null and void."[52] A reading of this fascinating document makes clear that, while real differences existed at the time of the Reformation and continue to exist today, much of our ostensible disagreement on the theology of the Eucharist was a result of talking past one another. In this regard, it is worth quoting Bishop Hanson's apposite observation: "It is a surprising but incontestable fact that today the theologians find it easier to agree than any other ecclesiastical group," because "unlike other Christians, they know too much to be divided by anything less than the truth."[53]

Of course, it was not always the case that theologians of different traditions were more likely than the rest of the faithful to agree with one another. In fact, "a century ago it was generally assumed that in any attempt of divided Christian bodies to come closer to each other the difficulties and obstacles would be provided by the theologians, whereas the ordinary rank-and-file would not find it difficult to understand each other."[54] This too speaks to the importance of a changed climate. When the basic stance of separated Christians is to maintain their identities by demonstrating the heresies of the other group, theologians will be the biggest obstacles to unity because they will be the best equipped for making such attacks. When, on the other hand, that basic stance changes to one of seeking mutual understanding, the

51. R. P. C. Hanson, "Eucharistic Agreement: An Ecumenical and Theological Consensus," in *A Critique of Eucharistic Agreement* (London: SPCK, 1975), 27.
52. Lehmann and Pannenberg, *Condemnations of the Reformation Era*, 116.
53. Hanson, "Eucharistic Agreement," 33.
54. Hanson, "Eucharistic Agreement," 33.

theologians will again be in the vanguard, being the most equipped to find real commonality under the layers of polemic and identity assertion that have built up over the centuries.

It seems, then, that underneath ecumenical agreement based on careful scholarship—as demonstrated, for example, by the recovery of the meaning of *anamnesis* by biblical scholars—the deeper cause of our rapid progress was a change in attitude. The modern world provided at least two goads in that direction. First of all, Christians in the modern world are more likely to move among Christians of different traditions in their daily life. Such intercommunication is the bane of caricature. Second, in an increasingly post-Christian culture, Christians of different traditions are more able to see one another as allies than as enemies.[55] As is well known, the beginning of the ecumenical movement was in the mission fields, where Christians of various Churches encountered one another and came to see the scandal of their division more clearly in non-Christian contexts. That the modern West is now essentially mission territory has done much to change the attitudes that separated Christians in that part of the world have toward one another.

It is certainly the case that, spurred on by such cultural factors, and enlivened by the efforts of a good many theologians and other Christians, the ecumenical movement has radically changed the face of Christianity. And eucharistic agreement is among the most impressive of its achievements. Nevertheless, the perceptive reader might be wondering if this is really the whole story. As remarkable as it was that a document like *BEM* could be produced within twenty years of Vatican II, the reverse of this coin is the fact that *BEM* is now almost forty years old, and relatively little has happened in terms of eucharistic agreement since. The early dialogues moved very quickly because so much of our disagreement was illusory. It did not take long for honest, industrious, and intelligent theologians to clear up many basic issues once the climate was right.

More Work to Do

On the other hand, we must note that the Churches are still divided, and that they are still divided on the question of the Eucharist. The average Catholic and the average Protestant still hold one another's eucharistic theologies in suspicion, or at least this is true among those with a basic awareness of their own Church's views. I suggest that there are a few factors at play here. For one thing, many Christians are simply unaware of the level of agreement

---

55. Both these ideas are presented in R. R. Williams, "Agreements: Their Sources and Frontiers," in *A Critique of Eucharistic Agreement* (London: SPCK, 1975), 18–19.

that has been possible. Others, aware that agreements have been signed, are suspicious of the contents of such agreements. Finally, despite the enormous strides made, the agreements themselves do not claim to be complete. Work remains to be done.

Transubstantiation, in particular, remains a stumbling block for ecumenical dialogue. While virtually every Christian community involved in ecumenical dialogue affirms Christ's eucharistic presence in some manner or other beyond the merely symbolic, Cardinal Kasper is correct to note that the lack of consensus on the term "transubstantiation" may well indicate deeper differences about real presence. At the very least, the role that the term plays in ecclesial identity formation will make it difficult for Christians to recognize the depth of their agreement on real presence as long as the question of transubstantiation remains unresolved. Before we begin our investigation of transubstantiation in earnest, then, it is important to look at three factors that have made consensus about the term itself difficult.

First of all, the ecumenical movement has, in general, avoided addressing it directly in its agreed statements. Consensus on transubstantiation per se was seen as unnecessary and fraught with controversy and was, therefore, eschewed in favor of (the relatively much easier) agreement about real presence. One reason, though it is only one, that consensus about transubstantiation has proved difficult is because it has not been attempted.[56] The dialogues were right, of course, that transubstantiation would be a very difficult issue on which to find consensus. We have already seen that the term is loaded with issues of ecclesial identity. We can now add that a further difficulty is that the term itself is esoteric and widely misunderstood—by both its proponents and its critics and in both popular and academic circles. Our second task in what follows is to look briefly at the nature of those misunderstandings. Third, those misunderstandings are rooted, to a large degree, in a radical shift in the dominant philosophical framework of Christian theology in Western Europe between the time of Thomas Aquinas and the Reformation. The emergence of nominalism by the late Middle Ages ensured that what the term "transubstantiation" meant for Luther and Calvin was quite different from what it had meant for Thomas Aquinas. What they, and all the Reformers with them, rejected was not what Thomas had affirmed.

---

56. I am speaking here of the publicly agreed statements of ecumenical dialogues, not of the work of the theologians in coming to these agreements. Many dialogues have, of course, dealt with transubstantiation "behind closed doors." But if they came to agreement there, this was not generally made explicit in the final public statements. The Christian people could not easily see the relationship between their own acceptance or rejection of transubstantiation and the agreements of the dialogues on real presence.

The Marginalization of "Transubstantiation"

It has been, by and large, the practice of the ecumenical movement, in its official documents, if not in its closed-door discussions, to ignore or marginalize the term "transubstantiation." And, indeed, some have lauded this decision as a move beyond what divides us. The Church of North India, in its official response to *BEM*, for instance,

> appreciates this statement for its careful avoidance of such controversial terms as "transubstantiation," "transignification," etc., and focuses attention on the central significance and experiential aspect of the Eucharist in terms of the "real presence" of Christ in this sacrament, which is likely to be acceptable to most of the WCC member Churches as a common understanding of the Eucharist.[57]

For its part, the ARCIC Agreed Statement on Eucharistic Doctrine chose to treat transubstantiation in a footnote, which read,

> The word *transubstantiation* is commonly used in the Roman Catholic Church to indicate that God acting in the eucharist effects a change in the inner reality of the elements. The term should be seen as affirming the *fact* of Christ's presence and of the mysterious and radical change which takes place. In contemporary Roman Catholic theology it is not understood as explaining *how* the change takes place.[58]

While we can leave a more careful parsing of this note for the next chapter, what is important for us here is that this attempt to downplay controversial and loaded terminology failed. In the *Elucidation* that followed the *Agreed Statement* in 1979, the commission noted that, in many of the responses it received,

> the word *become* has been suspected of expressing a materialistic conception of Christ's presence, and this has seemed to some to be confirmed in the footnote on the word *transubstantiation* which also speaks of *change*. It is feared that this suggests that Christ's presence in the eucharist is confined to the elements, and that the Real Presence involves a physical change in them.[59]

But it does not seem to be the case that a simple avoidance of the term would have solved ARCIC's problems, and, indeed, we will see that it did

---

57. Quoted in Wainwright, "Eucharist in the Churches' Responses to the Lima Text," 56–57. See also Scampini, "Sacraments in Ecumenical Dialogue," 680.

58. ARCIC, "An Agreed Statement on Eucharistic Doctrine," 31n2.

59. ARCIC, "Eucharistic Doctrine: Elucidation (1979)," in *The Final Report* (Washington, DC: US Catholic Conference, 1982), 20–21.

not solve *BEM*'s. Apparently expressing concern from a different direction, the Congregation for the Doctrine of the Faith (CDF) observed that "certain . . . formulations . . . do not seem to *indicate adequately* what the church understands by 'transubstantiation.'"[60] One suspects that both those who reject transubstantiation and those who accept it would have benefited from seeing it spelled out in more detail in the document, if for slightly different reasons.

And here, perhaps, is the most interesting twist: it may seem that the CDF—which wants an affirmation of transubstantiation, or at least of "what the church understands by [it]"—and those concerned that transubstantiation indicates a physical change—and therefore seek its repudiation—are approaching the document from diametrically opposed points of view; in point of fact, however, they are not. Rather, any formulations that actually do indicate "what the church understands by 'transubstantiation'" should reassure, rather than scandalize, those who are concerned that the term indicates a physical change. It would seem that the decision to avoid or marginalize the term actually created anxiety about it, while a decision to address it head-on would have relieved such anxiety.

I suspect that no one who reads ARCIC member Jean-Marie Tillard's eloquent exposition of transubstantiation in his article "Roman Catholic and Anglicans: The Eucharist"[61] will doubt that the commission had the capacity to address it head-on in a way that would have satisfied both the CDF and those Protestants concerned that transubstantiation indicates a physical change and a materialistic conception of presence. Instead, however, a rather lengthy back-and-forth between the commission and the CDF was required to convince Rome of the commission's intentions. And, though it eventually succeeded, the process surely left many feeling betrayed, hurt, and confused, as we shall see.

Adequately Indicated?

That the initial *Agreed Statement on Eucharistic Doctrine* was ambiguous is demonstrated by the fact that, while some evangelical Anglicans could write the commission with their concerns that the word "become," buttressed by the transubstantiation footnote, indicated a material presence and a physical

60. CDF/PCPCU, "Observations on the ARCIC Final Report," *Origins* 11 (May 6, 1982): 754 (emphasis added).

61. Tillard, "Roman Catholics and Anglicans," 171–78. This is an example of a commission doing excellent work "behind closed doors" but not displaying that work for the broader public in their official statements.

change, Bishop R. R. Williams, from that same wing of the Anglican Church, could write that

> what finally emerges is something very different from anything like transubstan-
> tiation (a subject reduced to a small footnote in the Anglican-Roman Catholic
> *Agreed Statement*) and it is not particularly like what one might call the Anglo-
> Catholic substitute for transubstantiation. Nor is it very much like the Lutheran
> doctrine of consubstantiation. The agreement rests on an assurance that Christ
> himself is really present and that the words of consecration (to use an old-
> fashioned form of expression) are still divinely authorized and spiritually valid.[62]

On Williams's reading of the document, the CDF is quite right to be concerned that Catholics might want reassurance. Catholics certainly wouldn't
sign up for "something very different from anything like transubstantiation."
On the other hand, many Catholics, especially those who have studied the
doctrine, would find that what Williams asserts in his last sentence here is,
in fact, *particularly like* transubstantiation.[63] And, if I may be so bold as to
speak for Lutheran readers, they too would affirm that the heart of their
eucharistic doctrine (whether they would use the term "consubstantiation"
or prefer something like "sacramental union") rests precisely on the idea
"that Christ is really present and that the words of consecration . . . are still
divinely authorized and spiritually valid."[64]

The commission was now faced with two, even three, groups. There were,
on the one hand, Catholics needing reassurance that what their Church understands by "transubstantiation" had been "indicated adequately." And there
were Anglicans, some of whom were worried that "transubstantiation" had
been allowed in through the back door and others who were grateful that it
had been marginalized! Neither of these latter groups, however, demonstrated
any knowledge about what the term in question actually means. But the commission, in its *Elucidation*, chose not to directly address the issue of transubstantiation. Instead, it wrote that

> *becoming* does not here imply material change. Nor does the liturgical use
> of the word imply that the bread and wine become Christ's body and blood
> in such a way that in the eucharistic celebration his presence is limited to the

---

62. Williams, "Agreements: Their Sources and Frontiers," 17.

63. See, e.g., Joseph Wawrykow, "Luther and the Spirituality of Thomas Aquinas," *Consensus* 19, no. 1 (1993): 89. For a recent Catholic articulation of transubstantiation that comes
remarkably close to defining transubstantiation in just this way, see Marshall, "Eucharistic
Presence of Christ."

64. See, e.g., *The Babylonian Captivity of the Church* (1519), in *LW* 36:30.

consecrated elements. It does not imply that Christ becomes present in the eucharist in the same manner that he was present in his earthly life. It does not imply that this *becoming* follows the physical laws of this world. What is here affirmed is a sacramental presence in which God uses the realities of this world to convey the realities of the new creation: bread for this life becomes the bread of eternal life. Before the eucharistic prayer, to the question: "What is that?," the believer answers: "It is bread." After the eucharistic prayer, to the same question he answers: "It is truly the body of Christ, the Bread of Life."[65]

Now, it must be said that this is a very satisfying paragraph to a Catholic.[66] In point of fact, it is a fairly good introduction to the meaning of "transubstantiation." On the other hand, it must also be said that, because the term itself goes unmentioned, it does not clear up the confusion about "transubstantiation" evident after the *Agreed Statement*. Does this explanation of "becoming," shorn of any connection with "transubstantiation," indicate that the commission is moving away from "transubstantiation"? The Catholic (not to mention the Anglican!) still doesn't know whether the term "transubstantiation" is avoided because it is being somehow repudiated, and the Anglican (not to mention the Catholic!) still doesn't know if "transubstantiation" implies material change, even if "becoming" doesn't. And neither the Anglican nor the Catholic is given the clear impression that Bishop Williams's contention—that "an assurance that Christ himself is really present and that the words of consecration . . . are still divinely authorized and spiritually valid" is "something very different from anything like transubstantiation"[67]—is, in fact, seriously mistaken. Had the commission adverted to the fact that the above-quoted paragraph aligns very precisely with what Catholics actually mean by "transubstantiation," both the Catholic and the Anglican reader could have been reassured.

It is interesting to note that, in its *Official Response*, the CDF also chooses to avoid the term "transubstantiation," though its concern that certain affirmations by the commission "are insufficient . . . to remove all ambiguity regarding the mode of real presence which is due to a substantial change in the elements,"[68] clearly demonstrates a concern to "indicate adequately what the church understands by [it]."[69] This insistence on the part of the CDF was not taken kindly by many in the ecumenical sphere, to whom it

65. ARCIC, "Eucharistic Doctrine: Elucidation (1979)," 21.
66. Cf. CDF/PCPCU, "Official Response," 39.
67. Williams, "Agreements: Their Sources and Frontiers," 17.
68. CDF/PCPCU, "Official Response," 43.
69. CDF/PCPCU, "Observations," 754.

sounded "as though non-Catholics are being asked for one-hundred percent agreement to the doctrines and practices of the Catholic Church," and "like a milder, toned-down version of the 'ecumenism of return.'"[70] The archbishop of Canterbury, George Carey, in his comments on the Roman Catholic *Official Response*, diplomatically (or not so diplomatically!) suggested that "in the case of the Roman Catholic Response, however, the question to our two Communions appears to have been understood as asking: 'Is *The Final Report* identical with the teachings of the Roman Catholic Church?'"[71] And the veteran Catholic ecumenist Francis Sullivan opined that "if the Vatican is going to continue to apply the criteria which it has used in judging the work of ARCIC-I, then I fear that the ecumenical dialogues in which the Catholic Church is involved have a rather unpromising future ahead of them."[72]

While I believe there is some merit to these concerns (for instance, Sullivan makes the important point that the Vatican Response gives the impression of criticizing ARCIC for not achieving things that ARCIC never claimed to achieve),[73] I cannot agree with Sullivan's conclusion that "what the CDF would require of an agreed dialogue statement is that it fully correspond to Catholic doctrine, and that, to do so, it must use the language in which the Roman Catholic Church has expressed that doctrine."[74]

The Rank and File

In fact, following one further clarification, Cardinal Cassidy indicated that the "appropriate dicasteries" (presumably the CDF and the Pontifical Council for Promoting Christian Unity [PCPCU]) found that the agreement reached by ARCIC I "is thus greatly strengthened, and no further study would seem to be required at this stage."[75] It is important for our purposes to look at what that final clarification had to say, specifically about transubstantiation:

70. Jeffrey T. VanderWilt, *A Church without Borders: The Eucharist and the Church in Ecumenical Perspective* (Collegeville, MN: Liturgical Press, 1998), 110. Cf. David Brown, "The Response to ARCIC-I: The Big Questions," *One in Christ* 28 (1992): 148–54; Gillian R. Evans, "Rome's Response to ARCIC and the Problem of Confessional Identity," *One in Christ* 28 (1992): 155–67.

71. George Carey, "Comments of the Archbishop of Canterbury on the Response of ARCIC-I," *One in Christ* 28 (1992): 48 (boldface original).

72. Francis A. Sullivan, "The Vatican Response to ARCIC-I," *One in Christ* 28 (1992): 231.

73. Sullivan, "Vatican Response," 225–26.

74. Sullivan, "Vatican Response," 228.

75. Cardinal Edward Cassidy, "Letter to the Co-chairs of ARCIC-II (March 11, 1994)," *Origins* 24 (October 6, 1994): 299.

Paul VI in *Mysterium Fidei* (AAS 57, 1965) did not deny the legitimacy of fresh ways of expressing this change even by using new words, provided that they kept and reflected what transubstantiation was intended to express. This has been our method of approach. In several places the Final Report indicates its belief in the presence of the living Christ truly and really in the elements. Even if the word *transubstantiation* only occurs in a footnote, the Final Report wished to express what the Council of Trent, as evident from its discussion, clearly intended by the use of the term.[76]

Why, after a back-and-forth of over two decades, did this seem to be enough for Rome? While some would suggest that the CDF finally browbeat ARCIC, and particularly the Anglican members of it, into a virtual acceptance of "transubstantiation,"[77] I want to suggest a different hermeneutic.

As we have already seen, transubstantiation, in its affirmation or denial, is an important identity marker for both Catholics and Protestants, even while many people in both groups do not clearly understand what the term entails. In such a context, the failure to address it explicitly is bound to rouse suspicion, not primarily in the Vatican, but among the faithful themselves, many of whom are suspicious that ecumenical dialogue is a matter of watering down the faith, or compromising truth for the sake of unity. And, it must be added, that by "the faithful," I do not mean merely the Catholic faithful. As is clearly indicated by the overview that ARCIC gives in the 1979 *Elucidation*, both Catholics and Anglicans were suspicious: worry was expressed that *anamnesis* was both too strong and too weak; concern was evident that Christ's presence, as expressed in the *Agreed Statement*, was both too real, and not real enough.[78] Those who wondered whether the "commission has been using new theological language which evades unresolved differences"[79] wanted to know whether there was a clear enough affirmation/denial of transubstantiation.

That the Christian people will not, by and large, accept agreed statements where they do not find their own faith articulated in the language in which they were formed is an essential consideration for ecumenism. It is not, I would suggest, a matter of the Vatican insisting on the language of the Catholic tradition for its own sake, but rather a recognition that, if the results of ecumenical dialogue are to take root among the Christian people, those people must be able to be clear that what a document is affirming is synonymous with their

76. ARCIC II, "Clarifications of Certain Aspects of the Agreed Statements on Eucharist and Ministry," *Origins* 24 (October 6, 1994): 302.

77. Cf. VanderWilt, *A Church without Borders*, chap. 4: "Ecumenism at Risk," esp. 109–13.

78. ARCIC, "Eucharistic Doctrine: Elucidation (1979)," 17–18.

79. ARCIC, "Eucharistic Doctrine: Elucidation (1979)," 18.

faith. It is not the case that the Vatican requires its dialogue partners to use Catholic language before agreement can be reached, though it is easy to see why many frustrated ecumenists have come to this conclusion. It is something rather more subtle, as careful attention to the CDF's language will indicate. As already related above, the Vatican's first response to ARCIC, its *Observations*, did not ask that "transubstantiation" be affirmed, but that "what the church understands by [it]" be *adequately indicated*.[80] This is actually a difference of some consequence.

It is undeniably the case that "transubstantiation" is a widely misunderstood term. But it is also undeniably the case that Catholics (or at least many Catholics) will not be convinced by any agreed statement that does not affirm it; and Protestants (or at least many Protestants) will not be convinced by any agreed statement with Catholics that does not deny it. What possible way forward can there be when one group insists on a certain term's affirmation while another group insists on its denial, and the vast majorities in both groups don't know what the term means? It seems to me that, in such a situation, someone must "adequately indicate what the church understands by 'transubstantiation.'" Without that, any agreement made by professional theologians seems unlikely to resonate with the Christian people.

It is certainly true that one can profess the perennial faith of the Christian Church regarding Christ's eucharistic presence without recourse to the term "transubstantiation." As many rightly point out, the term did not exist for the first thousand-plus years of Christianity, and Rome recognizes the Church's eucharistic faith in the Eastern Churches even when they do not make use of it. Nevertheless, it is important to note that neither the Church of the first millennium nor the Churches of the East have a rejection of transubstantiation in their foundational documents or their communal identity. When a term or concept has been the subject of controversy between two communities, it cannot be ignored or passed over in the same way as between two communities in which the issue never arose. What the Roman Catholic Church understands by "transubstantiation" needs to be adequately indicated, not because Protestants must affirm Catholic doctrine in every detail, but so that Catholics entering into agreements with Protestants can know that their faith is not being watered down or repudiated, and so that Protestants entering into agreements with Catholics can be assured that they are not thereby selling the Reformation farm. *Consensus on "transubstantiation" is important not because the word itself is essential for Christian faith but because, without such consensus, the Christian people won't know whether*

80. CDF/PCPCU, "Observations," 754.

official ecumenical agreements on the Eucharist have genuinely resolved our differences.

Is this dynamic not, in fact, what Fr. Tillard is hinting at when he writes the following? The theologians, he says,

> have to go on working out ways and means of showing that the traditional belief of their respective Churches is safeguarded in the common statements they, the theologians, elaborate. As long as the relationship between theology and official teaching remains what it is, this difficulty has to be faced; otherwise any unity ultimately reached would rest on a totally fruitless compromise instead of blossoming into the genuine *koinonia* of faith and life which we must envisage. It is no use having a consensus to which you merely append your signature: it has got to be a thing you can live by.[81]

Now, it is certainly a great ecumenical achievement that the commission was finally able to reassure the Vatican of its intentions, to the point where "no further study would seem to be required."[82] Nevertheless, it is difficult to avoid the conclusion that the way in which Rome was finally satisfied about ARCIC's treatment of transubstantiation left many parties confused. What, for instance, would someone of Bishop Williams's opinion take away from the claim that "even if the word *transubstantiation* only occurs in a footnote, the Final Report wished to express what the Council of Trent, as evident from its discussion, clearly intended by the use of the term"?[83] Would he feel he had been duped by the original *Agreed Statement*? Perhaps betrayed by the commission, or at least by Anglican commission members who seem to have lost their nerve? Or would he perhaps come to realize that "transubstantiation" doesn't mean what he originally thought it meant? If this latter, it can hardly be because its meaning was ever explicitly spelled out.

Even though ARCIC was eventually successful in reaching agreement on eucharistic presence, the process through which that achievement was arrived at undoubtedly left many Anglicans and Catholics confused and hurt. It is not my contention that this was entirely the fault of the commission. It is, in fact, a vocational hazard of the ecumenist. Any time one seeks consensus on contentious issues deeply rooted in communal identity, one risks rejection and confusion. And, as mentioned above, I do not imagine that the CDF's handling of the situation was entirely above reproach. But, regardless of how one apportions the blame for the shortcomings of the process, it seems clear that *the*

81. Tillard, "Roman Catholics and Anglicans," 131–32.
82. Cassidy, "Letter to the Co-chairs of ARCIC-II (March 11, 1994)," 299.
83. ARCIC II, "Clarifications," 302.

avoidance or marginalization of terms central to the consciousness and identity of divided Christians, however well intentioned, will not serve the ecumenical goal. That this is the case is also supported by the evidence regarding *BEM.*

Responses to BEM (Baptism, Eucharist, and Ministry)

As we have already seen, *BEM* chose to avoid the term "transubstantiation" completely. And while some groups, like the above-quoted Church of North India, applauded this decision, it left others confused. We need not wade through the whole history of the document and its reception in order to demonstrate this. A few representative quotes from the Churches' responses to *BEM* will suffice.

Several Churches express concern that *BEM* had somehow implied transubstantiation, or at least had not explicitly excluded it:

> The eucharist was to be in *remembrance* memorial and not re-enactment nor transubstantiation as advocated by sections of the church. If the miracle of transubstantiation operates, then the bread and wine now changed into actual flesh and blood of Jesus could no longer be said to be "memorial" as He is literally present and materially so in bread and wine. (The Moravian Church in Jamaica, V.170)

> Is the presence of Christ a matter of transubstantiation or of "transignification"? (The United Protestant Church of Belgium, III.171)

> But what precisely is the significance of the added words: "the sacrament of his real presence"? Do they mean that the bread which we eat and the wine which we drink *contain* the blood and flesh of the Son of Man? Is the formula intended to permit the possibility of belief in transubstantiation? If so, we could not subscribe to it. Or is it meant to say that the bread and wine are sacraments of the real *spiritual* presence of Christ? If so, then it conveys our convictions. Apparently the solution is to be found in the accompanying Commentary, namely, that the words are carefully chosen to allow both possibilities. And that is disquieting. (Union of Welsh Independents, III.273)

Some churches were concerned that the document's focus on *epiklesis* contained "hints of transubstantiation":[84]

> The shadow of transubstantiation clouds the analysis [of pericope 14 and its commentary concerning *epiklesis*]. (Union of Welsh Independents, III.274)

84. Tabbernee, "BEM and the Eucharist," 37.

> We cannot agree to the understanding of the *epiklesis* as consecrating the elements in the sense of a doctrine of transubstantiation. (Evangelical Church of the Rhineland V.79)

> In our churches there are reservations in particular against *epiklesis* of gifts in isolation, because of any "theology of transubstantiation" that might possibly lie in this. (Federation of the Evangelical Churches in the GDR, V.135)

One Church took a stance dramatically different from the one represented by the previous quotes:

> The document recognizes *anamnesis* as the essence of the eucharistic meal, whereas the Orthodox Church confesses as the essence of the eucharist the transubstantiation of the holy gifts. (Russian Orthodox Church, II.8)

These quotes raise all kinds of questions that need not detain us at length. What is important for us is to note the way in which transubstantiation functions in the imaginations of the responding Churches. Many Churches that are careful to reject transubstantiation make no attempt to define it. The Moravian Church of Jamaica, in its attempt at definition, seriously misses the mark. And even the Russian Orthodox Church, with its blunt affirmation of transubstantiation, gives at least the impression that transubstantiation is somehow incommensurable with *anamnesis*. In each case (if in different ways and to greater and lesser degrees), transubstantiation seems to function more as an identity marker than as a theological concept (even if the brevity of the United Protestant Church of Belgium's question makes its view a little more difficult to gauge).

The Catholic Response?

What, then, was the response of the Roman Catholic Church, which many of these other communities seemed to have in mind when crafting their own responses?

> On the one hand, we welcome the convergence that is taking place. On the other hand, we must note that for Catholic doctrine, the *conversion* of the elements is a matter of faith and is only open to possible new theological explanations as to the "how" of the intrinsic change. The content of the word "transubstantiation" ought to be expressed without ambiguity. For Catholics this is a central mystery of faith, and they cannot accept expressions that are ambiguous. (Roman Catholic Church, VI.21)

In order to understand this response we must recall the discussion of transubstantiation in ARCIC and the CDF/PCPCU's responses to it. I suggest that "express without ambiguity" here is functionally equivalent to "indicate adequately" in *Observations*. Rome wants to be sure that transubstantiation is articulated in such a way that the faith of Catholics is clearly and accurately expressed. Again, the concept or term "transubstantiation" per se is not being required of other Christians, though some have felt that this is the position of the CDF. In fact, this response indicates a difference between what is a matter of faith and what is a matter of theological opinion or explanation. What is a matter of faith for Catholics, highlighted by the use of italics (in original) here, is "the *conversion* of the elements."[85] This echoes the footnote in the original *Agreed Statement* from ARCIC, which claims that the term "transubstantiation" "should be seen as affirming the *fact* of Christ's presence and of the mysterious and radical change which takes place."[86] This is precisely what is highlighted here. What is not a matter of faith is the precise theological articulation of that presence and change. Other theological articulations can be attempted provided that they do not deny what is affirmed by, or what is the genuine "content" of, transubstantiation. That this is an appropriate reading of the response is supported by the fact that the CDF responded so favorably to ARCIC's mention of Paul VI's *Mysterium Fidei* when, in *Clarifications*, it wrote that "Paul VI in *Mysterium Fidei* (AAS 57, 1965) did not deny the legitimacy of fresh ways of expressing this change even by using new words, provided that they kept and reflected what transubstantiation was intended to express."[87]

Rome's evident concern for clarity on the question is consistent with what the Lutheran Egil Grislis concluded, after his reading of the responses: "The desire for further refinement of the understanding of the eucharist is a widespread one."[88] Geoffrey Wainwright, the Methodist theologian who chaired the session that approved *BEM*, agrees with Grislis[89] and gives a very helpful schema for the ways in which the various Churches need to contribute to the clarity sought by so many of the respondents:

85. Cf. Pope Benedict XVI, *God Is Near Us: The Eucharist, the Heart of Life* (San Francisco: Ignatius, 2003), 85–86: "What has always mattered to the Church is that a real transformation takes place here. Something genuinely happens in the Eucharist. There is something new there that was not before. Knowing about a transformation is part of the most basic eucharistic faith."

86. ARCIC, "An Agreed Statement on Eucharistic Doctrine," 31. Cf. A Lutheran–Roman Catholic Statement, "Eucharist as Sacrifice," 43; Kasper, *Harvesting the Fruits*, 186.

87. ARCIC II, "Clarifications," 302. Cf. Paul VI, *Mysterium Fidei*, #25 (http://www.vatican.va/holy_father/paul_vi/encyclicals/documents/hf_p-vi_enc_03091965_mysterium_en.html).

88. Grislis, "Eucharistic Convergence," 260.

89. Cf. Wainwright, "Eucharist in the Churches' Responses to the Lima Text," 54.

Once the question of the elements has been raised, it will not go away. In so far as erroneous answers threaten the faith, the question must be faced. It would be important that the Orthodox Churches explain to others what they mean by the transformation of the elements (*metabole*); that the Roman Catholic Church explore with others how what is "most aptly called transubstantiation" (Council of Trent) may otherwise be expressed; that those Protestants who deny any "essential change" in the elements state what they are thereby affirming. Here the dialogue remains open after the Lima text.[90]

Note that Wainwright also understands that the Roman Catholic response does not demand that other Christians subscribe to transubstantiation per se. Beyond that detail, Wainwright's broader conclusion here also matches my own—namely, if there is to be any rapprochement on the question of eucharistic presence between the Roman Catholic Church and various Protestant groups, then the issue of transubstantiation must be tackled head-on.

A Recent Breakthrough

In this regard, one can hardly be anything but greatly encouraged by the recent Fourth Agreed Statement of the Disciples of Christ–Roman Catholic International Commission for Dialogue, 2003–2009, called *The Presence of Christ in the Church, with Special Reference to the Eucharist*. This agreed statement is quite unique in its careful parsing of transubstantiation.[91] Transubstantiation is carefully located in its historical and theological context, and common misreadings of the doctrine are refuted. Its rejection at the time of the Reformation and its reaffirmation by the Council of Trent are briefly, but helpfully, described. And, finally, its rejection by the Disciples of Christ is relativized by the recognition that what they meant to reject, within their own philosophical context of Scottish commonsense realism, was "almost the opposite of what Aquinas had intended."[92] With this ecumenical heavy lifting done, the agreement reached on eucharistic presence lacks any ambiguity around the question of transubstantiation.[93]

90. Wainwright, "Eucharist in the Churches' Responses to the Lima Text," 65–66.
91. Disciples of Christ–Roman Catholic International Commission for Dialogue, "The Presence of Christ in the Church, with Special Reference to the Eucharist: Fourth Agreed Statement of the Disciples of Christ–Roman Catholic International Commission for Dialogue, 2003–2009," *Call to Unity* (October 2012): ##30–37.
92. Disciples of Christ–Roman Catholic International Commission for Dialogue, "Presence of Christ in the Church," #37.
93. Disciples of Christ–Roman Catholic International Commission for Dialogue, "Presence of Christ in the Church," esp. ##41–42.

Confusion about Transubstantiation

We have already seen, particularly in the responses to ARCIC and *BEM*, that confusion surrounding the term "transubstantiation" is a major factor in ecumenical disagreement about the Eucharist. But it is difficult to blame the Anglican and Protestant respondents who rejected transubstantiation without giving any indication of understanding it, if only for the simple reason that the reverse is so very often true of Catholics who accept it. In fact, this project had its genesis in my own recognition of my misunderstanding about transubstantiation.

Popular Misunderstanding

As a Catholic who professed transubstantiation, I was often confronted with pointed questions from Protestant friends. If Jesus's body really is present in the bread, they reasoned, would Jesus not have run out of body long ago? What did I think would be observed, they wondered, if a consecrated host were put under a microscope? Did Jesus get hurt if Catholics bit the host?[94] Most awkwardly, they pressed their point, if Catholics think they actually eat Jesus's body, do they follow their logic to its conclusion and profess that Jesus's body passes from our bodies in the natural way?

Looking back at these conversations now is a source of some embarrassment. I recall scrambling for answers without any reference to Scripture or Christian tradition and coming up with post hoc rationalizations quite similar to what any search engine can turn up on the internet: "God could always make more body for Jesus." Or, "Jesus could unconsecrate the host to preserve himself from the sacrilege of scientific investigation or the indignity of the processes of human digestion." I even once came upon a very sincere attempt to link all the pain Jesus ever felt in the mouths of communicants with his suffering on the cross. If the internet is any indication, the awkward kinds of ecumenical conversations I found myself in because of my poor understanding of transubstantiation are quite widespread. The fundamental problem is an attempt to articulate real presence in naturalistic or materialistic terms instead of sacramental ones.

The breakthrough for me came when, in meeting a professor to prepare for a class presentation on the Eucharist in ecumenical dialogue, I rather casually mentioned Christ's "physical presence." My professor stopped me and said, "But, Brett, that's a heresy!" Seeing the surprise on my face, she

---

94. Indeed, some older Catholics will recount being instructed not to bite the host for precisely this reason.

continued, "It's called capharnaism, named for the Jews at Capernaum who had misunderstood Jesus's claims in John 6."[95] I was both confused and excited. I had always, without thinking too deeply about it, imagined Christ's eucharistic presence in rather physical terms, and transubstantiation was a buttress for this imagining. As is evident from the questions they asked me, the same was true for my Protestant interlocutors. If such terms and images do not accurately represent transubstantiation, I thought, there was surely room for ecumenical movement on this sticky question. I started sending out email questionnaires and writing blog posts, and my suspicions were confirmed: many Catholics had been given to believe that to deny a physical or materialistic understanding of Christ's presence was to deny transubstantiation, and many Protestants felt that to affirm transubstantiation would be to affirm such a presence. Though I didn't know it quite yet, I had a research topic.

Confusion in the Academy Too

I began almost immediately, starting with my professor's suggestion that I write my final paper for that course on real presence. (By the time we met to discuss that paper after the semester's end, both of us thought that a dissertation topic was at hand.)[96] It was a revelation to find that the real presence presumed and expounded by the doctrine of transubstantiation was not a bare physical presence, but a rich interpersonal sacramental (i.e., predicated on the logic of sign) presence, with deep ecclesiological and eschatological resonances.[97] But,

95. Of course, not everyone who uses the adverb "physically" to describe Christ's presence is a heretic. And the term itself has not exactly been condemned as a heresy. (Trent distinguishes between Christ's "natural mode of existing" and the possibility of his being "sacramentally present" [Session 13, Chapter 1]. "Physical" is, etymologically at least, intimately connected with "natural.") It is only that the term can lead one to believe things about the real presence that are not the faith of the Church. "Physically present" is not theologically precise and can carry more than one meaning. Many people use it simply to mean "bodily" present, or "really, very, very" present. That is quite unobjectionable. The problem, however, is that using such a word, with no theological pedigree, can get one caught up in all the kinds of conceptual problems I had experienced and have since found all over the internet. And using it simply to mean "really, very, very" gives the impression that only the physical is really real, something completely at odds with a Christian worldview.

96. It didn't hurt that my professor had discovered, in the meantime, an appeal from Pope Benedict himself, made in a speech to ecumenists in Australia, to focus on the question of the Eucharist. Benedict XVI, "Address of His Holiness Benedict XVI" (presented at the Ecumenical Meeting, Crypt of St. Mary's Cathedral in Sydney, July 18, 2008), http://www.vatican.va/holy _father/benedict_xvi/speeches/2008/july/documents/hf_ben-xvi_spe_20080718_ecumenism_en .html.

97. My key sources for this first foray into the topic were F.-X. Durrwell, *The Eucharist: Presence of Christ* (Denville, NJ: Dimension Books, 1974); Benedict XVI, *God Is Near Us*; Herbert McCabe, OP, "Eucharistic Change," in *God Still Matters* (London: Continuum, 2005),

in my reading and writing, I very soon noticed other ecumenically interesting factors. Many Catholics were suspicious of transubstantiation thus understood, some even suggesting it sounded—horror of horrors—Calvinist! Furthermore, the confusion I had experienced and encountered at a popular level also existed in the academy. Though at a more refined level of discourse, there existed a subset of academic writing on the Eucharist that was concerned precisely with transubstantiation as a physical phenomenon.

It is not necessary to refute each author presented below point by point. Many of them have already been refuted and, in any case, it is hoped that the next chapter will equip any reader to see through any of the errors below that are not already obvious. But it is worth noting that, even in the academy, transubstantiation is misunderstood and misrepresented as supporting a more or less physical, rather than sacramental, presence and—here's the really interesting part—by both those who accept it and those who reject it. Perhaps the most famous (or infamous) example of this is the prolonged debate between Carlo Colombo and Filippo Selvaggi, SJ, after the latter's 1949 article, "Il concetto di sostanza nel dogma eucharistico in relazione all fisica moderna" (The concept of substance in eucharistic dogma in relation to modern physics).[98] In it, Selvaggi attempted to articulate transubstantiation with particular reference to the tiny building blocks of matter understood by modern physics, claiming that the substance of atoms and molecules, and not just that of bread, must be transubstantiated. Colombo, who was later to become Pope Paul VI's personal theologian, held that Selvaggi was confusing physics and metaphysics.[99] Richard Cipolla names Selvaggi's mistake with precision when he writes that "to talk of the transubstantiation of electrons is meaningless; it involves a gross misunderstanding of modern physics as well as a gross misuse of language."[100]

But Selvaggi was not the last Catholic theologian to somehow or other misread transubstantiation as a more or less physical phenomenon. In a

---

115–22; Tillard, "Roman Catholics and Anglicans"; Tillard, "Reflections on the Real Presence and Encountering the Lord in the Eucharist, Part 1," *Emmanuel* 81, no. 3 (1975): 106–13; Tillard, "Reflections on the Real Presence and Encountering the Lord in the Eucharist, Part 2," *Emmanuel* 81, no. 4 (1975): 156–63; and Tillard, "The Eucharist as the Bread and Sign of Brotherhood, Part 3," *Emmanuel* 81, no. 5 (1975): 204–12.

98. Filippo Selvaggi, SJ, "Il concetto di sostanza nel dogma eucharistico in relazione alla fisica moderna," *Gregorianum* 30 (1949): 17–45.

99. This debate is helpfully summarized in J. T. Clark, SJ, "Physics, Philosophy, Transubstantiation, Theology," *Theological Studies* 12 (1951): 24–51. Useful summaries of this debate can be found in Cyril Vollert, "The Eucharist: Controversy on Transubstantiation," *Theological Studies* 22, no. 3 (1961): 391–425.

100. Richard G. Cipolla, "Selvaggi Revisited: Transubstantiation and Contemporary Science," *Theological Studies* 35, no. 4 (1974): 671.

relatively recent article, Terence Nichols argues that "what makes the bread bread and the wine wine would seem to be precisely their chemical structures," and that Colombo's "purely metaphysical" articulation of substance in his debate with Selvaggi ends up "depriving it [substance] of any form or content, and so rendering it unintelligible."[101] And in a book published just as this work was going to press, Douglas Farrow suggests that "substance/accidents analysis, though a sort of common sense indispensable in ordinary thought, suffers philosophically from the fact that it depends on a distinction between primary and secondary matter that is no longer tenable, and from the fact that it cannot readily accommodate modern ideas of space and time."[102]

Germain Grisez runs into similar problems in "An Alternative Theology of Jesus' Substantial Presence in the Eucharist." After highlighting what he considers to be unintelligible in Thomas's account, Grisez articulates an awkward theory in which the bread and wine become "new *parts* of Jesus' body and blood,"[103] something completely alien to the tradition of the Church. According to Roch Kereszty, "Grisez ignores the philosophy of symbol because he fears that any symbolic interpretation would compromise the dogma of the ontological change in the Eucharistic elements."[104] This hampers Grisez's ability to read Thomas accurately because "unlike Grisez, Thomas knows about an intimate ontological connection not only between substance and accidents but also, in the context of Salvation History, between the sign and the reality signified by it."[105] Again, a theologian who treats transubstantiation without reference to its sacramental context ends up with false problems. It is interesting to note that Grisez himself finds that Thomas responds to one of Grisez's own objections by pointing out that the objection would only apply to substantial change (i.e., natural, physical change), but is irrelevant to transubstantiation. Nevertheless, because his own approach completely

---

101. Terence Nichols, "Transubstantiation and Eucharistic Presence," *Pro Ecclesia* 11, no. 1 (Winter 2002): 65.

102. Douglas Farrow, *Theological Negotiations: Proposals in Soteriology and Anthropology* (Grand Rapids: Baker Academic, 2018), 154. For an excellent, short rebuttal of the suggestion that modern physics makes transubstantiation meaningless or unintelligible, see Stephen Barr (himself a physicist), "Does Quantum Physics Render Transubstantiation Meaningless?," *First Thoughts* (blog), *First Things*, May 25, 2010, https://www.firstthings.com/blogs/firstthoughts/2010/05/does-quantum-physics-render-transubstantiation-meaningless.

103. Germain Grisez, "An Alternative Theology of Jesus' Substantial Presence in the Eucharist," *Irish Theological Quarterly* 65, no. 2 (2000): 123.

104. Roch A. Kereszty, OCist, "On the Eucharistic Presence: Response to Germain Grisez," *Irish Theological Quarterly* 65, no. 4 (2000): 349; Grisez was also refuted by Stephen L. Brock, "St. Thomas and the Eucharistic Conversion," *The Thomist* 65 (2001): 529–65.

105. Kereszty, "On the Eucharistic Presence," 349–50.

ignores the sacramental nature of Christ's presence, Grisez finds Thomas's response unconvincing.[106]

And, if Catholic scholars like Terence Nichols, Douglas Farrow, and Germain Grisez can so easily misconstrue transubstantiation, it should come as no surprise when Protestant scholar Horton Davies suggests that "transubstantiation" is "an Aristotelian term that is *negated by modern physics*."[107] Or when Fr. Joseph Classen, a nonspecialist writing a work of popular Catholic apologetics, describes smashing a guitar as "a transubstantial change."[108] Classen's work is interesting because, though it is not an academic book or article, neither is it a blog post or a conversation in a coffee shop. Classen's book went through an editorial process with a self-consciously orthodox Catholic publisher and was even endorsed by Raymond Cardinal Burke, then prefect of the Apostolic Signatura (a.k.a. the Vatican's Supreme Court), as "a plain-spoken and substantial presentation of the teaching of the Church" and "a reliable guide to those who want to deepen their knowledge of the faith."[109] Neither Cardinal Burke nor the editors at *Our Sunday Visitor* found anything out of place with Classen's rather glaring misrepresentation of "transubstantial change."[110] Presumably it is not caught by many of the book's readers either.

And what is of utmost importance for us here is the fact that it would make little difference whether those unwitting readers affirmed or denied transubstantiation. Confusion about transubstantiation exists in basically the same form (i.e., confusing it for a natural change) in both those who affirm transubstantiation and those who reject it. And this is true whether we are talking about people inside the Catholic Church, or people outside of it. It is

106. Grisez, "An Alternative Theology of Jesus' Substantial Presence in the Eucharist," 119–20.

107. Horton Davies, *Bread of Life and Cup of Joy: Newer Ecumenical Perspectives on the Eucharist* (Grand Rapids: Eerdmans, 1993), x (emphasis added).

108. Joseph F. Classen, *Meat and Potatoes Catholicism* (Huntington, IN: Our Sunday Visitor, 2008), 135–36.

109. Archbishop Raymond Burke, foreword to *Meat and Potatoes Catholicism*, by Joseph Classen (Huntington, IN: Our Sunday Visitor, 2008), 13.

110. Fr. Classen further muddied the waters with his attempt to buttress Church teaching about transubstantiation—in which, by definition, the accidents do not change—by reference to eucharistic miracles in which the very precise content of the miraculous claims is that the accidents *do* change. Such attempts to "prove" transubstantiation are quite common in popular Catholicism. I owe this observation to a very sharp confirmation student, Gabrielle Fournie, who asked me why her textbook, immediately after explaining that transubstantiation means that the physical characteristics of the eucharistic species remain unchanged, attempted to prove the truth of transubstantiation by reference to eucharistic miracles in which the physical characteristics *do* change. Now, whether certain miracle claims are legitimate need not detain us here. The point is that, even if legitimate, they would not be examples of transubstantiation, but of its opposite.

worth noting, however, that even though confusion about transubstantiation exists among both its adherents and its detractors, there is a way in which misunderstanding by those who self-identify as "faithful," "traditional," or "orthodox" Catholics is even more damaging to ecumenical understanding than misunderstanding by those Catholics who self-consciously reject Church teaching (even if they have not understood it). I certainly do not wish to suggest that a basic attitude in favor of Church teaching, an attitude that typically underlies hearty but inadequate affirmations of transubstantiation, is worse than a presumption against it. Far from it. The problem is simply that when Protestants encounter Catholics claiming to represent their own Church accurately, and who affirm transubstantiation by name but misrepresent it in explication, these Protestants are confirmed in their suspicion that what the Catholic Church affirms is, precisely, a physical rather than a sacramental change and presence. Protestants reject such articulations and, it must be said, they are right to do so.

But how do these just rejections relate to the original Protestant rejections of transubstantiation at the time of the Reformation? Were Catholics at the time also misrepresenting the doctrine? And, if so, why? Our final task in this chapter is to investigate, historically, how transubstantiation became so difficult to understand. What is the root of transubstantiation's propensity to be misunderstood? To this question we now turn.

The Corruption of Transubstantiation

Of course, it would be easy to suggest that transubstantiation's opacity is inherent in the doctrine itself. It is, after all, an attempt to articulate, though not to comprehend or explain away, a great mystery.[111] Many people express the belief that such a mystery is best left unarticulated due to the inadequacy of all human attempts to do so. Belief, such people often maintain, is more important than understanding. But the Catholic tradition has never shied away from attempts at such articulation when the content of the faith is threatened, however much it acknowledges the ultimately incomplete nature of such articulations. So, while C. S. Lewis makes an undeniably valid point when he writes, "The command, after all, was Take, eat: not Take, understand,"[112] theology must always respond to questions about the Christian faith with more than just an invitation to deeper faith. The temptation to fideism must be rejected. It is right that faith should seek understanding.

---

111. We will revisit this idea in the next chapter.
112. C. S. Lewis, *Letters to Malcolm: Chiefly on Prayer* (London: G. Bles, 1964), 136 (#19).

If we really want to understand the confusion about transubstantiation, we will need to look deeper than the simple fact that it deals with very mysterious subject matter. I suggest starting with history. The reason is this: transubstantiation did not come to be such a central aspect of Catholic eucharistic theology without reason. Rather, it became central because transubstantiation was, at least at one time, taken to be a highly intelligible and rationally satisfying response to those who protested that it was simply incoherent to claim that Christ's body and blood were *really* present in the consecrated bread and wine. Of course, by the time of the Reformation, it was no longer so satisfying. What had happened?

As we shall see in more detail in the next chapter, the language of "substance" enters the Church's eucharistic vocabulary as a result of the eleventh-century Berengarian controversy.[113] It provided a way to maintain that Christ's presence in the Eucharist was *real*, and not "merely" symbolic as Berengarius was suspected of teaching, while also maintaining the *sacramental*, as opposed to, say, a natural, material, or physical, manner of that presence. The term "transubstantiation" emerges in this context to describe the change that leads to Christ's "substantial" presence. At the Fourth Lateran Council, in 1215, the term makes its first appearance in official Catholic teaching.[114]

At this stage, the term still had a somewhat indeterminate meaning. Lateran IV had made no attempt to define it, but simply taught, in its statement against the Cathars and Albigensians, that "in this Church the priest himself is the sacrifice, Jesus Christ; and his body and blood are truly contained in the sacrament of the altar under the appearances of bread and wine—the bread being transubstantiated into his body and the wine into his blood by divine power."[115] The whole conceptual apparatus that would take definitive form in the work of Thomas Aquinas was not yet present, and the term was intended as a straightforward affirmation of real presence against those who denied it. It was not intended or understood as the canonization of transubstantiation over and against other attempts, such as consubstantiation or annihilation/succession, at articulating the mystery of Christ's "substantial" eucharistic presence. For the rest of the thirteenth century, theologians understood themselves to be well within the bounds of Church teaching even as they contemplated the strengths and weaknesses of the various articulations.[116]

113. See Henry Chadwick, "Ego Berengarius," *Journal of Theological Studies* 40, no. 2 (October 1989): 432.

114. James F. McCue, "The Doctrine of Transubstantiation from Berengar through Trent: The Point at Issue," *Harvard Theological Review* 61, no. 3 (July 1968): 392–93.

115. Quoted in McCue, "Doctrine of Transubstantiation," 393.

116. See McCue, "Doctrine of Transubstantiation," 392–95. See also Levy, "Eucharist in the Fourteenth and Fifteenth Centuries," 236.

Nevertheless, though Lateran IV's teaching about transubstantiation was not meant as a condemnation of alternative views of real presence, but rather as a condemnation of the denial of real presence per se, it is important to note that the theologians of the thirteenth century came down strongly in favor of transubstantiation. While there were subtle differences in the ways it was articulated by different authors, the basic consensus of thirteenth-century theology was that transubstantiation (the understanding that the substance of the bread and wine become the substance of Christ's body and blood) was preferable to consubstantiation (the understanding that the substance of the bread and wine remain with Christ's body and blood after the consecration) or to annihilation/succession (the understanding that God destroyed the substance of the bread and wine and replaced them with Christ's body and blood). Thomas Aquinas, writing in the middle of the century, is the first theologian to explicitly denounce consubstantiation as heresy, though his mentor Albert the Great came close.[117]

Enter Scotus

In the work of the great Franciscan theologian Duns Scotus, two things changed. First of all, Scotus, "contradicting all the recent great teachers,"[118] rejected the thirteenth-century consensus that preferred transubstantiation over the other articulations. In his mind, consubstantiation was more philosophically plausible. Second, and ironically, given his own preference for consubstantiation, Scotus is the first theologian to have interpreted Lateran IV's affirmation of transubstantiation as an explicit rejection of the other articulations. (While I have not seen any explanations for Scotus's novel interpretation of Lateran IV, could it perhaps be that the extent of the very consensus he was breaking, which included Aquinas's judgment that consubstantiation was heretical, had given him the impression that the Church had officially denounced it in 1215?) In any case, Scotus, then, feels bound by Church teaching to affirm transubstantiation despite the fact that it strikes him as less rationally satisfying than consubstantiation—and this he explicitly does.[119]

It should not surprise us, perhaps, that in our age theologians and historians of doctrine are far more interested in what I have called the second change, namely, Scotus's judgment about Lateran IV and his subsequent

117. McCue, "Doctrine of Transubstantiation," 395–99.
118. Gustave Martelet, *The Risen Christ and the Eucharistic World* (New York: Seabury, 1976), 141.
119. McCue, "Doctrine of Transubstantiation," 403–7. See also Levy, "Eucharist in the Fourteenth and Fifteenth Centuries," 236–37.

obeisance. Indeed, that James McCue, upon whose classic historical account I am largely depending, calls Scotus's view about Lateran IV the first change and his view about the plausibility of consubstantiation the second change[120] is indicative.[121] That Scotus would overrule his own reasoned conclusion because of the authority of the Church fascinates the contemporary mind. And, of course, McCue and others are right to flag this as a key shift given that Luther's rejection of transubstantiation was very much based on his coming to the same conclusion as Scotus: "The dogma of transubstantiation has no purpose and no support other than the authority of the Church."[122] In fact, a more or less direct line can be drawn from Luther back to Scotus via Pierre d'Ailly, Gabriel Biel,[123] and William of Ockham.[124] All of these thinkers took essentially the same position, the one difference being simply that once Luther had come to reject the authority of the Church on other grounds, his rejection of transubstantiation followed as a matter of course.[125]

But, as interesting and important a shift as Scotus's obedient acceptance of transubstantiation represents in the complicated relationship between faith, reason, and authority, a one-sided focus on this aspect of the problem leaves a key question uninvestigated—namely, "Why did Scotus find consubstantiation more plausible than transubstantiation?" In fact, the question can, and should, be put more broadly: "Why does the community of theologians, which in the thirteenth century almost unanimously considered transubstantiation more plausible, come, after Scotus, to be almost unanimous that consubstantiation is more plausible and that it would have to be affirmed had not the Church authoritatively taught otherwise?"

Indeed, while many scholars investigate Scotus's (or, following him, Ockham's or Wycliffe's) particular arguments against transubstantiation, I have not found any study that attempts to understand why, with Scotus, these arguments have suddenly become persuasive. This question is typically left unasked while the teaching of Scotus is simply juxtaposed with the earlier views. McCue is a good example of this approach. In some cases, however, it

120. McCue, "Doctrine of Transubstantiation," 403.

121. Ian Christopher Levy also uses this as his starting point when dealing with Scotus. Ian Christopher Levy, *John Wyclif: Sacramental Logic, Real Presence, and the Parameters of Orthodoxy*, Marquette Studies in Theology 36 (Milwaukee: Marquette University Press, 2003), 191–93.

122. McCue, "Doctrine of Transubstantiation," 407. Cf. Paul H. Jones, *Christ's Eucharistic Presence: A History of the Doctrine* (New York: Peter Lang, 1994), 98. Cf. Luther, *The Babylonian Captivity of the Church* (1520), in LW 36:29.

123. Heiko Oberman, *The Harvest of Medieval Theology: Gabriel Biel and Late Medieval Nominalism*, 2nd ed. (Grand Rapids: Eerdmans, 1967), 278.

124. See Levy, *John Wyclif*, 202–4.

125. Cf. Benedict XVI, "Problem of Transubstantiation," 228.

is tacitly assumed that Scotus found some kind of fatal flaw in the arguments of "a certain Doctor"[126]—namely, Aquinas. In these studies, Scotus appears to have blown transubstantiation's cover, exposing it for the philosophical fraud that it always was. Ian Christopher Levy, for example, writes that "once transubstantiation has been shown to be an inadequate way of explaining real presence it becomes a genuine stumbling block for theology, one that must be gotten round, rather than relied upon to explicate a mystery." A little further on, Levy continues, "While Scotus's emphasis on the divine will and the contingency of the created order does exalt revelation over natural reason, this must be considered in light of the fact that he examined explanations such as Aquinas's and found they lacked philosophical cogency."[127] What is interesting about this passage is that, while Levy explicitly acknowledges the broader philosophical context of Scotus's decision to accept transubstantiation simply on the authority of the Church—in other words, the exaltation of revelation over reason that results from Scotus's view of the divine will—there is no indication that something in Scotus's philosophical system might also have contributed to his rejection of transubstantiation. Rather, it is straightforwardly assumed that Scotus simply caught Thomas, and the rest of the thirteenth-century theological consensus, in a philosophical error. I suspect the truth is more complicated than that.

Univocity or Analogy

Many authors have contended that Scotus marks the beginning of the end for the great medieval Christian synthesis and the beginning of what we have come to recognize as modernity. Yale philosopher Louis Dupré,[128] evangelical scholar Hans Boersma,[129] Catholic theologian and popular evangelist Bishop Robert Barron,[130] the former secretary general of the Vatican's International

126. See McCue, "Doctrine of Transubstantiation," 403. Scotus does not refer to Thomas by name. Rather, he references the arguments of "quidam Doctor," whom Scotus's editors identify as Aquinas.

127. Levy, *John Wyclif*, 198.

128. Louis K. Dupré, *Passage to Modernity: An Essay in the Hermeneutics of Nature and Culture* (New Haven: Yale University Press, 1993), esp. 38–39, 174–75.

129. Hans Boersma, *Heavenly Participation: The Weaving of a Sacramental Tapestry* (Grand Rapids: Eerdmans, 2010), esp. 68–75.

130. Robert E. Barron, "Thomas Aquinas: Postmodern," in *Sacramental Presence in a Postmodern Context*, ed. Lieven Boeve and Lambert Leijssen (Leuven: Peeters, 2001), esp. 271; Barron, *The Priority of Christ: Toward a Postliberal Catholicism* (Grand Rapids: Brazos, 2007), esp. 12–14; Barron, "The Christian Humanism of Karol Wojtyla and Thomas Aquinas," in *Bridging the Great Divide: Musings of a Post-liberal, Post-conservative, Evangelical Catholic* (Toronto: Rowman & Littlefield, 2004), esp. 111–13.

Theological Commission Charles Morerod, OP,[131] and the school of thought
known as Radical Orthodoxy,[132] to name just a few, all assert that, with
Scotus, something changed in the history of philosophy that radically altered the way we conceive of the relationship between God and God's creation. And that change, says this chorus, can be summed up in one word:
univocity.

Since the work of Thomas Aquinas is generally acknowledged to be the
epitome of the medieval synthesis, the equilibrium of which was upset by
Scotus's univocal conception of being, and since Thomas's is also *the* classic
articulation of transubstantiation, the coherence of which was explicitly rejected by Scotus, it seems highly unlikely that the first has nothing whatsoever
to do with the second. Here, I suggest, is the place to begin the search for
the broader philosophical and theological context that led to the rejection
of transubstantiation from Scotus to Luther and beyond. So, what exactly is
univocity? How does it relate to the medieval philosophical and theological
synthesis as exemplified in the work of Thomas Aquinas? And, finally, what
does it have to do with transubstantiation?

The basic philosophical question at issue in the discussion of univocity is
"How can human beings speak about God?" Thomas Aquinas, with whom
Scotus was consciously breaking when he proposed a univocal concept of
being,[133] believed that God could never be put in any box or, in Aristotelian
terms, any "genus," even that of "being." This is because "God is so much
greater than we are that we cannot adequately comprehend God and talk
about him in straightforward language."[134] Thomas did not, however, deny
that we could speak about God in any meaningful way. Rather, he asserted,
human beings can talk about God by way of analogy and, in fact, only by
way of analogy. What does this mean? Robert Barron writes that

> because finite things come from God and are stamped by his creative power,
> they bear a resemblance to the divine reality and hence both God and creature
> can be described with the term "being." But because there is an infinitely great
> modal difference between that which exists through itself and that which ex-
> vists through another, the word *esse* [being] is ascribed to God and creatures
> only in the most cautious and qualified way. And it is important to note that
> this analogy between creatures is not predicated on the basis of their varying
> resemblance to some absolute of existence that precedes them, but rather

131. Morerod, *Ecumenism and Philosophy*, esp. 62–67.
132. James K. A. Smith, *Introducing Radical Orthodoxy: Mapping a Post-secular Theology*
(Grand Rapids: Baker Academic, 2004), esp. 96–103.
133. Barron, "Thomas Aquinas: Postmodern," 271.
134. Boersma, *Heavenly Participation*, 72.

on the participation of all finite things in the unparticipated to-be which is God.[135]

Because everything that exists (and that is not God) exists only by way of participation in God, whose very essence is to exist, we can speak about God by analogies with other existents. Or, as Hans Boersma explains, "The being of creation (as well as its truth, goodness, and beauty) was similar or analogous—and thus not identical—to the being (and the truth, goodness, and beauty) of the Creator. Analogy (or sacramentality) implies that, while creatures may be similar to the Creator, they are in no way identical to him."[136] Because there is beauty in creation, for example, we can speak about God as beautiful.[137] However, it is important to note that this move only works when it is understood that the beauty in creation does not account for itself but is grounded in a transcendent other. As Dupré writes, "Transcendence is not merely what lies beyond the world, but first and foremost what supports its givenness."[138] In other words, the whole system is predicated on the idea that anything that exists, exists by *participation* in God who is the ground of all reality. (To say, "anything that exists, exists by *participation* in God's existence, which is the ground of all reality" would be another way of saying precisely the same thing because God is, for Thomas at least, *ipsum esse subsistens*, that whose nature it is to be.)[139] God is not one more being among beings, but being itself, not one existent among existents, but the ground and goal of all existence (and existents). *To be*, therefore, means nothing more (and nothing less!) than to participate in God. From this conviction comes the term typically used to describe Thomas's approach to speaking about God: *analogia entis*, the analogy of being.

There are at least two further things worth highlighting about this way of speaking about God. The first is that, because God and creatures do not exist on the same plane of existence, because God is not one being among beings, they are never in competition with one another. In fact, the very opposite obtains. Because creatures only exist by way of participation in God, they can never be in a zero-sum game with God where, for example, if the creature is free God is bound, or vice versa.[140] Barron suggests that this understanding

135. Barron, "Thomas Aquinas: Postmodern," 269.

136. Boersma, *Heavenly Participation*, 70–71.

137. Of course, we can note in passing that such logic is exactly what leads to the classic Christian affirmation, made most famously by Augustine, that evil, properly speaking, does not exist.

138. Dupré, *Passage to Modernity*, 251.

139. See Barron, "Thomas Aquinas: Postmodern," 271–72.

140. For an exploration of the relationship between providence and freedom from this point of view, see the quote from Sertillanges in Morerod, *Ecumenism and Philosophy*, 157–58n8.

of the relationship between God and creatures functions as "a kind of herme-
neutical key to the Thomistic world. Whether the issue is the rapport between
nature and grace, the relationship between providence and human freedom,
the play between supernatural and natural causality, the clarifying principle—
sometimes stated, sometimes assumed—is just this non-competitive transcendence of God."[141]

Furthermore, this is not, for Thomas, simply one possible philosophical
framework he could have chosen from among many. As much as Thomas is
generally considered to be an Aristotelian, this is not from Aristotle.[142] Rather,
such a metaphysic is consciously understood as an outworking of revealed
truth—namely, that Jesus Christ is truly God and truly human.[143] It is, therefore, in Thomas's writings about the incarnation that we can find the basis
of this conviction.[144] As Barron writes elsewhere, "The radically nonworldly
character of God's being is paradoxically enough revealed precisely in the
act by which God enters the world. Were God a being in or alongside of the
universe, one of the natures in the world, God could not *become* a creature
without ceasing to be God or compromising the ontological integrity of the
creature he becomes."[145] In fact, Christian teaching is not simply that Jesus was
fully human, but even that he was more fully human than the rest of us. Far
from limiting his humanity, his divinity perfects it. Openness to God can never
detract from our being because God is the ground of our being. On this point
Barron quotes Irenaeus: "The glory of God is a human being fully alive."[146]

In summary, the first point to stress about the *analogia entis* is that, by
refusing to put God in a box, it preserves that radically other character of
God and, in doing so, preserves the intimate, noncompetitive relationship
between creatures and Creator. It maintains that God is not something else
or somewhere else, but "some*how* else."[147] The second consideration that is

141. Barron, "Thomas Aquinas: Postmodern," 270.
142. Robert E. Barron, "Thomas Aquinas's Christological Reading of God and the Creature,"
in *Bridging the Great Divide: Musings of a Post-liberal, Post-conservative, Evangelical Catholic*
(Toronto: Rowman & Littlefield, 2004), 98. Cf. Dupré, *Passage to Modernity*, 173.
143. Indeed, as David Burrell notes, the Christian doctrine of creation, so important for
Thomas's explication of transubstantiation (as we shall see), is rooted in the incarnation: "The
conundrum posed by the presence of the most high in our midst, in Jesus, brought the creator/
creature relation to a precise, indeed a personal focus." David B. Burrell, *Freedom and Creation
in Three Traditions* (Notre Dame, IN: University of Notre Dame Press, 1993), 60.
144. Barron, "Thomas Aquinas: Postmodern," 270. See also Morerod, *Ecumenism and
Philosophy*, 162, 169.
145. Barron, "Thomas Aquinas's Christological Reading of God and the Creature," 92. See
also Barron, *Priority of Christ*, 55.
146. Barron, "Thomas Aquinas's Christological Reading of God and the Creature," 95.
147. Barron, "Thomas Aquinas's Christological Reading of God and the Creature," 98.

important for us to understand about the *analogia entis* is that, while it makes it possible for us to speak about God in meaningful language, it is careful to emphasize that God remains forever beyond our comprehension. This is, of course, not unrelated to the first point, but it deserves its own treatment.

In *Heavenly Participation: The Weaving of a Sacramental Tapestry*, Hans Boersma argues that the type of ontology engendered by such a participative metaphysics as we saw in Thomas Aquinas is precisely a sacramental one. In the Christian sacraments, aspects of material creation *participate* in God's saving work. And they can do so because creation itself exists as a participation in God. As Boersma notes,

> The debates surrounding the real presence (or, we might say, participation) in the Eucharist were but the particular instantiation of a much broader discussion about real presence. While the church fathers and medieval theologians did look to the bread and wine of the Eucharist as the sacrament in which Christ was really present, in making this point they simultaneously conveyed their conviction that Christ was mysteriously present in the entire created order. Christ's sacramental presence in the Eucharist was, we might say, an intensification of his sacramental presence in the world.[148]

As lofty a doctrine of creation as this implies, it is essential, cautions Boersma, to understand that the world's participation in God is "*merely*" sacramental. This is because

> the doctrine of analogy does not just argue for similarity but also insists on the infinite *difference* between Creator and creature. In fact, *dis*similarity is the main point of the doctrine of analogy. Although there is a certain similarity between the way God is good and the way creation is good, nonetheless, an infinite difference remains—and never decreases, not even slightly—between the goodness of God and the goodness of creation. Therefore, the Fourth Lateran Council (1215) insisted that "between the Creator and the creature so great a likeness cannot be noticed without the necessity of noting a greater dissimilarity between them." The doctrine of analogy basically claimed that the connection between creation and Creator is *merely* sacramental in character. Yes, creation truly participates in its eternal Christological anchor; but this participation is strictly a gift of grace and in no way erases the Creator-creature distinction. In fact, sacramental participation *limits* the significance of the created order: its truth, goodness, and beauty are not its own, but are merely derived from the being of God.[149]

148. Boersma, *Heavenly Participation*, 26.
149. Boersma, *Heavenly Participation*, 71. For the quote from Lateran IV, Boersma cites Henry Denzinger, *The Sources of Catholic Dogma*, trans. Roy J. Deferrari (Fitzwilliam, NH: Loreto, 2002), 171 (no. 432). Cf. Colwell, *Promise and Presence*, 55.

In other words, the Christian affirmation that God is in all things is quite distinct from pantheism. To say that all things are grounded in God is not the same as saying that all things *are* God.

An Unlikely Coincidence?

Now, if we may anticipate the argument just a little, we can note something interesting in this last quote from Boersma—namely, that the same council that had first introduced the term "transubstantiation" into official Church teaching also laid the ground rules for the doctrine of analogy in talking about God. Perhaps we should not make too much of this. Transubstantiation, as defined by Lateran IV, was, as we have seen, still a rather loose concept. And it is certainly the case that the council did not present its teaching about transubstantiation and analogy in the same context or for the same purpose. We should not imagine that the council saw itself making any kind of explicit connection between the two. Nevertheless, if "the doctrine of analogy came to classical expression in the theology of Thomas Aquinas,"[150] the same is true of the doctrine of transubstantiation. While we cannot know if anyone at the council saw an explicit connection between the two doctrines, we can be sure that Thomas himself did not do his theologizing about the eucharistic presence without reference to the basic metaphysical conviction that so shaped the rest of his theology. And, again, both analogy (at least as Thomas understood and used it) and transubstantiation were rejected in the theology of Duns Scotus. It is hard to imagine that this is mere coincidence.

While Thomas Aquinas had insisted that God could not be put into any category, any genus, and that consequently God could only be spoken of by means of analogy, Scotus felt that this was incoherent. For Scotus, one could not make any meaningful analogy between two things unless there was some common background against which both could be measured.[151] And that background was "being." For Scotus, "something either has being or it does not. To say God exists and to say created objects exist is to say one and the same thing. All being is being in the same sense."[152] In other words, being is univocal. Univocity means that God *can* be put into a genus, the genus of being, which, of course, includes everything else. God and creation are both

---

150. Boersma, *Heavenly Participation*, 72.

151. Alexander Broadie, "Duns Scotus and William Ockham," in *The Medieval Theologians: An Introduction to Theology in the Medieval Period*, ed. G. R. Evans (Malden, MA: Blackwell, 2001), 251–56. Broadie is careful to point out that Scotus does not reject analogy completely, but rather invokes univocity as a way to make analogy coherent.

152. Boersma, *Heavenly Participation*, 74.

put into a "logical category that, in a real sense, transcends and includes them,"[153] and God becomes one being among many.

For this move, Scotus has been widely vilified. Barron writes that "the implications of this shift are enormous and, to my mind, almost entirely negative,"[154] and that the "consequence of this radical reconfiguration is obvious: God and the world, now drawn into too close a metaphysical intimacy, emerge as competitors. Sharing the same ontological background, God and creatures now become 'beings' necessarily pitted against one another antagonistically."[155] "Furthermore," writes Barron, "unanchored from their shared participation in God, no longer grounded in a common source, creatures lose their essential connectedness to one another. Isolated and self-contained individuals . . . are now what is most basically real."[156]

In *Introducing Radical Orthodoxy*, James K. A. Smith says that, for the Radical Orthodoxy movement, univocity represents a kind of "double idolatry."[157] In the first instance, by placing God within a genus, univocity reduces God. "God is subordinated to a higher concept, namely, that of being."[158] Second, univocity desacramentalizes nature. Nature no longer exists only by participation in God's being; rather, it exists independently of and alongside God's being.[159] If we recall Boersma's earlier point about eucharistic real presence as a particular instantiation of Christ's sacramental presence in all of creation, it should be getting clearer why Scotus's rejection of analogy is connected to his rejection of transubstantiation. Boersma puts it this way:

> If it is true that we can apply "being" to God and creatures *in the same way*, then "being" forms an overarching category in which God and creatures both share. With Scotus, we might say, it became possible to deny the sacramentality of the relationship between earthly objects and the Logos as their eternal archetype. No longer did earthly objects (as *sacramentum*) receive the reality (*res*) of their being from God's own being. No longer was there a mysterious reality hiding within what could be observed by the senses. The full reality of created objects could be seen, heard, touched, smelled, and tasted. The loss of analogy meant the loss of sacramentality.[160]

153. Barron, *Priority of Christ*, 13.
154. Barron, *Priority of Christ*, 13.
155. Barron, "Thomas Aquinas: Postmodern," 271. Following this insight, many suggest univocity is the basic ground of modern atheism. See, e.g., Martelet, *The Risen Christ and the Eucharistic World*, 140.
156. Barron, *Priority of Christ*, 14.
157. Smith, *Introducing Radical Orthodoxy*, 98.
158. Boersma, *Heavenly Participation*, 75.
159. Smith, *Introducing Radical Orthodoxy*, 98–99.
160. Boersma, *Heavenly Participation*, 75.

As important as Scotus's metaphysical innovation would be to the downfall of transubstantiation as a plausible articulation of real presence, it is important to note that he is not solely responsible. With univocity, Scotus had paved the way for nominalism, but he was not yet himself a full-blown nominalist. And, as the German study of the sixteenth-century condemnations significantly points out, "it was precisely the nominalist form of the doctrine of transubstantiation which [Luther] (and with him the Formula of Concord) combated; for, unlike Aquinas, the nominalists assumed that the substance of the bread ceased to be altogether, or was annihilated."[161] If we are to understand, then, what Luther and, with him, the entire Reformation were rejecting when they unanimously rejected transubstantiation, we need to see how univocity was followed by nominalism.

Nominalism

For our purposes, we can say that what univocity is to analogy, nominalism is to realism. Up to and including Scotus, the theologians of the Middle Ages were basically realists. That is to say, they affirmed the real existence of universals in which concrete existing things participated. So, human nature, for instance, is a real thing that both the author of this book and the readers have in common.[162] While this is already starting to slip away with Scotus's univocity, because it now becomes more difficult to imagine how two concrete things *participate* in something else that transcends them both, on this point William of Ockham marks the decisive break. For Ockham, "human nature" or even "being" itself are not real, but nominal. That is, they are merely abstractions conceived by the human mind and *named*—hence, nominalism—for purposes of thought and discourse. They do not reflect any actually existing reality beyond the mind. This is a function of Ockham's

161. Lehmann and Pannenberg, *Condemnations of the Reformation Era*, 96. Indeed, whether the reader finds my argument for the relationship between Scotus's opting for univocity and his negative judgment about transubstantiation to be compelling, or whether she shares Michael Root's suspicion of the "blame Scotus" narrative, noted in the foreword to this book, it remains the case that transubstantiation did undergo radical changes between the time of Thomas and the Reformation.

162. We need not imagine, however, that a full-blown Platonist idealism is the only alternative to nominalism. John Haldane describes Thomas's view as a kind of *via media* between "the view that everything that exists is individual, and the opinion that universals exist as such outside the mind" (Haldane, "A Thomist Metaphysics," 34). He explains, "Natures are many in things and one in the mind; but that as such, i.e. until a context has been specified, they are neither. Universality is only to be found in the intellect, but general species are nonetheless real: they are formed by abstraction from a plurality of formally identical natures existing in materially individuated substances."

famous razor. Ockham wants to pare away anything superfluous and, in his mind, universals were just that.[163]

But things are not so simple as this casual abandonment of universals suggests. The rejection of universals left a very important question unanswered—namely, "Why do the author of this book and its readers seem to have so much in common?" If there is no human nature per se, what accounts for the fact that we can say that there are roughly seven billion human persons? What ties them together into such a category? Ockham's answer is essential to understanding what happened to transubstantiation (and many other things besides!) in the hands of nominalist thinkers: the will of God.[164] In other words, voluntarism, recourse to God's bare will as an explanatory category, is concomitant with nominalism. The rejection of universals ends up putting a heretofore unimagined emphasis on the divine will. It is difficult to overestimate the impact of this move.

Voluntarism is a radical epistemological break with the medieval worldview exemplified in the work of Thomas Aquinas. For Thomas, will and reason were intimately related. It would have been impossible for Thomas to imagine that God could will something unreasonable. To do so would have been, simply put, unloving, and therefore impossible for God. With voluntarism it becomes possible to imagine God acting out of pure will without reference to reason. God's power, God's *potentia absoluta*, becomes the measure by which any theological assertion is judged. But this leads to theological chaos. As Gustave Martelet writes, with nominalism,

> there is no affirmation which is not destroyed by its own contrary. There is no earlier negation which cannot or must not in turn be changed into pure affirmation. Nothing can resist this inverting force which only, and which alone, appears to be a true definition of reason. . . . [In such a context] our only certainty will come solely from faith, which itself, moreover, is reduced to blind submission to the authority of the Church. Her decisions alone enjoy the right to stabilize an intellectual uncertainty which otherwise could be absolute.[165]

And, he continues,

> in such a climate of thought, earlier theological convictions concerning transubstantiation were not to remain unshaken. . . . Since the true principle of all things is solely the divine Power, how can *con*substantiation, which allows the

---

163. Boersma, *Heavenly Participation*, 80–81; Barron, *Priority of Christ*, 14. See also Dupré, *Passage to Modernity*, 104.

164. Boersma, *Heavenly Participation*, 81.

165. Martelet, *The Risen Christ and the Eucharistic World*, 140.

substance of the bread to co-exist with that of the body, be less acceptable than *trans*ubstantiation, which effects the conversion of the former into the latter, or than *annihilation*, which suppresses the substance of the bread; balancing miracle against miracle, which do you prefer?[166]

And, for reasons that will become clear, the nominalists preferred consubstantiation.

Several factors contributed to this preference, most of which have already been hinted at above. The final task of this chapter is to braid these loose threads into a sturdy cord upon which to hang our conclusion—namely, that what the Reformation rejected about transubstantiation was not what Thomas had taught.

The Transformation of Transubstantiation

The first thing to note is that Thomas's teaching about substance and accidents was a rather straightforward transposition of the patristic (and, particularly, Augustinian) categories of sign and signified, or, to put everything in the same order, of signified and sign.[167] To the patristic mind, real presence was possible because underneath the sign was the deeper reality in which the sign sacramentally participated. While Berengarius and those who disputed with him had "mortally wounded" such "symbolism,"[168] Thomas rearticulated the same basic conviction in ontological terms, using the newly minted Aristotelian language of "substance" and "accidents." Underneath the accidents—the sign—exists the substance—the signified, the deeper reality mediated by the sign. But while "substance" and "accident" are Aristotelian terms, the framework in which they were employed was far from pure Aristotelianism.[169] They were used by Thomas to convey the same participative metaphysics and sacramental ontology that underlay the early Church's convictions about Christ's real presence. As Louis Dupré writes,

> Even after Aristotle's philosophy became the chief conceptual instrument for articulating Christian theology and the category of efficient causality became

166. Martelet, *The Risen Christ and the Eucharistic World*, 141.
167. Indeed, we have already seen (p. 33 above) Kereszty's claim that "Thomas knows about an intimate ontological connection not only between substance and accidents but also, in the context of Salvation History, between the sign and the reality signified by it." Kereszty, "On the Eucharistic Presence," 349–50.
168. Henri de Lubac, *Corpus Mysticum: The Eucharist and the Church in the Middle Ages*, trans. Laurence Paul Hemming and Susan Frank Parsons (Notre Dame, IN: University of Notre Dame Press, 2007), 228.
169. Chadwick, "Ego Berengarius," 426. We will revisit this issue in more detail in chap. 2.

the principal one for defining the entire relation of the Creator to his creation, it did not yet denote a purely extrinsic relation as in its modern usage. Aquinas hesitated considerably between Plato's participation and Aristotle's efficient causality for conceptualizing the creature's dependence on God. Even in the later *Summa Theologiae* when he had mainly opted for the latter, he wrote: "Being is innermost in each thing and most fundamentally present within all things, since it is formal in respect of everything found in a thing. . . . Hence it must be that God is in all things, and innermostly."[170]

Though Berengarius had begun the exodus,[171] Aquinas still lived in a world where creation existed by participation in God. In fact, he was trying to halt the exodus. That Thomas explicitly applied this kind of thinking to his teaching about transubstantiation is clear. In a key passage, the significance of which is often overlooked, Aquinas writes that "the author of being is able to change that which is *being* in the one into that which is *being* in the other, by taking away what kept this from being that."[172] This is, in fact, a strong, if typically unrecognized, assertion of just the kind of sacramental ontology upon which the patristic view of real presence had been based. Such an articulation does not merely make the Church's traditional claim in a new context, it actually challenges the presuppositions of that context. It says that bread and wine can become Christ only because they are a part of creation, which already exists only by participating in Christ. This presupposition of the sacramental worldview is at the heart of Thomas's doctrine of transubstantiation and shows us that transubstantiation is not simply a modern answer to a modern question, as it would, almost necessarily, come to be read.[173] It is, rather, a challenge to a desacramentalized modernity, however incipient. In the face of Berengarius's mere symbolism and the ultrarealism of his opponents, Thomas uses transubstantiation to witness to a worldview in which a precisely *sacramental* presence is conceivable.

As we have already seen, the assertion of univocity undermines just this worldview. If things exist merely alongside of God but not by participation in

170. Dupré, *Passage to Modernity*, 173. The quote from Thomas is from *ST* I, q. 8, a. 1.

171. See Boersma, *Heavenly Participation*, 57.

172. *ST* III, 75.4 ad 3. A footnote at this point in the Blackfriars edition reads, "M.-T. Penido in *Le rôle de l'analogie en théologie dogmatique*, Paris, 1931, p. 437, says that the words of this reply are *the most profound words ever said on the possibility and nature of the Eucharistic conversion*" (emphasis original).

173. This is Benedict XVI's point when he writes that "it cannot be the case that the Body of Christ comes to add itself to the bread, as if bread and Body were two similar things that could exist as two 'substances,' in the same way, side by side." To highlight the distinction between the two kinds of things, a difference that gets lost in modernity, Benedict, like Calvin, prefers the metaphor of elevation. Benedict XVI, *God Is Near Us*, 86.

God, then a key aspect of Thomas's articulation becomes incoherent. What could it mean to say that the substance of the bread and wine *become* the substance of the body and blood of Christ by God *taking away* what *kept them from being Christ* if Christ is not already what is innermost to all of creation, the one through whom all things are made? Even abstracting from Thomas's subtle but essential point about "taking away," how can one understand eucharistic presence at all when Christ is not what is innermost in creation? The answer, already in Scotus, is clear: nonsacramentally.

Scotus's basic position is that, since both consubstantiation and transubstantiation would be theoretically possible for God, the more likely option is the one that would require fewer miracles and leave fewer *inconvenientia*. Consubstantiation wins on this reckoning because, if the substance of the bread and wine remain, there is no need to miraculously preserve the accidents in being without their proper subject. Furthermore, it avoids the inconvenience of deception in the sacrament, because in transubstantiation the accidents fail to signify their proper substance, but in consubstantiation they still do signify their proper substance.[174]

In response to this first concern, Thomas would respond that preserving the accidents without their proper subject is no extra miracle at all, but simply the outworking of the first and only miracle by which the substance of the bread and wine become the substance of Christ's body and blood.[175] But it is Scotus's second point that is of most interest for us here. According to Thomas, the sacrament does not contain any deception. Our senses perceive the signs of bread and wine, and those signs really are there.[176] The bread and the wine are essential to the sacrament precisely as signs. In fact, the continued presence of the bread and wine, as in consubstantiation, would obscure the signification proper to the sacrament because the sacramental signs would no longer lead only to the heavenly, but to the earthly as well; not to Christ's body and blood, as is proper to the sacrament, but to bread and wine.[177] We

174. Levy, *John Wyclif*, 193–95. Scotus even prefers annihilation over transubstantiation for similar reasons.

175. *ST* III, 77.5 corpus: "There is no new miracle; it all happens as a result of the original one." See below, pp. 120–21.

176. *ST* III, 75.5 ad 2: "There is no deception in the sacrament; the accidents, which are the proper object for our senses to deal with, are genuinely there. Our intellect, which is properly concerned with the substance of a thing, as Aristotle says, is kept by faith from being led into error."

177. McCue, "Doctrine of Transubstantiation," 401. McCue quotes Thomas's commentary on Lombard's *Sentences* as saying that the remaining presence of the bread and wine "would run counter to the meaning of the sacrament: the species would not, as a sign, lead to the true body of Christ, but rather to the substance of the bread" (Lib. IV, dist. Xi, a. 1, solution 1). It is clear that Thomas was not alone in this view among the thirteenth-century theologians who

see here an obvious consequence of the rejection of sacramental ontology implied by univocity: whereas for Thomas it would have been deceptive if the sacramental signs led to the earthly, for Scotus it is now deceptive if they lead only to the heavenly!

Nevertheless, as we have seen, Scotus opts for transubstantiation on Church authority (even while maintaining that the Eucharist must be an exception to the rule that the sacraments contain no falsity!).[178] But it is important to note that he does not opt for Thomas's version of it. Transubstantiation in Thomas was an insistence on a precisely sacramental presence. In Scotus it becomes one magic trick among the many conceivable magic tricks by which an omnipotent God might bring about the real, but rather unsacramental, presence of Christ's body and blood. Scotus reworks transubstantiation in order to overcome certain defects he saw in Thomas's position. This reworking is very telling. For Scotus, many of the aspects of Thomas's articulation are unsatisfactory precisely because they are too exclusively sacramental. Levy writes that, according to Scotus,

> despite what Aquinas says, God can make the same body simultaneously present in different locations, not just sacramentally, but locally and dimensively. After all, wherever God can make a natural substance exist in a way that is not in keeping with its natural mode of existence, he can surely make it exist according to its natural mode, since the latter would require one less miracle.[179]

That Scotus manages to articulate a way in which Christ can be dimensively present even as his dimensions are radically incommensurate with the dimensions of the consecrated bread and wine will not surprise the reader at this point. God, of course, could do it. It is not important for us to investigate these details.[180] What is more interesting and important for our purposes is to ask, "Why, exactly, would we want something other than a sacramental presence? Is the Eucharist not a sacrament? What would it even mean to eat Christ present according to his natural mode?" The answer, it seems clear, is that, once the sign no longer *really* participates in the signified, a sacramental

---

preferred transubstantiation to consubstantiation. McCue quotes Albert the Great, Thomas's teacher, three pages earlier: "It must be said that, though it is possible for a glorified body (and especially the body of the Lord) to be in the same place with the bread, there is a problem because of the nature of the sacrament, not because of the nature of the place. . . . For the accident would lead only to its own substance, and thus it would fail to function as a sign" (398).

178. Levy, *John Wyclif*, 195.
179. Levy, *John Wyclif*, 196.
180. The interested reader can see Levy, *John Wyclif*, 195–97, as well as Levy, "Eucharist in the Fourteenth and Fifteenth Centuries," 236–37.

presence is no longer a very *real* presence at all. If the Church's ancient faith that Christ is really present is to be maintained, sacramental presence will no longer suffice. It needs to be supplemented by something more, dare we suggest, substantial.[181]

Substance or Quantity?

But, as we have noted above and as we will investigate in detail in the next chapter, the term "substantial" entered the Church's vocabulary following the Berengarian controversy as a way to affirm a real *sacramental* presence. And we have also noted that it came to function, especially in Thomas, as a new way of saying "signified," while "accidents" came to function as a new way of saying "sign." We can now add that, in Thomas, as in Aristotle, there are several categories of accident, the first of which is the most basic. It is typically referred to as "quantity," and Thomas often calls it "the tendency to measure." What it means, basically, is that something takes up space. It is the most basic accident because, unless something is taking up space, it will not be in any spatial relationship with other things, nor will it have color, smell, and so forth. Without quantity, no other accidents are conceivable. It is so basic, in fact, that Thomas suggests that, once the substance of the bread and wine have become the substance of Christ's body and blood, the other accidents are able to subsist (miraculously, to be sure) in this first accident, the tendency to measure.[182]

The problem, however, emerges when quantity's admittedly basic nature ends up getting it confused with substance. As we saw earlier, the loss of analogy and sacramentality meant that "no longer was there a mysterious reality hiding within what could be observed by the senses. The full reality of created objects could be seen, heard, touched, smelled, and tasted."[183] That is to say, *substance as heretofore understood no longer existed.* There are only accidents, though one of them, the most basic one—*quantitas*—will now be identified with substance.[184] What this means, of course, is that "substance"

181. Cf. Leithart, "What's Wrong with Transubstantiation?," 307: "Even before Luther, the Thomistic doctrine was far from secure. Thomas's solution to the question of real presence had been, in fact, almost immediately undermined by Duns Scotus and William of Ockham, both of whom returned to an earlier, more realistic and physical conception of substance. This development is crucial for an understanding of Luther, who stands in the Ockhamist rather than the Thomist tradition." See p. 302 of Leithart's article for more details on this "earlier" conception of substance.

182. *ST* III, 77.2 corpus, ad 1.

183. Boersma, *Heavenly Participation*, 75.

184. Benedict XVI, "Problem of Transubstantiation," 233.

can no longer fill the role it filled for Thomas. It has crossed the aisle from the signified to the sign. According to Joseph Ratzinger this shift, which began in the late Middle Ages, became definitive in the work of Descartes,[185] and so, in modern parlance, substance has come to mean almost precisely what Thomas Aquinas meant by accidents.[186]

Of course, given that the loss of a participative metaphysics had rendered sacramental presence no longer satisfactory, the linguistic shift undergone by "substance" allowed it to keep its role in eucharistic theology—namely, that of guaranteeing the *reality* of the presence, even while that theology became less and less recognizable. Ratzinger writes,

> In the philosophical development of late Scholasticism, the Thomistic concept of transubstantiation had become intellectually untenable and inherently contradictory as a result of the extensive recasting of the Aristotelian categories that had taken place almost unnoticed in the leading schools. This process . . . had already started immediately after Thomas: the identification of substance and quantity, of substance and "mass," as we would say today. However, since in the celebration of the Eucharist nothing about the quantities changes perceptibly, the concept of transubstantiation had lost its meaning vis-à-vis the prevalent understanding of substance.[187]

And, like the loss of analogy, this change in the meaning of the term "substance" also favors consubstantiation over transubstantiation. If substance is simply quantity, then the substances of the bread and wine clearly remain, or, at the very least, we are deceived.[188]

Fideism

Now, after working through the philosophical shifts of the late Middle Ages and having looked at the rejection of transubstantiation in light of them, it is appropriate to return to the issue that our own age finds so fascinating that it tends to skip over the whole question we have just considered: the profession of belief in transubstantiation by those who find it incoherent or, at least, unsatisfying. There are those who would applaud these theologians for their

185. Benedict XVI, "Problem of Transubstantiation," 233; cf. Haldane, "A Thomist Metaphysics," 26.

186. Recall, in this regard, the discovery of the Disciples of Christ that what they rejected as transubstantiation was "almost the opposite of what Aquinas had intended." See above, p. 29.

187. Benedict XVI, "Problem of Transubstantiation," 227–28.

188. We can note, perhaps, that it is not only late medieval proponents of consubstantiation who, confusing accidents for substance, think that the sacrament contains a deception. Many contemporary Roman Catholics who affirm transubstantiation make precisely the same error.

obedience and fidelity. It is, after all, the vocation of the theologian to think with the Church. Nevertheless, there is something unsettling about the way this was gone about in late Scholasticism. For one does not get the sense that these theologians really *were* thinking with the Church. There was something strictly formal about their affirmations of transubstantiation. Because God's will was no longer intimately connected with reason in their systems, they could hold, at one and the same time, that transubstantiation was true, and that it was unreasonable. They never felt challenged to think that perhaps, if it was true, it was also reasonable. They had managed to inoculate their own views from any real challenge by Church tradition or authority. Ratzinger describes the situation this way:

> In a procedure typical of late Scholasticism and nominalism, theologians continued nevertheless to adhere to transubstantiation in a purely verbal way: whereas it is absurd, naturally considered, it must however be accepted in faith even contrary to this insight. This double-entry bookkeeping, in which the faith was no longer elaborated rationally and thought went its own way independent from it, while the formulas of theology were adhered to externally although they had become intrinsically absurd or meaningless—this double-entry bookkeeping is characteristic of that inner fragility which the situation of faith and Church in the late Middle Ages increasingly exacerbated.[189]

Though the theologians formally denied it, and found clever ways to avoid the charge,[190] it is hard to disagree with Martelet's assessment that "in those days fideism had taken up its abode in theology, before a complete human scepticism was to come as a quick reply to divine whim."[191]

It was, of course, the formality and sterility of late medieval nominalism against which Luther rightly rebelled. What we have seen here, in the case of transubstantiation, was merely a microcosm of what had happened to theology generally. The radical break between faith and reason had made theology an exercise of unnatural exteriority. And it was this barren exteriority that engendered Luther's breakthrough to interiority. Of course, this breakthrough also occurred in Catholic Spain with the likes of Teresa of Ávila, John of the Cross, and Ignatius Loyola, but in those cases it was expressed in the realm of spirituality, from which theology itself had been largely divorced. For Luther, on the other hand, interiority needed to be expressed in theology itself.

189. Benedict XVI, "Problem of Transubstantiation," 228.
190. See, e.g., Oberman, *Harvest of Medieval Theology*, 278; McCue, "Doctrine of Transubstantiation," 403.
191. Martelet, *The Risen Christ and the Eucharistic World*, 140.

As we shall see in chapter 3, with specific reference to his eucharistic theology, though Luther rejected nominalism (and for this reason never referred to his own theology of presence with the descriptor "consubstantiation," despite obvious resemblances), he was never able to pull himself completely from its gravity.[192] He rightly rejected late nominalism's version of transubstantiation (Thomas Aquinas would have seconded the motion!), but he had no way of knowing that this was far from what Thomas had meant by the term. And though other Reformers were less influenced by nominalism than Luther, it is fair to extend this judgment to the Reformation in general. In its rejection of transubstantiation, it was not the articulation of Thomas Aquinas that was rejected, but something that, as far back as Scotus, had already—explicitly—rejected Aquinas's articulation.

What all this means, from an ecumenical perspective, is that the rejection of transubstantiation by the Reformers in the sixteenth century need not be definitive for Catholic-Protestant understanding today.[193] Though, as we have seen, the rejection or affirmation of transubstantiation is central to the identity of many Protestants and Catholics, this is rarely based on familiarity with the theology of Thomas or even of Luther and Calvin. Indeed, as we shall see in the following chapters, without the opportunity to read Thomas, both Luther and Calvin end up reproducing much of what was essential to Thomas's articulation. Had they been able to read him and read him sympathetically, they may well have found his articulation of eucharistic presence quite amenable to their own purposes. On the other hand, Luther and Calvin (or at least Lutherans and Calvin) could not come to agreement on the nature of Christ's eucharistic presence themselves. Is it possible that Thomas could be of help here? Could it be the case that transubstantiation, far from being something Protestants must reject, could actually contribute to intra-Protestant understanding?

To answer such questions it is essential that we look at the thought, first of Thomas, then of Luther and Calvin in light of Thomas, in more detail.

---

192. The definitive study of this is still Oberman, *Harvest of Medieval Theology*. See also Dupré, *Passage to Modernity*, 203; Benedict XVI, "Problem of Transubstantiation," 228; Martelet, *The Risen Christ and the Eucharistic World*, 141. For a study on this question with particular reference to the Eucharist, see Thomas Osborne, "Faith, Philosophy, and the Nominalist Background to Luther's Defense of the Real Presence," *Journal of the History of Ideas* 63, no. 1 (2002): 63–82.

193. Cf. Lehmann and Pannenberg, *Condemnations of the Reformation Era*, 98–101.

2

Transubstantiation
in the Catholic Tradition

Origins of "Transubstantiation"

The first thing that it is necessary to investigate when looking at Thomas Aquinas and his articulation of transubstantiation is the historical context. We will not understand Thomas if we do not understand where the term "transubstantiation" came from and why it was so attractive to the Church of the High Middle Ages. In order to do this, we need to look at the eucharistic controversies that had both shaken the Western Church and shaped its eucharistic theology in the centuries before Thomas.

Though a careful exegesis of John 6 would seem to indicate that there have always been some Christians who have struggled with the Church's faith in Christ's eucharistic presence,[1] the fact remains that the Church managed to avoid any serious eucharistic controversy for almost a millennium. Given the radical nature of the Church's claim witnessed to by John 6, that, in itself, is remarkable. In the ninth century, however, the first tremors of the seismic shift that was to forever alter the landscape of eucharistic theology in the West began to make themselves felt.

The basic problem involves the translation of the Church's traditional faith into a new cultural and philosophical context. As we have already seen, especially in the work of Hans Boersma, patristic articulations of Christ's

1. Jenson, "Tenth Locus," 346.

real eucharistic presence were made within a worldview that was basically favorable to sacramentality. At issue was the relationship between symbol and reality. As a sacrament, the Eucharist is, by definition, symbolic. To the contemporary Roman Catholic invested in a theology of *real* presence, however, this statement is felt to be in immediate need of qualification.[2] To moderns, "symbol" is typically seen as opposed to "reality."[3] The Fathers of the Church had no such qualms. In the patristic age, "symbol" did not carry the implication of less-than-fully-real that it carries today.[4] Rather, in a Platonist worldview, the "dialectical relationship between the world of forms and the world of sense-experience means that the image or symbol cannot be thought of apart from the reality in which it participates."[5] This means that

> in the ancient world, a symbol had almost the opposite meaning of that which it has in modern culture. A symbol in ancient society is not primarily a pointer that represents something apart from the symbol. In ancient society, a symbol participates in that which it represents, so that it can almost be said to *be* that which it represents. Ancient thought does not distinguish in the way in which modern popular thinking does between symbol and reality. In antiquity, the symbol is the presence of that which it represents and mediates participation in that reality.[6]

This can be disorienting for the modern reader of patristic sources. Often coming to those sources anachronistically looking for either "realist" or "symbolist" theologies of eucharistic presence, the reader is baffled to find state-

2. Bruce Marshall, e.g., begins his dogmatic outline of the Eucharist by affirming that sacraments are signs and then, cognizant that such a statement requires serious explanation, devotes much of his essay to demonstrating just how real sacramental signs can be. See Marshall, "What Is the Eucharist? A Dogmatic Outline," in *The Oxford Handbook of Sacramental Theology*, ed. Hans Boersma and Matthew Levering (Oxford: Oxford University Press, 2015), 500–516.

3. Aidan Nichols writes that "calling the relationship between the elements and the divine-human victim 'symbolisation' *can* be given an acceptable meaning—so long as symbolisation is not defined over against identification, something which, for contemporary culture and consciousness in the West is, however, virtually inevitable" (*The Holy Eucharist: From the New Testament to Pope John Paul II* [Dublin: Veritas, 1991], 27).

4. A. Nichols, *Holy Eucharist*, 34–35.

5. Crockett, *Eucharist*, 82.

6. Crockett, *Eucharist*, 80. See also Robert Sokolowski, *Eucharistic Presence: A Study in the Theology of Disclosure* (Washington, DC: Catholic University of America Press, 1994), 198–99; Power, *Eucharistic Mystery*, 159; Colman E. O'Neill, OP, *Sacramental Realism: A General Theory of the Sacraments* (Wilmington, DE: Michael Glazier, 1983), 98. This explains why the Fathers could blithely accept metaphors about sculptures or paintings being the presence of historical figures when discussing eucharistic presence that seem to completely miss the point for us moderns. Indeed, Thomas himself follows them in this. See *ST* III, 73.5.

ments of both kinds side by side in the same author.[7] But, as David Power notes, the unselfconscious oscillation between calling the Eucharist "the body of Christ" and a "figure," "type," or "symbol" of the body of Christ indicates that the Fathers saw no contradiction in these two types of statements.[8]

While later theology would describe the medieval followers of St. Augustine as "symbolists" and the followers of St. Ambrose as "realists," the facts are that Augustine gives no indication of disagreement with Ambrose, the man who brought him into the Church, and that it is possible to find both "realist" statements in Augustine and "symbolist" statements in Ambrose.[9] Symbol and reality were not, in the patristic period, competing doctrines of eucharistic presence, but simply "different modes of expression within the framework of common presuppositions,"[10] namely, that symbols participated in the reality they were called upon to represent.

As we have already seen in chapter 1, such a participatory view of symbol and reality has obvious affinities with the Christian view of the relationship between God and creation.[11] And the implications of such a worldview for eucharistic theology are clear. As Boersma writes, "the very term 'real presence' is an indication of the deep impact that the Platonist-Christian synthesis exerted on the church's worship. The eucharistic body 'really' participated in the mystery of the unity of Christ himself."[12]

Though the Church's affirmation of Christ's eucharistic presence was always a "hard saying" (John 6:60),[13] and the early Christians *were* sometimes accused of cannibalism, a worldview that included a participatory metaphysics allowed Christians themselves both to give full scope to symbol *and* reality in their understanding of the Eucharist and to avoid any serious dissension

7. Cf. Crockett, *Eucharist*, 83. Crockett's schema includes not only "realist" and "symbolical," but also "spiritualistic."

8. Power, *Eucharistic Mystery*, 146.

9. See Crockett, *Eucharist*, 87–88; James T. O'Connor, *The Hidden Manna: A Theology of the Eucharist* (San Francisco: Ignatius, 2005), 53–56; Power, *Eucharistic Mystery*, 146.

10. Crockett, *Eucharist*, 83.

11. Indeed, for this reason, Boersma's basic goal in *Heavenly Participation* is the recovery of what he calls the Platonist-Christian synthesis. See esp. pp. 33–51.

12. Boersma, *Heavenly Participation*, 51. Later Boersma adds, "Everyone understood that God most truly gives himself in the body of Christ in the eucharistic celebration. Thus, people experience participation in heavenly realities—in the eternal Son of God himself—nowhere as gloriously as in the Eucharist itself. Heaven and earth, nature and the supernatural come together in the real presence of Christ on the altar. In a very important sense, the general sacramental ontology—the participation of natural, created existence in the Christological anchor provides the basis for the real presence of Christ in the Eucharist" (57). See also Power, *Eucharistic Mystery*, 149.

13. Cf. O'Connor, *Hidden Manna*, 95–97; Robert E. Barron, *Eucharist* (Maryknoll, NY: Orbis, 2008), 99–101.

within their own ranks about eucharistic presence. As that worldview was eclipsed in the Western Church (note that the East has never had a major dispute about the Eucharist), the untroubled coexistence of symbol and reality in eucharistic theology was lost.

In the worldview of the Germanic tribes that had come to dominate what had once been the Western Roman Empire, symbol did not have the same participatory relationship to reality that it had had for the Platonist Greeks. For these peoples, like modern Westerners, symbols were related to the realities they signaled in a merely external fashion.[14] This, of course, had serious ramifications for eucharistic theology. Whereas for the Christians in the patristic period, eucharistic realism was guaranteed by symbol, it now seemed to be in direct conflict with symbol.[15] Appropriating the Church's tradition in this new situation would prove a difficult and contentious undertaking.

Corbie

The first discernible hints of the problem show up at the Benedictine Abbey of Corbie, in France, in the 830s. The abbot Paschasius Radbertus composed the first known systematic treatise on the Eucharist in the history of theology, *De corpore et sanguine Domini*, for the education of his monks. It has been described as a combination of Augustinian sacramental theology and "popular realism,"[16] and its overriding concern was to affirm the identity between the body of Christ present in the Eucharist and the historical body of Christ, born of the Virgin Mary and crucified for our salvation.[17] While most commentators argue that Paschasius was an able enough interpreter of Augustine to be cleared of charges of ultrarealism, or capharnaism,[18] it is true that he gives his critics some ammunition with his suggestion that the sacramental species function as a veil to protect the communicant from the

14. Edward J. Kilmartin, *The Eucharist in the West: History and Theology* (Collegeville, MN: Liturgical Press, 1998), 79.

15. See Crockett, *Eucharist*, 106–7: "As long as the symbol is the means by which the community participates in the reality that it signifies, there is no problem in using symbolical and realist language simultaneously. Once the unity between the symbol and the reality begins to dissolve, however, the presence of the reality seems to be threatened when symbolical language is used."

16. Heron, *Table and Tradition*, 92.

17. A. Nichols, *Holy Eucharist*, 59.

18. A. Nichols, *Holy Eucharist*, 59; Nathan Mitchell, *Cult and Controversy: The Worship of the Eucharist outside Mass* (New York: Pueblo, 1982), 78; Mark G. Vaillancourt, "Sacramental Theology from Gottschalk to Lanfranc," in *The Oxford Handbook of Sacramental Theology*, ed. Hans Boersma and Matthew Levering (Oxford: Oxford University Press, 2015), 188; Lawrence Feingold, *The Eucharist: Mystery of Presence, Sacrifice, and Communion* (Steubenville, OH: Emmaus Academic, 2018), 236.

horror of eating raw flesh and his uncritical appropriation of grossly carnal legends from popular piety.[19]

Furthermore, his hearty defense of what would come to be called eucharistic realism struck at least some of his contemporaries as "novel and exaggerated."[20] One of these contemporaries was the emperor Charles the Bald, grandson of Charlemagne, who requested clarification on the issue from another monk at Corbie, the theologian Ratramnus.[21] The question Charles put to Ratramnus, whether Christ was present in figure or in truth, highlighted quite explicitly the issue that would bedevil eucharistic theology from that point on—namely, how does the Eucharist's symbolic nature relate to the Church's claim that Christ is *really* present?

Ratramnus's thought is a bit slippery. In his response to the falsely dichotomous question put to him by the emperor, Ratramnus concluded that Christ was present in figure, not in truth.[22] And while his decision led to accusations of heresy for denying Christ's presence,[23] most scholars reject this interpretation.[24] Ratramnus did not deny that something objective changed in the Eucharist at the consecration but, since he had defined "truth" as that which is evident to the senses, he was forced to affirm the alternative, Christ's presence in "figure."[25] In point of fact, Ratramnus's theology was, in certain ways, more traditional than Paschasius's. In its more nuanced consideration of sign and its rejection of the kind of crude materialism that occasionally crept into Paschasius's work, it was more properly sacramental.[26] However, the unfortunate rejection of Christ's presence in "truth," and the consequent denial that the eucharistic body could be identified with Christ's historical body, ensured that Ratramnus would not emerge as the voice of the tradition. Ratramnus, as Aidan Nichols puts it, "set out to combat the Paschasian notion of a supernatural transformation of the bread and wine extending to their very appearances, veiled though this be to our sensory perception; in pruning back a theological excess, he cut too deep into the sap-bearing trunk of the Church's

---

19. De Lubac, *Corpus Mysticum*, 160. Nathan Mitchell recounts an especially ghastly narrative including a vision of an angel descending to an altar with a knife and dismembering a small child. See Mitchell, *Cult and Controversy*, 78–79.

20. Walsh, *Sacraments of Initiation*, 297. See also Mitchell, *Cult and Controversy*, 80; Kilmartin, *Eucharist in the West*, 88.

21. Mitchell, *Cult and Controversy*, 80–81.

22. A. Nichols, *Holy Eucharist*, 60.

23. O'Connor mentions Geiselmann in this regard. See O'Connor, *Hidden Manna*, 91n43.

24. John H. McKenna, *Become What You Receive: A Systematic Study of the Eucharist* (Chicago: Hillenbrand, 2011), 174.

25. O'Connor, *Hidden Manna*, 93.

26. Mitchell, *Cult and Controversy*, 82.

eucharistic faith."[27] Neither articulation from Corbie was satisfactory, but these ambiguities in Ratramnus cost him the field, and a Paschasian realism gained increasing hold of eucharistic theology in the years that followed.

If Ratramnus's weakness was a rejection of Christ's presence in "truth" that could easily be misread as a denial of Christ's real presence, buttressed by a denial of identity between Christ's eucharistic and historical bodies,[28] Paschasius's weakness was "a failure to take the sacramental signs with full seriousness."[29] This was especially evident in his teaching that our senses are miraculously preserved from seeing Christ physically on the altar.[30] Such a suggestion leaves little room for the signs of bread and wine to function sacramentally and turns them into mere disguises. And, though Paschasius's views had gained hegemony in Western eucharistic theology, his failure in this regard would necessarily provoke a reaction in a Western Church whose towering patristic authority was St. Augustine himself, the key features of whose eucharistic theology included a careful analysis of the relationship between sign and the reality signified.[31] That the reaction would emerge in the person of Berengarius of Tours, a man of acerbic temper, ever ready to castigate opponents even in the highest places, certainly contributed to the sensation it caused in the eleventh-century Church.[32]

Ego Berengarius

By the time of Berengarius, Ratramnus's work on the Eucharist had been mistaken for that of John Scotus Eriugena.[33] A popular teacher in Tours, Berengarius took up Ratramnus's arguments, under Eriugena's already suspect name, against the Paschasian realism prominent in his day, but with a new twist. Berengarius was one of the leading proponents of a new way of thinking that was sweeping Western Europe at the time, that of dialectic.[34]

---

27. A. Nichols, *Holy Eucharist*, 61.

28. Ratramnus actually posits a dual body of Christ to account for this. See Martelet, *The Risen Christ and the Eucharistic World*, 129.

29. Mitchell, *Cult and Controversy*, 76.

30. A. Nichols, *Holy Eucharist*, 60.

31. Cf. Crockett, *Eucharist*, 109. See also Kilmartin, *Eucharist in the West*, 97.

32. Chadwick, "Ego Berengarius," 428. See also Margaret Gibson, "The Case of Berengar of Tours," *Studies in Church History* 7 (1971): 61. While most treatments of the subject deal with the theological nuances, this fascinating article is interested in the politics surrounding the Berengarian controversy.

33. O'Connor, *Hidden Manna*, 94. Eriugena was one of the most important thinkers of the early Middle Ages (ca. 810–ca. 877); he was suspected of teaching a purely symbolic presence of Christ in the Eucharist. His work on the Eucharist is not extant.

34. See de Lubac, *Corpus Mysticum*, 227–28.

The rather unselfconscious lack of participatory metaphysics that informed Charles the Bald's poorly put questions to Ratramnus was now elevated to a science and ensconced in theology. Roch Kereszty explains that the conflict,[35] which began at Corbie,

> grew into a crisis of faith when, with the spreading of a rationalist dialectic, the meaning of symbol was reduced to a mere noetic sign. In this context, the consecrated elements do not participate in the reality of the body and blood but simply point to them. In the new climate the traditional words, *symbolum, figura, sacramentum,* could no longer express the faith of the Church as had been possible, albeit imperfectly, in the context of Christian Platonism.[36]

Though he considered himself an heir of Augustine, Berengarius's dialectical method made him incapable of truly understanding the bishop of Hippo. "The new dialecticians," indicts Henri de Lubac in his classic study *Corpus Mysticum,*

> were only capable of dissociating a reality that was believed to have been united for ever by those geniuses of ontological symbolism, the Fathers of the Church. At the hands of Berengar, the sacramental synthesis disintegrated. . . . On the one hand, there was a real body—whether earthly or heavenly—which could only be understood *sensibly*; on the other, there was a spiritual body, which no longer had real corporality nor, to be frank, any objective existence. On the one hand, there was the idea of a substantial presence, which came to an end for us when Christ returned to heaven; on the other, a power bereft of the pregnant significance that it still had for the theologians of the previous age. . . . All the symbolic inclusions were transformed, in his understanding, into dialectical antitheses. Thus he constantly separated what tradition unified.[37]

It is true, in any case, that Berengarius's formulas met with vigorous objection in the theological community. The tragedy of this situation, however, lies in the failure of the orthodox party to apprehend neither the real threat

35. It is perhaps worth noting, as Gary Macy does, that, "if there was a controversy at Corbie in the mid-ninth century, it was a very quiet one. A few mumblings by other theologians, which may or may not have been directed at the two monks, are the only witnesses to the struggle. No council was held; Paschasius remained as abbot, Ratramnus remained a well-respected theologian. As far as can be determined, the two men went on living together in peace, attending the same liturgy, but obviously thinking about it in quite different ways" (*The Banquet's Wisdom: A Short History of the Theologies of the Lord's Supper,* 2nd ed. [Akron: OSL Publications, 2005], 90).
36. Kereszty, *Wedding Feast of the Lamb,* 131–32.
37. De Lubac, *Corpus Mysticum,* 226.

posed by Berengarius's dialectic nor the genuine insight his protests contained. Instead, they mirrored Berengarius's errors back to him.[38] And this is also what makes the Berengarian controversy interesting for our purposes. As we shall see, the task of transubstantiation was precisely to put back together what Berengarius, in unwitting collusion with his opponents, had separated.

For Ratramnus, the rejection of Christ's presence in "truth" did not amount to a rejection of the Church's faith, precisely because he had defined "truth" to mean simply that which was apprehended by the senses. Berengarius, on the other hand, was understood by his contemporaries to have rejected real presence, despite his protests to the contrary, because his rejection of a presence apprehended by the senses seemed to include a rejection of anything objectively real.[39] "Berengar's major difficulty appeared to have been an inability to conceive of the presence of the body and blood of Christ in any but physical terms, and this sort of presence he simply could not accept in the Eucharist."[40] The rift between symbol and reality that was already discernible at Corbie had become, with Berengarius, an unbridgeable chasm. Whereas Paschasius could acknowledge the role of symbol and Ratramnus could affirm a deeper reality beyond the sacramental signs, Berengarius's attempts at securing Christ's real presence after his radical division of sign from reality were unconvincing.[41] While Berengarius was right to reassert the symbolic reality of the sacrament, "the possibility of a symbol that actually makes present the reality signified never seemed to have crossed his mind."[42]

Furthermore, while Berengarius's dialectical methodology ended up solidifying the separation of symbol and reality, his argument from grammar and logic also contributed to the suspicion he aroused. According to Berengarius, the words "Hoc est enim corpus meum" lose any sense if the "hoc" in question is no longer bread. In Henry Chadwick's pithy summary, "To assert that the consecrated bread and wine are Christ's body and blood necessarily implies that they exist to be so. X cannot be Y if no X exists to be Y."[43] But, read through a dialectical either/or, as opposed to a symbolic inclusivity, the affirmation of the continued presence of bread and wine amounted to a denial

---

38. A. Nichols, *Holy Eucharist*, 65–66.

39. See McCue, "Doctrine of Transubstantiation," 386. Henry Chadwick argues that "to classify [Berengarius] as a 'mere symbolist' would be misleading" ("Ego Berengarius," 421).

40. Gary Macy, *The Theologies of the Eucharist in the Early Scholastic Period: A Study of the Salvific Function of the Sacrament according to the Theologians, c. 1080–c. 1220* (New York: Clarendon, 1984), 43.

41. Mitchell, *Cult and Controversy*, 141.

42. McKenna, *Become What You Receive*, 174.

43. Chadwick, "Ego Berengarius," 423.

of any genuine ontological change in the elements and an insufficiently objective view of Christ's presence. Berengarius's articulations "seemed to remain
at the level of an interior psychological event."[44] His fellow theologians, and
eventually the whole Church, recoiled.

Under pressure from Berengarius's theological opponents in Normandy
(Berengarius lived in the south of France during a time of tension between
the north and south),[45] Pope Nicholas II summoned Berengarius to Rome in
1059. There he was made to swear an infamous oath, drafted by the redoubt-
able Cardinal Humbert of Silva Candida, which is known to posterity by its
first two words in the Latin, *Ego Berengarius*:

> I Berengarius, . . . acknowledging the true and apostolic faith, anathematize
> every heresy, especially that one for which heretofore I have been infamous
> . . . and I confess with mouth and heart that . . . the bread and wine which are
> placed on the altar are not merely a sacrament after consecration, but are rather
> the true body and blood of our Lord Jesus Christ—and that these are truly,
> physically [*sensualiter*] and not merely sacramentally, touched and broken by
> the hands of the priests and crushed by the teeth of the faithful.[46]

Lawrence Feingold diplomatically dubs this a "less than perfect formulation."[47]
Aidan Nichols calls the oath "draconian" and "a source of some embarrassment."[48]
Robert Barron calls it "frank, even gross" and "almost cannibalistic."[49] Gary
Macy writes, "The oath of Berengar is clear, blunt, and forceful. It is also, theo-
logically, a disaster."[50] Even James O'Connor, almost the only contemporary
theologian willing to defend the *Ego Berengarius*,[51] concedes that "the graphic

---

44. Mitchell, *Cult and Controversy*, 145. In this regard Berengarius's theology has drawn
comparisons to transignification, the inadequacy of which is usually seen to lie precisely in this
lack of objective reality. See Barron, *Eucharist*, 127.

45. Readers interested in the political context of the dispute should see Gibson, "The Case
of Berengar of Tours"; Mitchell, *Cult and Controversy*, 137–51.

46. Quoted from Mitchell, *Cult and Controversy*, 137. Mitchell references DS 690.

47. Feingold, *Eucharist*, 242.

48. A. Nichols, *Holy Eucharist*, 62.

49. Barron, *Eucharist*, 112.

50. Gary Macy, "The Theological Fate of Berengar's Oath of 1059: Interpreting a Blunder
Become Tradition," in *Treasures from the Storeroom: Medieval Religion and the Eucharist*
(Collegeville, MN: Liturgical Press, 1999), 22.

51. O'Connor, *Hidden Manna*, 178. I am aware of only one other contemporary theologian
who has defended the oath. See Alvin F. Kimel, "Eating Christ: Recovering the Language of Real
Identification," *Pro Ecclesia* 13, no. 1 (Winter 2004): 82–100. Ironically enough, the oath's most
famous defender is Martin Luther, who lamented, "Would to God that all popes had acted in
so Christian a fashion in all other matters as this pope did with Berengar in forcing this confession" (*Confession concerning Christ's Supper* [1528], in *LW* 37:300–301).

nature of the words required that they be put in their sacramental context by later theologians."[52]

The problems with the oath are at least twofold. First of all, the adverb *sensualiter* locates Christ's eucharistic presence in the realm of the five senses. The presence is thus imagined in a completely nonsacramental manner. The category of sign has become utterly superfluous,[53] and it becomes difficult to distinguish the eucharistic banquet from cannibalism. Second, to speak of Christ's body being broken by hands and ground by teeth, besides the cannibalistic overtones, raises serious questions about the nature and location of Christ's risen body. Did not the resurrection rule out such possibilities?[54]

Upon his return to France, Berengarius, quite understandably, repudiated the oath on the grounds that it was taken under duress.[55] But, more than that, he launched an attack on the oath itself, highlighting its weaknesses in ways that his opponents could not easily refute. Guitmond of Aversa, for example, acknowledged Berengarius's rejection of the various implications of a naturalistic change due to the incorruptibility of Christ's risen body.[56] And everyone came to agree with Berengarius that it is only the sacrament of Christ's body that is broken and chewed, not the body itself.[57] Those who would defend eucharistic realism now had the added task of defending a poorly written and theologically inept, but still rather official, Church statement.

Lanfranc of Bec, later archbishop of Canterbury and one of the aforementioned "Norman theologians," was Berengarius's most formidable opponent. Upon Berengarius's repudiation of the oath, Lanfranc continued the cause of the orthodox camp, publishing his own *De corpore et sanguine Domini* in 1063.[58] Something decisive occurs in this work of Lanfranc. Faced with the task of denouncing Berengarius's error while also defending an unfortunate, and now widely circulating, Church document, Lanfranc made a distinction using Berengarius's own language against him.

Enter "Substance"

The term "substance" had long existed in Christian theology and in philosophy generally. It is used in the Nicene Creed, for instance, to express the

52. O'Connor, *Hidden Manna*, 179.
53. Jones, *Christ's Eucharistic Presence*, 80.
54. Macy, "Theological Fate of Berengar's Oath," 22–23; Jones, *Christ's Eucharistic Presence*, 80.
55. A. Nichols, *Holy Eucharist*, 63.
56. Chadwick, "Ego Berengarius," 429.
57. See Macy, "Theological Fate of Berengar's Oath." Humbert's formulation actually originally drew from a gloss on Augustine's commentary on John 6 that had referred not to Christ's physical body, but to "the sacrament of the body and blood of Christ" (A. Nichols, *Holy Eucharist*, 63).
58. Mitchell, *Cult and Controversy*, 145.

relationship between the Father and the Son: *consubstantial*, of the same being. In general philosophical terms it indicated that which something really is, in itself. While it later became closely associated with the Aristotelian categories that were used to hone it with such precision by later theologians, the idea of substance per se was not an Aristotelian imposition on Christian thought as is often supposed.[59] As Liam Walsh notes,

> In a general way, the word seems to have been used in Christian theology to identify a real and distinctive feature of something, that is to say what it really is. Christ is *duplicis substantiae* (of twofold substance) because he is truly man and truly God. The language of faith would seem to have a particular need for a word that allows it to differentiate between what things are and what they might simply seem to be.[60]

In Berengarius's mind, substance was linked absolutely to empirical qualities. Like a modern materialist, for Berengarius it made no sense to distinguish between what a thing was, in itself, and its material reality.[61] Following this line, and using the language of "substance," "he denied that the bread and wine could become the body of Christ without having to undergo any change in 'appearance.' The consecration could not act upon the nature of things, as it was maintained it did, since there was no modification in the sensible elements."[62] This was the opening that Lanfranc needed. Granting Berengarius's point that the appearances do not change, Lanfranc—using St. Ambrose's teaching that, as creator of the universe, Christ has the power to change one thing into another[63]—put forward what would eventually become the doctrine of transubstantiation—that is, that the deepest reality, the substance, does change, while the appearances do not.[64] As Martelet puts it, Berengarius was "the unfortunate discoverer of his own Waterloo."[65]

Before continuing the historical narrative, it is important to note that this marks the beginning of a recovery of the sacramental that was lost in Humbert's

---

59. Kereszty, *Wedding Feast of the Lamb*, 133; Walsh, *Sacraments of Initiation*, 300–301; Power, *Eucharistic Mystery*, 211.

60. Liam G. Walsh, OP, "An Ecumenical Reading of Aquinas on the Eucharist," in *Liturgia et Unitas*, ed. M. Klöckener and A. Join-Lambert (Freiburg: Universitätsverlag Freiburg Schweiz, 2001), 236.

61. Kereszty, *Wedding Feast of the Lamb*, 132.

62. Martelet, *The Risen Christ and the Eucharistic World*, 133.

63. It certainly helped Lanfranc's cause that he caught Berengarius misquoting Ambrose on just this issue! Mitchell, *Cult and Controversy*, 146.

64. A. Nichols, *Holy Eucharist*, 63.

65. Martelet, *The Risen Christ and the Eucharistic World*, 134.

formula.[66] Though he is ostensibly defending Humbert's formula against Berengarius's rejection of it, Lanfranc is, in fact, the first in a long line of "medieval commentators on *Ego Berengarius* (1059) [who] explained it in terms that validated Berengar's objections."[67] While on the surface it might look finicky, and even, to modern eyes, implausible, the distinction Lanfranc makes between substance and appearances is actually a rough, at this stage, translation of the patristic relationship between reality and symbol. Later theologians, including Thomas Aquinas, would be highly influenced by Lanfranc's distinctions and carefully refine them in their own development of eucharistic theology.[68]

The loss of the connection between symbol and reality had hampered theology's ability to take the symbols of bread and wine seriously because to do so necessarily seemed to degrade the reality of Christ's presence. They had become nothing more than veils to protect communicants from being horrified by the sight of raw flesh and to exercise faith.[69] And while these unfortunate explanations became traditional, so that they appear almost pro forma even alongside the recovery of the sacramental sense in Lanfranc and those who follow him, Lanfranc's distinction allowed symbol back into the sacrament while protecting reality.[70]

The New Language

It is true, of course, that translation is an imperfect science. The happy coexistence of symbol and reality in the patristic period flowed out of a sacramental worldview built on symbolic inclusions, not dialectical distinctions. Substance and appearances (or, later, accidents) become useful for sacramental theology through distinction, not inclusion, and this has consequences for any theology that depends on them.[71]

---

66. Indeed, it was this loss of the sacramental that had come with the dominance of a Paschasian realism that Berengarius was already protesting, however inadequately. As Martelet, who is in general quite favorable to Paschasius, points out, it was with Paschasius in mind that *sensualiter* made its appearance in the first *Ego Berengarius* (*The Risen Christ and the Eucharistic World*, 132).

67. Chadwick, "Ego Berengarius," 443. See also 423. Indeed, while Berengarius's solutions were inadequate, his questions might have had a better hearing if not for "the dissidence of his personality" (428).

68. Mitchell, *Cult and Controversy*, 149.

69. De Lubac, *Corpus Mysticum*, 241–42.

70. Mitchell, *Cult and Controversy*, 150; Kilmartin, *Eucharist in the West*, 144.

71. Cf. de Lubac, *Corpus Mysticum*, 229:

> The beautiful considerations of the past, the symbols flowing with doctrinal richness were in their turn relegated to second place, though without in any way being formally repudiated. Only another dialectic could triumph over a dialectic whose aim was insidious negation, to which it was no longer enough to oppose simple recourse to the Almighty.

In the first instance, it means that the system itself is less organic and flexible, and more technical and rigid. While the Fathers could often talk unselfconsciously about the reality of bread and wine even after the consecration, in this new language such talk was in serious danger of countering the reality of Christ's presence in the elements, as we have already seen in the case of Berengarius.[72] Precision of terminology became more important than it had been heretofore. Second, as is the case in many instances of translation, and certainly in those where technical precision has become paramount, the possibility of misunderstanding greatly increases. In order to convey the richness that the concepts had in their original language, the new language must introduce a multitude of careful distinctions and qualifications. The resulting machinery ends up with so many tiny moving parts that it breaks very easily and requires a high level of expertise to repair.

Indeed, though the machine itself was not yet fully constructed by Lanfranc, Berengarius seized upon one of its more vulnerable parts in his rejection of Lanfranc's arguments. If the bread and wine really do not persist, argued Berengarius, then the signs necessary for the Eucharist to be truly a sacrament are gone.[73] "Here we are at the heart of the opposition between these two theologians," writes Nathan Mitchell. "For Berengarius, the sacrament is destroyed if bread and wine are changed into something else; for Lanfranc, the sacrament is destroyed if bread and wine are not changed into something else."[74] As we have already seen in chapter 1, Berengarius will not be the last to use this argument against what will become transubstantiation.[75]

Though, as we shall see in our study of Thomas, Berengarius's objection was taken to heart in future articulations, it was not seen as decisive. Lanfranc's articulations were taken up and further refined by other theologians, notably Guitmond of Aversa and Alger of Liège, and Berengarius found himself before another papal council in Rome in 1079 where he was forced to swear a second *Ego Berengarius,* quite possibly drafted, at least in part, by Guitmond:[76]

After a series of tentative attempts, it would be ready, two centuries after Berengar. Its weapons would be forged. The dialectic of substance and accidents . . . would correspond to the dialectic of the sign and the reality. Sacramental realism would no longer be anything but that which symbolism augmented, and persistent faith in a real presence of Christ in the sacrament would be protected, for further centuries, by a sacramental theology with quite other appearances and implications.

72. Cf. Walsh, "Ecumenical Reading of Aquinas on the Eucharist," 233.
73. A. Nichols, *Holy Eucharist,* 64.
74. Mitchell, *Cult and Controversy,* 147–48.
75. Cf. pp. 50–51 above.
76. Chadwick, "Ego Berengarius," 432; O'Connor, *Hidden Manna,* 110.

I, Berengar, believe with my heart and confess with my mouth that the bread and wine which are placed on the altar are changed in their substance (*substantialiter converti*) into the true flesh and blood of Jesus Christ, by the Holy Prayer and the words of our Redeemer. They are thus, after consecration, the true body of Christ, born of the Virgin Mary, which was offered, and hung on the Cross, for the salvation of the world, and which sits on the right hand of the Father, and the real blood of Christ, which was shed from his side—and they really are this, not only by virtue of the sign and the power of this sacrament, but in their peculiar nature and their substantial reality.[77]

Notably absent is the grossly carnal language of the first *Ego Berengarius*. Instead of *sensualiter* (usually rendered "physically" in English) we have *substantialiter*, and there is no mention of Christ's body being broken or crushed. Though Berengarius was not happy with the new adverb, since for him substance could not be separated from appearances, "the new formula of 1079 was [otherwise] altogether simple for Berengarius to accept. In fact, therein lay the problem for him: it was eminently reasonable."[78] Though Berengarius tells us that he only swore with grave mental reservations (because of *substantialiter*), this new oath effectively ended the controversy. It was not open to the criticisms easily leveled against the first *Ego Berengarius*, and while theologians would continue to feel the need to explain this first away, with the new language of "substance" at hand, that job became much easier.[79]

The Emergence of "Transubstantiation"

By the middle of the next century, the term "transubstantiation" itself appears. It refers to the substantial change of bread (and wine) into Christ's body (and blood) originally posited by Lanfranc and the "*substantialiter converti*" of the second *Ego Berengarius*. Roland Bandinelli, the future Pope Alexander III, is often credited with coining the term, but this is not certain and the literature mentions other possibilities for its origin.[80] In any case, the

---

77. Quoted from A. Nichols, *Holy Eucharist*, 64. Nichols references DS 700: the work of Alberic of Monte Casino.

78. Chadwick, "Ego Berengarius," 434, 435; A. Nichols, *Holy Eucharist*, 64.

79. Gary Macy traces the slow but unmistakable move away from a literal defense of the oath and concludes that "within one hundred years after the oath had been written, Peter Lombard had effectively reversed the literal meaning of the oath through reinterpretation. Within another hundred years, this interpretation had become the standard and accepted theological understanding of the oath." Macy, "Theological Fate of Berengar's Oath," 28. Calvin would note the same dynamic (*Inst.* 4.17:1372–73 [12]): "But Peter Lombard, even though he toils hard to explain away this absurdity, inclines rather to a more divergent opinion."

80. See, e.g., Power, *Eucharistic Mystery*, 245; Crockett, *Eucharist*, 118; Chadwick, "Ego Berengarius," 440. Other candidates include Stephen of Autun and Hildebert of Lavardin (see

term had become so widespread and commonly accepted by the beginning of the thirteenth century that the Fourth Lateran Council could, in 1215, use the term casually and without definition in its document asserting, against the Cathars and Albigensians, that only duly ordained priests can consecrate the Eucharist.[81]

From at least the ninth century onward, theologians had struggled to assert a eucharistic realism that was fully sacramental. By Berengarius's time the situation was quite serious, as demonstrated by both his own rejection of sacramental realism and the oath drafted by Cardinal Humbert in support of a decidedly unsacramental realism. As Henri de Lubac has highlighted, Berengarius's error was simply inverted by some of his opponents: "While their aim was to contradict him the more convincingly, they foolishly followed him into his own territory, without realizing the danger that awaited them there. . . . It could be said that the ultra-orthodox party fell into the trap that had been set for them by the heretic, or again, that they allied with him in mutilating the traditional teaching."[82] Pitting symbol against reality was a "fatal dichotomy that should have been refuted from the outset."[83] But, instead of rejecting the dichotomy, Berengarius's opponents rejected half of it—sacramental symbolism—and emphatically embraced the other half—reality—even if "reality" was thereby reduced to the merely physical.[84] Hans Boersma situates this "false dichotomy" regarding the sacrament within its larger cultural philosophical framework:

> The false dichotomy, "whose hypothesis ought to have been refuted from the outset," was that of a universe in which sacrament no longer participated in its reality, in which nature became dislodged from the supernatural. Whether the focus was on the former or the latter, both parties took for granted the underlying desacramentalized universe that would characterize modernity. The Platonist-Christian synthesis was about to unravel.[85]

Because we know Berengarius's thought mostly through the writings of his opponents, and because, as with Ratramnus, certain aspects of it strike us as slippery or inconsistent, it is difficult to know if we are representing

---

Jones, *Christ's Eucharistic Presence*, 113n49). This latter is currently given the honor in the Wikipedia entry for "Transubstantiation" (as of April 19, 2019), where, in his own entry, he is also listed as a possible student of Berengarius!

81. See above, p. 36.
82. De Lubac, *Corpus Mysticum*, 223.
83. De Lubac, *Corpus Mysticum*, 223.
84. Benedict XVI, *God Is Near Us*, 84; cf. Mitchell, *Cult and Controversy*, 144.
85. Boersma, *Heavenly Participation*, 58.

him accurately in every detail.[86] Whether or not we are in a position to understand his theology completely, however, one thing is clear: Berengarius forced eucharistic theology in the eleventh century and beyond to take the sacramental character of Christ's presence seriously. Though the tradition did not accept his claim that the bread and wine remained essentially unchanged, Berengarius's challenges to naturalistic readings of the change forced the tradition to develop a much better understanding of what it actually meant to affirm change in the elements. Furthermore, his insistence on the resurrection, though it did not convince theologians that Christ's body was incapable of real presence on our altars, did result in a clearer idea of the relationship between Christ's historical, risen body and his body present in the Eucharist.[87] The questions Berengarius put to his opponents continued to provide grist for the mill of treatises on the Eucharist for generations and contributed to the ever more careful distinctions theologians made about Christ's eucharistic presence.[88]

Henry Chadwick has convincingly argued that

> in the context of the twelfth-century post-Berengarian debates transubstantiation was a term offering a way of escape. On the one hand, it had the merit of affirming Christ's presence in the Eucharist to be more than a metaphorical or subjective way of speaking. Although Berengar would not have conceded that he intended no more than a metaphor, he had certainly scared many into supposing that in the end his programme for the reform of Eucharistic theology by getting back to Augustine would mean this. On the other hand, transubstantiation met the necessity of explaining away Pope Nicholas II's *Ego Berengarius* of 1059. It went hand in hand with a quest for a via media between affirming the presence *spiritualiter* and affirming it *corporaliter* or *sensualiter*, and encouraged the adverb *sacramentaliter*, thereby conveying the simultaneity of sign and *res* [reality]. To affirm that Christ's presence in the Eucharist was "sacramental" was felt to offer a middle way between a representative symbolism and Humbert's too gross physicality.[89]

86. See Chadwick, "Ego Berengarius," 424. Cf. A. Nichols, *Holy Eucharist*, 65. Nichols notes an "ambivalence" in the writings of Berengarius: "Sometimes he affirms a real presence of Christ, while denying that this involves the outright conversion of the elements into Christ's body and blood—this will be, later, the moderate Reformation position of Luther. At other times, he anticipates such 'left-wing' Reformation teaching as that of Zwingli, saying, in effect, that the consecrated elements are only tokens." Cf. Chadwick, "Ego Berengarius," 436.

87. Mitchell, *Cult and Controversy*, 150. See also A. Nichols, *Holy Eucharist*, 62.

88. Chadwick, "Ego Berengarius," 441.

89. Chadwick, "Ego Berengarius," 445; see also the response by Christopher Kiesling to Ross MacKenzie, "Reformed Theology and Roman Catholic Doctrine of the Eucharist as Sacrifice (with Response by Christopher Kiesling)," *Journal of Ecumenical Studies* 15, no. 3 (Summer 1978): 439.

This is certainly correct. And Chadwick is also correct to note the irony in the fact that many Protestants balk at transubstantiation as representing a kind of grossly physical interpretation of eucharistic presence when, in fact, it developed precisely as a way to affirm real presence while avoiding the carnal connotations of the first *Ego Berengarius*.[90]

I would like to add, however, that transubstantiation was more than just a way of escape out of a theological problem. It was, in fact, a rebellion against the desacramentalized universe of Berengarius and Humbert that made such a theological problem possible in the first place. It is impossible to undo history.[91] After Berengarius, one could not simply return to the affirmations of the Fathers of the Church. A new language was needed to convey the traditional Christian conviction about the Eucharist in this new context. Transubstantiation provided a way of talking about Christ's real presence, but it also, necessarily, carried with it implications about what it means for something to be *real* at all.[92] The relationship between God and creation is in the background of any discussion of eucharistic presence.[93] Let us keep in mind, then, as we look at how transubstantiation came to classic expression in the work of Thomas Aquinas as an articulation of real, sacramental, presence, the implications that such a presence holds for what Christians think about reality generally.

Transubstantiation and Real Presence

Before investigating Thomas's exposition of transubstantiation in detail, it is important to locate the doctrine of transubstantiation in relationship to Christian faith in Christ's eucharistic presence. As we have seen, many Christians profess Christ's eucharistic presence without reference to any doctrine of transubstantiation and, in fact, the term did not exist for much of

90. Chadwick, "Ego Berengarius," 442; cf. A. Nichols, *Holy Eucharist*, 67: "Chadwick has pointed out the touch of paradox in the circumstance that this doctrine of a change of metaphysical substance arose from the need to avert Humbert's 'materialistic and naturalistic interpretation of eucharistic change and reception.' . . . We shall not be far wrong in finding additionally in these words a plea to separated Western Christians to find in the dogma of transubstantiation an equilibrium and repose amidst the clashing possibilities which eucharistic thinking has engendered."

91. Cf. Wainwright, "Eucharist in the Churches' Responses to the Lima Text," 65; Benedict XVI, "Problem of Transubstantiation," 228–31.

92. O'Neill, *Sacramental Realism*, 162.

93. Robert E. Barron, "Creation, Transubstantiation, and the Grain of the Universe: A Contribution to Stanley Hauerwas's Ekklesia Project," in *Bridging the Great Divide: Musings of a Post-liberal, Post-conservative, Evangelical Catholic* (Toronto: Rowman & Littlefield, 2004), 215.

Christian history. Calvin seized upon this fact for his own polemic when he wrote, "For transubstantiation was devised not so long ago; indeed not only was it unknown to those better ages when the purer doctrine of religion still flourished, but even when that purity already was somewhat corrupted."[94] What Calvin did not know was that, rather than being an endorsement of the first *Ego Berengarius*, with which he explicitly links it,[95] transubstantiation was rather, as we have seen, an attempt to recapture a precisely sacramental understanding of Christ's presence that was completely lacking in Humbert's formula. This historical context is essential for understanding transubstantiation's theological context.

Transubstantiation is not, as is sometimes suggested, the "how" of real presence, in the sense that it somehow explains real presence.[96] Rather, tran-

---

94. Calvin, *Inst.* 4.17:1375 (14). Calvin later adds, "Even in Bernard's time, although a blunter manner of speaking had been adopted, transubstantiation was not yet recognized. And in all ages before this comparison flitted about on everybody's lips, that the spiritual reality is joined to bread and wine in this mystery" (*Inst.* 4.17:1377 [15]). This latter comment, of course, highlights the concern of the Reformers that transubstantiation denied the persistence of the bread and wine.

95. Calvin, *Inst.* 4.17:1372–74 (12–14). Chadwick writes that "Calvin (*Inst.* IV 17 12 f) regards Ego Berengarius as the naked truth about transubstantiation which sophisticated schoolmen vainly tried to provide with a decent figleaf of qualifications. It did not occur to him that for Alexander III and Innocent III the merit of transubstantiation was that it did not entail the 'sensualiter' theme of Humbert's formula" ("Ego Berengarius," 442n53).

96. Karl Rahner, SJ, "The Presence of Christ in the Sacrament of the Lord's Supper," in *Theological Investigations IV: More Recent Writings* (Baltimore: Helicon, 1966), 300–305. Rahner offers a nuanced discussion of this issue with the help of a distinction between logical and ontic explanations:

> The *logical* explanation of a statement about a given matter would be a statement which makes the statement to be explained clear, that is, more definite and unmistakable, by interpreting it on its own terms, that is, without appealing to matters distinct from the matter to be explained. The logical explanation—to put it crudely for the moment— explains by giving precisions, but does not affirm anything else in explanation of the matter in hand. (300)

> The *ontic* explanation of a statement about a given matter would be the explanation which asserts *something else* than the matter in question, but something which is capable of rendering it intelligible, and so preserving it from misunderstandings, by giving it for instance indications of its cause, of the precise, concrete way in which it came about and so on. I have explained the darkness before my eyes ontically when I connect the statement, "it grows dark before my eyes" with the switching off of the light or a physiological atrophy of the nerve of sight. (301)

Transubstantiation is a logical explanation, not an ontic one, and so

> the function of this doctrine is not to explain the real presence by accounting for *how* it takes place, so that the manner of its coming, understood in itself as *another* process, would explain how the real presence came to be. Transubstantiation as a dogma, means more than just any sort of a real presence, but it does not affirm anything more than the real presence which is there when what is given is understood as the presence of the body of Christ. It is a way of formulating the truth that the body is present, and it is correct

substantiation says *what* happens—that, despite appearances, the bread and wine really do become Christ's body and blood—and it seeks to show that such a claim is not simply unintelligible. It does not seek to explain some arcane process by which bread and wine become Christ's body and blood. Thomas is quite clear on this. For him, the only proper response to the question "*How* do the bread and wine become Christ's body and blood?" is "By the power of God."[97] This answer contains within itself two other answers found in the tradition and in Thomas—namely, "By the word of Christ"[98] and "By the power of the Holy Spirit."[99] As we shall see, the former of these was particularly emphasized by Luther, the latter by Calvin.

Rather than answering the question "How do the bread and wine become Christ's body and blood?" transubstantiation answers the questions "What does it mean to say that the bread and wine become Christ's body and blood?" and "What is the intelligible content of the claim that that which appears to the senses to be bread and wine is, in fact, Christ's body and blood?" These are, of course, properly *theological* questions. "Theology helps bring out the intelligibility of the deposit of faith."[100]

The question for theology is not, in the strict sense, "How did God create the universe?" There can be only one answer to such a question, and we have

---

and significant so far as it explains and defends that truth. But it is not an explanation which reduces the truth to something else which could be grasped in its own distinct content. (302–3)
Cf. Matthew Levering, *Sacrifice and Community: Jewish Offering and Christian Eucharist* (Malden, MA: Blackwell, 2005), 165. Levering takes up the critique of the great Russian Orthodox theologian Sergius Bulgakov in his chapter on transubstantiation (pp. 115–67). Bulgakov understands transubstantiation to be an answer to the question of *how* the bread and wine become Christ's body and blood. See, in particular, pp. 122–23, 151n95.

97. *ST* III, 75.4 corpus. The term "how" is not, of course, univocal. While it is correct to deny that transubstantiation attempts to answer the question "How is Christ present?" in the sense of "How does it come about that Christ is present?," it does contribute to answering the question "In what way is Christ present?" That is the sense in which Herbert McCabe uses the term "how": "If you ask: How is Christ present to us in the Eucharist, the answer I believe must be that he is present because the food and drink have become his body. If, however, you ask how his body is present, the answer is that it is present sacramentally." "Transubstantiation and the Real Presence," in *God Matters* (London: Continuum, 2005), 117. The answer to the questions "How have the food and drink become his body?" and "How did his body come to be present sacramentally?" remains "By the power of God."

98. *ST* III, 78.5.

99. *ST* III, 75.1 ad 1; 78.4 obj. 1, ad 1.

100. Robert Sokolowski, "The Eucharist and Transubstantiation," in *Christian Faith and Human Understanding: Studies on the Eucharist, Trinity, and the Human Person* (Washington, DC: Catholic University of America Press, 2006), 95; See also Walsh, *Sacraments of Initiation* (1st ed.), 271–72: "Theologically the issue is not just a matter of fact: it is also a matter of understanding the fact affirmed by faith."

already seen it: "By God's power." (We can note in the case of creation, as well, the presence of both Word and Spirit as expressions of God's power.) But, given the affirmation of faith that God *did* create the universe, the properly theological question is, "What does it mean to say that God created the universe? What is the intelligible content of such a claim?" Theology does not ask, "How did Christ rise from the dead?" By faith we know only that, by God's power, God *did* raise Christ from the dead. But theology must ask, "What does it mean to say that Christ rose from the dead? What is the intelligible content of such a claim?" A theologian cannot, strictly speaking, answer the question "How can Jesus be fully human and fully divine?" But a theologian can help us to understand how this claim is not simply nonsense or a contradiction in terms.[101] A theologian can help us to understand what it means to say that Jesus is fully human and fully divine. The theologian can identify the intelligible content of such a claim of faith.

If real presence is an article of faith, then transubstantiation is, quite simply, *fides quaerens intellectum*, faith seeking understanding.[102] It is, in other words, theology. And the relationship between real presence and transubstantiation is the relationship between faith and theology. Transubstantiation's role is simply to articulate the intelligible content of the claim that the bread and wine become Christ's body and blood when the Church follows Christ's command to "Do this in memory of me." It emerges when it does, historically speaking, because it was at that time that this particular claim of faith was being rejected precisely as unintelligible. When an article of faith is challenged as incoherent, often enough because it is being misunderstood and misrepresented, as in the present case, faith needs theology if it is not to lapse into skepticism or fideism.[103]

---

101. As Elizabeth Anscombe writes, apropos transubstantiation, "When we call something a mystery, we mean that we cannot iron out the difficulties about understanding it and demonstrate once for all that it is perfectly possible. Nevertheless we do not believe that contradictions and absurdities can be true, or that anything logically demonstrable from things known can be false. And so we believe that there are answers to supposed proofs of absurdity, whether or not we are clever enough to find them." "On Transubstantiation," in *Ethics, Religion and Politics*, The Collected Philosophical Papers of G. E. M. Anscombe 3 (Oxford: Blackwell, 1981), 109. See also Feingold, *Eucharist*, 259–60.

102. Cf. Benedict XVI, "Problem of Transubstantiation," 242; Lehmann and Pannenberg, *Condemnations of the Reformation Era*, 101.

103. This is not to say that transubstantiation per se is the only theology of real presence that can save faith in Christ's eucharistic presence once that faith has been challenged. And Christian unity requires only that faith, not theology, be held in common. On the other hand, any theology of real presence that does effectively safeguard the Church's faith is bound to have much in common with transubstantiation. In fact, I would assert, any such theology would have so much in common with transubstantiation that the remaining differences would not

In such a context, theology's task is to clear away misunderstanding, though not with an eye to fully disclosing the mystery, for that is impossible. Theology's task, rather, is to locate the mystery.[104] Or, as Fergus Kerr writes, "Correctly understood . . . transubstantiation does not *explain* but rather *protects* the mystery."[105] And Jean-Marie Tillard says that Thomas sought to "give a certain intelligibility both to the realism and to the mystery of the presence."[106] Theology must advert to poor understandings and false problems,[107] but without presuming to fully explain what is, by definition, beyond human understanding. Any theology of Christ's eucharistic presence that purports to explain away the mystery of Christ's presence fails by that very fact. That is why Karl Rahner could write that the magisterium correctly rejected certain interpretations of "substance" and "species" by which "transubstantiation was made very understandable, much too understandable."[108] Protestant and Orthodox writers are correct, therefore, to caution Catholics against any rationalistic explanations of eucharistic presence,[109] though they are mistaken if they assert that transubstantiation represents such an explanation.[110] On the other hand, it must be admitted that some Catholics have fallen into the trap of understanding transubstantiation in this way, and so Orthodox and Protestant writers are not simply tilting at windmills. As Elizabeth Anscombe admits, "It was perhaps a fault of the old exposition . . . that [it] was sometimes offered as if it were supposed to make everything intelligible. Greater learning would indeed remove that impression."[111]

---

reach so deep as to impair Church unity on the question. Safeguarding the Church's faith in real presence is the true heart of the ecumenical matter.

104. Hütter, "Transubstantiation Revisited," 27.

105. Fergus Kerr, OP, "Transubstantiation after Wittgenstein," *Modern Theology* 15, no. 2 (April 1999): 119; cf. Lewis, *Letters to Malcolm*, 133 (19); see also Kelly, "Eucharistic Doctrine of Transubstantiation," 64.

106. Tillard, "Roman Catholics and Anglicans," 174.

107. Cf. Levering, *Sacrifice and Community*, 146.

108. Rahner, "Presence of Christ in the Sacrament of the Lord's Supper," 305. In particular, these interpretations equated "concrete reality" with "accident," and "religious interpretation" with "substance." These make transubstantiation much too understandable as a subjective reality. As we saw with Humbert, there is also the temptation to make Christ's presence much too understandable as an objective reality.

109. As Alexander Schmemann does. See Levering, *Sacrifice and Community*, 122n20.

110. As, for example, the Greek Orthodox bishop Methodius Fouyas does. See Hunsinger, *Eucharist and Ecumenism*, 74. The Reformed theologian Peter Leithart, though he gets Thomas wrong at certain key points (see 79n118 below), is absolutely correct when he notes that Luther was incorrect in his assessment of Thomas and that "Thomas did not claim to have explained the mystery of the Eucharist." Leithart, "What's Wrong with Transubstantiation?," 310. See also Gustave Martelet on Franz Leenhardt in Martelet, *The Risen Christ and the Eucharistic World*, 108–9.

111. Anscombe, "On Transubstantiation," 109.

The aforementioned ARCIC footnote to which transubstantiation was relegated was, therefore, absolutely correct when it claimed that "the term should be seen as affirming the fact of Christ's presence and of the mysterious and radical change which takes place. In contemporary Roman Catholic theology it is not understood as explaining *how* the change takes place."[112] On the other hand, the word "contemporary" risks giving the wrong impression. As true, and even important, as the statement is regarding the *how*, it can be read as suggesting that traditional (as opposed to contemporary) Catholic theology, including Aquinas and Trent, *did* understand the term as an explanation of "*how* the change takes place." This is both inaccurate and likely to make more traditional Catholics, or at least those traditional Catholics unaware that it is inaccurate, unnecessarily skittish about accepting ARCIC's conclusions.

Transubstantiation and Aristotle

In any case, the proper understanding of the relationship between transubstantiation and real presence as that of theological articulation to affirmation of faith is essential for clarifying one final preliminary issue—namely, the role of Aristotelian philosophy in transubstantiation. Protestants since Martin Luther have denounced transubstantiation as an inappropriate subservience of Christian theology to pagan, or at least antiquated, philosophy.[113] They have lately been joined in this by some Orthodox theologians and many Catholics as well.[114] According to this critique, transubstantiation is untenable either because it is not sufficiently biblical, taking its basic framework and terminology from a philosophy of nature and not from the Scriptures, and/or because it is outdated, being based in a philosophy of nature long since abandoned by contemporary believers. But these critiques fail to appreciate the role Aristotle actually plays in Aquinas's articulation of transubstantiation.

Such critiques imagine Thomas trying to solve a kind of Aristotelian logic puzzle; Thomas is often critiqued for being a bad Aristotelian because he

112. ARCIC, "Eucharistic Doctrine (1971)," in *The Final Report* (Washington, DC: US Catholic Conference, 1982), 14n2.

113. *The Babylonian Captivity of the Church* (1520), in *LW* 36:29. For a contemporary example, see Leithart, "What's Wrong with Transubstantiation?," 296–306. This was also a concern of the Tractarian movement in the Church of England. See Tillard, "Roman Catholics and Anglicans," 170.

114. According to Levering, the Orthodox Bulgakov criticizes (an unwitting misrepresentation of) transubstantiation as philosophically crude, "on the grounds that idealist philosophers such as Hegel and Kant have moved philosophy beyond this Aristotelian theory of substance" (Levering, *Sacrifice and Community*, 124).

ends up with a solution that is impossible within an Aristotelian universe—namely, accidents that continue to subsist without their proper substance.[115] As the Catholic philosopher P. J. FitzPatrick writes, "Transubstantiation is a eucharistic application of Aristotelian terms which abuses them to the point of nonsense—it is 'Aristotelian' only in the sense that forged money is 'money.'"[116] This is also indicated by Luther's accusation that Thomas knew "neither his philosophy nor his logic," and did not understand Aristotle, who spoke so differently than Thomas about subjects and accidents.[117] On the other hand, Thomas is often criticized for being much too good an Aristotelian, far too bound by Aristotelian strictures to capture the heart of the Christian faith. So Peter Leithart writes that "Aristotelianism thus controls not only the speculative periphery of Thomas's doctrine, but his explication of the dogmatic core as well," and, he later continues, "under the force of his Aristotelian framework, he sharply opposed figure and reality [so that] [t]here is no room in Thomas's mind for a doctrine that affirms both the reality of Christ's presence and the symbolic character of the elements."[118]

115. Alasdair Heron, e.g., suggests that Thomas's non-Aristotelian answer using Aristotelian language and categories is "a prima facie incoherence which cannot simply be passed over as insignificant." See *Table and Tradition*, 99. And, following Heron, see Jones, *Christ's Eucharistic Presence*, 104.

116. P. J. FitzPatrick, *In Breaking of Bread: The Eucharist and Ritual* (New York: Cambridge University Press, 1993), 11. This quote appears in the book's first chapter, "Against Transubstantiation," pp. 1–48.

117. *The Babylonian Captivity of the Church* (1520), in LW 36:29.

118. Leithart, "What's Wrong with Transubstantiation?," 300, 303. It must be said that Leithart's reading of Thomas on this question is fatally impaired by his suggestion that, when Thomas asks, "Is the body of Christ really and truly present in this sacrament or only in a figurative way or as in a sign?" (3a. 75, 1), Thomas is pitting reality against symbol. Leithart believes that the "only" in Thomas's question indicates a strong either/or between real presence and symbol. It is clear, however, given Thomas's earlier definition of sacraments as belonging to the order of signs (see *ST* III, 60), that Thomas is using "only" to ask whether, given the obviously symbolic nature of the sacrament, there is not something *more* than what can be accounted for merely by reference to signs. His affirmative answer does not deny the symbolic, but simply insists that the symbolic is not, in itself, sufficient to account for the reality of Christ's presence. Read *without* the "only," the question would pose the false dichotomy that Leithart rightly rejects. The "only" allows Thomas to affirm the symbolic without denying the real: the presence is symbolic without being "only" symbolic, i.e., not real. For Thomas, the real is more than the merely symbolic, but it is not opposed to it. Cf. Power, *Eucharistic Mystery*, 222; Crockett, *Eucharist*, 117. Crockett, who, it might be worth noting, is not a Catholic himself, writes, "Thomas employs the principle of causality not in order to negate the symbolic character of the sacraments, but in order to make clear in the medieval context what was obvious in the patristic context, namely, that the sacraments as signs participate in the reality that they signify and are not 'mere' signs." See also Kelly, "Eucharistic Doctrine of Transubstantiation," 57. Kelly writes, regarding the decrees of Trent, that "the use of the word 'only' before 'sign' and 'figure' attests that this substantial presence is at the same time a sacramental presence."

So, which is it? Is transubstantiation in Thomas too Aristotelian or not Aristotelian enough?

The answer becomes clear when we see that Thomas is not, in fact, trying to solve an Aristotelian logic puzzle at all. There is no question of finding an earthly philosophy that can adequately explain Christ's eucharistic presence. Like the resurrection, the central point is that we are dealing here with something beyond what is possible within our earthly systems.[119] Or, as Herbert McCabe writes, "Important theological ideas are invariably expressed through the breakdown of philosophical concepts."[120] Like resurrection, real presence breaks any earthly system, and so any good theology of real presence must do likewise. According to the demands of his subject matter, Thomas is simply not *doing* philosophy, Aristotelian or otherwise. Thomas may be *using* philosophy, but he is *doing* theology. In fact, Thomas himself commented on the role of philosophy in theology, suggesting that the theologian who uses philosophy does not mix wine with water, but turns water into wine.[121] Thomas knew he was transforming Aristotle.

This distinction puts Thomas's use of Aristotle in its proper place. Thomas is not using Aristotle because he believes that Aristotle's categories can somehow explain Christ's eucharistic presence. In fact, as we shall see, Thomas has already dramatically reshaped Aristotle's categories long before he gets to the question of transubstantiation. Like relatively recent theologians who attempt to articulate Christ's eucharistic presence using categories taken from phenomenology because such categories are deemed accessible to contemporary people, Thomas "fostered an intellectual understanding in line with the Aristotelian interest of the times."[122] The reason Thomas's articulation has been judged more successful in expressing the faith of the Church than phenomenological articulations like transignification is not because the Church prefers Aristotle to phenomenology,[123] but rather because Thomas "broke" Aristotle more effectively than theologians in the last century were able to

119. Cf. Walsh, *Sacraments of Initiation* (1st ed.), 276.

120. Herbert McCabe, OP, "Transubstantiation," in *God Matters* (London: Continuum, 2005), 146.

121. On the relationship between philosophy and theology in Aquinas, see Mark D. Jordan, "Theology and Philosophy," in *The Cambridge Companion to Aquinas*, ed. Norman Kretzmann and Eleonore Stump (Cambridge: Cambridge University Press, 1993), 232–51. On the water and wine metaphor, see pp. 235, 247–48.

122. Power, *Eucharistic Mystery*, 240. Cf. Disciples of Christ–Roman Catholic International Commission for Dialogue, "Presence of Christ in the Church," para. 33: "Aquinas used Aristotle's philosophy, which was popular in the universities of his day and hence had an apologetic value."

123. Cf. A. Nichols, *Holy Eucharist*, 114: "The Church's teaching office has no authority to impose a philosophical system."

"break" phenomenology.[124] Few have understood this dynamic better than the Dominican theologian Herbert McCabe:

> It is important to recognize that in using Aristotelean language St Thomas is not giving an "Aristotelean" explanation of the Eucharist. He uses it because it was the common philosophical currency of his time; but he uses it to give account of something that simply could not happen according to Aristotle. Transubstantiation, like creation or incarnation, does not make sense within the limits of the Aristotelean worldview. St Thomas uses Aristotle's language, but it breaks down in speaking of the Eucharist. It doesn't break down because there is some more accurate language in which the whole thing can be explained. It breaks down because it is language. We are dealing here with something that transcends our concepts and can only be spoken of by stretching language to the breaking point. We are dealing here with mystery.[125]

Thomas's willingness to recast Aristotle according to the biblical picture of God and God's relationship to creation is a key reason why Thomas's theology has outlasted the popularity of Aristotle's philosophy of nature. In order to understand the way in which Thomas recasts Aristotle, and the implications of such a recasting for his treatment of transubstantiation, we need to look at two related issues: first, the relationship between God and creation and, derivatively, the relationship between *esse*, being, and substance and accidents.

Breaking Aristotle

According to McCabe, the eminent twentieth-century Thomist Étienne Gilson argued that "the notion of *esse* (existence over against the possibility that nothing whatever might have existed) came to medieval European thought not from classical Greek philosophy, but from the biblical doctrine of creation."[126] For Aristotle, there was no creation. Matter was coeternal with God, and there was no possibility that it might not have ever existed. As such, his philosophy of nature did not need to be able to account for the idea of creation *ex nihilo*. For Aristotle, matter can take on new forms, as when the matter of a sandwich becomes the matter of a human body or the matter of a

---

124. G. Egner (a pseudonym now known to be P. J. FitzPatrick) suggests that transignification does not abuse phenomenology to the same degree that transubstantiation abuses Aristotle. "Some Thoughts on the Eucharistic Presence," in *God Matters*, by Herbert McCabe (London: Continuum, 2005), 135–36. While FitzPatrick means this as a compliment, it is, to my mind, a sure sign of transignification's inadequacy.

125. McCabe, "Eucharistic Change," 116–17.

126. Herbert McCabe, OP, "The Eucharist as Language," in *God Still Matters* (London: Continuum, 2005), 125.

tree becomes the matter of a door, but it cannot come to exist where nothing existed before. Aristotle's whole philosophy of nature is predicated on the idea of change in something already existing, but it has no room for the giving of existence in the first place: What, indeed, would existence be given to?

Thomas's answer to this problem can be found in his *De potentia*, where he writes that "God, giving being, simultaneously produces that which receives being. And thus it does not follow that his action requires something pre-existing."[127] According to Robert Barron,

> This implies something remarkable, viz. that the creature is the act by which it is created. It seems as though a principal conceit of Aristotelian metaphysics, the view that substance is fundamental and relationship accidental, is overturned in this context. It appears as though the relationship between creator and creature is what is primary and elemental whereas the "substances" involved—God and the world—are derivative, metaphysically secondary. The giver/receiver language, inextricably tied to a metaphysic of substance, cannot be applied to the act by which finitude itself is constituted.[128]

While Thomas will use the language of "substance" and "accident" in his account of transubstantiation, it is essential to note how they function differently for Thomas than for Aristotle. The possibility that there might not have been anything at all, something unthinkable for Aristotle, adds another level to Thomas's metaphysics.[129] Because of his Christian theology of creation, Thomas insists that the deepest ontological category is not substance but the concrete act of existence—in other words, that something has been given existence and is being held in existence by God.[130] Accordingly, then,

> transubstantiation is not at all the point at which Aquinas's reading of Aristotle becomes problematic: rather, transubstantiation indicates the extent to which Aquinas's re-inscription of Aristotle's physics is total, so that it very naturally concurs with everything else Aquinas has to say in this regard. Aquinas breaks company with Aristotle not over transubstantiation, but in the matter of the eternity of the world, which for Aquinas cannot be, since "in principio creavit Deus cælum et terram."[131]

127. *De potentia*, q. 3, a. 1, ad. 17. Quoted in Barron, "Thomas Aquinas: Postmodern," 274.
128. Barron, "Thomas Aquinas: Postmodern," 274–75.
129. McCabe, "Eucharist as Language," 125.
130. For an excellent explanation of this dynamic, see A. Nichols, *Holy Eucharist*, 69–70.
131. Laurence Paul Hemming, "After Heidegger: Transubstantiation," *Heythrop Journal* 41 (2000): 172; cf. E. L. Mascall, "Egner on the Eucharistic Presence," *New Blackfriars* 53, no. 631 (December 1972): 542. Mascall mentions Thomas's views on celestial motion, the unmoved mover, and the relationship between body and soul as other areas where his Christian theology

If the world is not eternal, but only exists because it is given its being by God, who alone is eternal, then the autonomy of substances, absolute for Aristotle, is only relative for Thomas. Let us look a little closer.

For Aristotle, accidents are those aspects of reality that do not exist autonomously, or in themselves. For instance, in order for us to see the color red, there must be some independently existing thing that is red. Red cannot exist independently. To invoke a grammatical metaphor, in order to have any concrete meaning, adjectives need nouns. Red needs an apple (or a house, or a stop sign). Technically speaking, red *subsists* in an apple. Substances, on the other hand, are those things in which accidents subsist. They themselves do not subsist in anything. In other words, they exist autonomously.[132] This is technical language, of course, and some will find it off-putting, but, in the final analysis, all it really means is that substance answers the question "What is that?"[133]

Many have argued that, because substance is really just a technical way of affirming that there is actually some existing thing, it is a misconception to suggest that it is no longer accessible to contemporary Christians. Thus Herbert McCabe:

> If you tell somebody what sort of a thing something is (a horse, an electron, etc.) you are telling him of its substance. If you are giving him further information (where it is, how high it is, how intelligent it is, etc.) you are telling him its accidental characteristics. It is important to an Aristotelian that a thing may lose some accidental characteristic (it may move, shrink, grow stupider, etc.) without ceasing to be the same identical thing; whereas if it should lose its substance, its essential character, it perishes, it ceases to be this thing and turns into something else (as when the horse dies, it is no longer a horse but has changed into a corpse). This seems a fairly common-sense account at least of the organic world in which it is usually fairly easy to agree on what sorts of things there are (horses, onions, human beings) and not too difficult to observe them beginning to exist (being born or whatever) and ceasing to exist (dying). *It differs considerably from our modern physicist's way of talking but it seems bizarre to claim that it is unintelligible to us.*[134]

As McCabe's fellow Dominican Aidan Nichols observes, "No one is rational who cannot ask, What is it? or see the meaning of that question."[135] And

---

requires him to radically reconfigure Aristotle and then concludes, "It is not surprising, therefore, if in order to formulate a satisfactory doctrine of the Eucharistic presence, he handled the Aristotelian doctrine of substance and accidents with equal brutality."

132. Walsh, *Sacraments of Initiation*, 308.
133. Tillard, "Roman Catholics and Anglicans," 160.
134. McCabe, "Eucharistic Change," 116 (emphasis added).
135. A. Nichols, *Holy Eucharist*, 75.

Frederick Bauerschmidt has puckishly said that "one does not need Aristotle to understand substance. One simply requires the object permanence one would expect from a two-year-old."[136] In other words, substance is not a category imposed on how we experience the world, but derived from it.[137]

All of this is quite true in as far as it goes. Substance is meant to simply denote the concrete existing thing itself. And this is true for both Aristotle and for Thomas, despite their differences concerning creation. We must be careful, however, not to imagine that the basic intelligibility of the term "substance" somehow makes transubstantiation rather straightforward. In other words, because some have rejected transubstantiation on account of substance's supposed incoherence does not mean that clarification about substance is enough to explain the meaning of transubstantiation. It remains true that transubstantiation is, as Robert Barron puts it, "Aristotelian nonsense."[138]

But transubstantiation is not simply nonsense for Thomas because, while substances exist autonomously for Aristotle, not subsisting in anything else, for Thomas substances only exist autonomously of other *created* realities.[139] They still rely utterly upon God for their own existence.

> Precisely by virtue of being created, the world composed as it is of substances with their accidents, is a world which only endures because it constantly receives being. God who is infinite actuality, *actus purus*, communicates being, the act of being, to creatures as the deepest foundation of their existence. So as to draw attention to the fact that substances with their accidents are dependent for their own ground on God, Thomas describes them as *entia*, "be-ings," from the verbal participle of *esse*, *ens*: finite participations in the infinite *esse* or act of being which God, as Creator, is.[140]

So, while substance means simply the concrete existing thing for both Aristotle and Thomas, the implications of being a concrete existing thing are quite different for Thomas than for Aristotle. What it means for a thing *to be* is different when everything exists by participation in God's existence. Any

---

136. Bauerschmidt made the comment to me in private conversation, though he indicated that he uses this illustration when he teaches about transubstantiation.

137. See Richard J. Connell, "Substance and Transubstantiation," *Angelicum* 69 (1992), esp. 6–7, 17; cf. Haldane, "A Thomist Metaphysics," 21; Feingold, *Eucharist*, 259, 276.

138. Barron, "Creation, Transubstantiation, and the Grain of the Universe," 218.

139. Cf. Benedict XVI, "Problem of Transubstantiation," 236: "From this perspective [that of belief in creation], however, one can assert a twofold substantiality of created being: the general substantiality of the creature based on the fact that, while it is 'being from elsewhere,' it is nevertheless 'being in its own right'; as something created, it is not God but, rather, is posited in the autonomy of an independent, non-divine being that exists for itself."

140. A. Nichols, *Holy Eucharist*, 69–70.

autonomy in creation is given and therefore cannot be absolute. Something's independence is, in fact, dependent. As we have already seen in the previous chapter, sacramental presence—the participation of a sacramental sign in a deeper, divine reality—of which transubstantiation is an articulation, depends on just such biblical metaphysics.[141]

While any talk of dependence on a given metaphysics can raise ecumenical hackles, this should not. It is naïve to imagine that one operates without any metaphysics whatsoever. Everyone operates with basic presuppositions about reality and, in particular, God's relationship with creation.[142] For Christians, those presuppositions ought to be formed by Scripture. As we have seen, for Thomas Aquinas, Aristotle was used in order to reassert the traditional relationship between symbol and reality in a new cultural context, but not before being radically reworked in order to convey the biblical worldview in which all of creation is utterly dependent upon the Creator of heaven and earth. Joseph Wawrykow writes that "what we have [in Thomas] is a critical appropriation of non-Christian work, done in the perspective and on the basis of the full commitment to Christian truth."[143] As we will see in more detail as we begin to look at Thomas's work in earnest, it was only within this biblical Christian worldview that Thomas could make use of Aristotle's categories to articulate a theology of Christ's eucharistic presence. But it is not only a matter of reworking Aristotle's categories in order to be able to say something impossible in a purely Aristotelian system. Because transubstantiation is only possible once Aristotle has had to make room for the Creator, "the Eucharist itself . . . is a perpetual reminder of the transcendence and power of God."[144] Transubstantiation witnesses to the God who creates and sustains all of reality, and who communicates with us precisely through created reality. As Gustave Martelet writes,

> Transubstantiation is not an isolated mystery that could be regarded as arbitrary; it is a direct consequence of the structure of a world created in Jesus Christ. Things undoubtedly have their own substantial consistency, but the world is ordered around a mystery which "resumes or brings together everything" (Eph. 1:10). The Eucharist is the *sacramental* emergence of this mystery.[145]

141. See above, pp. 42–44; Boersma, *Heavenly Participation*, 26.

142. "No one can avoid philosophical presuppositions, and the more seriously the theologian takes them, the more free he is of them." Morerod, *Ecumenism and Philosophy*, 161; see also xxiii. Cf. Christopher Kiesling, OP, "Roman Catholic and Reformed Understandings of the Eucharist (with Reformed Response by Ross MacKenzie)," in *The Eucharist in Ecumenical Dialogue* (New York: Paulist Press, 1976), 82–83.

143. Wawrykow, "Luther and the Spirituality of Thomas Aquinas," 86.

144. Sokolowski, "Eucharist and Transubstantiation," 103.

145. Martelet, *The Risen Christ and the Eucharistic World*, 112–13.

Transubstantiation in the *Summa Theologiae*

Having situated transubstantiation theologically and clarified the role of Aristotelian categories in its articulation, we are now in a position to investigate transubstantiation in Thomas's mature work, the *Summa Theologiae*. In fact, the questions on the Eucharist, 73–83, are almost the last thing we have from Thomas's pen. The next question, on the sacrament of reconciliation, was left unfinished at Thomas's death. Of particular interest are questions 75, 76, and 77, which address, respectively, the change of the bread and wine into the body and blood of Christ—that is, transubstantiation; how Christ exists in this sacrament—that is, the nature of real presence; and the accidents that remain in the sacrament—that is, the persisting physical reality of the bread and wine. We will treat them in order, though not without reference to other questions that are of concern for our treatment. The overriding theme of our investigation will be how Thomas is using transubstantiation to articulate a precisely sacramental presence of Christ in the Eucharist,[146] and this for two reasons: first of all, because this respects what we have learned from our historical investigation—namely, that transubstantiation arose in response to a false dichotomy between reality and symbol that effectively ignored the sacramental nature of Christ's eucharistic presence; and second, because many Reformers, especially Calvin, believed that, by denying the persistence of the substance of bread and wine, transubstantiation led to an unsacramental view of Christ's presence that ignored the symbolic value of the bread and wine.[147]

Question 75: A Unique Kind of Presence

That this is an appropriate theme is confirmed immediately when we look at the first article of question 75.[148] It asks, "Is the body of Christ really and

146. Walsh, "Ecumenical Reading of Aquinas on the Eucharist," 227, 234. Cf. Matthew Levering, who writes that the "exposition of a sacramental mode of bodiliness is the task of the doctrine of 'transubstantiation'" (*Sacrifice and Community*, 141).

147. This concern is also reflected in the Anglican Thirty-Nine Articles, which claim that transubstantiation "overthroweth the nature of a sacrament" (article 28). Luther, on the other hand, does not pursue this point; but he is concerned that the (substances of the) bread and wine remain because it is more philosophically coherent (given his nominalist background) and follows the pattern of the incarnation. An understanding of how transubstantiation articulates a precisely sacramental presence is a good starting point for resolving this issue as well.

148. In fact, it is confirmed even before that. Thomas chooses to treat the matter of the sacrament—that is, the bread and the wine—in question 74. As Liam Walsh writes,

> To express the complementarity of things and words in the making of a single sign of faith, medieval theology had borrowed an analogy from Aristotelian philosophy (60, 7 ad 2). The thing/action was seen to have a role in the sign like matter, because its

truly in this sacrament or only in a figurative way or as in a sign?" In order to understand this question properly, it is important to go back a few chapters to look at, first, Thomas's definition of sacrament and, second, Thomas's classification of the Eucharist as a sacrament. Thomas gives us his definition of a sacrament in question 60. In article 1 of that question, Thomas affirms that sacraments belong to the general category of signs. In article 2, he specifies further, "The term 'sacrament' . . . is applied to that which is a sign of a sacred reality inasmuch as it has the property of sanctifying men."[149]

Having defined sacraments as signs in question 60, Aquinas first asks, when he turns specifically to the Eucharist in question 73, "Is the Eucharist a sacrament at all?" Liam Walsh points out that

> the theological method of Thomas in this first question 73 about the Eucharist— one of giving intelligible shape to the tradition of faith about the Eucharist by applying the technical categories of sacramentality to it—has to be kept in mind for understanding all the rest of his eucharistic theology. Otherwise one will get things like his theory of transubstantiation and some remarks he makes about sacrifice quite out of perspective.[150]

The second objection is the most important for our purposes. In it, the objector suggests that the Eucharist is not a sacrament because "in all the sacraments of the New Law that which strikes our senses is what brings about the hidden effect of the sacrament. . . . But in the Eucharist the accidents of bread and wine do not bring about either Christ's actual body and blood or Christ's mystical body."[151] By highlighting "that which strikes our senses," the objector is hearkening back to Thomas's earlier definition of sacraments as signs. The suggestion here is that, because the accidents of bread and wine—in other words, the signs—do not bring about Christ's presence, they do not function sacramentally.

---

signification is open to, in potency to many determinations; whereas the words have a role like form, because they determined the signification in one particular direction. Thomas uses this model of analysis to structure his theology of the Eucharist. The bread and the wine are the matter of the sacrament; the words of Jesus spoken over them at the Last Supper are the form. The matter only signifies in conjunction with the form. When Thomas analyzes the matter of the Eucharist in IIIA qq. 74–77 he is analyzing it as an element of signification. *This is very clear in q. 74, where his reflections on the bread and wine are entirely symbolical. It must also be true—although this had been too seldom noted by commentators—of the remaining questions.* (Walsh, "Ecumenical Reading of Aquinas on the Eucharist," 232 [emphasis added])

149. *ST* III, 60.2 corpus.
150. Walsh, *Sacraments of Initiation*, 305–6.
151. *ST* III, 73.1 obj. 2.

In his response, and using the example of baptism, Thomas shows that the other sacraments do not function in the way that this objection presumes: "It is not because of the natural power of the water that any spiritual effect is caused in Baptism, but because of the power of the Spirit which is in the water."[152] The objector had imagined that sacraments, being signs, had the power to convey grace merely by signifying. But, Thomas points out, such signification is not, in itself, enough. The "natural power of the water," which, we can note, would be enough to signify, must be accompanied by "the power of the Spirit" if baptism is to have its "spiritual effect." And, Thomas continues, "what the power of the Spirit is to the water of Baptism, that the very body of Christ is to the appearances of bread and wine. These are only operative because of the very body of Christ that they contain."[153]

In order for something to be a sacrament it must belong to the order of sign, but it can be no "mere" sign, for sacraments also bring about or "cause" grace and for that, the natural sign value alone is insufficient.[154] Aquinas addresses this issue in question 62, article 1, "Are the sacraments a cause of grace?" The first and third objections are the most important for us here. The first notes that, since sacraments are, by definition, signs, they cannot also be causes, for signs are effects rather than causes. The third objects that it is not proper to attribute the cause of grace to any creature, since God alone can cause grace. In order to answer these objections, Thomas introduces the distinction between a principal and an instrumental cause.

According to Thomas, it is not enough to imagine, as some do, that "when the sacraments are applied God produces grace in the soul."[155] Such an external connection between the sacraments and grace "does not attribute any further force to them beyond that of a sign."[156] It is not enough that God works alongside the signifying sacraments. Rather, God works through and with them, as a carpenter uses an ax. While it is true, in a sense, to say that an ax is the cause of what is built using an ax, this does not mean that the carpenter is thereby excluded. Rather, the carpenter is more fundamentally

---

152. *ST* III, 73.1 ad 2.
153. *ST* III, 73.1 ad 2. Cf. Walsh, "Ecumenical Reading of Aquinas on the Eucharist," 230.
154. As David Power writes, "Aquinas made it clear that the sacramental has a reality beyond what is explained through sign-activity as such. What happens, though known through signs, cannot be wholly accounted for through their operations as signs. What takes place in sacramental action is in the realm of being, not only in the realm of sign and understanding, where signs by their nature work. One can learn through signs of what takes place, but without reducing the reality to the intelligibility expressed through signs" (*Eucharistic Mystery*, 222). See also Marshall, "What Is the Eucharist?," 504–12.
155. *ST* III, 62.1 corpus.
156. *ST* III, 62.1 corpus.

the cause of what is built than is the ax. The carpenter is the principal cause, but the ax is merely an instrumental cause.

And so, in response to the first objection, Thomas acknowledges that a principal cause cannot also be a sign, but an instrumental cause, "in virtue of the fact that it is not only a cause but in some sense an effect too, inasmuch as it receives its initial impetus from the principal agent,"[157] can be both a sign and a cause. Sacraments are signs by their own natural power, but they are causes insofar as their natural significatory power is used as an instrument by God.[158]

The distinction between principal and instrumental cause also leads to the answer to the third objection. While it is true that only God causes grace, it is false to imagine that the means by which God causes grace are somehow in competition with God. Just as both my pen and I write a letter without being in competition, so God and the sacraments cause grace without being in competition. They are not causes in the same sense and, indeed, the instrumental cause is utterly dependent upon the principal cause.[159]

It is probably important to note, since Thomas's metaphors are taken from the physical realm and can therefore give the impression of grace as a kind of "product," that Thomas does not understand grace as some kind of quantifiable stuff.[160] Rather, he says, "grace is nothing else than a certain shared [participata!] similitude to the divine nature."[161] In other words, sacraments don't "cause" grace by producing some sort of ethereal matter that is applied to the soul; rather, they grant us participation in God's own life.[162]

157. ST III, 62.1 ad 1.

158. In a very helpful article, Nathan Lefler highlights how the often misunderstood relationship between sign and cause in Aquinas's sacramental theology is clarified by the introduction of the category of person. It is because a person—namely, God—uses the sacramental signs that they are also causes ("Sign, Cause, and Person in St. Thomas's Sacramental Theology: Further Considerations," Nova et Vetera, English Edition 4, no. 2 [2006]: 381–404, esp. 392–99). Cf. Walsh, "Ecumenical Reading of Aquinas on the Eucharist," 229–30; and Joseph Wawrykow, "The Sacraments in Thirteenth-Century Theology," in The Oxford Handbook of Sacramental Theology, ed. Hans Boersma and Matthew Levering (Oxford: Oxford University Press, 2015), 222–23.

159. The distinction between principal and instrumental causes follows from, but is not identical with, Aquinas's basic distinction between primary and secondary causality that allows him to grant genuine freedom and agency to created agents. See Burrell, Freedom and Creation in Three Traditions, 97–101.

160. Liam Walsh responds very effectively to concerns that Thomas views grace as a kind of product. See his "The Divine and the Human in St. Thomas's Theology of Sacraments," in Ordo Sapientiae et Amoris: Image et Message de Saint Thomas d'Aquin à Travers Les Récentes Études Historiques, Herméneutiques et Doctrinales (Fribourg: Éditions Universitaires Fribourg Suisse, 1993), esp. 347–48.

161. ST III, 62.1 corpus.

162. Contemporary writers have profitably used metaphors taken from human communications, rather than from construction, to convey Thomas's views on this. See, e.g., McCabe,

With this understanding of Thomas's theology of the sacraments in general, we are now in a position to properly understand the first article in question 75, "Is the body of Christ really and truly in this sacrament or only in a figurative way or as in a sign?" Thomas is not here endorsing the false dichotomy between symbol and reality that was at the root of the Berengarian controversy. He is not suggesting that, if the presence is real, it is not predicated on the symbolic character of the elements.[163] Rather, the "only" indicates that Thomas is opposing real presence with a presence, rejected already in question 62, that "does not attribute any further force to them beyond that of a sign." Given that sacraments are signs, as per Thomas's definition in question 60, the question is, "Is the Eucharist *only* a sign, or is it also something more?"

It is important to attend to the objections to real presence and Thomas's responses to them, for these will indicate what Christian faith affirms, or, perhaps better, what it does *not* affirm, when it insists that Christ is really and truly present in the Eucharist. The objections Thomas gives against "real" presence are four: first, that Christ said, in John 6:63, that the spirit gives life but the flesh is of no avail; second, that Christ's body is risen and therefore in heaven; third, that a body can be in only one place at a time; and fourth, that Christ's body needed to ascend so that the Holy Spirit could come. Nevertheless, Thomas finds it both theologically necessary—because the sacrifice of the New Law must contain something more than the sacrifices of the Old Law[164]—and promised in Scripture—particularly in Jesus's promise to abide in those who eat his flesh and drink his blood—that Christ is really and truly present. It is a point of interest that Thomas here mentions that Berengarius, not having understood the necessity of real presence, was the "first to hold this erroneous view,"[165] that Christ is only present symbolically.

Having established the necessity of holding that Christ is really present, Thomas indicates why the objections given do not hold. It is here that we begin to get an understanding of the unique kind of presence to which transubstantiation leads. To the first objection, Thomas grants that Christ is there "spiritually, that is, invisibly and by the power of the spirit."[166] But that, of course, does not

---

"Eucharist as Language"; McCabe, "Sacramental Language," in *God Matters* (London: Continuum, 2005), 165–79.

163. As Peter Leithart mistakenly suggests in his "What's Wrong with Transubstantiation?," 303. See 79n118 above.

164. *ST* III, 75.1 corpus. For an analysis of transubstantiation that highlights its relationship to the sacrificial aspect of the Eucharist, see Matthew Levering's chapter "Transubstantiation" in *Sacrifice and Community*, 115–67.

165. *ST* III, 75.1 corpus.

166. *ST* III, 75.1 ad 1.

mean "only as in a mystical symbol."[167] Spiritual presence is not synonymous with mere symbolic presence nor is it the opposite of real presence.[168] Furthermore, the flesh is only of no avail when understood in a crude manner, "as if it had been torn from a carcass or sold in a butcher's stall,"[169] as Jesus's audience at Capernaum had understood him. Of course, to Christians who believe in the incarnation, the flesh is of great avail: the Word was made flesh!

The answer to the next three objections is essentially the same—namely, that they all imagine a natural, local presence and not a sacramental presence. Of course, Thomas grants that, according to Christ's natural appearance, he is ascended into heaven and locally present only there. But Christ's presence in the sacrament is unique. "The body of Christ is not in this sacrament in the way a body is in place."[170] Its dimensions do not correspond to the dimensions of the consecrated bread and wine, and Christ is not on different altars as if he were in several places at once. Problems related to such concerns are, as we shall see in more detail in questions 76 and 77, false problems that misunderstand the nature of sacramental presence. Nevertheless, Thomas is careful to point out that, "although it is true that every sacrament is a sign," he does not mean to say that "Christ is only symbolically there" (note the "only" again); rather, he is there "in a way that is proper to the sacrament."[171] As Frederick Bauerschmidt points out,

> Thomas denies that Christ is present only symbolically in the elements of the Eucharist, but he also denies that Christ's presence is a *physical* one—that is, that Christ's body is present, for example, in the same way in which it was present in Mary's womb or on the cross. If this were the case, then Christ's body could not be present on many altars at the same time. Nonetheless, Thomas still wants to claim that the body that is present in the Eucharist is the same one that was in Mary's womb and that hung on the cross. This apparent contradiction is the result of a distinction Thomas makes between *what*—or, better, *who*—is present, and in *how* this presence occurs. What Thomas wants to say is that Christ's presence in the Eucharist is *neither* purely symbolic *nor* physical; rather it is a way of being present that is unique to the sacrament of the Eucharist.[172]

167. *ST* III, 75.1 ad 1.
168. Frederick Christian Bauerschmidt, *Holy Teaching: Introducing the* Summa Theologiae *of St. Thomas Aquinas* (Grand Rapids: Brazos, 2005), 290n16. Cf. de Lubac, *Corpus Mysticum*, 161: "'To *understand spiritually*' had for a long time described a condition of rectitude, but now [after the eucharistic controversies], on the contrary, had come to describe a form of deviance."
169. *ST* III, 75.1 ad 1. Aquinas is quoting Augustine here.
170. *ST* III, 75.1 ad 3.
171. *ST* III, 75.1 ad 3.
172. Bauerschmidt, *Holy Teaching*, 289–90n15. We needn't worry that Bauerschmidt is using "how" to explain eucharistic presence rationalistically. In fact, he is rejecting two

Essentially, Thomas is engaged here in dispelling the false dichotomy between symbol and reality.[173] Some, imagining that real presence can mean only physical, natural, or local presence, suggest that such a presence is impossible for several reasons. Thomas acknowledges that such presence, as they understand it, is, in fact, impossible, but gives no ground on the reality of Christ's presence. Christ's presence in the Eucharist is real, but unique. He will spend the next three questions exploring what sort of presence this unique presence is, or, perhaps better, what it is not.[174] As Cyril Vollert, SJ, writes, "A good way to approach an understanding of what the Church affirms by transubstantiation is to see what it denies; for the dogma intends to discard several notions of change which are inadequate in the case of the Eucharist."[175]

Since there is no perfect analogue with which we could compare the change that takes place in the eucharistic conversion, Thomas often starts with a comparison and then proceeds to point out where the analogy works, and where it fails. The method of proceeding is one of *via negativa*:[176] we can learn something from stating what transubstantiation is not, though we can never state exactly what it is in a way that will satisfy human reason. As we have already seen, that is not the method of theology in approaching a mystery of the faith.

In the remaining articles of question 75, Thomas sets up two different comparisons in order to give us a better idea of what transubstantiation means by demonstrating what it does not mean. The first is between transubstantiation and two other theoretical possibilities considered by Scholastic theology, consubstantiation and annihilation. The second is between transubstantiation and two other existing realities, natural change and creation *ex nihilo*. We shall address these two comparisons in order.

---

ways of explaining the presence, two "hows," that would be rationalistic. See also 74–75n96 above.

173. See Walsh, "Ecumenical Reading of Aquinas on the Eucharist," 234:

The theology of sacrament that Thomas developed allowed him to attribute both signification and realism to the Eucharist. It is a sign, and everything to be said about it is being said about a sign. Bread and wine are to be changed in the Eucharist so that Christ's body and blood can be truly given in them as in a sign. The sign becomes effective sign of the ultimate reality of the Eucharist, which is the mystical body of Christ (*res tantum*), when it becomes reality as well as sign (*res et sacramentum*) of the personal body and blood of Christ, which it makes visible, tangible and "receivable" in bread and wine.

174. Levering describes this process as "metaphysical *ascesis*," purifying our minds of "attachment to our imagistic understanding of 'bodily'" (*Sacrifice and Community*, 150; see also 146, 151, 155). Cf. Power, *Eucharistic Mystery*, 222–25; Wawrykow, "Luther and the Spirituality of Thomas Aquinas," 90–91, 96.

175. Vollert, "The Eucharist: Controversy on Transubstantiation," 416–17.

176. Br. Jeffrey Gros, FSC, "The Roman Catholic View," in *The Lord's Supper: Five Views*, ed. Gordon T. Smith (Downers Grove, IL: IVP Academic, 2008), 17.

Consubstantiation?

In article 2, Aquinas asks whether the substance of the bread and wine remains after the consecration. Though Thomas (like Luther after him) does not use the term here, this possibility is typically known as consubstantiation because, according to it, the substance of the bread and wine would exist with (*con*) the substance of Christ's body and blood. Thomas gives four reasons for rejecting this possibility, the first of which is the most important.[177] Since the body and blood of Christ are not present before the consecration but they are present after it, Thomas reasons, they must somehow come to be present. "But a thing cannot be where it was not before, except by being brought in locally or by something already there being changed into it."[178] And, since it is impossible that Christ be locally moved—that would imply leaving heaven, passing through space, and being available in only one location at a time—the only way Christ could come to be in the sacrament is by the change of the substance of the bread into the substance of his body (and of the substance of the wine into the substance of his blood). But "what is changed into something else is no longer there after the change,"[179] and so the bread and wine are no longer present.

We must be careful here not to fall into the trap of imagining Thomas trying to solve an Aristotelian logic puzzle. While it is true that Thomas phrases his argument in terms of metaphysical possibilities, we have already seen that he does not feel bound by the strictures of Aristotle's philosophy of nature. He is using these metaphysical tools to better understand the mystery by ruling out inadequate conceptions of it, not to overdetermine it rationalistically. The important thing to note is that, in his rejection of the local movement hypothesis, Thomas is highlighting the precisely sacramental nature of the presence. The problems with local movement—that is, that it contradicts the ascension and Christ's presence in heaven, that it imagines Christ zipping through space, and that it cannot address the fact of Christ's presence on numerous altars at one time—are precisely the kinds of problems Thomas rejected as false problems in article 1. They misunderstand

---

177. The other reasons Thomas gives are that the words of institution, "This is my body," fit only awkwardly if the bread and wine remain, that worship of the consecrated host would constitute idolatry, and that eating the bread would break the Church's rules concerning fasting before the Eucharist. These reasons are less than decisive. Others have reasoned that "This is my body" also fits awkwardly if there is no bread and wine. (See, e.g., Stephenson, *Lord's Supper*, 105.) Also, the remaining presence of the accidents seems to complicate the final two reasons. If worship of bread is a problem, is not the worship of the accidents of bread a problem? And does not eating the accidents of bread break the fast?

178. *ST* III, 75.2 corpus.

179. *ST* III, 75.2 corpus.

eucharistic presence as physical or naturalistic and so miss the essentially sacramental character of a presence predicated on the sign value of the bread and wine. Consubstantiation, then, is not rejected simply because it is metaphysically absurd, though Thomas clearly believes that it is,[180] but because it is unsacramental.[181] In fact, one of the objections (the third) suggested that the substances should remain in order for the sacramental signification to obtain, but Thomas replies that accidents, being what are discerned by the senses, are all that is needed "to bring out what the sacrament signifies."[182] Walsh argues that

> the most important thing about this reply is not the discrete evocation of the Aristotelian distinction between substance and accident, and the consequent suggestion that the *species* of the Eucharist—the continuing visibility of bread and wine—have the metaphysical status of accidents. The really noteworthy thing is the sacramental role that Thomas gives to the bread and wine: they are able to exercise signification because the change that has occurred in them does not affect the part of their make-up that manifests what bread and wine are and what can be done with them, i.e. that they can be eaten and drunk for human nourishment and conviviality.[183]

We have here an articulation of the patristic sign-signified relationship in a new context.[184]

180. Walsh points out that whether the bread and wine remain depends on what exactly one means by bread and wine. Thomas talks not about bread and wine but about the substances of bread and wine. In so doing he is being very precise, metaphysically speaking. And since one concrete existing thing cannot, at the same time and in the same way, be another concrete existing thing, he finds it impossible that the substance of the bread and wine persist (Walsh, *Sacraments of Initiation*, 307–8). Whether, and in what way, a Catholic following Thomas might be willing to affirm the persistence of bread and wine will be dealt with in the next section, when we look at the concerns of the Reformers. See also Benedict XVI, "Problem of Transubstantiation," 236–38.

181. Indeed, as we have already seen in the case of Scotus, a preference for consubstantiation leads to a less than sacramental articulation of Christ's presence. See above, pp. 49–51. George Hunsinger correctly recognizes that this is the Catholic concern with consubstantiation (*Eucharist and Ecumenism*, 77).

182. *ST* III, 75.2 ad 3.

183. Walsh, "Ecumenical Reading of Aquinas on the Eucharist," 238.

184. Kelly, "Eucharistic Doctrine of Transubstantiation," 61–62. Cf. Crockett, *Eucharist*, 118: "Thomas employs the principle of causality not in order to negate the symbolic character of the sacraments, but in order to make clear in the medieval context what was obvious in the patristic context, namely, that the sacraments as signs participate in the reality that they signify and are not 'mere' signs." As we have already seen, after Berengarius, theology was much less free to affirm the persistence of bread and wine in general terms. Now things had to be parsed very carefully to avoid giving the impression of a purely symbolic presence. See above, pp. 68–69, 72–73. Cf. Walsh, "Ecumenical Reading of Aquinas on the Eucharist," 233.

Annihilation?

The third article of question 75 asks whether the substance of the bread is annihilated or otherwise ontologically reduced. As we have seen, after Lateran IV used the term "transubstantiation" without defining it, many understood the term to indicate an annihilation/replacement theory of eucharistic conversion.[185] Thomas rejects such an interpretation. At the heart of his rejection is his understanding of God's relationship with creation. In the *sed contra*, he quotes Augustine, who notes that "God is not the cause that anything should tend toward non-existence."[186] Thomas goes on to indicate how an annihilation theory would lead to many theoretical problems regarding time and space. For instance, would annihilation occur only once Christ is present? In such a case there would be an instant where Christ and the bread exist alongside one another, but this was rejected in the previous article. Or would annihilation occur before Christ is present? In this case there would be an instant where neither Christ nor the bread would be present, "a most undesirable situation."[187] Finally, he adds, it is not suitable that the form of the sacrament, "This is my body," should cause a reduction or annihilation that it does not signify.

As in the previous article, Thomas highlights the metaphysical difficulties of the proposed alternative with an eye to clarifying sacramental presence. The bread and wine cannot be added to or destroyed. They themselves must become (the sacrament of) Christ's body and blood.[188] While it is a common critique of transubstantiation that it does away with the bread and wine, Thomas's rejection of the annihilation theory highlights the importance of the bread and wine in the sacrament. It is not that they are done away with, but rather that they are used by God precisely as sacraments.[189] Their transformation is not one of degradation, as imagined by annihilation, but of lifting up: it is they themselves that have become Christ's body and blood. As Joseph Ratzinger writes, "The Lord takes possession of the bread and wine;

185. See above, pp. 36–37.
186. *ST* III, 75.3 sc.
187. *ST* III, 75.3 corpus.
188. "In the moment of transubstantiation, the bread and wine are not annihilated but rather assumed by Christ through the power of the Holy Spirit to become effective signs of Christ's body and blood. The change is so complete that the bread and wine no longer exist in themselves as bread and wine; therefore they are no longer 'substances'" (Kereszty, *Wedding Feast of the Lamb*, 214–15).
189. "Aquinas does not hold that transubstantiation consists in the annihilation of the bread and its replacement by the body of Christ. This would indeed, as the Thirty-Nine Articles put it, take away the nature of a sacrament. For Aquinas the Eucharist is sacramental just because it is bread that becomes the body of Christ" (McCabe, "Transubstantiation," 154n3).

he lifts them up, as it were, out of the setting of their normal existence into a new order; even if, from a purely physical point of view, they remain the same, they have become profoundly different."[190] Here, in fact, we can see an eschatological theme in transubstantiation, an anticipation of Christ as all in all, and we are reminded of what we heard earlier from Gustave Martelet— namely, that "transubstantiation is not an isolated mystery" but "the *sacramental* emergence" of the mystery that is, even now, restoring the universe.[191]

A Unique Kind of Change

Having rejected both consubstantiation and annihilation/replacement, Thomas turns, in article 4, to consider more closely the idea that the bread and wine themselves become the body and blood of Christ and asks, "Can the bread be turned into the body of Christ?" It is at this point that Thomas's break with Aristotle becomes crystal clear. All three objections are from Aristotle's philosophy of nature and read a bit like variations on a theme. First, we are told, such a change does not "obey the general law of change" because in every change,

> there is a subject which is first of all in potentiality to, and then actuated by, the final actuation. As Aristotle puts it, *change is the actuation of that which is still in potentiality* (to the final actuation). But there is no subject underlying the substance of the bread and the substance of the body of Christ, because it is of the nature of substance *not to be in a subject*, as Aristotle says.[192]

This requires some translation for readers not familiar with Aristotelian physics. Substances, for Aristotle, are made up of form and matter. Matter is the potency out of which existing things emerge, and form is the organizing principle that makes such potency into one thing or another.[193] So, for example, wood is a form that organizes plant cells; or, table is a form that organizes wood. (Note that one and the same thing, wood, in this case, can be both matter and form depending on the angle from which it is viewed. That is, matter does not mean simply physical reality in general as it has come to mean today. It is, rather, a relational reality. Furthermore, a nonphysical reality

---

190. Benedict XVI, *God Is Near Us*, 86.
191. Martelet, *The Risen Christ and the Eucharistic World*, 112–13. See above, p. 85.
192. *ST* III, 75.4 obj. 1 (emphasis original).
193. See Haldane, "A Thomist Metaphysics," 26: "What we are recognizing in the analysis of substantial change is the fact that one aspect of reality is the natural potential for the successive reception of structuring substantial principles. Prime matter is not any kind of stuff but the empirical condition for the existence of material particulars."

like numbers, for instance, can be the matter for an equation in which they are organized according to a certain principle, a form.) In order to speak of change, there must be some subject that undergoes the change, some *thing* that changes. The change may be accidental, as when a red door is painted blue while remaining one and the same door, or it may be substantial, as when a door is burned and becomes smoke and ash and embers. In either case, there is something that becomes something else. In the first example, the door became blue, maintaining its matter and form, and therefore its substance. In the second, the matter of the door was organized by a new form and became the matter of smoke and ash and embers.

When the first objection says that such a change is impossible because there is, by definition, no subject underlying substance, it is simply saying that such a change is impossible because *there is no something that becomes something else.* We cannot speak of change if literally *nothing* changes. It is worth highlighting, I think, just how precisely this objection maps onto the incredulity of our contemporaries when they are faced with claims like transubstantiation. Within their worldview, as within Aristotle's physics, the claim is simply meaningless. Nothing happens.[194]

Objections 2 and 3 simply offer more specific examples of the same basic problem. According to the second, the bread cannot become the body of Christ unless the form of Christ begins to exist in the matter of the bread. This is what happens naturally, for instance, if Christ eats bread. The matter that once was organized by the form "bread" comes, by the natural process of digestion, to be organized by the form "body." Obviously this is not what happens at the consecration. The third notes that two realities of the same order cannot be changed into one another. A door may change from red to blue, but red itself does not change into blue. Nor does a door become a table, though the matter of a door may become the matter of a table. This is another way of saying that there must be an underlying subject, but Thomas introduces a further problem: "Now just as two contrary forms are essentially opposed as being the very sources of formal difference, so also two individuated parts of matter are essentially opposed as being the very sources of individual distinction. Therefore, it cannot be that the individuated matter of this bread should become the matter which gives its individuation to the body of

194. Cf. Benedict XVI, "Problem of Transubstantiation," 235: "Viewed from the perspective of physics and chemistry, absolutely nothing takes place in the gifts—not even somewhere in a microscopic realm; considered physically and chemically, after the transformation they are exactly the same as they were before it. Only great speculative naïveté and a complete misunderstanding of what faithful Catholic thinking means by transubstantiation could contest this statement."

Christ."[195] In other words, the difficulty extends beyond the problem of turning bread into a body without an underlying subject because it includes the problem of turning this particular concrete existing piece of bread into a very particular concrete preexisting body. In the *Summa contra Gentiles*, Thomas expresses this particular problem with a very succinct example that will help us to understand, precisely by demonstrating its unimaginability, what is at issue. "Nature cannot," he says, "bring it about that this substance becomes that substance, that this finger, for example, become that finger."[196] Indeed, it is hard to know what it would mean for *this* finger to become *that* finger.

Thomas's reply begins by noting, as we have already seen in articles 2 and 3, that because Christ's risen body is beyond change there is no other way for Christ's body to become present than by something already present becoming Christ's body.[197] Nevertheless, such a change "is not like any natural change, but it is entirely beyond the powers of nature and is brought about purely by God's power."[198] We have already noted that this is the only real answer to the question of *how* Christ becomes present. Aristotle's objections apply to natural change, but do not apply in this case. It is like, says Thomas quoting Ambrose, the virgin birth, whereby Christ's body also entered the world in an impossible way, naturally considered. Furthermore, says Thomas, quoting Chrysostom, the words of Jesus in John 6:63—"The words that I have spoken to you are spirit and life"—so often quoted against transubstantiation, indicate that the bread of life discourse is "not to be taken in a carnal sense or according to the laws of nature."[199]

Now an appeal to God's power may well be in order, but it does not serve to make the idea of eucharistic change much more intelligible. Fortunately for us, Thomas is not content simply to claim that God does it, but he also wants to show that it is in some sense doable, if not naturally. It is here that our previous investigation of how Thomas differed from Aristotle on God's relationship to the world becomes important.

To insist that bread and wine are the kinds of things that can become, even if only by the power of God,[200] the body of Christ (annihilation and, perhaps to a lesser extent, consubstantiation insist the opposite) is to say something about God's relationship to created reality more generally. Creatures, being

195. *ST* III, 75.4 obj. 3.
196. *SCG* IV, 63.7.
197. As Levering puts it, "If the two terms of the conversion are Christ's body and blood, and bread and wine, then it is the second term that must change" (*Sacrifice and Community*, 141).
198. *ST* III, 75.4 corpus.
199. *ST* III, 75.4 corpus.
200. Cf. *ST* III, 75.8 ad 4: "This change does not occur because of passive ability in the creature to be this or that, but solely through the active power of the creator."

limited, can only change one thing into another by changing the form. We can burn a door, or eat a sandwich. In other words, changes such as creatures can work would be subject to the Aristotelian objections we have already looked at. But God's action, not being limited even by the genus of "being," "reaches out to the whole extent of the being of a thing." (Recall how Scotus, who had insisted on the univocal nature of being, and therefore put God in the genus "being," also found transubstantiation philosophically untenable.)[201] Therefore, God can effect a change at a deeper level than Aristotle's (or the contemporary materialist's) philosophy of nature supposes to exist: "not merely a changing of form, so that different forms follow one another in the same subject, but the changing of the whole being of a thing, so that the complete substance of this is changed into the complete substance of that."[202] Such a change "does not belong to the natural kinds of change, and it is called by a name proper to itself—'transubstantiation.'"[203] In other words, the very term "transubstantiation" is here very consciously articulated as something impossible within Aristotelian physics, which did not understand God as the Creator of the universe whose unlimited power extended to the concrete act of existence that makes a thing to be what it is. Accidental and substantial changes are both possible for Aristotle (and for the modern materialist), but transubstantial change is not. Transubstantiation is, quite consciously, trans-Aristotelian.

Thomas replies to the first two objections, then, by pointing out that they apply to different kinds of change than that understood by the Church to occur at the consecration of the Eucharist. But recall the third objection: How can one make this concrete existent to be that concrete (and preexisting) existent, since they cannot have any common matter upon which a change could be predicated? Thomas's reply here deserves careful attention. He writes that "the power of an infinite agent which bears on the whole being of a thing can bring about such a change. To the form of each thing and to the matter of each thing the nature *being* is common; and the author of being is able to change that which is *being* in the one into that which is *being* in the other, by taking away what kept this from being that."[204] To speak of change presumes something in common between the two terms of the change—in other words, something that changes. But, according to Aristotle's categories, there is nothing in common between (this concrete existing) bread and the (concrete preexisting) body of Christ that could render the term "change"

---

201. See above, pp. 40, 45–50.
202. *ST* III, 75.4 corpus.
203. *ST* III, 75.4 corpus.
204. *ST* III, 75.4 ad 3.

meaningful in this case.[205] On the other hand, from a biblical perspective on creation, God made everything and holds everything in existence—that is, God gives every existing thing *being*. Or, we could say, everything that exists exists by participation in God's being. And so God, who is therefore already the innermost reality of every existing thing,[206] and the author of being, can bring about a change at the level, unknown to Aristotle, of being—the level at which everything is here and now being given existence, being created, by God. As the author of being, God is the only one in whose power it is to determine being, and the question at the heart of transubstantiation is one of being proper.

The Eschatological

We must also note the startling final clause: "by taking away what kept this from being that"! The elevation of the bread and wine into the sacraments of Christ's body and blood is here presented as a kind of loss. But what, precisely, do they lose? The answer is, as we shall see in more detail later when we treat question 77, their independence. Their creaturely autonomy has been subsumed so as to make them utterly transparent to the ground and goal of creation. They become signs of the Alpha and the Omega, him in whom the universe was made (John 1) and who will be all in all at its consummation (1 Cor. 15). Their loss of being is simultaneously their elevation to the highest level of being. The bread and wine image the gospel paradox that those who lose their lives for his sake will find it. All of this is only meaningful, of course, within a biblical worldview that does not see creation as being in competition with God but as existing by participation in God, so that God, as the last thing of every creature, is not the threat of annihilation, but the promise of fulfillment.

Indeed, though he is rarely explicit about it, Thomas's theology of the Eucharist is thoroughly informed by an eschatological sensibility.[207] In the first question on the Eucharist, question 73, Thomas reflects that it is suitable

205. For a detailed investigation of this issue, written in response to concerns voiced by Germain Grisez in his "An Alternative Theology of Jesus' Substantial Presence in the Eucharist," see Brock, "St. Thomas and the Eucharistic Conversion."

206. See above, p. 49.

207. For an enlightening look at transubstantiation with explicit reference to eschatology, see David W. Fagerberg, "Translating Transubstantiation," *Antiphon* 6, no. 3 (2001): 9–13. On the other hand, Douglas Farrow's proposals regarding transubstantiation in his recent *Theological Negotiations* follow from his conviction that transubstantiation is insufficiently, even completely, non-eschatological. Farrow intuits that transubstantiation has more eschatological potential than consubstantiation or annihilation/replacement (146n3) but seems unaware of any sources that explore this potential, many of which (such as Martelet, *The Risen Christ and the Eucharistic World*, and Ratzinger, "Problem of Transubstantiation") we engage in the present work.

for the Eucharist to have several names since its significance is related to the past, because it commemorates the passion of Christ and is therefore called a sacrifice; the present, in which it draws the Church together and is therefore called communion; and the future, because it "prefigures that enjoyment of God which will be ours in heaven," and is therefore called viaticum and also Eucharist.[208] It is worth noting that the primary term Thomas takes for this sacrament—namely, "Eucharist"—is explicitly understood by him as eschatological in its implications. Gilles Emery, OP, writes that "the attention paid to this eschatological dimension is fully consistent with the deep movement of St. Thomas's theology toward the vision of God, toward the plenary revelation of the mysteries in the fulfillment of the Church: This is exactly what Thomas puts at the heart of his doctrine of the Eucharist."[209]

This eschatological dynamic is important to keep in mind as we continue to follow Thomas along the *via negativa*. In article 8, Thomas compares transubstantiation with natural change and with creation *ex nihilo* in order to clarify our thinking further. This comparison serves to highlight the uniqueness of transubstantiation while also drawing out its intelligibility in terms of things already known. It also demonstrates further, now explicitly through the comparison with creation *ex nihilo*, that Aristotle's categories are not determinative for transubstantiation.[210]

Transubstantiation, Natural Change, and Creation Ex Nihilo

Because each of these three actions has an order of terms—that is, there is one term before (bread, air, nothing) and another term after (the body of Christ, fire, being)—they are compared as changes, though it is important to note that creation *ex nihilo* is not, properly speaking, a change. As we have already seen, to speak meaningfully of change requires some *thing* that changes, but the first term of creation is nothing. While it is tempting to imagine nothing as a very vague kind of something out of which God created the universe, Thomas is under no such illusions.[211] In any case, Thomas

208. *ST* III, 73.4. Cf. *ST* III, 60.3 corpus, where Thomas talks about this threefold signification, in terms of past, present, and future, for sacraments generally.

209. Gilles Emery, OP, "The Ecclesial Fruit of the Eucharist in St. Thomas Aquinas," *Nova et Vetera* 2, no. 1 (2004): 60.

210. Bauerschmidt, *Holy Teaching*, 290n17: "This article, however, shows that Aquinas's understanding of Eucharistic conversion is primarily rooted not in Aristotle's metaphysics, but in a biblical metaphysics of creation from nothing, something that is quite alien to Aristotle."

211. See McCabe, "Transubstantiation," 148:
Aquinas himself was fully aware of the dangers of such a reification of "nothing" and he is careful to point out (Ia, 45, 1, ad 3) that "God made the world out of nothing" does not mean that "nothing" was what he made the world out of, it means that God did not

exploits the fact that each of the three actions has an order of terms in order to draw attention to the ways in which transubstantiation is both like and unlike natural change and creation *ex nihilo*.

Because the first term in creation *ex nihilo*, nonbeing, is so unique a metaphysical (non)category, it is difficult to fit into any analogy. Creating something from nothing is a totally unique act. And Thomas has already emphasized, in article 4, that it is precisely the act of having *being*—that is, of existing—that gives God something to work with, so to speak, in the eucharistic conversion. Thomas is consistent, then, in denying that creation *ex nihilo* can be properly called a change, because there is literally nothing to be converted. There is no first term that actually becomes the second term. Bread becomes the body of Christ and air becomes fire, but nonbeing does not become being. Nevertheless, despite its unique status, creation *ex nihilo* does have one thing in common with transubstantiation: in neither transubstantiation nor in creation *ex nihilo* "is there any underlying subject present to each extreme term. But the contrary of this is observed in all natural changes."[212] This means that both of these acts are the preserve of God alone acting without reference to secondary causes.[213]

Just as any temptation to imagine creation as a kind of natural change, by thinking of nothing as some sort of thing, for instance, must be avoided, so must any temptation to understand transubstantiation as a natural change. Robert Barron notes that two common misunderstandings of transubstantiation—as either a "clandestine chemical change in the bread or a metaphysical sleight of hand whereby one set of substances is whisked away and, under cover of the accidents, replaced by another" or "a projection of the meaning-creating capacity of the community"[214]—both miss the mark because they

---

make the world out of anything. The difficulty is simply that to a good Aristotelian this just means that God did not make the world. Aquinas wants to eat his cake and have it; he wants to say that God made the world while denying that he made it in any sense we can understand of the verb to make. . . . This kind of trick is characteristic of theologians' language. Aquinas became very interested in this right at the beginning of the *Summa Theologiae* (cf. Ia, 13, 3 and 5). He saw that we were always saying things like "God is good—but not in any way that we can understand goodness."

In other words, Thomas speaks about God by analogy. See above, pp. 40–43.

212. *ST* III, 75.8 corpus.

213. Robert Barron draws out an important consequence of this commonality: "It is the noncompetitively transcendent God, capable of affecting being at the most fundamental level, who alone is capable of both creation and transubstantiation. In both cases, the deepest grain of reality—God's sheerly generous and nonviolent gift—is made manifest. . . . Were the eucharistic transformation a this-worldly change, it would never function as an adequate representation of God's nonviolent love" ("Creation, Transubstantiation, and the Grain of the Universe," 218–19). Both creation and transubstantiation, properly understood, highlight that God's relationship with creation is one of gratuity, not manipulation.

214. Barron, "Creation, Transubstantiation, and the Grain of the Universe," 216.

would be types of natural change.[215] The comparison Thomas makes with creation, which, as we have seen, is at the root of Thomas's differences with Aristotle, serves to highlight the difference between transubstantiation and any kind of natural change, whether such change is articulated with Aristotelian terminology or in the language of contemporary physics and chemistry.

Nevertheless, despite the radical difference between transubstantiation and natural change, there are two commonalities between them that Thomas finds instructive. In the first place, in both transubstantiation and natural change one of the two extremes is converted into the other. So, while nonbeing cannot change into being, bread can change into the body of Christ and air can change into fire. This is not to say that they do so in the same way. Indeed, as we have seen, the bread is changed into Christ's body at a deeper level of reality than can be affected in natural change, that of being proper, so that this substance might become that substance (instead of the matter of this substance becoming the matter of that substance as happens in natural change). That is why this particular change has a name all its own, transubstantiation. Nevertheless, unlike creation *ex nihilo*, both transubstantiation and natural change can be properly understood as conversions because one term really does change into the next.

The second aspect that transubstantiation has in common with natural change is that something persists through the change. As we have seen, natural change can take two forms, accidental and substantial. In accidental change, the substance persists. In substantial change, the matter persists, taking on a new form. Hence, because of the persistence of some "subject," we can identify what came after with what came before. *That door* was red but now it is blue. Or, *that (matter)* which was a sandwich is now (matter which is) my body. But, in transubstantiation, neither the substance nor the matter persists. Rather, the accidents of the bread and wine persist and through them we are able to identify what comes after with what came before; in other words, we can affirm the "bread" and "the body of Christ" are the two extreme terms of the *same* conversion.[216] Because of this, we can say things like "The bread is the body of Christ," not in the sense that the substances of the bread and wine persist—that is, are unchanged by the consecration—but in the sense that precisely that aspect of creation—that something participating in God's being—which was the bread and wine is now the body and blood of Christ.

215. Barron, "Creation, Transubstantiation, and the Grain of the Universe," 215, 218. Of course, the first of these is closer to what Thomas has in mind in this article. The second is dealt with by Thomas in article 1 of question 75, where he insists that the presence is more than merely symbolic.
216. See Brock, "St. Thomas and the Eucharistic Conversion," 540–41.

What we see, then, in the juxtaposition of transubstantiation with creation and natural change is a unique reality—a unique presence (i.e., a sacramental one) predicated on a unique change, transubstantiation. But it is not unique in the sense that it is unrelated to the rest of creation or God's relationship to it.[217] Rather it is the unique presence in history of the new creation, which, like transubstantiation, is both the pure act of the creator God and the genuine conversion, not the annihilation, of the existing creation. Though different from natural change, transubstantiation is nonetheless a real conversion because it takes the existing created reality seriously. In this we can again see the eschatological import of transubstantiation. God's new creation is none other than the original, purified and redeemed.[218] As Ratzinger writes regarding eucharistic change, "This capacity things have for being transformed makes us more aware that the world itself can be transformed, that it will one day as a whole be the New Jerusalem, the Temple, the vessel of the presence of God."[219]

Furthermore, beyond serving as a kind of identity marker for that which has become the body and blood of Christ, and therefore making the terms "change" or "conversion" meaningful in the case of transubstantiation, the accidents have another important, and obviously related, function. While in their persistence through the change the accidents highlight the eschatological dynamism of the sacrament by providing the link between creation and the new creation,[220] the presence that follows upon the change is also utterly dependent upon the persistence of the accidents.[221] A sacramental presence is a presence that is predicated on the logic of sign.[222] Signs are the tools God

217. See Alexander Schmemann's critique of transubstantiation in his *The Eucharist: Sacrament of the Kingdom* (Crestwood, NY: St. Vladimir's Seminary Press, 1987), 33–34.

218. I must respectfully disagree with Matthew Levering's assertion that "for Aquinas, the eucharistic conversion is a miraculous this-worldly change, not an eschatological event" (*Sacrifice and Community*, 133; see also 134). By "this-worldly change" Levering does not mean "natural change," which he calls, rather, a "this-worldly *mechanism*" (141, emphasis original). He is simply trying to emphasize the genuine bodiliness of Christ's eucharistic presence (cf. 152–53). In any case, I find the suggestion that transubstantiation is not an eschatological reality because this-worldly realities—namely, the bread and wine—*really* change, to be based on a false dichotomy. Every this-worldly miracle, beginning with the resurrection of Christ, is an eschatological event. Perhaps Tillard's comment, "We must immediately stress that [Christ's paschal humanity] is present in a manner which does not pertain to the natural order of things, yet the purpose of this presence is specifically to communicate with the natural order," is helpful in this regard ("Roman Catholics and Anglicans," 159).

219. Benedict XVI, *God Is Near Us*, 86–87.

220. See Walsh, "Ecumenical Reading of Aquinas on the Eucharist," 239. Cf. Farrow, *Theological Negotiations*, 158. In contrast to Walsh, and to the whole thrust of the interpretation pursued here, Farrow asserts that "substance/accidents analysis closes off . . . an eschatological interpretation."

221. Cf. Fagerberg, "Translating Transubstantiation," 11–12.

222. See Walsh, "Ecumenical Reading of Aquinas on the Eucharist," 232–35.

uses to impart grace, to give us a share in the divine life, through the sacraments. The accidents of the bread and wine are the signs that make Christ's eucharistic presence possible precisely as a sacramental presence.[223] It is to the nature of this presence that Thomas turns in question 76. He will concentrate even more specifically on the accidents in question 77.

Question 76: Purifying Our Imagination

Transubstantiation, being an utterly unique kind of change, leads to an utterly unique kind of presence. As a nonphysical, nonempirical kind of presence, it is impossible for us to imagine since our imaginations deal precisely in the physical and empirical—that is, things we can picture (image) in our minds.[224] Nevertheless, there is a great temptation for us to try to imagine Christ's eucharistic presence. When we do this, we are met with all kinds of conceptual problems. In question 76, Thomas walks us through a series of these conceptual problems in order to purify our imaginations of ideas that are not appropriate for sacramental presence.

The first four articles all address the issue of the presence of the *whole* Christ and the problems presented by such an affirmation. First of all, it does not seem that Christ's soul or divinity could be present in a sign that is said to be simply his body. Indeed, a separate symbol for blood seems to indicate that not even that is included in the symbol for his body, to say nothing of bones, nerves, or other parts of Christ's body. In what sense, then, can we suggest that the whole Christ is present in the sacrament? Here Thomas introduces the idea of concomitance, which provides the basis of his response for each of the first four articles. He writes,

> There are two ways in which a part of Christ can be in [the sacrament]. The first way is as an immediate result of the sacramental sign; the second is by way of natural concomitance. . . . Because, wherever two things are actually joined together, wherever you have one, the other has to be. It is only by an act of our mind that we separate things that are really joined together.[225]

Christ's body, then, is present in the species of the bread "as an immediate result of the sacramental sign"; that is, the bread specifically *represents* Christ's body. The same is true of Christ's blood and the species of wine. Whatever else there is of Christ, whether spiritual realities such as his soul

223. *ST* III, 75.2 ad 3. See also Levering, *Sacrifice and Community*, 144–45.
224. Cf. *ST* III, 76.7 corpus.
225. *ST* III, 76.1 corpus.

and divinity, or physical realities like his bones and nerves, is present in the Eucharist not because it is effectively symbolized in itself, but simply because his body cannot be genuinely present without it. While signs function in the mental realm where we can make certain distinctions, the reality conveyed by the signs is not, in reality, available in pieces, but only as an integral whole. To receive Christ's body without his soul, for example, would imply receiving his dead body, whereas, in his risen body, his soul is always united with his body.[226]

Thomas applies this basic logic of concomitance to several related problems. For instance, in article 2 he argues that Christ's body is present in the species of the bread by the power of the sacramental sign, but in the species of the wine by concomitance, while the reverse is true for Christ's blood. And, while this means that the communicant receives the whole Christ in receiving either the bread or the wine, there is an essential sacramental significance in having both species. First of all, Christ's passion, wherein his body and blood were actually separated, is well represented by the twofold consecration and, second, Christ can be given to the faithful as their food and drink, thereby fulfilling the promise of John 6.[227]

Thomas also invokes concomitance to address the obvious incompatibility of the dimensions of Christ's body with the dimensions of the bread. It "is obvious to our senses"[228] that the dimensions of the bread (and wine) remain, and Thomas has no patience for the idea that this would imply some kind of deception in the sacrament. As he noted in article 5 of the previous question, "There is no deception in this sacrament; the accidents, which are the proper object for our senses to deal with, are genuinely there."[229] But if the whole Christ truly is present in the sacrament, then it is not only the case that his soul and divinity are present alongside his body and blood, but it is also the case that the dimensions of that body, and all its other accidents, are present as well. If these were lacking, we could not properly say that the sacrament contains the whole Christ.

226. This is entirely consistent with the biblical understanding in which "body" indicated the whole embodied person, not merely the physical category "body" abstracted from the rest of what made a person a person. As David Power writes, "The *body* in Semitic language refers to the person as one who expresses self, acting and communicating with others. The *blood* is the life-principle and its use highlights the fact that life is a gift, sacred in such a way that it belongs to God and can be taken away only by God" (*Eucharistic Mystery*, 38).

227. *ST* III, 76.2 ad 1. Thomas gives no indication of developing the idea of concomitance as a justification for restricting the cup to the ordained, as is sometimes suggested. In fact, his suggestion that a twofold signification is valuable so that the faithful may be given Christ's body as food and his blood as drink seems quite unlikely under such a pretense.

228. *ST* III, 75.5 corpus.

229. *ST* III, 75.5 ad 2.

Thomas's response to this dilemma is twofold. First of all, the dimensions of Christ's body "are not in this sacrament as a result of the effectiveness of the sacramental sign."[230] They are not specifically indicated by the bread or wine as the substance of Christ's body and blood are. Therefore they must be in the sacrament in the same way as everything else that is not the direct effect of the sacramental sign itself—namely, by concomitance. The dimensions of Christ's body are essential aspects of it that, while they can be conceived of independently in the mind, must exist along with Christ's body wherever it occurs in reality.

Alasdair Heron has suggested that concomitance is a "further doctrine" introduced so that transubstantiation "is not to leave us, so to speak, with the mere body and blood of Christ rather than his whole person and saving power."[231] But it is not a supplementary doctrine so much as an observation—namely, of the fact that to say Christ's body is present is to imply that the whole Christ is present precisely in "his whole person" and with his "saving power." Concomitance is a clarification that highlights the sacramental nature of Christ's presence. Consuming a body naturally (like eating a steak) is not to commune with a person. But the terms "body" and "blood," as used by Christ at the Last Supper and in the tradition of the Church, are in themselves symbolic realities representing, so to speak, the person (body) and life (blood) of Christ and his life-giving sacrifice (emphasized by their separate consecration).[232] That traditional Catholic piety refers to Christ as present "body, blood, soul, and divinity" demonstrates that, despite frequent misapprehension of the doctrine of transubstantiation, the idea of concomitance has succeeded in helping people to think more in terms of communion than of cannibalism.

After establishing their presence by means of concomitance, the second thing Thomas points out is that the dimensions are not in the sacrament in the normal way in which dimensions are present; rather, they are present in the mode of substance. While dimensions normally exist "whole in the whole and parts in the parts," substance exists "whole in the whole and whole in every part." For example, while the dimensions of my body exist only in my whole body, the dimensions of my finger exist only in my finger and not in my toe. On the other hand, the substance of my body exists in the whole of me and in every part of me, at least inasmuch as such parts remain part of the whole. (The substance of my body is not in my fingernail clippings or on

---

230. *ST* III, 76.4 corpus.
231. Heron, *Table and Tradition*, 99.
232. Power, *Eucharistic Mystery*, 38.

the barbershop floor!) The substance of my body, that aspect which the intelligence apprehends so that it can say, "That is your body," is, in principle, not divisible. To take another example, the substance of water is present in every part of water so that, whether one is looking at a molecule or an ocean, one can rightly say, "This is water." Or one can remark, "That is bread," whether one is talking about a tiny crumb or a whole loaf, because the substance of bread is equally present in the part and in the whole.[233] Furthermore, because the dimensions of Christ's body are present in this way, whole in the whole and whole in every part, they are not in any competition with the remaining dimensions of the bread, which continue to exist in the way that it is normal for dimensions to exist. In fact, Christ's dimensions exist wholly in each part of the species of the bread, as we shall see presently.

The Language of Common Sense

Two things are worth noting at this point. First of all, though we do not typically use the language of "substance" in our everyday lives, the way it is used here does reflect the way that people actually talk about reality. We do call bread "bread" and water "water," regardless of the amount, and whether present in pieces or in a whole. And our everyday language recognizes that my body is in some sense genuinely present in each of its parts even while the dimensions of each of the parts are only commensurate with themselves and the dimensions of the whole are only commensurate with the whole. Thomas is not here imposing Aristotle on eucharistic theology so much as using Aristotle to help us see more clearly how it is that we actually talk about reality and to use our everyday categories (whether we recognize them as such or not) to make Christ's eucharistic presence more intelligible.[234]

Second, it is important to recognize that these categories that we use to talk about everyday things presume a certain logic that could rightly be called symbolic. While we have come to imagine that symbol and reality are somehow mutually exclusive categories, this is not actually reflected in the way we apprehend reality from day to day. We apprehend the substance of a thing, what a thing *is*, by following the lead of our senses, but we do not mistake what our senses tell us for being the thing itself. Our senses read signs (symbols), the attributes of things, so that our intellects may affirm the things in themselves (reality). So, while our tongue perceives sweetness and our eyes perceive white granules, our intellect apprehends sugar, and this is how we

233. *ST* III, 76.3 corpus.
234. This is what John Haldane means when he describes Thomist metaphysics as "descriptive" rather than "revisionist" ("A Thomist Metaphysics," 21). See also Feingold, *Eucharist*, 276.

refer to it in conversation. We do not call it "sweetness" or "whiteness," for that would be only a very partial aspect of the reality in question and not the reality itself. Indeed, even if we did not know its common name, we would not request "sweetness" for our coffee, but rather that sweet, white, granulated *thing*. We know, in other words, the difference between adjectives and nouns. But we also know that adjectives (signs) are not exclusive of nouns (things). Rather, they presume them.

Thomas was keenly aware of this dynamic and, in fact, his theology of the sacraments is predicated upon it. The first reason Thomas gives for the necessity of sacraments "is taken from the way in which human nature functions in achieving knowledge of spiritual or intelligible realities. It has the special property of arriving at this knowledge deductively through its experience of physical and sensible realities."[235] It is not merely that "spiritual" things, in the sense of "those things that pertain to religion," must be arrived at by some indirect route. No, anything "intelligible" is arrived at through the senses. Nevertheless, such intelligibility is not to be reduced to sense perception. Other animals sense things without deducing from that experience intelligible realities. The capacity for such deduction is a "special property" of human nature.

All of this background will help us to see how Thomas's response to the question posed in article 3, "Is the whole Christ under each and every part of the species?" is so important for understanding Christ's eucharistic presence as sacramental. He writes,

> Since the body of Christ is in this sacrament because of the effectiveness of the sacramental sign and its quantitative dimensions as the result only of a natural concomitance, the body of Christ is here as if it were just substance, that is, in the way that substance is under dimensions, and not in any dimensive way, i.e., not in the way that the dimensive quantity of a body is under the dimensive quantity of the place that contains the body. Now it is clear that the whole nature of any substance is under any part of the dimensions that contain it; for example, under any part of air you have the whole nature of air and under any part of a loaf you have the whole nature of bread; and this is equally true whether the quantity is actually divided into parts (as when the air is divided or the loaf is cut into pieces), or it is not actually divided, but only potentially so. You are to think then of the whole Christ as being present under each and every part of the bread, even when the host remains unbroken.[236]

235. *ST* III, 61.1 corpus.
236. *ST* III, 76.3 corpus. Cf. *ST* III, 77.4: "Can the sacramental species cease to exist by decomposition?"

Because Christ's sacramental presence is not dimensive, because his body parts do not correspond to certain parts of the consecrated bread, but rather exist in the same way that the substance of the bread from which it came once existed, questions that presume a dimensive presence are shown to be false problems. Broken, or potentially broken, hosts lead neither to a multiplicity of Christs (or, as the first objector worried, to an infinity of Christs) nor to a division of Christ. Instead, as David Power writes, "Of a large or a small loaf, of a whole loaf or part of a loaf, of a slice or of a crumb, one says that it is bread. In the sacrament, the substance is that of Christ's body, not that of bread. Given the difference, the rules of predication are the same. Of anything that retains the external qualities of bread one says that it is the body of Christ."[237] What this means, in terms of clarifying sacramental presence, is that, *as long as the symbol exists, so does the presence*. Sacramental presence is predicated on the logic of symbols. Whenever that is forgotten or ignored, often in an attempt to highlight the realism of Christ's presence by those who understand symbol and reality to be exclusive, false problems emerge.[238] But when this principle is adhered to, the false problems evaporate. We shall see this again as we move forward.

A Local Presence?

Thomas's next step, in article 5, is to deny that Christ is "locally" present in the sacrament. This follows upon at least two things that we have already seen—namely, that Christ did not come to be in the sacrament by local motion and that Christ's dimensions need not correspond in any way to the dimensions of the bread, both of these things having been rejected as unsacramental. In this article, however, Thomas introduces a further distinction between natural presence and sacramental presence by drawing out an implication of the fact that, in transubstantiation, there is not a subject common to both terms. He asks us to

> note also that the substance of Christ's body is not the subject of the dimensions of the bread as the substance of the bread was. The bread by reason of the dimensions was localized in a place, because it was related to a place by dimensions that were its own. But the substance of Christ's body is related to that place by dimensions that are not its own; and, contrariwise, the dimensions of Christ's body are related to that place only in so far as the substance of his

237. Power, *Eucharistic Mystery*, 223.
238. This is essentially Roch Kereszty's assessment of Germain Grisez's critique of transubstantiation. See Kereszty, "On the Eucharistic Presence," esp. 348–50; see also Grisez, "An Alternative Theology of Jesus' Substantial Presence in the Eucharist."

body is. But that is not the way in which a body is localized. Hence, Christ's body in this sacrament is in no way localized.[239]

Christ's own dimensions, being present by concomitance and only in the mode of substance, cannot fulfill their normal function of localizing Christ's body, and the dimensions of the bread, not having Christ's body as their proper subject, also cannot fulfill this function. What remains to be said is simply that what *is* present locally is none other than the dimensions of the bread.

This distinction between the relationship that the bread had with its own proper accidents and the relationship that Christ's body has with the accidents of the bread is of dual significance. In the first place, by leading to a nonlocal presence, it resolves all kinds of issues that arise when the presence is imagined in a physical or material way. Second, it serves to highlight the value of the bread and wine precisely as signs. We will treat these two issues in order.

The remaining three articles in question 76 are a working out of what the nonlocal presence affirmed in article 5 means in response to three further questions. In the first, article 6, Thomas asks whether Christ is present in a mobile way, that is, in a way that he can be moved. In order to answer this question, Thomas makes another important distinction: "Now it is not the same thing for Christ to be, simply, and for him to be under the sacrament; because when we say that he is under the sacrament we mean that he has a relationship [*habitudo*] to the sacrament."[240] This allows Thomas to say two things. First of all, "according to this mode of his being under the sacrament, Christ is not moved locally in any strict sense, but only after a fashion."[241] Christ, being beyond change, including movement, in heaven, cannot be moved. On the other hand, he can be said to be moved, but only in the sense that that with which he has a sacramental relationship is moved. Second, and perhaps more importantly, just as Christ does not come to be present in the sacrament by local motion, neither does he cease being present by local motion. Because he cannot "be directly subject to any other kind of change, precisely as he exists in this sacrament,"[242] there is only one way by which his presence can cease:

> God, whose being is unfailing and immortal, ceases to be in a corruptible creature by the fact that the corruptible creature has ceased to be. In the same way, since Christ has unfailing and immortal being, he does not cease to be under the sacrament because of any ceasing-to-be on his part. Nor does he cease to be

239. *ST* III, 76.5 corpus.
240. *ST* III, 76.6 corpus.
241. *ST* III, 76.6 corpus.
242. *ST* III, 76.6 corpus.

under the sacrament because of any local movement, as is clear from what has already been said, but simply because the sacramental species have ceased to be.[243]

In other words, Christ's sacramental *relationship* to the species, a relationship so determinative that we must say he is *really* present by it, ends when there are no more species with which to be in sacramental relationship. Or, as we have seen, when the symbol is gone, so is the presence.

What such a sacramental presence means becomes even clearer in article 7, where Thomas asks whether Christ's body, "as it is under this sacrament," could ever be seen by the eye. Thomas answers that "the body of Christ, as it is under this sacrament, cannot be seen by any bodily eye." The objectors had imagined that certain heavenly eyes, and especially Christ's own eye, could somehow pierce the veil of the sacramental species by means of which we are prevented from seeing Christ's body, but Thomas answers that there is simply no veil to pierce: "It is not just that [the sacramental species] are a sort of covering, preventing us from seeing him in the way a bodily veil hides what it veils; it is rather because Christ's body has no connection with the ambient of this sacrament through its own proper accidents, but only by means of the sacramental species."[244] In the unique way in which Christ is present, it is not so much that we cannot see, as it is that there is simply nothing *to see*. This is because the way in which Christ's body is present is "as if it were just substance," and substance "cannot be seen by the bodily eye, nor is it the object of any sense, nor can it be imagined; it is only open to the intellect."[245] Hence, when angels or demons "see" the body of Christ in the sacrament, it is not by some special sense perception (indeed they do not have sense perception at all!), but by faith, which has informed their intellect. Indeed, faith is also the only way in which *we* can "see" Christ in the sacrament.[246]

243. *ST* III, 76.6 corpus.
244. *ST* III, 76.7 ad 1.
245. *ST* III, 76.7 corpus.
246. Thomas notes that "the eye of the intelligence" is "called so by analogy" (*ST* III, 76.7 corpus). See McCabe, "Transubstantiation," 152:

> It is not that God tricks us—so that while all our criteria for decision make us think that it is bread, he has secretly switched the "inner reality" to make it zinc or flesh. On the contrary the consecration is God's quite public announcement that here these criteria no longer apply. It makes no more sense to ask whether this is bread than to ask whether God is bread—of course both these questions *could* be asked within the realm of metaphor. It *appears* that we have here a fit subject for our ordinary criteria. It is only because we have faith in the consecrating word of God that we know the criteria cannot sensibly be applied. If we did not know this we would make the mistake of applying them (as the unbeliever does) and then naturally we would say that this is bread and not anything else.

Finally, in article 8, Thomas addresses the question of eucharistic miracles, the appearances of which would often seem to undercut the idea that Christ's presence is not a natural presence. After (wryly) noting that some such apparitions are only in the eye of the beholder, he goes on to address those that have not merely a subjective, but an objective basis. Thomas does not deny that such apparitions are possible, but he does deny that they present Christ in his natural form. Thomas is committed to the idea that the risen Christ is naturally in heaven and in heaven only. Instead, such miracles must be only "a miraculous change in the other accidental quantities, for example, the shape and colour, etc., . . . in order to express a certain truth [remember, for Thomas, there must be no deception in the sacrament!] . . . that the body and blood of Christ are really present in the sacrament."[247] Furthermore, as long as the dimensions of the species remain, Christ's sacramental presence remains, even if some of the accidents change. The same rule applies for apparitions as for anything else—as long as the species are recognizable as the species of bread and wine, Christ's presence remains.

Before moving on to our second consideration, we can note also that an important implication of Christ's nonlocal presence also shows up in question 81, where Thomas is considering the hypothetical situation of what would happen to a host reserved from the Last Supper during Christ's passion. The relationship between Christ's natural body and his sacramental body is not symmetrical. While everything that is "attributed to Christ as he is in himself may be attributed to him both under his own proper appearance and as present in the sacrament, for instance to live, to die, to suffer, to be alive or not alive, and the like," the reverse does not hold. So,

> whatsoever is his in relationship to external bodies can be attributed to him as existing under his own proper species, but not as present under the sacrament, thus to be mocked, spat upon, scourged, and crucified. Hence the verse:

> When reserved in the pyx he can grieve
> from within, yet cannot be hurt from without.[248]

Indeed, the idea that Christ might suffer whatever becomes of the host is rather widespread in some Catholic circles, demonstrated most famously by

---

Cf. *ST* III, 75.5 corpus, where Thomas argues that "in taking the body and blood of our Lord in their invisible presence, we increase the merit of our faith." Levering treats this in *Sacrifice and Community*, 139. See also Kelly, "Eucharistic Doctrine of Transubstantiation," 62.

247. *ST* III, 76.8 corpus.

248. *ST* III, 81.4 corpus. The verse Thomas quotes is from his teacher, Albertus Magnus.

anecdotes about children being instructed not to bite the host for fear that Christ would be hurt by their teeth.[249] But transubstantiation is not the ground of such misconceptions. Rather, properly understood, it explains why such concerns are misplaced.

The Importance of the Sacramental Signs

But, beyond resolving issues that emerge when Christ's presence is misunderstood in a physical or materialistic way, the distinction between the relationship that the accidents of bread have with their proper substance and the one they have with the body of Christ also serves to highlight their character as signs. As McCabe writes, "It is an important part of St Thomas's teaching on the Eucharist that the accidents of bread and wine cease to be the appearances of bread and wine, but this is not because they become the misleading appearances of something else. They cease to function as appearances at all, they have become signs, sacramental signs through which what is signified is made real."[250] Recall Thomas's insistence that there be no deception in the sacrament. We see what were once the appearances of bread and wine because they really are there. Nevertheless, they are no longer there *as* the appearances of bread and wine. And, because their relationship to Christ's body is not the same as their relationship to the substance of bread, neither are they the appearances of Christ. They are, rather, sacramental signs of Christ.

While some critics have suggested that transubstantiation involves a collapse between sign and signified, and so fails to adequately translate the traditional faith of the Church as seen in the Fathers,[251] the fact that the species of the bread and wine do not localize Christ's body and blood because they do not have the same relationship with them as they had with their own proper accidents actually prevents such a collapse.[252] If, on the other hand, Christ's body and blood were supposed to function as a proper subject for the accidents, because of the demands of Aristotelian natural philosophy, sign and signified *would* collapse. Ironically, then, the fact that the accidents persist without a proper subject—generally seen as a great weakness of transubstantiation because it is so non-Aristotelian—actually ends up preserving the sign-signified distinction necessary for a properly sacramental understanding.

249. Cf. Kelly, "Eucharistic Doctrine of Transubstantiation," 60.

250. McCabe, "Eucharistic Change," 118.

251. See, e.g., MacKenzie, "Reformed Theology and Roman Catholic Doctrine of the Eucharist as Sacrifice (with Response by Christopher Kiesling)," 433. Cf. Kiesling's response on p. 439.

252. Hunsinger sees this clearly (*Eucharist and Ecumenism*, 58).

And so, though the accidents of the bread and wine remain throughout the change, their mode of existence has changed radically because of their new *relationship* to the body and blood of Christ. Existing without a proper subject, they can become pure signs. Ratzinger puts it this way, and again connects the whole discussion with eschatology:

> The sacramental word does not produce a physical transformation (that would have to be brought about through physical operations), but, rather, through God's mighty benevolence it causes things to be changed from autonomously existing things into mere signs that have lost their creaturely peculiarity and exist no longer for themselves but only for him, through him, in him. Thus they are now in their *essence*, in their being, *signs*, as they were previously in their essence *things*. And they are in this regard truly "trans-substantiated," affected at the deepest and most intimate level, in their being, in what they truly are in themselves. What has happened here does not affect the physical phenomenon as such, but it reveals the provisional character of the merely physical as "accident" and points to the distinctive reality that is encountered here and that now of course lends an entirely new meaning and a new value to the physical elements. The potential that in principle lies hidden in all creatures—the fact that they can and should be signs of His Presence—becomes here through the sacramental word a reality in the highest degree.[253]

It is to the physical elements, "the accidents remaining," the signs, that Thomas turns in question 77.

Question 77: Free-Floating Accidents?

The first article of question 77 really is, in a sense, the whole question. After a small clarification is made in article 2, the remaining six articles exist to show how the answer to article 1 resolves the many difficulties imagined to surround the question of the remaining accidents. More than anything, they are a matter of the application of the principles enunciated in article 1 and clarified in article 2. As such, article 1 deserves our careful attention. It asks, "Do the remaining accidents have no subject?"

Remember that, according to Aristotle, an accident is something that exists only in a subject, and not in itself. Within an Aristotelian framework, then, the accidents must have a subject by definition. But we know that the substance of bread is not their subject, since it has become the body of Christ. Furthermore, we know from question 76, article 5, that the relationship between the accidents of the bread and the body of Christ is not the same as that which

---

253. Benedict XVI, "Problem of Transubstantiation," 237.

once existed between the bread's accidents and its substance. Indeed, "it is obvious that those accidents do not inhere in the substance of Christ's body and blood, because the substance of the human body could not be affected by accidents of this kind, and it is further impossible that Christ's body, now glorious and immune from suffering change, should so be altered as to receive these qualities."[254] The body of Christ cannot be the subject of the accidents because it is nonsense to imagine Christ "could be affected by accidents of this kind." Indeed, to imagine that would be something like turning Christ into bread, rather than the other way around.[255] And furthermore, as we have repeatedly seen, Christ's glorified body cannot change, but for it to be affected by the accidents of bread and wine would constitute change.

But if the accidents do not inhere in the substance of the bread or in the substance of Christ's body, in what do they inhere? Thomas has no use for those who would imagine that they must, therefore, inhere in the surrounding air. Not only does that lead to several logical problems of its own, but it is not at all indicated by the form of the sacrament itself. No, rather than inventing some such explanation, Thomas prefers to

> conclude that the accidents in this sacrament do not inhere in any subject. God's power is able to bring this about. Seeing that all effects depend more on the first cause than on secondary causes, God, who is the first cause of both substance and accident, by using his infinite power, is able to conserve an accident in being, even when the substance which hitherto as its immediate cause was keeping it in existence has disappeared. In this way also he is able to produce what are effects of other natural causes without actually employing these causes, as when he formed a human body in the Virgin's womb without male seed.[256]

Remember, when Thomas appeals to God's power, he is not satisfied simply to let the matter rest there. If God could do it, it must be, in some sense, do-able. That is, it must not be merely nonsense. But to work against definitions *is* nonsense. God can't make a four-sided triangle.[257] In order to understand why Thomas thinks it is possible for God to hold accidents in existence without a proper subject, which, according to Aristotle at least, is against their

254. *ST* III, 77.1 corpus.
255. Cf. Heron, *Table and Tradition*, 98; and Christopher Kiesling's response in Ross Mac-Kenzie, "Reformed and Roman Catholic Understandings of the Eucharist (with Roman Catholic Response by Christopher Kiesling)," in *The Eucharist in Ecumenical Dialogue* (New York: Paulist Press, 1976), 77.
256. *ST* III, 77.1 corpus.
257. This example is taken from Frank Sheed, *Theology and Sanity* (San Francisco: Ignatius, 1993), 35. See also Feingold, *Eucharist*, 273–74.

definition, we must go back to our treatment of how Thomas's fundamental view of reality diverged from Aristotle's because of Thomas's commitment to the biblical doctrine of creation.[258]

For Aristotle, substances are absolutely autonomous, subsisting, by definition, in themselves and themselves alone. But for Thomas, with his biblical doctrine of creation, no mere creature can be said to be absolutely autonomous. Substances may be autonomous relative to other creatures, but they still depend for their existence upon the act of existence given by the Creator. Their very independence is *given* and, therefore, dependent. It is still useful, of course, to distinguish substance and accidents. "Red" is a different kind of a thing than "ball." But it is essential to note that the addition of a whole metaphysical layer, that of "being," changes what existence means for both "red" and "ball." While "red" still exists by its participation in "ball," both "red" and "ball" only exist by participation in God. That, indeed, is the only way that anything the essence of which is not existence—that is, anything that is not God—exists.

That is why Thomas explains, after invoking God's power, that, since "all effects depend more on the first cause than on secondary causes, God, who is the first cause of both substance and accident, by using his infinite power, is able to conserve an accident in being, even when the substance which hitherto as its immediate cause was keeping it in existence has disappeared."[259] As John Milbank and Catherine Pickstock explain,

> since participation in Being is the most fundamental ontological dimension of creation, the real distinction of essence and existence can in theory sustain finite reality before and without the division of substance and accident. And this explains why free-floating accidents are possible, although it would have been better to say that the remaining accidents have passed beyond the contrast of substance and accident. They are neither essential—since they are not God; nor are they non-essential—since they manifest God and His creation.[260]

This is why we could say, when we looked at Thomas's startling claim in article 4 of question 75—namely, that "the author of being is able to change that which is *being* in the one into that which is *being* in the other, by taking away what kept this from being that"—that what the author of being takes away from the bread and wine is precisely their independence.[261] Substance is that which exists independently, even if only relatively so for Aquinas. Therefore,

---

258. See above, pp. 81–83.

259. *ST* III, 77.1 corpus.

260. John Milbank and Catherine Pickstock, *Truth in Aquinas* (London: Routledge, 2001), 106.

261. See above, p. 100.

to lose substance, to have it taken away, while retaining accidents is simply to have lost independence. The bread no longer exists in itself, but only in Christ, through whom God made the world. Ratzinger puts it this way:

> Bread and wine participate first of all in the general autonomy of created being; they share in the fundamental "substantiality" that belongs to the created thing as an independent being beside divine Being. Transubstantiation, however, signifies that these things lose their creaturely independence, that they cease to exist simply in themselves in the manner befitting a creature, and instead become *pure* signs of his presence.[262]

We can further note that, as we saw in chapter 1, because God does not belong to any genus, not even that of "being," the loss of such independence is not destructive of the creature. (Endorsing a theory of annihilation would have indicated the opposite.)[263] God is not in competition with the creature so that every increase in the creature is matched by a corresponding decrease in God. Rather, the opposite obtains. This is why F.-X. Durrwell can write that "by calling the eucharist the true Bread, the language [of the liturgy, based on John 6] reflects the mystery better than by saying: the eucharist is no longer bread."[264]

And, given the nominalist insistence that God belongs in the genus "being" and nominalism's rejection of transubstantiation, it is fascinating to note that, in his response to the objection that accidents cannot, by definition, exist without a subject, Thomas invokes God's unique metaphysical status:

> *Seeing that being is not a genus, existence cannot be of the essence of either substance or accident.* It is not right then to define substance as "that which exists of itself without inhering in a subject" or to define accident as "that which exists in a subject"; one should say that to the definition or essence of a substance "it pertains to have existence without inhering in a subject," and that to the definition or essence of an accident, "it pertains to have existence in a subject." Now in this sacrament the fact that the accidents exist without actually inhering in a subject is not because their essence has been changed but because they are being kept in existence by God.[265]

This is perhaps the most explicit acknowledgment from Thomas that his Christian understanding of God and creation radically alters his view of substance

---

262. Benedict XVI, "Problem of Transubstantiation," 236–37.

263. See above, pp. 95–96.

264. Durrwell, *Eucharist*, 34. Thomas himself acknowledges such liturgical usage; cf. *ST* III, 77.6 ad 1.

265. *ST* III, 77.1 ad 2 (emphasis added).

and accidents. Because it is not of their essence to exist—that is, because their existence is *given* by something beyond themselves—substance and accidents simply cannot be defined in the way that Aristotle defined them. And, because God is the one who gave the accidents their existence in the first place, God can continue to keep them in existence even without their proper substance. In other words, God can keep in existence that which he is already keeping in existence, if in a new way.

Many Miracles?

Now, because God holds the accidents of bread and wine in existence miraculously, there is a serious temptation to attribute anything done by or to the species (i.e., their actions and passions) to a miracle and so multiply miracles ad infinitum. But Thomas does not imagine God constantly intervening in the subsequent history of the species to ensure that they continue to behave as the species should. Rather, the original miracle suffices to explain everything that follows from it. As Thomas writes in article 4, explaining how it is that the species can decompose, "The ceasing-to-be of the species is nothing miraculous but quite natural; however, it presupposes the miracle which took place at the consecration, namely, that these sacramental species hold on to the being which they had when they inhered in a subject. In the same way a blind man who is miraculously given his sight, sees naturally."[266]

In order to further illustrate the principle that the "species hold on to the being which they had when they inhered in a subject," Thomas had already, in article 2, asked whether the dimensive quantity of the bread and wine, itself an accident, is the subject in which the other accidents inhere.

That something has dimensive quantity simply means that it takes up space or, as Thomas says, that it is "extended." Thomas affirms that the other accidents do inhere in the dimensive quantity of the species because it is unique among the accidents. Even when a (proper) substance is present, "all the other accidents cling to the substance through the medium of the quantity; for this reason we say that the immediate recipient of colour is the extended surface."[267] In other words, red may not be able to exist independently of a ball (or an apple, or a house), but it can only exist in the ball because the ball takes up some (*particular*) space.[268] Furthermore, dimensive quantity, even in the presence of a proper subject, is the source of individuation; it

---

266. *ST* III, 77.4 ad 3.
267. *ST* III, 77.2 corpus.
268. "For it is of the very definition of a dimension to be *quantity having position*" (*ST* III, 77.2 corpus [emphasis original]).

marks off one thing from another. "The reason why a thing is in one thing and in one thing only is because that thing, undivided in itself, is divided off from everything else."[269] Dimensive quantity is so basic, in fact, that some people were led "to think that the dimensions of a body were its very substance, as we read in Aristotle."[270] (As we have already seen in chap. 1, this exact problem, confusion between dimensive quantity and substance, was not limited to Aristotle's contemporaries. Its presence within nominalism was a major factor in making transubstantiation unintelligible by the time of the Reformation.)[271]

Of course, Thomas himself is careful to distinguish between substance and dimensive quantity. As basic as "big" or "small" are, they remain adjectives, not nouns. In the normal course of things there must be some *thing* that is big or small. And this is why accidents do not support other accidents. Even though color inheres in its substance through quantity, color does not normally inhere in quantity itself. One does not say, "Look at that red big!" The noun is missing. Nevertheless, since in this case it has been granted for accidents to persist without a subject, quantity, since it is that through which the other accidents normally inhere in a subject, "can be the immediate subject which sustains another accident."[272]

This move is quite important sacramentally for at least two reasons. First of all, though we may not notice it at first, by highlighting the fact that it remains given to the species to take up space, Thomas is emphasizing that they remain in the realm of the senses wherein something must exist if it is to be properly sacramental. Having lost their independence and identity, the species of bread and wine, because they retain dimensive quantity, can continue to exist only and precisely sacramentally—that is, as signs. Indeed, without their independence, they can exist as *"pure* signs."[273] Second, by grounding the other accidents in the dimensive quantity by virtue of transubstantiation (in the consecration "everything that pertains to matter is granted to the dimensive quantity"),[274] the need for further miracles to explain the actions and passions of the species is obviated. Since dimensive quantity was a medium through which other accidents "clung to" substance, it is not miraculous if they cling to it now given that all the accidents have been given (miraculously to be sure) to continue existing *as if* they had a subject.

269. *ST* III, 77.2 corpus.
270. *ST* III, 77.2 corpus.
271. See above, pp. 52–53.
272. *ST* III, 77.2 ad 1.
273. Benedict XVI, "Problem of Transubstantiation," 237.
274. *ST* III, 77.5 corpus.

And so Thomas can affirm that the species can change things outside themselves (article 3), decompose (article 4), generate other substances such as ashes or dust (article 5), nourish (article 6), break without breaking Christ himself (article 7), and, in the case of wine, mix with other liquids (article 8). And all of this happens quite naturally, without recourse to further miracles.[275] As Thomas puts it, "It does not seem reasonable to say that anything happens miraculously in this sacrament except as a result of the consecration. . . . There is no new miracle; it all happens as a result of the original one."[276] It would be tedious to investigate the arguments for each individual affirmation since they all follow on the principles already enunciated in articles 1 and 2. Nevertheless, it will be helpful to look at two final issues in question 77 before moving on. First, article 7 deserves special attention because it does not simply ask whether the species can be broken just as ordinary bread is broken, but also considers the oath of Berengarius which professed that, in the Eucharist, Christ's body was broken by the priest and crushed by the teeth of the faithful. Second, we will look at articles 4 and 8 together because, in their consideration of when Christ ceases to be present in the species, they highlight an important aspect of sacramental presence.

Berengarius Redux

The third objector in article 7 suggests that the fraction should not be attributed to the species, but to Christ's body itself, in accordance with the oath of Berengarius. Thomas rejects this suggestion for two reasons. First of all, Thomas affirms that Christ's risen body is beyond change and cannot be affected by us in any way. Therefore, to claim to break his body is to misunderstand the nature of that body. We have already seen that this basic affirmation is at the heart of Thomas's articulation of sacramental presence and his rejection of a natural presence. Thomas's second reason for rejecting this suggestion follows from something else we have seen earlier, in question 76, article 3. Because

275. Cf. Heron, *Table and Tradition*, 98, who writes that transubstantiation "involves not only one but two distinct miracles." The second, for Heron, is precisely the maintenance of the accidents without their proper substance, which Thomas explicitly denies a second miracle here. Heron does not address Thomas's claim that transubstantiation is only one miracle, but goes on to write, "When one has followed the theory thus far, it becomes hard to suppress the question whether something must not have gone wrong further back in the chain of reasoning if such a loose-ended conclusion is the result. No doubt God *could* do what is here suggested, but that is not really the question. The issue is, rather, how many miracles a theologian (or indeed a church) is entitled to assume in order to sustain a theological hypothesis." Thomas would have agreed with Heron that the multiplication of miracles would be a problem for a theory of real presence. In fact, that is precisely why Thomas avoids such a multiplication.

276. *ST* III, 77.5 corpus.

Christ is present in the mode of substance—that is, whole in the whole and whole in every part—his body is "present in all its completeness under every part of the quantity, as we saw above, and that runs counter to the whole idea of being broken into parts."[277] To affirm that Christ's body is broken at the fraction is, therefore, not only to misunderstand the nature of his risen body, but also the nature of his sacramental presence. And so Thomas can conclude that "this is the sense in which we should understand Berengarius's profession of faith; the fraction and the chewing with the teeth refer to the sacramental species, underneath which the body of Christ is really present."[278] And so Thomas, like the long line of commentators before him, affirms the oath of Berengarius in a sense quite the opposite of that intended by its author.[279] At the very least, he put the words of the oath "in their sacramental context."[280]

Final Clarifications

In articles 4 and 8 Thomas deals with the questions of the decomposition of the species, and the possibility of mixing the consecrated wine with other liquids, respectively. While these questions may seem arcane, they are actually quite practical. Ministers who actually work with the consecrated species need a way of understanding how Christ's presence relates to real-life situations such as decomposition or mixing. Furthermore, on top of informing liturgical practice concerning such matters, Thomas's answers clarify even further how we are to understand Christ's presence as sacramental rather than natural.

In both articles Thomas responds to objections of the Aristotelian sort (e.g., the lack of the proper substance makes change impossible because there could be no subject in the imagined change) with the blunt affirmation that our senses detect these changes. Since we see (or perhaps smell) the species decomposing or the consecrated wine being mixed with other liquids, we know that they can, in fact, decompose or be mixed. As obvious as that seems, the Aristotelian objections allow Thomas to reflect upon such decomposition and mixing in helpful ways.

We have already seen that it is in article 4 that Thomas articulates the important principle that changes in the species following the consecration are not miraculous themselves because the species have already been granted to exist *as if* they had a subject, and so they are like the blind man who sees

---

277. *ST* III, 77.7 corpus.
278. *ST* III, 77.7 ad 3.
279. See Chadwick, "Ego Berengarius," 443; Macy, "Theological Fate of Berengar's Oath," 28.
280. O'Connor, *Hidden Manna*, 179. See above, pp. 65–66.

naturally even if his sight was restored miraculously. This observation essentially covers all the objections.

Nevertheless, it is important for Thomas to highlight the implications of such natural decomposition for Christ's presence in the species. Christ's presence, as we have seen, can be said to remain for as long as the substance of the bread or wine could be said to remain. Qualitative changes, such as slight changes in color or taste, which would not be enough for us to cease identifying the species as bread or wine, do not affect Christ's presence. Nor do quantitative changes, such as the division of the species into smaller parts, provided those parts remain large enough to be identified by us as bread and wine. On the other hand, should qualitative changes be so great as to lead us to say, "This is no longer bread," or "This is no longer wine" (were the species not consecrated), Christ's sacramental presence ceases. His sacramental presence was a *relationship* to a creature that no longer exists and, therefore, the presence no longer exists. The same is true of quantitative changes. If the species of bread or wine are so subdivided as to no longer be recognizable as bread or wine, we no longer affirm Christ's presence in the remaining particles.

We can add here that the identification of bread and wine need only take place at a commonsense level. Highly precise modern instruments that could detect particles that once belonged to the bread or wine are not a cause of concern as might be suspected. Our noses, for instance, can detect such tiny particles, but we do not concern ourselves that, in smelling wine, we have inhaled it. It follows, therefore, that instruments more precise than our noses are not detecting bread and wine any more than our noses are. The Church will, of course, prefer to err on the side of caution out of reverence, but there is no need for excessive scruples in this area.

Article 8 is essentially a specialized form of the same question as article 4. It is of particular importance because water actually is intentionally mixed with the wine in the liturgical celebration. While our senses tell us that the consecrated wine can be mixed, and we know that we needn't concern ourselves with Aristotle's worry about the lack of a subject, it is still practically important for Thomas to articulate what happens to Christ's presence when the consecrated wine is mixed. What is at issue here is the amount of foreign liquid added to the consecrated wine. And though the discussion looks rather abstract, Thomas's conclusion is really quite commonsense. If the amount of foreign liquid is great enough that what is produced by the mixing would be something other than wine, then Christ's sacramental presence ceases. If, on the other hand, a tiny amount (like the amount of water used in the liturgy) is added that is not enough to say that the wine (were it there) is no longer present, Christ's sacramental presence remains. This is, in fact, how we talk about wine, or whatever else, in everyday language. A cup of wine with a teaspoon of water is identified as wine, but a cup of wine in a gallon of water is just dirty water.

Karl Rahner makes this point well in a contemporary idiom. Imagine, he asks,

> if one made a molecule of some substance radio-active, so that it remained in principle recognizable, and added it to the wine to be consecrated, this molecule—supposing it was not an absolutely foreign body with regard to wine, but for instance a molecule of alcohol—would also be consecrated and hence also transubstantiated. If this molecule, which is still recognizable, were removed from the field of wine—it does not matter whether the procedure is possible or not, technically—Christ would no longer be present under it, though chemically and physically nothing had happened but an accidental change of locality in the molecule. This is so obvious, that it is now even possible and quite easy technically to separate such a tiny quantity of "wine," by a purely quantitative division, that there can be no question of wine any longer in the ordinary sense of human language. The real presence of Christ then ceases under this tiny quantity, though it is chemically exactly the same as the larger quantity from which it was taken. The tiny quantity needs only be so small, for instance, that it can no longer be seen. Hence St Thomas sees quite correctly (III, q. 77, a. 4) that a purely quantitative reduction of the species of wine can prevent one calling it wine any longer—though chemically it remains "the same" as before for a long time—and thus the presence of Christ ceases. Hence St Thomas correctly denies (III, q. 77, a. 8c) that a small amount of consecrated wine still indicates the presence of Christ if it is mixed with a large amount of non-consecrated wine. "This" concrete consecrated wine no longer exists as something separate and distinguishable from the human point of view, even though "physically" and "chemically" it exists in exactly the same way as before.[281]

The central point to emphasize, particularly from an ecumenical perspective, is that, while such technical language and obscure metaphors can look very much like rationalizing the mystery of the Eucharist, they are, in fact, a very careful work of demythologizing, and therefore protecting, it. Even within the forms of the academic discourse of his day, Thomas is actually giving very commonsense answers to questions that honest people have to this day. How do we deal with crumbs in the eucharistic celebration? What do we make of the microscopic fragments that inevitably leave the species of

---

281. Karl Rahner, SJ, "On the Duration of the Presence of Christ after Communion," in *Theological Investigations IV: More Recent Writings* (Baltimore: Helicon, 1966), 315. Cf. O'Connor, *Hidden Manna*, 287–88n14.

bread and wine? How is Christ's presence affected by human digestion? And so forth. Someone who has understood Thomas's articulation of sacramental presence knows that they needn't worry that Jesus would have long ago run out of body to feed us with or be harmed by our teeth or stomach acid. And they certainly won't be afflicted by the scruples of the stercoranists who fretted about the digestion and eventual expulsion of Christ. Digestion is, after all, merely a (qualitative) form of decomposition. And so, when digestion makes the species no longer recognizable as bread, Christ's sacramental presence ceases. Microscopic fragments that break off, like the tiny particles that allow us to smell the wine, for example, are the product of a quantitative form of decomposition. They too are no longer capable of *signifying* Christ's presence. And, in a presence that is genuinely sacramental, that is the determining factor.

Furthermore, it is worthwhile to note that the principles laid out in these two articles are the norm for determining how to deal with remaining species after the celebration of the Eucharist: whatever is *recognizable* of the species should be consumed or reserved. In fact, the small amount of wine remaining in the chalice, after all that can be drunk has been, is dealt with exactly as article 8 imagines: it is mixed with such an amount of water that it would no longer be considered wine. The liquid produced by this practice is treated reverently, but it is not the same as the blood of Christ. A similar practice is used in the cases of qualitative changes in the bread. A consecrated host that has undergone a kind of qualitative change that would make it unfit for human consumption is placed in water in order to dissolve so that there we can say with certainty that it is no longer bread—in other words, the body of Christ.[282]

Those who are concerned that transubstantiation neglects the value of the symbolic in the sacraments should find all of this reassuring. While the great care with which Catholics treat the consecrated species highlights the seriousness with which we take the claim that Christ is really present, the logic that dictates such practices is completely sacramental. Though transubstantiation posits a presence that is much deeper than the merely symbolic, it does not thereby posit an unsacramental presence. Real as it is, Christ's sacramental presence operates on the logic of symbol, not on the level of chemistry or physics. When the symbol has ceased, so has the presence.

---

282. I became familiar with this practice when an auxiliary bishop in Toronto recommended this course of action with a host that appeared, at least to some parishioners, to be turning into flesh. The host in question had been coughed up after it had been presented to a communicant. No matter what the reason for the change in appearance, the host was clearly unfit for future consumption and was dissolved in a glass of water.

Question 78: The Words of Consecration

Question 78 addresses the form of the Eucharist—that is, the words of consecration, "This is my body" and "This is the chalice of my blood." Though
we need not investigate this question in great detail for our purposes, there
are a few salient points that it will be helpful to consider. We have already
seen the comparison that Thomas makes between transubstantiation and
creation in question 75, especially in article 8. This comparison also emerges
in Thomas's consideration of the form of the sacrament because of the role
of the word of God in both creation and transubstantiation. In article 2, an
objector suggests that the form of the sacrament is not suitable because it
does not use the imperative as one would expect given Ambrose's dictum that
the word of Christ that consecrates the sacrament is the same word by which
the universe was made. If God creates saying, "Let there be light," a more
suitable form of the sacrament would be "Be this my body."[283]

While, as so often, the importance of this question is lost on contemporary readers, Thomas is making an important point about the nature of the
sacrament that remains relevant today:

> The word of God was effective in the first creation of things and that self-same
> word is effective here, but the mode of operation is different. Here it works
> through a sacramental mystery, it is effective through a sign. And so it is that
> the form should signify the final effect of consecration by the verb to be, in the
> indicative mood and the present tense. In the creation of things God's word was
> purely and simply effective; it worked through the command of his wisdom.
> For that reason the word of the Lord at the creation of things is expressed by
> a verb in the imperative mood.[284]

Though we are quite happy to take the scriptural witness to Christ's words at
face value, and so would not see much use in debating the imperative versus
the indicative mood in the words of consecration, Thomas's point about how
God's creative word functions differently in the sacrament than in creation is
important. In creation *ex nihilo* there could be no intermediary, no *nothing*
to become creation,[285] no instrument to work through. In the sacrament, on
the other hand, God is adapting his communication to the human condition,
as Thomas affirmed in question 60. That means that the same word of God,
which needed no intermediary to create the universe, functions differently

283. In the original Latin this objector prefers "Hoc *sit* corpus meum" to "Hoc *est* corpus
meum."
284. *ST* III, 78.2 ad 2.
285. See above, pp. 101–2.

here for our sake. Because we need signs,[286] God's word here "works through a sacramental mystery, it is effective though a sign."[287] Again, the sacramental aspect that is the key to understanding transubstantiation shows itself.[288]

The same sacramental dynamic shows up in article 3. Here the question at issue is whether, in the words of consecration, "there is any created power which produces the consecration." Thomas's basic answer is to apply the distinction between principal and instrumental cause that we investigated above.[289] The words of consecration, uttered by the priest, are effective because "being the words of Christ himself, it is by his will they derive from Christ an instrumental power."[290] And so we can say at one and the same time that "it is by the power of the Holy Ghost and by it alone that the bread is changed into the body of Christ," and that there is "the presence of an instrumental power in the form of this sacrament."[291]

In his response to the third objection, that the change is instantaneous though the words of consecration are not, Thomas notes that "the above-mentioned words by which the consecration is brought about work in a sacramental way. This means that the power of changing which is found in the formal part of these sacramental signs, depends on them fully signifying, and that only happens at the utterance of the last syllable."[292] That is to say, the exact sacramental principle that we saw applied to the matter of the sacrament (i.e., the species of bread and wine) applies to the form of the sacrament (i.e., the words of consecration). In both cases, the sacrament is only constituted when the sign is whole and recognizable. Just as a microscopic piece of complex carbohydrate floating as dust in the air does not indicate Christ, neither does "This is my bod . . ." In both cases the signification is impaired or incomplete, and so Christ's presence is not manifested.[293]

---

286. "The divine wisdom provides for each reality according to its condition. . . . Now it is connatural to man to arrive at a knowledge of intelligible realities through sensible ones, and a sign is something through which a person arrives at knowledge of some further thing beyond itself. Moreover the sacred realities signified by the sacraments are certain spiritual and intelligible goods by which man is sanctified. And the consequence of this fact is that the function of the sacrament as signifying is implemented by means of some sensible realities" (ST III, 60.4 corpus).

287. ST III, 78.2 ad 2.

288. For more on this, see Brock, "St. Thomas and the Eucharistic Conversion," 561–62.

289. See above, pp. 88–89.

290. ST III, 78.4 corpus.

291. ST III, 78.4 ad 1.

292. ST III, 78.4 ad 3. See also Wawrykow, "Luther and the Spirituality of Thomas Aquinas," 105n41.

293. There is, of course, the danger that such a focus on the words of consecration can end up isolating Christ's presence from its broader liturgical context. Contemporary Catholic eucharistic theology is sensitive to this concern. As Tillard writes, "Serious theological thinking

Article 5 of question 78 wonders whether the words of consecration are true. The basic issue here is what the term "this" in the phrase "This is my body" is supposed to indicate. It makes no sense if it means "This bread is the body of Christ," for the substance has not yet become the body of Christ and, even if it had, then it would no longer be bread. Nor is it useful to say, "This body is the body of Christ." Nor could it mean that the accidents are the body of Christ, since they obviously are not. Thomas answers that, since the words are effective, rather than simply indicative, as the other proposals presume, the "this" in question indicates "that what is contained under these species, which was once bread, should now be Christ's body."[294]

While purely grammatical arguments about the "this" in question are bound to be inconclusive, given the utterly unique nature of the claim being made and the limitations of human language,[295] it is important, from an ecumenical perspective, to recognize Thomas's view of the function of God's word in the sacrament. That is, it is essential to note the importance of the fact that Thomas finds the determining factor for this argument in the character of God's word as effective and not merely indicative. As we saw in article 4, Thomas puts great stock in the fact that the words of consecration are Christ's own words. Now, in article 5, he asserts that "just as the idea in the practical intelligence does not presuppose the thing we are thinking about, but rather brings it into existence, so the truth of the Eucharistic formula does not presuppose the thing it signifies but rather causes it; it is in this way that the word of God is related to the things called into being by that word."[296]

Again we see how the whole doctrine of transubstantiation is rooted in a biblical theology of creation. God's relationship with creation is through his word, which does not merely signify but rather causes being. God's word is not indicative but performative. This adds another layer to our previous considerations concerning God's capacity to produce a change in the Eucharist at the level of being. It is through God's creative word that God is able to change creation at the level of being because it is through God's word that created being exists in the first place. As Robert Barron puts it, Aquinas "said that

---

has broken with the far too narrow vision that tries to identify the exact utterance after which the presence would be achieved. Today's understanding sees the efficacy of the Spirit and the Word . . . as extended through the whole anaphora." Quoted in Jenson, *Unbaptized God*, 30; see also Kelly, "Eucharistic Doctrine of Transubstantiation," 65. The point here is simply to indicate that Thomas's reasoning is utterly sacramental.

294. *ST* III, 78.5 corpus.

295. Cf. Calvin, *Inst.* 4.17:1384 (20): From the fact that "bread is called body in a sacramental sense . . . it follows that Christ's words are not subject to the common rule and ought not to be tested by grammar."

296. *ST* III, 78.5 corpus.

God does not know things because they exist (as we do) but rather that things exist because God knows them."[297] Barron also highlights how the preface to the Gospel of John identifies Jesus with God's creative word and how the Gospels in general show Jesus's word having the same performative power as the words by which God created the universe.[298] He concludes,

> Jesus was not one prophet among many; he was the incarnate Word of God. Therefore, his words had the power to create, to affect reality at the deepest possible level. Since what *he* says *is*, the words, "this is my body" and "this is my blood" effectively change the bread and wine into his body and blood. Like all divine utterances, they *produce* what they say. The same Word that spoke the elements of bread and wine into existence in the first place now speaks them into a new mode of being, changing them into the bearers of Christ's sacramental presence.[299]

The category of "word" is essential to understanding transubstantiation at several different levels. First of all, transubstantiation is an attempt to answer all kinds of questions that emerge when God's word in Scripture, "This is my body," is taken seriously. Second, God's creative word, by which the universe was made, literally *informs* the elements of bread and wine, making them to be sacraments of Christ's presence. Finally, sacraments, like words, are a means of communication. Indeed, it is because of this that St. Augustine referred to them as "visible words," and Herbert McCabe could write that "the reason [Christ] can be present at many *Eucharists* is that his body is present in the mode of language—rather as meaning is present to a word."[300] Sacramental presence is a presence that *communicates*. Transubstantiation does not posit, as some have supposed, a kind of static presence like that of an inanimate object. Christ is not in the Eucharist as a thing, but as a person.[301] His body must be present because, like all of our bodies, it is an essential prerequisite for any human communication. Indeed, that is why the Word became flesh.

But, like the incarnation, Christ's eucharistic presence is not an end in itself. Rather, it is intended to communicate something more. If the incarnation is finally oriented to bringing human persons into communion with the very trinitarian life of God, Christ's bodily eucharistic presence is oriented to the mystical body of Christ, the Church. Because the nature of Christ's eucharistic presence was an area of such concern in Thomas's day, and because Thomas

297. Barron, *Eucharist*, 129.
298. Barron, *Eucharist*, 129–30.
299. Barron, *Eucharist*, 130.
300. McCabe, "Transubstantiation and the Real Presence," 118.
301. Benedict XVI, "Problem of Transubstantiation," 238–39.

therefore addressed this question in such detail, we can get the impression that the whole of his eucharistic theology can be reduced to the question of transubstantiation.[302] Nevertheless, it is important to recognize that, while Thomas spent a great deal of time and energy considering transubstantiation,[303] he does not treat it as an isolated mystery. In fact, even as we have highlighted the sacramental nature of Christ's presence in Thomas's exposition, we can now conclude by noting how, for Thomas, Christ's sacramental presence was itself a sacrament of something more.

Res Tantum: *Transubstantiation and the Church*

Perhaps one of the more esoteric aspects of medieval sacramental theology is the classification of *sacramentum tantum, res tantum*, and *res et sacramentum*. Liam Walsh explains:

> The *sacramentum tantum* is the external ritual; the *res tantum* is the divine grace that is given to those for whom the sacrament is celebrated; the *res et sacramentum* is an intermediate level on which the persons taking part in the sacraments are spiritually qualified by the sacraments they are receiving, or have already received, to join with Christ in making the sacred actions that signify and realize his grace.[304]

In the sacrament of the Eucharist these indicate the signs of bread and wine, including their ritual usage (*sacramentum tantum*), the communion of charity in Christ's ecclesial body (*res tantum*), the Church, and the substantial presence of Christ's body under the appearances of bread and wine (*res et sacramentum*).[305] What we have had to say so far has pertained to the relationship between the *sacramentum tantum* and the *res et sacramentum*—that is, between the signs of bread and wine and Christ's sacramental presence. But

302. Cf. Bruce D. Marshall, "The Whole Mystery of Our Salvation: Saint Thomas Aquinas on the Eucharist as Sacrifice," in *Rediscovering Aquinas and the Sacraments*, ed. Matthew Levering and Michael Dauphinais (Chicago: Hillenbrand, 2009), 40–44. Marshall highlights the fact that Thomas says very little about eucharistic sacrifice, as compared with the Eucharist as a sacrament, but that this does not imply that Thomas therefore saw sacrifice as unimportant.

I am aware that a similar impression can be given by a book such as this. Because it takes up the controversial question of transubstantiation it must, of necessity, address it in great detail. By working on one question in detail because it is an area of misunderstanding, I do not wish to imply that it is the only area of importance in eucharistic theology.

303. Interestingly, Thomas uses the term "transubstantiation" eighty-eight times in his commentaries on Peter Lombard's *Sentences*, an early work, but only four times in the *Summa*. See Walsh, "Ecumenical Reading of Aquinas on the Eucharist," 239.

304. Walsh, "Ecumenical Reading of Aquinas on the Eucharist," 231n4.

305. See *ST* III, 73.6 corpus.

the fact that Christ's sacramental presence is not *res tantum*, but rather *res et sacramentum*, indicates that it is not the final goal of the sacrament but is, in fact, itself the sign of a deeper, indeed ultimate, reality.[306]

This is an essential, though underappreciated, feature in Thomas's theology of the Eucharist.[307] It is of particular ecumenical significance given recent ecumenical convergence around communion ecclesiology.[308] No articulation of real presence that isolates Christ's personal presence in the elements from his ecclesial body will be ecumenically acceptable. Fortunately, though it is overshadowed by the immense detail with which Thomas felt he needed to articulate transubstantiation, Thomas's eucharistic theology did not isolate Christ's sacramental and ecclesial bodies, but understood them as intimately connected.[309] For Thomas, "the sign becomes effective sign of the ultimate reality of the Eucharist, which is the mystical body of Christ (*res tantum*), when it becomes reality as well as sign (*res et sacramentum*) of the personal body and blood of Christ, which it makes visible, tangible and 'receivable' in bread and wine."[310] For Thomas, it is only because Christ is really present that the Eucharist can properly signify the mystical body. To him, it would be inconceivable to play off Christ's eucharistic body and Christ's ecclesial body against each other in a kind of zero-sum game. The emphasis on eucharistic realism in Thomas does not derogate from his sense of the Church as Christ's body, but rather supports it. As Gilles Emery writes,

> Insisting on the truth of Christ contained in the Eucharist, Thomas constantly reminds us that the true Body of Christ is also the sign, the representation, the likeness, the exemplar, and the figure of his mystical body, which is the Church; in other words, it is the sign and the cause of that which the Eucharist procures. He never fails to attribute to the *corpus verum* the fundamental structure of the *res et sacramentum*: The true Body of Christ is at once *signum* and *res*. As sign, the Body of Christ denotes unity, the gathering of the multitude of members in unity. Ecclesial realism appears deeply rooted in eucharistic realism. Thus, showing the fittingness of the institution of this sacrament, Thomas closely

306. Rahner highlights this very effectively in "Presence of Christ in the Sacrament of the Lord's Supper," 310–11.

307. Crockett is an exception to this pattern and begins his treatment of Aquinas with an acknowledgment of the relationship between the Eucharist and the Church in Thomas. See his *Eucharist*, 114–15.

308. See Paul McPartlan, "*Ut Unum Sint*: Eucharist and Ecumenism," in *The Mystery of Faith: Reflections on the Encyclical Ecclesia De Eucharistia*, ed. James McEvoy and Maurice Hogan (Dublin: Columba Press, 2005), esp. 348.

309. See, in particular, Emery, "Ecclesial Fruit of the Eucharist in St. Thomas Aquinas"; see also Walsh, "Ecumenical Reading of Aquinas on the Eucharist," 228–31.

310. Walsh, "Ecumenical Reading of Aquinas on the Eucharist," 234.

links the substantial *conversion* of the bread and wine into the Body and Blood of Christ (transubstantiation) and our own *conversion* in Christ who is the end [*finis*] of this conversion.[311]

To understand more deeply why Thomas so links eucharistic and ecclesial realism, it is important to note that the level of *res et sacramentum*, the same intermediate level at which Thomas places Christ's eucharistic body, is also the level at which he places sacramental characters. Baptism (as well as confirmation and ordination) has a kind of structural value in the Church. In question 63, article 3, Thomas argues that the baptized are configured to Christ's priesthood so that they might participate in his perfect worship of the Father. (Confirmation and ordination add further specifications to such participation.) Such configurations are what the Catholic tradition means by "sacramental character." These "enable people to be and to act sacramentally in the name of Christ, for their own and others' sanctification; they make the Church in its members be the sacrament of Christ; they create the sacramental relationships within which the grace of the Holy Spirit is given and the Body lives."[312] "But," continues Walsh,

> people can only be the sacrament of Christ in this way when Christ, their head, is himself with them in the Church. What Thomas is saying, by locating the eucharistic presence of Christ on the level of *res et sacramentum*, is that the Eucharist realizes the Church because it is nothing less than Christ himself, personally present in his individual body among his personally present members, as the Head and bodily source of all the sanctifying activity that is being received and given in the Church.[313]

Indeed, as Walsh points out, Thomas's first use of the adjective "substantially" to describe Christ's eucharistic presence is in an explicitly ecclesial context. In his discussion of the preeminence of the Eucharist among the sacraments in question 65, Thomas highlights that Christ's presence in the

311. Emery, "Ecclesial Fruit of the Eucharist in St. Thomas Aquinas," 47. Emery himself includes a footnote at this point saying, "This is not an exaggerated term: the use of the faithful is the end (*finis*) of this sacrament (*ST*, III, q. 74, a. 2); cf. *ST*, III, q. 74, a. 2, ad 2: *finis effectus*." Gerard Kelly highlights that Thomas gets this from St. Augustine; see Kelly, "Eucharistic Doctrine of Transubstantiation," 67. Boyd Taylor Coolman shows how the basic threefold framework Thomas operated within developed in the previous century in "The Christo-Pneumatic-Ecclesial Character of Twelfth-Century Sacramental Theology," in *The Oxford Handbook of Sacramental Theology*, ed. Hans Boersma and Matthew Levering (Oxford: Oxford University Press, 2015), 201–17.

312. Walsh, "Ecumenical Reading of Aquinas on the Eucharist," 231.

313. Walsh, "Ecumenical Reading of Aquinas on the Eucharist," 231.

Eucharist is something more than the way he is present in the other sacraments. While Christ can be said to be present in the other sacraments because they are instruments by which he builds up the Church, Christ must be *personally* present in the Eucharist as head of his body, the Church, if it is to be truly his body. It is to distinguish this presence from the kind of instrumental presence that can be affirmed of the other sacraments that Thomas invokes "substantially," so often understood as ignoring or downplaying the relationship between the Eucharist and the Church by isolating Christ's eucharistic presence,[314] for the first time.[315] Without Christ's *real* presence, the Church cannot *really* be his body.

"Quid Sumit Mus?" and Transignification: Two Test Cases for Understanding

We have already noted that the doctrine of transubstantiation is, in many ways, a matter of saying what does *not* happen in eucharistic presence or change. It is a kind of *via negativa*. It may be fruitful, then, to conclude our study of Thomas by putting two questions to transubstantiation to see what the doctrine does not mean. These two questions are from very different eras, but the connection between the two of them should become apparent in the course of our treatment of them.

The question "Quid sumit mus?" or "What does a mouse consume?" came to be an important test question for eucharistic understanding in the Middle Ages. It was not merely the product of an age worried about mice in the tabernacle. Rather, it allowed theologians to make certain important distinctions about how they understood Christ's presence in the Eucharist.

In question 80, article 3, Thomas is treating the question "Can only the upright receive Christ sacramentally?" In it, he argues against those who would suggest that, should someone approach the sacrament unworthily, Christ's presence would cease before they could consume it. While the unworthy may not consume Christ spiritually, says Thomas, Christ's body remains present under the species as long as the species persist, whether they are consumed by a just person or by a sinner, and so all consume Christ sacramentally, if not spiritually.

---

314. See, e.g., Jones, *Christ's Eucharistic Presence*, 110–11.

315. Walsh, "Ecumenical Reading of Aquinas on the Eucharist," 229. Cf. Coolman, "Christo-Pneumatic-Ecclesial Character." Coolman is keen to highlight the integrated nature of medieval sacramental theology (note his title!) over against suggestions that it treated grace as a product or that it isolated Christ's eucharistic presence from its broader theological context.

It is in this context that Thomas's answer to the question "Quid sumit mus?" appears. In responding to the third objector, who had suggested that sinners do not receive because animals (who are less offensive to God than sinners!) do not, Thomas writes,

> Even were a mouse or dog to eat the consecrated host, the substance of Christ's body would not cease to be under the species so long as the substance of the bread remained. . . . All the same, that the animal eats the body of Christ sacramentally cannot be held, since it is not of a nature to use it as a sacrament. Hence in point of fact Christ's body is accidentally consumed, not sacramentally, as when one consumes a host not knowing it was consecrated.[316]

Here, in response to what must strike the contemporary reader as a very strange question, Thomas again articulates the truly sacramental nature of Christ's presence. It is a given for Thomas, as we have seen, that Christ does not somehow depart from the species. As long as the species persist, no matter the circumstance, Christ's presence remains. But it is a unique presence. With a natural presence, to eat the accidents is to eat the substance. Were a mouse to eat the accidents of bread, it would consume the substance of bread as well. But, as demonstrated above, the relationship between Christ's substance and the accidents of bread is not like the relationship those accidents had with their own proper substance.[317]

The accidents of the bread and wine are not in a relationship of subsisting in Christ's body and blood, but rather a relationship of signifying Christ's body and blood. But that means that any access to Christ's body and blood can only be had by one who has read the sign. That is why it is not only the mouse who does not access Christ's body and blood, but the ignorant human as well. That the mouse does not consume Christ because "it is not of a nature to use it as a sacrament" means, simply, that mice can't read human signs. And, when consuming the Eucharist, a mouse is like the ignorant human who can read the sign, but hasn't.

Thomas is careful to insist that the presence of Christ persists even while it is "accidentally" consumed by the illiterate mouse in order to avoid the conclusion that the presence is not so real after all. His insistence is like that of someone who insists that the paintings on the ceiling of the Sistine Chapel exist even when the only people present are blind. There is no question about the reality or the splendor of Michelangelo's work, only an impairment in attaining to it.

316. *ST* III, 80.3 ad 3. See Farrow, *Theological Negotiations*, 154n27.
317. *ST* III, 76.5 corpus. See above, pp. 110–12.

If I may attempt a contemporary analogy, radio waves exist, whether we discern them or not. To pick up radio waves, one needs an antenna. Furthermore, to pick up more than just static, one's antenna must be set to the proper frequency. Human persons have sacramental antennae; mice do not. If humans are like radios in this analogy, mice are like toasters. That they cannot pick up radio waves in no way derogates from the existence of such waves. Humans, on the other hand, can have their radio tuned to the correct frequency, or not. Someone on the wrong frequency will not pick up the wave in question, just as the person ignorant of consecration will not consume Christ sacramentally. Finally, it is only those with their antennae correctly tuned who will pick up the wave. In the same way, it is only those who are aware of Christ's presence, because they both *can* and *have* read the signs, who can consume him sacramentally, for good or ill.

The twentieth-century theologians who proposed the idea of transignification (and transfinalization) were trying to capture, in a contemporary idiom, something very much like Thomas's answer to "Quid sumit mus?"[318] They wanted to be able to affirm the deep reality of Christ's eucharistic presence through signs while avoiding any crudely physical or materialistic understandings of that presence that often accompanied popular ideas about transubstantiation. In order to achieve this, they proposed to talk about eucharistic change in terms of meaning rather than of substance, which had, they suggested, become unintelligible to contemporary people.[319]

The great advantage of this manner of talking is that it does, in fact, quite effectively rule out the possibility that the eucharistic change and presence be understood in a crudely physical or materialistic way. Sacraments in general, and the Eucharist in particular, are matters of communication. As such, meaning is a very appropriate category under which to discuss them.[320] On the other hand, when presented as an alternative to transubstantiation, these articulations risk giving the impression that transubstantiation indicates precisely the crude presence that it itself was developed to rule out. In the encyclical *Mysterium Fidei*, Pope Paul VI suggested that these new formulations were useful as clarifications of, but not as alternatives to, transubstantiation:

> As a result of transubstantiation, the species of bread and wine undoubtedly take on a new signification and a new finality, for they are no longer ordinary

318. The classic introduction to this question remains Edward Schillebeeckx, OP, "Transubstantiation, Transfinalization, Transfiguration," *Worship* 40, no. 6 (1966): 324–38.
319. Cf. McCabe, "Eucharistic Change," 116. See above, pp. 83–84.
320. McCabe, "Eucharistic Change," 117; cf. Walsh, "Ecumenical Reading of Aquinas on the Eucharist," 232–33.

bread and wine but instead a sign of something sacred and a sign of spiritual food; but they take on this new signification, this new finality, precisely because they contain a new "reality" which we can rightly call ontological.[321]

According to Paul VI, transignification failed not because meaning is an inappropriate category for understanding the eucharistic presence, but because it was not always clear that the meaning reached by these articulations plumbed the full depths of reality.

Aware of this deficiency, the theologians promoting transignification had argued that what happened in the Eucharist was not merely community meaning-making wherein a group of people decided to understand what they once understood to be bread and wine as the body and blood of Christ, but rather that it was God and God alone who had determined the new meanings of the bread and the wine.[322] And what God determines something to mean, it does, in fact, mean. As Herbert McCabe points out, if this is understood radically enough, it becomes impossible to distinguish from transubstantiation, "for if God deems something to happen it must happen, and come about in the created world."[323]

On the other hand, it is not at all clear that transignification lends itself to such a radical interpretation. It is quite possible that, instead of imagining God's power reaching into the very depths of reality, we simply imagine reality itself in a shallower way. Regarding such a flattened view Ratzinger writes,

> That is in fact the poverty of our age, that we now think and live only in terms of function, that man himself is classified according to his function, and that we can all be no more than functions and officials, where being is denied. The significance of the Eucharist as a sacrament of faith consists precisely in that it takes us out of functionality and reaches the basis of reality.[324]

The reason that this danger is inherent in transignification and not in transubstantiation is because transignification starts with what we humans can do. We can change the meanings of things based on culture and context. We can make a piece of cloth to be a national flag or a piece of metal to be a wedding ring. Our ability to transignify is, it would seem, part of the definition of being human. It is concomitant with our use of language and symbol in the building

321. Paul VI, *Mysterium Fidei*, #46. See Bruce Marshall's concerns that *Mysterium Fidei* has not been heeded ("Eucharistic Presence of Christ," 50).

322. Edward Schillebeeckx, OP, *The Eucharist* (London: Sheed & Ward, 1968), 150–51.

323. McCabe, "Eucharistic Change," 117.

324. Benedict XVI, *God Is Near Us*, 88.

and shaping of culture. To attribute the change in the Eucharist to transignification is to start from the wrong end. Though it will be qualified in the end with the assurance that it is not a matter of human meaning-making, but of God's meaning-making, transignification is, nevertheless, understandable in completely human terms.

Transubstantiation, on the other hand, can be nothing other than a work of God.[325] It is not something we do every day that, in this particular case, is given added depth because it is an action of God. Rather it is something completely impossible for us in any circumstance, exceedingly more like the act of creating the universe from nothing than deeming that a colored cloth represents a nation. A change at the level of being itself is not within our capacity. Indeed, we can't even imagine it.

The truth of transignification—and it is, of course, completely true that the meaning of the bread and wine do change at the consecration while their physical reality remains unaltered—therefore, can only be properly understood within the context of transubstantiation. Robert Barron puts it this way:

> And since God's speech affects what it says, it is appropriate to describe *this* transsignification of the bread and wine as ontologically transformative, a change at the level of being. When Aquinas insists that this "change" be referred to as *transsubstantiatio*, he is not recommending that Aristotelian metaphysics is the only or even the best conceptual framework for understanding this mystery; rather, he is insisting that we are dealing with a phenomenon so unique that it can only be compared to creation, that properly supernatural act which only God can in principle perform.[326]

And so, far from being an imposition of pagan philosophy on Christian theology, or an articulation of an unsacramental presence that fails to respect the value of the symbols or the reality of the ascension, transubstantiation is rather a completely sacramental articulation of real presence that depends on and witnesses to a biblical view of the relationship between God and creation that is shared by Catholics and Protestants alike. That it is also compatible with many of the affirmations of the Reformers about Christ's eucharistic presence is what I hope to demonstrate in the rest of this book, as we turn to the eucharistic theologies of Martin Luther and John Calvin.

325. Walsh, "Ecumenical Reading of Aquinas on the Eucharist," 239, writes, "Ecumenical theology might be helped by recognizing that Thomas allows the word *transubstantiatio* into the theology of the Eucharist because he believes that the Eucharist is a sacrament and that a sacrament is primarily the work of God, of the coming of the Kingdom."

326. Barron, "Creation, Transubstantiation, and the Grain of the Universe," 218; cf. Walsh, "Ecumenical Reading of Aquinas on the Eucharist," 232–33.

3

Martin Luther

It has become standard practice to discuss Martin Luther's theology of the Eucharist by referring to the various stages in his development. These are enumerated differently in different sources,[1] but all agree that the most important development is the change of the target of Luther's critiques that occurred around 1524.[2] Before this time, Luther was concerned, as we saw at the beginning of our first chapter, with the Roman Catholic doctrine of the Eucharist and the "three captivities" he discerned therein—namely, withholding the cup from the laity, transubstantiation, and the idea of the Mass as a sacrifice. This front was almost completely abandoned, however, when Luther took up his controversy with the Swiss Reformers, particularly those centered in Zurich under the leadership of Ulrich Zwingli, which would be one of his major preoccupations for the rest of his life. As far as Luther was able to discern, Zwingli and his followers completely denied the doctrine of real presence, making the Lord's Supper into a mere memorial of Christ's atoning death while leaving Christ himself as far from the worshipers as heaven is from earth. This Luther could not countenance, and the full force

---

1. See, e.g., Ralph W. Quere, "Changes and Constants: Structure in Luther's Understanding of the Real Presence in the 1520's," *Sixteenth Century Journal* 16, no. 1 (Spring 1985): 47–48, who articulates four phases in Luther's development of the role of signification in the Eucharist. See also James F. McCue, "Luther and Roman Catholicism on the Mass as Sacrifice," *Journal of Ecumenical Studies* 2, no. 2 (Spring 1965): 209, who articulates three stages based on Luther's main theological emphasis in his writings of a given period.

2. Jones, *Christ's Eucharistic Presence*, 119. See also Mark D. Thompson, "Claritas Scripturae in the Eucharistic Writings of Martin Luther," *Westminster Theological Journal* 60, no. 1 (Spring 1998): 25. Thompson suggests the decisive shift occurred in 1523.

of his theological (and rhetorical!) acumen was redirected away from Rome
and directly at Zurich.[3]

While we must not skip over Luther's earlier works entirely, what will be of
most value for our study are his writings against the Swiss, often derided by
Luther as "Enthusiasts" or "Fanatics," *Schwärmerei* in the original German.
The reason for this is that, in responding to the Swiss, Luther is responding
to the same basic problem as Thomas Aquinas—and indeed as Cardinal
Humbert, however ineptly—had been compelled to respond several centuries
earlier. The Swiss claim was essentially the claim of Berengarius—namely, that
to say that Christ is *really* present in the Eucharist is simply nonsensical and
therefore untrue. It is incoherent, agree Berengarius and the Swiss, to suggest
that that which is obviously bread and wine can be meaningfully called the
body and blood of Christ in a more than symbolic way. As Johannes Oecolampadius, one of Zwingli's chief collaborators, put it, "That the symbolic
bread is the flesh of Christ is so abhorrent to the mind of all believers that
no one of us has ever truly believed it. . . . This idea of mangling the flesh
the mind so rejects that one would not dare to chew but would spit it out
of one's mouth."[4] Luther's writings against the Swiss are, therefore, of the
most importance when comparing his eucharistic theology to that of Thomas
Aquinas because it is in those writings that Luther confronts the problem
with which medieval theology had to struggle after Berengarius: How is it
not simply nonsense to claim that Christ is really present in the Eucharist?

As we shall see, in responding to this problem Luther often had recourse to
many of the same arguments and strategies as Thomas Aquinas, even though
the styles of their theologies are quite radically distinct.[5] In order to better
discern the similarities in Luther and Thomas, it is important to notice that

3. That Luther correctly understood Zwingli has been disputed. For an account of the
debate between Luther and Zwingli that takes account of such claims, see Brian A. Gerrish,
"Discerning the Body: Sign and Reality in Luther's Controversy with the Swiss," in *Continuing the Reformation: Essays on Modern Religious Thought* (Chicago: University of Chicago
Press, 1993), esp. 66–69. See also chap. 4, "Luther and Zwingli," in Crockett, *Eucharist*, 128–47.

4. Oecolampadius, "Rearguard or Supplement concerning the Eucharist," in *Zwinglis Sämtliche Schriften*, 4:493, quoted in Kurt K. Hendel, "*Finitum Capax Infiniti*: Luther's Radical Incarnational Perspective," *Currents in Theology and Mission* 35, no. 6 (December 2008): 429n39.

5. "Otto Pesch . . . wrote a massive comparison of the doctrine of justification in Thomas
Aquinas and Martin Luther, concluding that their differences were more a matter of theological
style than of theological substance. Thomas wrote sapiential theology and Luther existen-
tial, but their views on grace and justification were remarkably similar." David C. Steinmetz,
"The Catholic Luther: A Critical Reappraisal," *Theology Today* 61 (2004): 192–93. Steinmetz
refers his readers to Otto Hermann Pesch, *Theologie der Rechtfertigung bei Martin Luther
und Thomas von Aquin: Versuch eines systematisch-theologischen Dialogs* (Mainz: Matthias
Grünewald, 1967).

Luther is not only responding to the same problem to which Aquinas and the eucharistic theology of the High Middle Ages had responded. In fact, his own theological development on this question maps remarkably closely onto the development of Catholic theology that we have already investigated at the beginning of the previous chapter. Like the early Church, Luther begins by serenely accepting Christ's eucharistic presence and expounding upon its ecclesiological significance. Only when faced with the claim that Christ's presence in the Eucharist is incoherent does he have recourse to metaphysical speculation. Accordingly, we will begin our investigation by looking at Luther's early works, with a special focus on his rejection of transubstantiation.

Next, we will look in some detail at the most important issues in his debates with the Swiss because this will highlight just how much he has in common with Thomas, despite appearances to the contrary. Then we will carefully compare Luther's own articulations of real presence with those of Thomas in order to discern just how close the two thinkers came to one another. Finally, we will look at the question of the persistence of the bread and wine, especially given that this is perhaps the most salient difference between Luther and Thomas in the popular mind, in two specific contexts. First, we will look at the persistence of the bread and wine with reference to Luther's ideas about signs and signification in the Eucharist; and, second, we will ask whether the Catholic denial of their persistence in transubstantiation really does offend the dogma of the incarnation or, conversely, whether Luther's affirmation of their persistence offends the doctrine of transubstantiation.

Real Presence without Transubstantiation

In his earliest works on the Eucharist, Luther seems to take transubstantiation for granted, or at least to let it go unchallenged. He is not much interested in philosophical subtlety, but simply affirms real presence as the result of a change in the elements. In his 1519 work *The Blessed Sacrament of the Holy and True Body of Christ, and the Brotherhoods*, Luther understands this change, and the resulting presence, as undergirding the sacrament's function of effecting Christian unity. Because Christians commune with Christ, really present in the Eucharist, they are in communion with one another. Communion in his body makes us one body in him.[6] This theme is, of course, completely traditional (being the argument of St. Paul in 1 Corinthians 10–11), entirely consonant with Augustine's ecclesial theology of the Eucharist, and

---

6. *The Blessed Sacrament of the Holy and True Body of Christ, and the Brotherhoods* (1519), in *LW* 35:59–60.

of a piece with Thomas Aquinas's identification of the unity of the Church as the *res tantum*, the final goal, of the sacrament.[7] The contemporary Cistercian theologian Roch Kereszty calls this work "a beautiful testimony to a revitalized Catholic understanding that has been enriched by a return to biblical and Augustinian theology,"[8] and he quotes Luther favorably to show that the Reformer not only accepts transubstantiation at this point but also "perceives and expounds its anthropological and ecclesial significance": "For just as the bread is changed [*vorwandelt*] into his true natural body and the wine into his natural true blood, so truly are we also drawn and changed into the spiritual body, that is, into the fellowship of Christ and all saints and by this sacrament put into possession of all the virtues and mercies of Christ and his saints."[9]

It must be noted that Luther does not use the term "transubstantiation," however. And while Kereszty sees Luther's affirmation of "change" as sufficient evidence that he accepts transubstantiation, others suggest that Luther's use of the term *vorwandelt* indicates that he is already moving away from it. In his collection of Luther's writings, Timothy Lull includes the following footnote at this point:

> *Vorwandelt.* While this term and the imagery involving change are associated with the doctrine of transubstantiation, it is clear that, through rejecting all scholastic speculation concerning substance . . . , Luther is already beginning to call into question that very doctrine which within a year he was to condemn as "the second captivity of the sacrament" (LW 36, 28–35). Cf. Charles E. Hay (trans.) Reinhold Seeberg's *History of Doctrines* (Grand Rapids: Baker, 1952), II, 286, n. 1, "Literally, transubstantiation is here retained, but really Luther is only concerned to hold fast the idea that the body is 'in' the bread."[10]

Whether one sides with Kereszty, on the one hand, or Lull and Seeberg, on the other, it must be admitted that, on such a question, we can do no more than conjecture. Our initial judgment, that Luther takes transubstantiation for granted, or at least allows it to go unchallenged at this point, stands. The more important point is that Luther's thoroughly ecclesial theology of the Eucharist, buttressed by the fact that he felt no need to engage in metaphysical

---

7. See above, pp. 130–33.
8. Kereszty, *Wedding Feast of the Lamb*, 139. See also Thomas J. Davis, *This Is My Body: The Presence of Christ in Reformation Thought* (Grand Rapids: Baker Academic, 2008), 25.
9. Kereszty, *Wedding Feast of the Lamb*, 139.
10. Martin Luther, "The Blessed Sacrament of the Holy and True Body of Christ, and the Brotherhoods," in *Martin Luther's Basic Theological Writings*, ed. Timothy Lull (Minneapolis: Fortress, 1989), 252n27.

speculation, is utterly patristic. Luther's earliest stage of eucharistic theology mirrors the Church's earliest stage of eucharistic theology.

A year later, when Luther does attack transubstantiation in *The Babylonian Captivity of the Church*, he explicitly appeals to the patristic Church in his rejection of metaphysical speculation and philosophy. "Moreover," he writes, "the church kept the true faith for more than twelve hundred years, during which time the holy fathers never, at any time or place, mentioned this transubstantiation (a monstrous word and a monstrous idea), until the pseudo philosophy of Aristotle began to make its inroads into the church these last three hundred years."[11] At this stage, Luther saw no need for philosophy in a theology of real presence. In fact, he explicitly rejected it: "Why do we not put aside such curiosity and cling simply to the words of Christ, willing to remain in ignorance of what takes place here and content that the real body of Christ is present by virtue of the words. Or is it necessary to comprehend the manner of the divine working in every detail?"[12] All that was required was that "the words of God . . . be retained in their simplest meaning as a far as possible."[13] If Christ said, "This is my body," then that is what it is. "For my part," Luther maintains, "if I cannot fathom how the bread is the body of Christ, yet I will take my reason captive to the obedience of Christ [2 Cor. 10:5], and clinging simply to his words, firmly believe not only that the body of Christ is in the bread, but that the bread is the body of Christ."[14] While Luther has now moved from assuming, or at least not explicitly rejecting, transubstantiation to a forceful public denunciation of it, his basically patristic model remains: real presence is strongly affirmed, while metaphysical speculation is eschewed. The difference is that Luther is now explicitly professing these positions in a polemical context rather than simply operating according to them in a pastoral one.

What is essential to note is that both the patristic Church and Luther (and Eastern Orthodoxy, for that matter) could afford to do their eucharistic theology without reference to metaphysics as long as no one raised the Berengarian question about coherence. But when once someone says, "It is simply nonsense to call this bread and this wine the body and blood of Christ," ontological speculation becomes unavoidable for those who want to reaffirm

---

11. *The Babylonian Captivity of the Church* (1519), in *LW* 36:31. Cf. Pelikan, *Christian Tradition*, 4:200: "Luther's acceptance of the real presence and rejection of transubstantiation made his position analogous to that of medieval theology before transubstantiation had become official; in short, Luther had, despite his polemics against Peter Lombard, retained the Lombard's eucharistic doctrine."

12. *The Babylonian Captivity of the Church* (1519), in *LW* 36:33.

13. *The Babylonian Captivity of the Church* (1519), in *LW* 36:30.

14. *The Babylonian Captivity of the Church* (1519), in *LW* 36:34.

the historic faith of the Church. To say what is possible or impossible, what is coherent or incoherent, is to make an ontological claim, wittingly or not. And the response to such a claim will not be satisfactory if it is not made on the same level as the claim itself. If a person believes it is simply nonsense to call the bread and wine the body and blood of Christ, no amount of appealing to the Scriptures and the tradition will do without a demonstration that what one finds in the Scriptures and Christian tradition is actually a meaningful claim.

A New Berengarius?

In this respect, what medieval theology met in Berengarius is precisely what Luther met in Zwingli. The Church's initial response, represented by Humbert's blunt affirmations in the first *Ego Berengarius*, was found to be inadequate not simply because of its crudity, though that was certainly a problem, but because mere affirmation, no matter how forceful, cannot answer the question of coherence.[15] If the metaphysical quandaries of the Berengars and the Zwinglis of the Church are to be answered, the answer cannot eschew metaphysics. Real presence will not be accepted as true until it is seen to be both meaningful and possible. *Luther's recourse to philosophy in his debate with the Swiss, then, can be seen as paralleling the development of transubstantiation in the medieval Western Church's response to the Berengarian crisis.* What had once been affirmed on the witness of Scripture and the enduring faith of the Church now had to be defended in a new context and with new weapons. As Luther himself wrote in 1528 in the *Confession concerning Christ's Supper*, one of his most important anti-Zwinglian tracts, "I am not speaking now from Scripture. But we must use our reason or give way to the fanatics."[16] In order to avoid devolving into fideism or skepticism, faith must seek understanding. Having rejected transubstantiation in favor of a simple adherence to the words of Scripture, Luther was now forced to *replace it* in order to uphold adherence to the words of Scripture. History cannot be undone. Once the question of coherence is raised, it cannot go unanswered.[17]

---

15. Indeed, Luther's forceful affirmations unencumbered by metaphysics are not completely unlike Humbert's infamous formula, which Luther himself endorsed. See *Confession concerning Christ's Supper* (1528), in *LW* 37:300–301: "Would to God that all popes had acted in so Christian a fashion in all other matters as this pope did with Berengar in forcing this confession."

16. *Confession concerning Christ's Supper* (1528), in *LW* 37:224.

17. Cf. Benedict XVI, "Problem of Transubstantiation," 228: "Once a question has made its appearance, it cannot be taken back; the previous situation is irrevocably gone. After the question of transubstantiation has been raised, one can no longer speak about the Eucharist as if this question did not yet exist." See also pp. 230–31: "And it becomes obvious that it is

We should be careful, however, not to portray Luther's change of tactics on this question as a complete rupture. Already in the *Babylonian Captivity*, the seeds of his later theologizing on the question of Christ's presence are apparent. Furthermore, even in his later anti-Zwinglian works Luther is quite cautious about the claims he is willing to make from philosophy, and the primacy of the Word of God in his thought is consistently maintained.[18] Like transubstantiation, properly understood, Luther's theology of the real presence respects the mystery of the Eucharist.[19] Like Thomas before him, Luther does not intend to demonstrate *how* Christ is present in the sense of describing some process or mechanism.[20] Indeed, Luther forcefully repudiates any such attempts, writing, "But how this takes place or how he is in the bread, we do not know and are not meant to know."[21] Rather his goal is simply to demonstrate that the claim of real presence is neither incoherent nor impossible.[22] If that can be demonstrated, no barrier remains to accepting Christ's words at the Last Supper and the perennial faith of the Church at face value. In this, Luther is the unwitting heir of Thomas Aquinas and the doctrine of transubstantiation.

---

problematic to attempt to return to biblical simplicity at a moment when the human mind had irrevocably abandoned this simplicity and was able to preserve the old and original articles of faith only by articulating them in something new. History allows no return, and this becomes particularly clear in Luther's Eucharistic teaching as well."

18. *Confession concerning Christ's Supper* (1528), in *LW* 37:207. Cf. Osborne, "Faith, Philosophy, and the Nominalist Background," 64: "Luther differs from his scholastic predecessors in that he uses philosophy not to develop theological conclusions but only to attack errors about the Bible, and so the concern here is with Luther's use of Nominalist doctrines about presence in his attack on the sacra-mentarians' [*sic*] belief that Christ cannot be present both at the right hand of God and in the Eucharist at the same time." See also Stephenson, *Lord's Supper*, 22: Luther "never supposed that this christologically developed argument for the *possibility* of the real presence, which he set forth 'beyond the call of duty' [*zum Überfluß*] did anything to *establish* this article of faith. The *Great Confession* of 1528 indicates the limited apologetic value of Luther's proof of the communicated omnipresence. Furthermore, it makes clear that, even if he were unable to respond to the first Swiss objection, he would still have confessed the real presence on the *sole* basis of the sacred text and with appeal to divine omnipresence."

19. Osborne, "Faith, Philosophy, and the Nominalist Background," 72: "Luther's arguments about place do not explain away the mystery of Christ's presence, but they show that there is no contradiction in believing the Scriptures and the Creed when they say that Christ is present in the Lord's Supper and at God's right hand."

20. See Paul R. Hinlicky, "Christ's Bodily Presence in the Holy Supper—Real or Symbolic?," *Lutheran Forum* 33, no. 3 (Fall 1999): 28.

21. *That These Words of Christ, "This Is My Body," etc., Still Stand Firm against the Fanatics* (1527), in *LW* 37:29.

22. Hunsinger, *Eucharist and Ecumenism*, 29–30; Kenneth R. Craycraft, "Sign and Word: Martin Luther's Theology of the Sacraments," *Restoration Quarterly* 32, no. 3 (1990): 162–63; Jones, *Christ's Eucharistic Presence*, 132; Egil Grislis, "The Manner of Christ's Eucharistic Presence according to Martin Luther," *Consensus* 7, no. 1 (January 1981): 13. See also *Confession concerning Christ's Supper* (1528), in *LW* 37:223–24.

Nominalist Transubstantiation

Recall from chapter 1 that Luther's condemnations of what he called the second captivity were much milder than his condemnations of the first and third captivities.[23] Because he was an ardent supporter of the doctrine of real presence, and because transubstantiation was intended to support that doctrine, Luther found it at least tolerable.[24] What he would not tolerate was its imposition by Church authority.[25] And, while it might be permissible as a private theological opinion, Luther felt the doctrine of transubstantiation failed on at least two counts. First of all, the imposition of pagan philosophical categories seemed to corrupt and obscure the witness of Scripture, and, second, the denial of the reality of the bread seemed counter to the logic of the incarnation on which the sacrament was necessarily based. Christ's humanity did not need to be transubstantiated into divinity in order for God to be really present in Jesus of Nazareth.[26]

Beneath these two objections, however, lies a deeper issue. Recall also that between the time of Aquinas and Luther, the word "transubstantiation" had come to mean something quite different from what it meant in Thomas's articulation.[27] Read through nominalist lenses, transubstantiation came to mean virtually the opposite of what it had meant for Thomas. But Luther was trained in the nominalist school. And even though he forcefully rejected nominalist theology on many issues, and especially on justification, he was never free of many of its premises.[28] Indeed, in the case of eucharistic theology,

> like the nominalists, Luther rejects "any permanent quantity separate from the substance" as sustainer of the accidents remaining after transubstantiation, because the quantity cannot be divided from the substance. On the other hand,

---

23. See above, pp. 1–4.

24. Indeed, John Stephenson has argued, following Tom Hardt, that Luther refrained from condemning transubstantiation in his public preaching and lectures in order not to scandalize the faithful for whom the doctrine often simply meant an affirmation of real presence (Stephenson, *Lord's Supper*, 95). Cf. Luther's comments in *The Babylonian Captivity*: "I rejoice greatly that the simple faith of this sacrament is still to be found, at least among the common people. For as they do not understand, neither do they dispute whether accidents are present without a substance, but believe with a simple faith that Christ's body and blood are truly contained there, and leave to those who have nothing else to do the argument about what contains them" (*LW* 36:32).

25. *The Babylonian Captivity of the Church* (1520), in *LW* 37:30, 35.

26. *The Babylonian Captivity of the Church* (1520), in *LW* 36:35.

27. See above, pp. 52–55.

28. Benedict XVI, "Problem of Transubstantiation," 228; see also David C. Steinmetz, "Luther among the Anti-Thomists," in *Luther in Context* (Grand Rapids: Baker, 1995), 56–57.

it was precisely the nominalist form of the doctrine of transubstantiation which he (and with him the Formula of Concord) combated; for, unlike Aquinas, the nominalists assumed that the substance of the bread ceased to be altogether, or was annihilated. Consequently, the result of taking over the empirical concept of substance from late scholasticism was a *misinterpretation of transubstantiation*, which saw it as meaning a physical transformation (*conversio physica*) or a spatial encapsulation of Christ's body and blood.[29]

That Luther's rejection of transubstantiation in *The Babylonian Captivity* was determined by nominalist presuppositions—his own and those of the specific articulation of transubstantiation that he rejected—is readily apparent. He begins his critique of transubstantiation by referencing the prominent nominalist theologian Pierre d'Ailly, a student of Ockham's, the "learned Cardinal of Cambrai" who, according to Luther, "argues with great acumen that to hold that real bread and real wine, and not merely their accidents, are present on the altar, would be much more probable and require fewer superfluous miracles—if only the church had not decreed otherwise."[30] But Thomas had insisted that transubstantiation was only *one* miracle, the transformation of the bread and the wine into Christ's body and blood, with everything else following from that as simple corollaries.[31] The nominalist version of transubstantiation, however, had become overgrown with superfluous miracles, beginning with the annihilation of the bread and wine, something Thomas had explicitly rejected.

Luther refers to the next miracle in nominalist transubstantiation when he writes that those who profess transubstantiation "have been driven to pretend that a new substance is created by God for those accidents on the altar, all on account of Aristotle, who says: 'It is the nature of an accident to be in something,' and endless other monstrosities. They would be rid of all these if they simply permitted real bread to be present."[32] Indeed, it follows from annihilation that something new would need to be created to take the

29. Lehmann and Pannenberg, *Condemnations of the Reformation Era*, 95–96 (emphasis added); cf. Stephenson, *Lord's Supper*, 100–101n84.

30. *The Babylonian Captivity of the Church* (1520), in *LW* 36:29.

31. *ST* III, 77.5 corpus. See above, pp. 120–21. Cf. Stephenson, *Lord's Supper*, 102–3. Stephenson, who extols Luther's nominalist view about "substance" (100–101), criticizes transubstantiation for consisting of two distinct miracles. He seems unaware that it was the nominalist version of transubstantiation that posited a second miracle, not Thomas's "realist" version.

32. *The Babylonian Captivity of the Church* (1520), in *LW* 36:32. Lawrence Feingold notes that Luther "also seemed to have various misunderstandings of transubstantiation, thinking that it implied an additional miracle of the annihilation of the substances of bread and wine or the creation of a new substance in which the accidents of bread and wine could inhere, notions to which he rightly objected but that are totally foreign to the Thomistic account" (*Eucharist*, 294).

place of the annihilated substance.[33] The problems of intelligibility inherent in such a formulation were precisely why Thomas felt the need to reject annihilation as a possibility.[34]

Of course, as we have already seen, nominalism was content to bypass concerns about intelligibility by recourse to divine power.[35] That Luther was critiquing precisely this kind of theology is demonstrated by the following, rather opaque, text:

> If a "transubstantiation" must be assumed in order that Christ's body may not be identified with the bread, why not also a "transaccidentiation," in order that the body of Christ may not be identified with the accidents? For the danger remains if one understands the subject to be "this white or this round is my body." And for the same reason that a "transubstantiation" must be assumed, a "transaccidentiation" must be assumed, because of this identity of subject and predicate. If however, merely by an act of the intellect, you can do away with the accident, so that it will not be regarded as the subject when you say, "this is my body," why not with equal ease transcend the substance of the bread, if you do not want it to be regarded as the subject, so that "this is my body" is no less in the substance than in the accident? After all, this is a divine work performed by God's almighty power, which can operate just as much and just as well in the accident as it can in the substance.[36]

This passage will be fatally misread if it is not understood from the start that Luther is being sarcastic here, answering the fool according to his own folly, so to speak. And, because Luther is here mocking his opponents, we should be careful not to discern too much about his own view from it. Nevertheless, several pertinent points may be highlighted. First of all, the appeal to God's power is a clear sign that Luther is mocking the nominalist version of transubstantiation that was accepted on the authority of the Church despite consubstantiation's advantage in the area of intelligibility, the credibility gap being filled by appeals to God's absolute power.

33. "From a Nominalist perspective transubstantiation requires two actions of God, namely, the annihilation of the substance of the bread and the placement of Christ's body under the species. Therefore, consubstantiation would be a simpler account of Christ's Eucharistic presence. If Christ's body were present along with the substance of the bread annihilation would not have to occur" (Osborne, "Faith, Philosophy, and the Nominalist Background," 64–65). Cf. David C. Steinmetz, "Scripture and the Lord's Supper in Luther's Theology," *Interpretation* 37, no. 3 (July 1983): 255.

34. Cf. *ST* III, 75.3.

35. See above, pp. 47–48.

36. *The Babylonian Captivity of the Church* (1519), in *LW* 36:33–34.

There is more to the passage than this, however. Luther may be mocking nominalism's flagrant appeals to divine power, but he too is operating within nominalism's categories. Luther, like the nominalists, so blurs the distinction between substance and accidents, a distinction absolutely essential for Thomas's articulation, that he is able to talk about them as if they are the same *kind* of thing. Substance no longer transcends particular accidents but behaves as simply one more of them. But if substance does not transcend accidents, it can simply be transcended as if it were one more accident and the substance of the bread and wine can be said to remain just as the accidents are said to remain. Or, in Luther's sarcastic reversal, if transubstantiation is required, so is transaccidentiation.

Luther is exactly right, of course. Because nominalism has blurred the distinction between substance and accidents, transubstantiation *is* indistinguishable from transaccidentiation. Thomas could not have disagreed. But, in Thomas's realist metaphysics, that which something is (substance) *does* transcend its particular characteristics (accidents) and cannot, therefore, be simply transcended in the same way that such characteristics are. Rather, for something's very being to be transcended is for it to *become* something else. Perhaps we should not read too much into a passage in which Luther is being sarcastic, but it is worth noting the irony in Luther's suggestion that the *substance* of the bread be *trans*cended. According to Thomas, eucharistic change is a substantial change, but not a kind of clandestine natural substantial change. Rather, it is a unique change that is "called by a name proper to itself—'transubstantiation,'"[37] a change in which the substance is not, strictly speaking, transformed—that is, it does not become something new because its matter has been given a new form, as in natural changes—but is rather transcended.

Luther's two basic theological concerns about transubstantiation—an exaggerated role for philosophy in theology and its failure to follow an incarnational pattern—are, of course, not unaffected by these considerations. Luther could not avoid the impact of his own philosophical presuppositions in his theologizing and, as we shall see, may have been less frequently misunderstood by his contemporaries on the question of eucharistic presence had he been more conscious of and explicit about them from the start.[38] And new light is shed on the question of the persistence of the substance of the bread and

37. *ST* III, 75.4 corpus.

38. Grislis, "Manner of Christ's Eucharistic Presence according to Martin Luther," 14: "Of course, he had to organize his insights of faith, and here at times the use of philosophical concepts was inevitable. Perhaps it is ungrateful to wish that a great biblical theologian could have been more conversant with philosophical theology. Had that been the case, philosophy

wine when it is seen that the term "substance" is being used in a very different way by Luther, who affirms their persistence, than by Thomas, who denies it. As Joseph Ratzinger writes, "'Transubstantiation' forms no antithesis at all to 'consubstantiation,' if the latter is simply supposed to mean the bread and wine as physical-chemical entities continue to exist unchanged."[39] We will need to return to the question of transubstantiation's relationship to the pattern of the incarnation and the persistence of the bread and wine after we have had the opportunity to investigate Luther's later works on eucharistic presence.

Luther and the Swiss

As we have already mentioned, the bulk of Luther's writings on the Eucharist (and I use the term "bulk" quite deliberately!) were produced during his lengthy debate with the Swiss Reformers. Luther believed that the Swiss completely rejected any sense of Christ's presence beyond what they could conjure in their own minds, to Luther an act of works righteousness on par with the Roman idea of the Mass as sacrifice,[40] while for their part the Swiss suspected Luther of cannibalism and capharnaism given his often blunt insistence on the reality of Christ's presence. It was in responding to these charges that Luther further developed his theology of real presence.

In response to his concerns that the Catholic understanding of the Mass as a sacrifice was a form of works righteousness, Luther developed his emphasis on the Mass as a testament. James McCue sums up the idea of the Mass as testament in one sentence: "At the Last Supper Christ bequeaths to us what is to be won on Calvary; in the mass we receive this inheritance."[41] Luther drew a sharp distinction between giving and receiving in the Lord's Supper. In the Mass we receive this great gift from God, but we offer nothing. But real presence remains just as important in this emphasis as it was for Catholics with the emphasis on the Mass as sacrifice. If, for Catholics, Christ must be present precisely to guarantee the reality of the sacrifice (which, without the presence of Christ, could be nothing more than blasphemous playacting), for Luther Christ must be present in order to guarantee the gift character of the Supper.[42] Without Christ's presence, the Supper becomes just one more

---

would not have been employed as the very last resort—and Luther would have been less often misunderstood."

39. Benedict XVI, "Problem of Transubstantiation," 237.
40. Gerrish, "Discerning the Body," 60.
41. McCue, "Luther and Roman Catholicism on the Mass as Sacrifice," 215.
42. Cf. Hunsinger, *Eucharist and Ecumenism*, 104–5.

human work.[43] This is the reason Luther was so scandalized by the Swiss denial of real presence.

While agreeing with Luther about the sole sufficiency of Christ and his work for our salvation, Zwingli drew the opposite conclusion about the Eucharist. While for Luther the Eucharist was the place wherein we could lay hold of Christ and his promise of forgiveness and salvation, for Zwingli sacraments, at least if they were imagined to actually achieve something, were a distraction, an addition to Christ, and so an affront to the idea of salvation through Christ alone.[44] For Zwingli, the eucharistic symbols could not convey Christ really present, but could only representatively point to Christ absent. As Crockett writes,

> Historically, therefore, Zwingli represents the point at which the symbolical and spiritualistic traditions in eucharistic thought threaten to become antirealist and even antisacramental. This does not mean that for Zwingli the eucharist is unimportant. It means that the tension is now broken between two strains in the eucharistic tradition, which up to this point had belonged together.[45]

While ecumenical theology, in general, is not particularly sympathetic to Zwingli (Calvin himself was appalled at Zwingli's "profane" approach to the Supper),[46] it is worth noting two ecumenically salutary aspects of his teaching. First of all, Zwingli's rejection of real presence seems to be a rejection of a capharnaitic understanding of real presence.[47] While he may falsely represent his opponents as capharnaites,[48] he is correct to insist that any acceptable articulation of the Lord's Supper must be able to discriminate between the Eucharist and cannibalism. Inasmuch as the more realist traditions are wont to follow Humbert's blunt affirmations in popular piety, if not in theology or doctrine, Zwingli stands as a warning. While he himself seems to have tragically, Luther would suspect even deliberately,[49] misunderstood and misrepresented the Catholic and Lutheran positions on real presence, the fact remains that many Christians today with a basically Zwinglian view of the Eucharist are responding to similar misunderstandings, and those who would

---

43. Gerrish, "Discerning the Body," 60; Jones, *Christ's Eucharistic Presence*, 129.
44. Crockett, *Eucharist*, 135.
45. Crockett, *Eucharist*, 137–38.
46. Brian A. Gerrish, "Luther and the Reformed Eucharist: What Luther Said, or Might Have Said, about Calvin," *Seminary Ridge Review* 10, no. 2 (Spring 2008): 13.
47. Jones, *Christ's Eucharistic Presence*, 122.
48. See *That These Words of Christ* (1527), in *LW* 37:93; *Brief Confession concerning the Holy Sacrament* (1544), in *LW* 38:301.
49. *Brief Confession concerning the Holy Sacrament* (1544), in *LW* 38:292, 301.

promote a realistic understanding of Christ's eucharistic presence do well to recognize this.

The second aspect of Zwingli's thought that is ecumenically helpful is his ecclesial reading of the sacrament. Zwingli did not simply reject the Church's theology of the Eucharist in favor of a purely memorial meal.[50] Rather, not unlike the early Luther, he maintained and reemphasized an ecclesial realism that was often overshadowed by medieval eucharistic piety centered on the consecrated host. Zwingli's exegesis of 1 Corinthians 10:16–17 ("The cup of blessing that we bless, is it not a sharing in the blood of Christ? The bread that we break, is it not a sharing in the body of Christ? Because there is one bread, we who are many are one body, for we all partake of the one bread") "led him to a realism with respect to the Church that he denied with respect to the elements. The body of Christ that is eaten spiritually by faith transforms the community that receives it into the body of Christ, the Church. The body of Christ is not in the bread, but in the Church."[51]

Ecclesial realism, we have already insisted, is a perfectly traditional theme in eucharistic theology. If the Eucharist is not oriented toward building up the body of Christ, but becomes merely a matter of individualistic piety, then it has been rendered useless, even counterproductive. Zwingli is right to highlight this feature of eucharistic theology, especially in a context where individualistic piety often obscured the ecclesial import of the sacrament. But, again, Zwingli makes a tragic false dichotomy. The same tradition that had fought to hold together symbol and reality had also always held together eucharistic and ecclesial realism.[52] For the Fathers, like Irenaeus and Augustine, as for Thomas Aquinas and Martin Luther, Christ's real presence in the Eucharist was the guarantee, even the cause, of his presence in the gathered community. The ecclesial body could not expect to exist without its head. In Zwingli, however, the relationship between Christ's presence in the elements and his presence in the Church is severed. Gerrish writes that, from Luther's point of view, the Swiss "mistook the fruit for the institution of the Supper, and so took away the only means by which the spiritual [i.e., ecclesial] body could be established."[53] In Zwingli, eucharistic and ecclesial presence came

50. Egil Grislis points out that, in this emphasis, Zwingli follows Thomas Aquinas, for whom the idea of memorial meal was actually quite important. Aquinas, however, held memorial within a richer theological context than Zwingli ("Eucharistic Presence of Christ," 25–26).

51. Crockett, *Eucharist*, 139. Brian Gerrish is skeptical, however, of scholars (he mentions Julius Schweizer) who would suggest that Zwingli's realism with regard to the Church is so high that it might be called a transubstantiation of the people. See Gerrish, "Discerning the Body," 66–69.

52. De Lubac, *Corpus Mysticum*, 256.

53. Gerrish, "Discerning the Body," 72.

to be seen as alternatives, understood as opposed to one another rather than interdependent. Again, for Zwingli, Christ's presence in the eucharistic elements distracts from the true value of the sacrament; for Luther, Christ's presence guarantees it.

Marburg

Facing a theological splintering of the Reformation that would imply a political splintering of Protestant Germany, Landgrave Philip I of Hesse called a colloquy at Marburg Castle to attempt to reach accord on the question of eucharistic presence. It was here that the basic issues between Wittenberg and Zurich became clear. Luther and Zwingli were unable to come to agreement at Marburg, and the basic questions that emerged there continued to shape the debate between Luther and the Swiss for the rest of Luther's life, and even, if to a lesser extent, to the present day.

We will look at three distinct, but obviously interrelated, areas of disagreement. First of all, there is the disagreement about the relationship between faith and reason in the interpretation of Scripture already hinted at in our earlier comments about the question of coherence. Second, there are christological disagreements that have a bearing on the meaning and possibility of Christ's presence in the elements. And finally, there is confusion about the role of signs and signification in the Eucharist.

Like Berengarius before him, Zwingli did not seem able to conceive of any real presence of Christ in the eucharistic elements that was not grossly carnal and materialistic. Anyone who proclaimed a real presence in the elements was suspect. In 1526 he wrote, "I am wont to call my antagonists cannibals."[54] With such a conception of real presence, it is no surprise that Zwingli was enthusiastic about the ideas of the Dutchman Cornelius Hoen, whose work on the Eucharist Zwingli published at Zurich.[55] Hoen claimed that the famous "is" in Jesus's words at the Last Supper, "This *is* my body," is to be understood as "signifies," as in other places in the Gospels where Jesus speaks of himself in metaphor: "I am the door," "I am the vine," and so forth. According to this exegesis, Jesus could not have actually meant, "This is my body," but rather, "This (bread) signifies my body."[56]

---

54. Letter of March 1526 to Urbanus Regius, in *Huldreich Zwinglis sämtliche Werke, Bd. IV, Werke April 1525–März 1526*, ed. Emil Egli, Georg Finsler, Walther Köhler, and Oskar Farner, Corpus Reformatorum 91 (Leipzig: Heinsius, 1915–27), 933:18. Quoted in Stephenson, *Lord's Supper*, 3.

55. Gerrish, "Discerning the Body," 62.

56. Jones, *Christ's Eucharistic Presence*, 125.

Zwingli also famously buttressed his claim that Jesus could not have actually meant "This *is* my body" by his exegesis of John 6:63: "It is the spirit that gives life; the flesh is useless. The words that I have spoken to you are spirit and life." According to Zwingli, these words, spoken by Jesus immediately after the bread of life discourse in which Jesus claims, "My flesh is true food and my blood is true drink. Those who eat my flesh and drink my blood abide in me, and I in them" (6:55–56), indicate that Jesus could not have meant either the bread of life discourse or the eucharistic words of institution literally. Eating Christ's flesh—cannibalistically conceived—is of no avail. Rather, eating Christ is a metaphor for believing in Christ.[57]

To Luther, Zwingli's method was perfectly backward. One must not start with what one finds reasonable and then search for an exegesis that agrees with one's profane conclusions: "But this is not Christian teaching, when I intrude my own ideas into the Scripture and compel Scripture to accord with them. On the contrary, the Christian way is to make clear first what the Scriptures teach and then compel my own ideas to accord with them."[58] For Luther, one must take the word of God at face value, reducing it to metaphor or symbolization only when the scriptural context itself, and not profane reason, manifestly compels it.[59] It is clear from Scripture that Jesus's words about being a door or a vine are meant metaphorically, but that is not at all the case with respect to the words of institution. Therefore, they cannot be treated as an equivalent case.[60]

Moreover, insists Luther, if profane reason is to be the determining factor in biblical interpretation, Christ's presence in the Supper is not the only thing threatened. Rather, the whole incarnational economy must be rejected.[61] That God should become one of us in the womb of the Virgin Mary and die for our sins on a cross is absurd and impossible by our own lights.[62] Zwingli's exegetical method, consistently applied, ends by undermining the gospel itself:

57. Crockett, *Eucharist*, 136.
58. *The Adoration of the Sacrament* (1523), in *LW* 36:283.
59. *The Adoration of the Sacrament* (1523), in *LW* 36:280; *That These Words of Christ* (1527), in *LW* 37:32. See also Steinmetz, "Scripture and the Lord's Supper in Luther's Theology," 67.
60. *Confession concerning Christ's Supper* (1528), in *LW* 37:287–88; cf. *The Adoration of the Sacrament* (1523), in *LW* 36:280–86.
61. See Crockett, *Eucharist*, 141.
62. See *The Sacrament of the Body and Blood of Christ—Against the Fanatics* (1526), in *LW* 36:338:

> To this first point I might say equally well that it is not reasonable that God should descend from heaven and enter into the womb; that he who nourishes, sustains, and encompasses all the world should allow himself to be nourished and encompassed by the Virgin. Likewise that Christ, a king of glory [Ps. 24:10], at whose feet all angels must

For if we permit such violence to be done in any one passage, that without any basis in Scripture a person can say the word "is" means the same as the word "signifies," then it would be impossible to stop it in any other passage. The entire Scripture would be nullified, since there is no good reason why such violence should be valid in one passage but not in all passages. In that case one could say: That Mary is a virgin and the mother of God is equivalent to saying that Mary signifies a virgin and the mother of God. Likewise: Christ is God and man; that is, Christ signifies God and man. Likewise Rom. 1[:16]: the gospel is the power of God and so forth; that is, the gospel signifies the power of God. See what a horrible mess this would lead to. Therefore, since such violence cannot be allowed in other passages of Scripture, it cannot be allowed here either, that Christ's body is signified by the bread; because the words stand there clear, unadorned, and plain: "This is my body"—unless one can adduce clear and definite passages to prove that the word "is" should mean "signifies."[63]

Furthermore, argued Luther, John 6:63 is of no help to Zwingli's cause and, indeed, Zwingli's interpretation of it leads down exactly the same path as his reading of "is" as "signifies" in the institution narratives. It is clear in John 6:63 that Jesus is not, with the phrase "the flesh is useless," denouncing physical realities as opposed to spiritual realities. That is gnosticism. Rather, "all is spirit, spiritual, and an object of the Spirit, in reality and in name, which comes from the Holy Spirit, be it physical or material, outward or visible as it may; on the other hand, all is flesh and fleshly which comes from the natural power of the flesh, without spirit, be it as inward and invisible as it may."[64] As William Crockett writes, for Luther, "Spirit is not opposed to the bodily and the earthly, but the realm of 'spirit' is the sphere of God's activity in Christ through the power of the Spirit. 'Flesh' does not mean the bodily and the earthly, but human life under the dominion of sin and death."[65] Indeed,

---

fall and before whom all creatures must tremble, should thus humble himself below all men and allow himself to be suspended upon the cross as a most notorious evil-doer and that by the most wicked and desperate of men. And I might conclude from this that God did not become man, or that the crucified Christ is not God.

63. *The Adoration of the Sacrament* (1523), in *LW* 36:280. If Luther's claims here seem far-fetched, it should suffice to point out that many of the conclusions he posits have since been drawn in various (mostly, but not exclusively, Protestant) theological circles.

64. *That These Words of Christ* (1527), in *LW* 37:99.

65. Crockett, *Eucharist*, 143. Cf. Steinmetz, "Scripture and the Lord's Supper in Luther's Theology," 257. See Davis, *This Is My Body*, 59:

To speak of Luther's theology as incarnational carries with it a number of implications because of Luther's understanding of incarnation. The most important implication is that, when the Bible speaks of the Spirit as over against the flesh, this cannot mean the Spirit over against the body. Since Christ came to reveal God in a body, it is clear that the bodily can serve as the means by which the spiritual—meaning the things of God—is

how could one make any sense of John 6 as a whole if Zwingli's exegesis were to be preferred? For if the flesh is of no avail in Zwingli's sense, what is the point of the incarnation, upon which Jesus insists so strongly in that chapter? "For if the flesh is not present in the sacrament because the flesh is of no avail, neither is it in his mother's womb, precisely for the same reason that it is of no avail."[66] Indeed, the whole economy of salvation is endangered by such a reading:

> If the flesh of Christ is not spirit, and therefore is of no avail since only the Spirit is profitable, how can it be profitable when it was given for us? How can it be useful if it is in heaven and we believe in it? If the reasoning is correct and adequate, that because Christ's flesh is not spirit it must be of no avail, then it can be of no avail on the cross or in heaven either! For it is quite as far from being spirit on the cross and in heaven as in the Supper. But since no spirit was crucified for us, therefore Christ's flesh was crucified for us to no avail. And since no spirit, but Christ's flesh ascended into heaven, we believe in an unprofitable flesh in heaven. For wherever Christ's flesh may be, it is no spirit. If it is no spirit, it is of no avail and does not give life, as Zwingli here concludes.[67]

David Steinmetz suggests that "when Zwingli . . . protested against Roman Catholic and Lutheran doctrines of the Eucharist by citing John 6:63, he took hold of a sword that cuts both ways."[68] Even preaching is an act of the flesh! According to Steinmetz, Luther's protest against Zwingli's exegesis is important because the logical conclusion of Zwingli's rejection of flesh "is to leave the Christian nothing but mental prayer and wordless contemplation."[69] But Christianity is a religion of the flesh.

---

revealed. The spiritual has to do with the execution of God's will; the flesh is the totality of sinful impulses that turn one away from God's will to one's own selfish will. Thus, flesh and spirit have to do with one's basic disposition in life, not with materiality and nonmateriality. In Luther's understanding, the incarnation means that God's Word truly is a concrete, visible, bodily word.

66. Cf. *That These Words of Christ* (1527), in *LW* 37:82. Luther expounds on this theme at length, pp. 82–89.

67. *Confession concerning Christ's Supper* (1528), in *LW* 37:246–47. Zwingli, of course, disagreed with Luther's assessment, insisting that "the flesh of Christ profiteth very greatly, aye, immeasurably, in every way but . . . by being slain, not eaten. Slain it has saved us from slaughter, but devoured it profiteth absolutely nothing." "Commentary on True and False Religion," in *The Latin Works of Huldreich Zwingli*, ed. Clarence Nevin Heller (Philadelphia: Heidelberg Press, 1929), 3:209. Quoted in Hendel, "Finitum Capax Infiniti," 423n11. Of course, as Zwingli conceived of eating Christ's flesh—i.e., cannibalistically—both Luther and Thomas would have to agree that it would indeed profit nothing. But they would also insist that Christ is not eaten cannibalistically in the sacrament and so Zwingli's objection is irrelevant.

68. Steinmetz, "Scripture and the Lord's Supper in Luther's Theology," 263.

69. Steinmetz, "Scripture and the Lord's Supper in Luther's Theology," 264.

Given their exegetical differences over such christologically dense texts as John 6, it will come as no surprise that Luther and Zwingli operated from quite divergent Christologies and that these divergences would seriously impact their theology of the Eucharist.[70] Indeed, Zwingli's conviction that Christ's presence in the elements was impossible was consistent with his understanding of the resurrection and ascension that had, for him, removed Christ's body from the world.[71] Christ could not be present in the Eucharist because he was present at the right hand of the Father. Luther's Christology, on the other hand, was utterly incarnational. God had irrevocably joined humankind, and material creation in general, in the incarnation.[72] The presence of God in Christ, and therefore Jesus's presence in creation, was the foundation of our salvation, and Luther would not suffer it to be removed.[73] For Luther, the ascension to God's right hand did not remove Christ from creation, but joined him to the power that is omnipresent in creation.[74]

These differing christological emphases can be traced to the patristic debates about the relationship between Christ's human and divine natures:

The Alexandrian theologians emphasized the unity of the person of Christ, whereas the Antiochene theologians emphasized the distinction between the natures. This same difference in emphasis is evident in the Reformation controversies over the Lord's Supper. Luther holds to the Alexandrian Christology, which stresses the unity of the person of Christ, whereas Zwingli emphasizes the distinction of natures. The Alexandrian theologians held that the attributes of each nature are communicated to the other nature because of the unity of the person of Christ. Luther takes up this position and develops it in his own way. What it means for Luther in relation to the doctrine of the real presence is

70. Mickey Mattox is attentive to the connections between Christology and eucharistic theology in "Sacraments in the Lutheran Reformation," in *The Oxford Handbook of Sacramental Theology*, ed. Hans Boersma and Matthew Levering (Oxford: Oxford University Press, 2015), esp. 279–80.

71. Jones, *Christ's Eucharistic Presence*, 127.

72. Hendel, "Finitum Capax Infiniti," 430: "In responding to the Swiss assertion that the flesh is of no avail and that it would be inconsistent with Christ's glory to be present in bread and wine, Luther formulated a theology of creation and incarnation which affirms matter as God's good creation, which emphasizes God's immanent presence in all created things and which maintains that God accomplishes God's saving work precisely through material means. The Reformer thus clearly differentiated himself from his sacramental opponents by insisting that the finite is capable of holding the infinite, *finitum est capax infiniti.*" Norman Nagel qualifies this statement, writing, "It is not that the finite is capable of containing the infinite, but that the infinite is capable of placing itself in the finite." Nagel, "The Incarnation and the Lord's Supper in Luther," *Concordia Theological Monthly* 24, no. 9 (September 1953): 642.

73. Nagel, "The Incarnation and the Lord's Supper in Luther," 640. See also *Confession concerning Christ's Supper* (1528), in *LW* 37:218–19.

74. *That These Words of Christ* (1527), in *LW* 37:57.

that the attribute of "omnipresence" or "ubiquity" (i.e., the capacity to be in many places [*ubique* = everywhere] at once) that belongs to the divine nature of Christ is communicated to the human nature of Christ. This means that the human nature of Christ is not confined to a physical space "at the right hand of God," but can dwell in many hearts and can be present in many places in the sacrament of the altar. Zwingli, and the Swiss theologians generally, held that since Christ is ascended into heaven, his human nature is in heaven and cannot be present in the sacrament. The body of Christ remains in heaven, and cannot, therefore, also be in the bread. This presupposes a Christology in which the divine attribute of ubiquity is not communicated to the human nature because of the distinction of the natures in Christ.[75]

Depending on whether the distinction between Christ's two natures (Zwingli) or the unity of Christ's person (Luther) is emphasized, resurrection and ascension end up with diametrically opposed implications for eucharistic presence. They become either the end of Christ's bodily relationship with history, or the foundation for its continuation. To Zwingli, "the ascension means that the humanity of Christ is no longer accessible to me in my space and time," while for Luther,

> Christ does not go away. He remains in our space and time. What changes in the ascension is not the fact of Christ's presence but solely the mode of that presence. . . . The ascension does not point to the absence of the humanity of Christ at the right hand of God. Rather it celebrates the ubiquitous presence of the God-man, Jesus Christ, and the universal accessibility of that saving presence through preaching and the sacraments.[76]

It is interesting to note that Luther's view on the ascension was not, by his own description, literal.[77] At Marburg he had asked Zwingli, "Should one not rather assume a trope in the sentence 'He ascended into heaven' and leave the text of the Lord's Supper as it is? For figurative speech could much more conveniently be found in the word 'heaven' which, as is generally acknowledged, in Scripture is used in various meanings."[78] While Luther took the words of institution literally, it was Zwingli who took the ascension to

75. Crockett, *Eucharist*, 141–42. Cf. Craycraft, "Sign and Word," 163.

76. Steinmetz, "Scripture and the Lord's Supper in Luther's Theology," 262.

77. Cf. Gerrish, "Discerning the Body," 61: "More exactly, the only sign Luther has discovered is not the sacrament but the ascension. To say that Christ has gone up to heaven and sits at the right hand of God means that he is above all creatures—and in all and beyond all." Gerrish then quotes *LW* 36:342: "That he was taken up bodily, however, occurred as a sign of this."

78. Hermann Sasse, *This Is My Body: Luther's Contention for the Real Presence in the Sacrament of the Altar* (Minneapolis: Augsburg, 1959), 249.

the right hand of the Father literally.[79] According to Luther, "The Scriptures teach us, however, that the right hand of God is not a specific place in which a body must or may be, such as on a golden throne, but is the almighty power of God, which at one and the same time can be nowhere and yet must be everywhere."[80] Luther and Zwingli were agreed about one thing, however: it was not possible to accept both a literal ascension and a literal institution of the Supper. For both men, these two ideas were mutually exclusive, and the issue became how to determine which to take literally and which to take figuratively.

Luther's question to Zwingli at Marburg highlighted his own way of resolving that difficulty. Scripture itself, insists Luther, teaches that the ascension is figurative. As Paul Hinlicky observes, for Luther, "it cannot be decided *a priori* on the basis of the notion that 'to be' is a metaphor meaning 'to signify.' For one could [appeal to] this principle just as easily to insist that the statement, 'Christ is at the right hand of God,' is symbolic or metaphorical."[81] Rather, it must be decided on the basis of the scriptural text. The question must be, "Which idea does Scripture present as metaphorical?" One wonders, however, whether the dichotomy between Luther and Zwingli here is not a false one. Is it, in fact, necessary to insist that only one of the ascension and the institution can be taken literally? Is there no way to affirm the realism of both the ascension and the Eucharist? And would not such an articulation be ecumenically desirable? According to Thomas Davis,

> Looking back, people might think that Luther or Zwingli, for example, were miles apart on the question of Christ's presence in the Eucharist. But in at least one regard they absolutely agreed: the word "is" in the phrase "This is my body" could have only one meaning. This style of thinking carried over into their other disagreements as well: language was flattened out into a linear one-to-one correspondence between sign (and words are signs) and thing. Even if Luther thought something should be understood allegorically, for example, there was only one proper allegorical interpretation: all others were false. Perhaps it is helpful to know that, instead of being peculiar to these particular theological discussions among these theologians, this way of viewing language and signs was part of a larger cultural shift, one that required, in a sense, a literal reading of signs in order for that reading to be considered authoritative. There was, in other words, a *push* toward the literal in the world of the sixteenth century.[82]

79. Jones, *Christ's Eucharistic Presence*, 130.
80. *That These Words of Christ* (1527), in *LW* 37:57.
81. Hinlicky, "Christ's Bodily Presence in the Holy Supper—Real or Symbolic?," 26.
82. Davis, *This Is My Body*, 16–17.

To take something literally, then, was to strip it of all other meaning. That is why Luther and Zwingli could not imagine taking both eucharistic presence and the ascension "literally." If Christ was "literally" in one place, he could not be "literally" in any other. In such a flattened picture, "presence" can mean only one thing. It is not possible to be present in different modes in different places. Christ is either in heaven, and therefore not in the bread, or everywhere, and therefore in the bread as well. A more layered reading would avoid such an impasse and allow Christ's ascension and eucharistic presence to be taken "literally."[83] As Ratzinger writes about Luther and Calvin (who was in basic agreement with Zwingli about the ascension, if not all of its implications),

> Our reflections thus far, however, lead also now to the correction of Calvin's local understanding of the Lord's being [in heaven], just as on the other hand we can preserve the element that correctly kept him back from a simple agreement with Luther's ubiquity doctrine. So we will now say that certainly no natural ubiquity is to be attributed to Christ, and on this point Calvin is right as opposed to Luther. But no local limitation to an imaginary heavenly place should be attributed to him either. Nowhere does the Risen One have a physically restricted place that can be designated. As the Risen One, he has entered into a new mode of existence and participates in God's might, by virtue of which he can give himself to his own whenever and wherever he wishes.[84]

And, of course, in another time, under another metaphysics, or perhaps another semiotics, Thomas Aquinas had no qualms about affirming both a "literal" ascension and eucharistic presence.[85]

Replacing Transubstantiation

Just as Luther's incarnational emphasis had contributed to his rejection of transubstantiation, because in his reading consistency with the incarnation

---

83. For a very instructive analysis of the language used to describe eucharistic presence, see Hunsinger's excellent subsection "Mode of Rhetoric" in *Eucharist and Ecumenism*, 52–64, esp. 59: "Because the term 'literal' is essentially a rhetorical category entangled in a very problematic semantics, it would probably be better to leave it to one side. Matters that are already very difficult are only hopelessly obscured if one discussion partner claims to have a 'literal' view of 'real presence' which is supposedly superior for that reason to the views of others."

84. Benedict XVI, "Problem of Transubstantiation," 240.

85. Hunsinger, *Eucharist and Ecumenism*, 23: "Aquinas was able to accomplish something that neither Luther nor Calvin ever quite managed. He was able to hold together, convincingly, a robust definition of 'real presence' with an equally robust definition of 'local presence' [in heaven]. He was able, that is, to satisfy two conditions that are indispensable for any proposal that would hope to resolve eucharistic conflicts."

mandates that the (substances of) bread and wine remain, it now provided a basis for his argument against the Swiss that real presence is, in fact, possible. Christ's body, an essential aspect of his human nature, is now available in the hearts of the faithful and in the sacrament because it has been joined to his divinity, which is present in all creation, by the incarnation, and seated at God's right hand, which indicates God's power over all creation, in the ascension.[86] What had started as an analogy between the Eucharist and the incarnation, in Luther's earlier work rejecting transubstantiation, was expanded into an explanation of the possibility of eucharistic presence in his later polemics against the Swiss.[87] Several scholars have noted that this explanation is functionally equivalent to (the invocation of substance in) the doctrine of transubstantiation.[88] And, it is essential to keep in mind, this equivalence extends to the fact that neither Luther nor Thomas is giving an explanation of how eucharistic presence occurs; they agree that the answer to that is simply, "By the word of Christ." (Indeed, both Luther and Thomas make the explicit link between the power of Christ's words to effect his eucharistic presence and the words of creation.)[89] Instead, they are giving an explanation in the sense of demonstrating that the claim is both possible and meaningful.

Recall, now, that Luther's theological development here mirrors the history of Western eucharistic theology in the centuries preceding him. Faced with the claim that real presence is incoherent (or, if coherent, objectionable

---

86. It is difficult to determine the precise relationship Luther saw between the incarnation and the ascension in grounding Christ's omnipresence. On the one hand, the communication of attributes, which means, for Luther, that Christ's humanity (including his body) is present wherever God is present, is a function of the incarnation (*This Is My Body* [1527], in *LW* 37:66; Stephenson, *Lord's Supper*, 253n32). On the other hand, in his debates with Zwingli about the ascension, Luther argued that God's right hand, to which Christ had ascended, was a figural way of saying "everywhere" (see above, pp. 157–58; *That These Words of Christ* [1527], in *LW* 37:57).

87. Heron, *Table and Tradition*, 112, 118.

88. Alasdair Heron argues that Luther's explanation, though differing in detail from transubstantiation, "is strikingly similar in pattern and end-result, the divine omnipresence playing the role which non-spatial *substantia* fulfilled in Aquinas' account" (*Table and Tradition*, 118). See also Lehmann and Pannenberg, *Condemnations of the Reformation Era*, 98; Jones, *Christ's Eucharistic Presence*, 130.

89. See above, pp. 128–29, for Thomas. Cf. *ST* III, 78.5 corpus; see also *Confession concerning Christ's Supper* (1528), in *LW* 37:181:

But if they [the words of institution] are true words, then we confidently reply: Even the fanatical spirit [i.e., Zwingli] must acknowledge that Christ gave his body in the Supper. For they are action-words which Christ spoke at the first administration, and he did not lie, when he said "Take, eat, this is my body," just as the sun and moon came to be when he said, Genesis 1[:14], "Let there be a sun and moon," and it was no lying word. So his word surely is not merely a word of imitation, but a word of power which accomplishes what it expresses, Psalm 33[:9], "He spoke, and it came to be," especially because it was first spoken here, and was meant to be an action-word.

and disgusting) and impossible, Luther turns to philosophy, in his case the nominalist (and specifically Ockhamist) philosophy in which he was trained, to demonstrate its possibility. It will be important to look at his explanation in some detail in order to see how it relates to Thomas's articulation of transubstantiation.

Luther's Philosophy

In order to demonstrate the possibility of Christ's presence in the elements of the Eucharist, Luther combines his Alexandrian Christology, which emphasizes the unity of Christ's person—so that where his divinity is, so is his humanity, including his body[90]—with the nominalist articulation of different possible modes of presence.[91] It is important, however, to recognize that Luther does not borrow from nominalism whole cloth, so to speak. Besides certain subtle differences in his understanding of the various modes of presence, Luther also differs from his nominalist predecessors in his basic attitude toward the relationship of philosophy to theology.[92]

While Luther is using philosophy to simply try to demonstrate that eucharistic presence is not impossible to those who would assert otherwise, the nominalists were discussing eucharistic presence at a time when all affirmed it and used philosophy to try to understand it more precisely.[93] In this, Luther is again closer to Thomas Aquinas than to late nominalism. Though Thomas had a more positive view of the role of philosophy in theology than Luther, his articulation of transubstantiation was more about showing that the claim of real presence is coherent than in nailing down precisely what kind of presence it is. In fact, as we have seen, Aquinas's articulations are of the negative variety, and in this he is followed by the Council of Trent: sacramental presence is unique. The change that leads to such presence is called by a name all its own. It is not like any other presence that we know or experience. Thomas says much more about what the presence is not than he says about what it is.[94] What John Stephenson says about Luther's approach applies equally well to Thomas: both men use philosophy to distinguish "the presence proclaimed in the words of institution from certain caricatures or spurious substitutes thereof."[95]

---

90. See Osborne, "Faith, Philosophy, and the Nominalist Background," 70.
91. See *Confession concerning Christ's Supper* (1528), in *LW* 37:215–23.
92. Osborne, "Faith, Philosophy, and the Nominalist Background," 76.
93. Osborne, "Faith, Philosophy, and the Nominalist Background," 81.
94. See above, p. 92, on *via negativa*.
95. Stephenson, *Lord's Supper*, 248.

While Luther was closer to Thomas in his intention, he was, nevertheless, closer to the nominalists in his articulation. Thomas was aware of the various modes of presence—circumscriptive, definitive, and repletive—later taken up by the nominalists and Luther, and he denied that Christ was present in the Eucharist circumscriptively or definitively:

> According to Thomas, circumscriptive presence is the presence whereby an ordinary body is in a place, and definitive presence describes how a body which itself does not have extension can be said to be present at a particular location. Since an angel does not have a body, it cannot be present anywhere circumscriptively, although it can be present definitively when it acts on a body which is present circumscriptively. According to Thomas, Christ's body is present neither circumscriptively nor definitively in the Eucharist, since it is only circumscriptively present in heaven.[96]

The nominalists, while agreeing with Thomas that Christ was circumscriptively present only in heaven, disagree with Thomas about the *possibility* of two bodies being circumscriptively present in the same place. While, for Thomas, bread and wine cannot be in the same place as Christ's body and blood in the exact same way as Christ's body and blood[97] (transubstantiation—saying that the accidents of bread coexist with the substance of Christ's body—is a way of saying that two things can exist in the same place if they exist there in different ways), for the nominalists two things can be in the same place in the same way not naturally, but, as always, by God's power.[98]

Though the nominalists did not believe Christ was circumscriptively present in the Eucharist, due to his presence in heaven, they did affirm his presence definitively. The problem with such an assertion, from Thomas's perspective at least, is that Christ's body does have extension and parts and thus *is not the kind of thing that can be present definitively*, since that is the manner of presence for things without extension, like angels or souls.[99] The reader will not be surprised

---

96. Osborne, "Faith, Philosophy, and the Nominalist Background," 76. I assume that Osborne has merely slipped in his terminology when he asserts that a body without extension and an angel (which does not have a body) are both the subjects of definitive presence. Whatever the case, his basic point remains.

97. Cf. Benedict XVI, "Problem of Transubstantiation," 237–38.

98. Osborne, "Faith, Philosophy, and the Nominalist Background," 77. See above, pp. 47–48.

99. As Osborne notes, "The oddity of the Nominalist position on the Eucharist is the belief that a body which does have parts, namely Christ's body, can be present in a location without its parts being distinct from each other. In the Eucharist Christ's foot and his eye are both present even though they are not spatially distinct from each other. It is even possible that Christ uses his eye in the Eucharist to see his surroundings" ("Faith, Philosophy, and the Nominalist Background," 77). This is a significant difference from Thomas's affirmation that Christ's body parts

at the nominalist response here: if God can make two bodies circumscriptively present in the same place, he can surely override the problem of extension by doing the same with different parts of the same body![100] Definitive presence has become, in such an articulation, not the kind of presence attributed to nonbodily, nonextended things, but simply a disguised circumscriptive presence. In other words, it is exactly the kind of presence Thomas rejected in his rejection of consubstantiation, a presence conceived of merely as a solution to a logic puzzle, and a presence that takes no account of its sacramental context.[101]

While it must be admitted that Luther inherited some of the weaknesses of this articulation—his own articulation can also lose its grip on the sacramental as we shall see when we look at signs and signification—he cannot be indicted in the same way as the nominalists for the simple reason that his use of philosophy was always consciously and explicitly subordinated to revelation. While the nominalists got caught up in the *how* of real presence, thereby losing sight of the mystery, Luther was always simply concerned with the *that*. Luther repeatedly asserts, throughout his discussions on the nature of Christ's presence, that he is only attempting to show that it is not nonsense to affirm a presence different from the circumscriptive presence with which the Swiss take issue.[102] When the philosophy he inherits leads to unwelcome conclusions or misunderstandings by his opponents, he explicitly distances himself from such conclusions.[103]

For Luther, circumscriptive presence is when "the space and the object occupying it exactly correspond and fit into the same measurements." It is what Thomas rejected when he rejected "local" presence, and Luther rejects it as well. Definitive presence, in Luther's articulation, occurs when "the object or body is not palpably in one place and is not measurable according to the dimensions of the place where it is, but can occupy either more room or less."[104] This is the way in which Luther *suggests* (i.e., he does not insist on this) that Christ is present in the Eucharist. It is important to note that Luther's understanding of "definitive" is not Thomas's. For Thomas, definitive presence applies to things without extension. It describes how we can say that things like angels or souls are present. For Luther, like his nominalist teachers, it has become more like a disguised circumscriptive presence. So,

---

are present by concomitance, i.e., because they are included in what is effectively symbolized. The sacramental logic of concomitance does not lead to the suggestion that Christ's parts are operative in the eucharistic species as if naturally present. Cf. pp. 110–12 above.

100. Osborne, "Faith, Philosophy, and the Nominalist Background," 78.

101. See above, pp. 93–94.

102. E.g., *Confession concerning Christ's Supper* (1528), in *LW* 37:214–19.

103. See, e.g., *Brief Confession concerning the Holy Sacrament* (1544), in *LW* 38:301.

104. *Confession concerning Christ's Supper* (1528), in *LW* 37:215.

for example, definitive presence is the kind of presence ascribed to Christ as he passed through the rock sealing the tomb (though the biblical witness says the rock was rolled away, not that Christ passed through it!), or the door into the upper room, or even as he was born of a virgin.[105]

The pictures such examples conjure up, of one circumscriptive presence superimposed on another, are partly responsible for the Swiss conviction that Luther really did believe in a circumscriptive or local presence, even though he himself denied it. Luther knew that Christ was not present in a local manner, but he did not have the philosophical tools to make this case convincingly, since the nominalist heritage from which he learned his philosophy had not been satisfied with a sacramental presence and consequently articulated a basically local and circumscriptive presence, however clandestine, under a different name. The Swiss, for their part, agreed with the nominalists that any presence that could be called "real" was somehow local, if covertly so for the nominalists, the difference being that what the nominalists accepted, the Swiss rejected.

Nevertheless, it is important to recognize that Luther's rejection of circumscriptive presence and affirmation of definitive presence parallels Thomas's distinction between accidents and substance in transubstantiation, at least in intention. Both articulations recognize that the bread is present in one way and Christ's body is present in a different way that is not in direct competition with the bread. Presence according to the accident of quantity *is* local presence, which *is* circumscriptive presence. Both men reject such presence. Presence according to substance, *per modum substantiae*, though not exactly definitive presence, shares important features with it. According to Thomas, definitive presence is the proper way of talking about the presence of things that do not have extension. Since Christ's body does have extension, it is not present definitively for Thomas. On the other hand, the substance of Christ's body does not have extension per se, but only through its proper accidents, and so presence *per modum substantiae* is not completely unlike Thomas's idea of definitive presence. For Luther, definitive presence includes the presence of things with extension, like Christ's body and, though this makes it too close to circumscriptive presence for his opponents, his intention is obviously exactly the same as Thomas's presence *per modum substantiae*—namely, to affirm a real presence that is not crudely local, but that is nonetheless intimately related to the elements of bread and wine themselves.[106]

---

105. *Confession concerning Christ's Supper* (1528), in *LW* 37:216, 221–23. Cf. Osborne, "Faith, Philosophy, and the Nominalist Background," 74.

106. Cf. Jones, *Christ's Eucharistic Presence*, 132: "Christ's body can be present in the bread in an uncircumscribed manner and the bread can be present in a circumscribed manner." While

And, even if in certain articulations Luther's understanding of definitive presence was difficult to distinguish from a clandestine circumscriptive presence, it is important to understand that Luther complemented his nominalist ideas about definitive presence with his belief in Christ's omnipresence, called repletive presence in the nominalist scheme. A year before Luther appealed to the nominalist distinctions between circumscriptive and definitive presence in the *Confession concerning Christ's Supper*, he had written about Christ's presence in the supper in relation to his ubiquity as the God-man in *That These Words of Christ, "This Is My Body" etc., Still Stand Firm against the Fanatics*. It is sometimes assumed in the public imagination, and even by certain theologians,[107] that Luther taught that Christ was present in the Eucharist by the mere fact of his ubiquity. It is more accurate to say that Luther believed Christ's omnipresence made his eucharistic presence possible.[108] In other words, Christ's eucharistic presence is not simply one more instance of his ubiquity, but is, rather, a presence specific to the sacrament. While not yet articulating it as "definitive" in this earlier work, Luther notes that Christ's presence in the door or the gravestone was not simply a function of his ubiquity.[109] And Christ does not pass through a door in the same sense in which he is already in the door in any case!

The question arises, however, of how we are to understand a presence that is based on Christ's ubiquity but is not simply a function of it. What distinguishes Christ's presence in *this* bread from Christ's presence in any of the other food I consume? Luther's response here helps us to see not only the difference between Christ's omnipresence as the God-man and his eucharistic presence, but it also shows that his ideas about definitive presence must not be taken to equate Christ's presence in the Supper with Christ's presence in the door. There is a difference for Luther between nominalist definitive presence and what we might call, following Stephenson, "sacramental definitive presence."[110] Indeed, when Luther says that Christ is present in the words of the preacher in the same way that he is present in the Supper,[111] this also

---

Jones suggests that this distinction allows Luther to avoid transubstantiation, the fact is that he only manages to avoid it by replicating its most basic feature.

107. Stephenson, *Lord's Supper*, 251, believes this process began already with Melanchthon and accuses Robert Jenson of the same mistake. Ratzinger too gives this impression of Luther. Benedict XVI, "Problem of Transubstantiation," 230.

108. Stephenson writes, "From the matrix of His bodily repletive presence . . . the almighty God-man gives Himself into His sacramental definitive presence" (*Lord's Supper*, 253).

109. Osborne, "Faith, Philosophy, and the Nominalist Background," 71. Cf. *This Is My Body* (1527), in *LW* 37:66.

110. Stephenson, *Lord's Supper*, 253. While this happy phrase is Stephenson's, the reflections on it that follow are my own.

111. *The Adoration of the Sacrament* (1523), in *LW* 36:278; *The Sacrament of the Body and Blood of Christ—Against the Fanatics* (1526), in *LW* 36:348. Cf. Hunsinger, *Eucharist and Ecumenism*, 33.

mitigates against an understanding that Christ is present in the bread as he is present in the door. How could one be present in words in the same way one is present in a door? The inadequate image of one circumscriptive presence superimposed on another does not appear here. When Luther compares Christ's eucharistic presence to both his definitive presence in a door *and* to his presence in the words of the preacher, are we not justified in concluding that his ideas are more properly sacramental than his inherited philosophical categories allowed him to express?

"For You"

Indeed, Luther's answer to the question "What is the difference between Christ's presence in this bread and Christ's presence in every piece of bread?" is not unlike a subtle distinction made by Thomas Aquinas to guarantee the sacramental character of transubstantiation. For Luther, the key distinction is that, according to the words of institution, Christ is present in the Eucharist "for you." "It is one thing if God is present," writes Luther, "and another if he is present for you."[112] And so, while Christ is present in your cabbage and your soup, he is not present there in the same way he is present in the sacrament:

> So too, since Christ's humanity is at the right hand of God, and also in all and above all things according to the nature of the divine right hand, you will not eat or drink him like the cabbage and soup on your table unless he wills it.[113] He also now exceeds any grasp, and you will not catch him by groping about, even though he is in your bread, unless he binds himself to you and summons you to a particular table by his Word, bidding you to eat him.[114]

Christ's word does not, however, merely announce a presence that preexisted the proclamation. It is not a matter of merely being informed that you are eating Christ, whereas before you simply ate Christ in ignorance.[115] Rather,

---

112. *That These Words of Christ* (1527), in *LW* 37:68.

113. This is an example of the careless terminology that sometimes confused Luther's opponents. Of course, Luther does not believe that, even when Christ does will to be eaten in the sacrament, that he is eaten therein "like the cabbage and the soup on your table." In fact, he explicitly states otherwise. See *That These Words of Christ* (1527), in *LW* 37:100.

114. *That These Words of Christ* (1527), in *LW* 37:69.

115. Grislis, "Manner of Christ's Eucharistic Presence according to Martin Luther," 10n20; Gerrish, "Discerning the Body," 60. On this point, Ratzinger seems to oversimplify Luther's position when he writes that, for Luther, "the word of institution teaches us to seek and find in a particular piece of bread the Christ-Body which in and of itself is present everywhere and therefore also in *every* piece of bread" ("Problem of Transubstantiation," 230). On the other hand, Ratzinger says something quite similar later in the same article when he writes, "The potential that in principle lies hidden in all creatures—the fact that they can and should be sign

Christ's word of promise actually *determines* the kind of presence available to the communicant. According to Egil Grislis, for Luther "the words of institution not only announce but also effect the Eucharistic presence."[116] Grislis then cites the sage advice of Karl Rahner that serves as a helpful rule of thumb for navigating Luther's often imprecise and inconsistent articulations:

> Luther's effort to bring in the doctrine of ubiquity to explain the real presence of the body of Christ is a theological after-thought, which should not be used as the invariable starting-point to explain and restrict the view which Luther wished to have maintained with regard to the sacrament, *because the explanation should be brought into line with what is to be explained, and not vice versa.*[117]

In other words, if Luther did not mean, by his doctrine of ubiquity, to make Christ's sacramental presence just one more example of Christ's omnipresence, we are not justified in drawing that conclusion from it, even if he is not always careful and consistent in his formulation.

Rather, as we have seen, Luther meant to highlight a presence that was uniquely sacramental. His use of different comparisons and illustrations (remember the door and the preached word) was not intended to precisely articulate Christ's presence, but merely to show that it is not impossible or absurd to talk about a real presence that is not a circumscriptive presence. In this context, Luther's emphasis on the "for you" of the words of institution has an irreplaceable role. It is irreplaceable not only because it distinguishes repletive presence from definitive presence, but because it also distinguishes definitive presence in general from what we have called sacramental definitive presence. And, in this respect, it functions much like Thomas Aquinas's suggestion that transubstantiation is a matter of "taking away what kept this from being that."[118]

Omnipresence?

Recall how, in Thomas's metaphysics, the biblical doctrine of creation had forced a total reimagining of Aristotle's hylomorphism. Thomas could not be

---

of His Presence—becomes here through the sacramental word a reality in the highest degree" (237). Ratzinger is at least partially justified, however, because Luther's articulation tends to ignore the sign value of the sacrament (as we shall see below) and consequently makes the presence grounded in ubiquity less than fully sacramental.

116. Grislis, "Manner of Christ's Eucharistic Presence according to Martin Luther," 10n20. See also, in this regard, Stephenson (*Lord's Supper*, 97), who highlights the validity of the idea of "change" in the Lutheran understanding of the consecration.

117. Rahner, "Presence of Christ in the Sacrament of the Lord's Supper," 295 (emphasis added).

118. *ST* III, 75.4 ad 3. See above, pp. 99–100.

content with an understanding of things as matter taking first this form, then that form. Rather, because the universe is not eternal, but created, Thomas insisted that at the root of every creature was its act of existence given by God. In this way we saw that, for Thomas, "God is in all things, and innermostly."[119] Compare this with Luther, who wrote that

> God is no such extended, long, broad, thick, high, deep being. He is a super-natural, inscrutable being who exists at the same time in every little seed, whole and entire, and yet also in all and above all and outside all created things. . . . Nothing is so small but God is still smaller, nothing is so large but God is still larger, nothing is so short but God is still shorter, nothing so long but God is still longer, nothing so narrow but God is still narrower, and so on. He is inexpressible being above and beyond all that can be described or imagined.[120]

The doctrine of transubstantiation in Thomas Aquinas is, therefore, also dependent on a sense of God's omnipresence, even if that omnipresence is not articulated in the same way as in Luther. For Luther, omnipresence is a function of the incarnation and ascension,[121] and therefore more directly linked to Christ's body; for Thomas it is a function of creation and is linked with Christ's body because of God's capacity as creator to determine the nature of reality by the Word which is incarnate in Christ.[122] So, for example, Aquinas's affirmation of Christ's local presence in heaven is inconsistent with Luther's figurative interpretation of the ascension. It should be noted, however, that Thomas does not naïvely picture Christ sitting on a "golden throne." Rather, a realistic interpretation of the ascension implies, for Aquinas and for the Catholic tradition following him, that Christ's presence in the world must now be a function of transcendence and not of immanence, as it had been during his earthly life and ministry. In this affirmation, it is not as different as it might at first glance appear from Luther's view, as described, for instance, by David Steinmetz: "God is near; that is his immanence. God's presence is

---

119. See above, p. 49.
120. *Confession concerning Christ's Supper* (1528), in LW 37:228.
121. See above, p. 161n86.
122. The Catholic view, on the other hand, also features accents from both incarnation and ascension. For Thomas, the possibility of eucharistic presence is grounded in the fact that the Word that became flesh in Christ is the Word through which God created the universe. (See above, pp. 99–100.) On the other hand, contemporary Catholic commentators like Martelet and Ratzinger highlight the necessity of Christ's ascension in his capacity to give himself wherever he pleases. (See, e.g., Benedict XVI, "Problem of Transubstantiation," 240; Martelet, *The Risen Christ and the Eucharistic World*, esp. part 3, "Resurrection of Christ and Eucharist.")

inaccessible apart from his Word and sacraments; that is his transcendence."[123] For both Luther and the Catholic tradition, the ascension means that Christ's relationship to creation continues in a new mode centered in the ministry of the Church, the ministry of word and sacrament.

For Thomas, transubstantiation by "taking away" is a revelation of God's presence at the heart of creation. The signs of bread and wine lose their independent existence and now exist purely as signs of God's presence.[124] But this constitutes a real—though not physical, material, local, or circumscriptive—change in the elements. Christ's mode of presence through the sacramental signs is not simply the mode of presence of God in creation now revealed by the words of institution. It is a new mode, proper to the sacrament. Because it prefigures the eschatological future of all creation, it cannot simply reveal creation's present status. The already cannot be equated with the not-yet. God is omnipresent, but not yet omnipresent in the way in which God will be "all in all" at the consummation of history. Transubstantiation too is based on God's presence in all of creation, and on Christ's participation in that presence, but it is not simply the revelation of what already is. There is a genuine change, and not merely an announcement of God's preexisting presence, that makes the elements a revelation of what is still to come.

But in this do we not see an important parallel with Luther's emphasis on the "for you" of the words of institution? When Christ designates *this* bread as his body, he does not merely identify his repletive presence, but rather determines his sacramental definitive presence. For both Thomas and Luther, Christ's presence in the eucharistic elements depends on a kind of omnipresence but cannot be simply identified with that omnipresence. And so John Stephenson, the contemporary Lutheran theologian of the Eucharist, can favorably quote Matthias Scheeben, the eminent nineteenth-century German Catholic theologian, who wrote concerning transubstantiation,

> Yet by the very fact that it [the body of Christ] serves as the instrument of an exclusively divine operation it shares in the omnipresence of God. . . . Accordingly, is it not once again clear that Christ's sacramental mode of existence is utterly supernatural, seeing that it is a participation in a mode of existence proper to a higher substance, indeed the very highest, the divine substance?[125]

123. Steinmetz, "Scripture and the Lord's Supper in Luther's Theology," 264; cf. Davis, *This Is My Body*, 60.
124. Benedict XVI, "Problem of Transubstantiation," 236–37.
125. Matthias Joseph Scheeben, *The Mysteries of Christianity*, trans. Cyril O. Vollert (St. Louis: Herder, 1946), 474. Quoted in Stephenson, *Lord's Supper*, 253n32. Stephenson has other issues with Scheeben, however. He writes that Scheeben "betrays a defective grasp of the historical data by alleging that Lutheran confession of the communicated omnipresence arose

And Ratzinger can claim that, while "certainly no natural ubiquity is to be attributed to Christ,"[126] there is "a correct intention hidden in the ubiquity doctrine. . . : The Lord, who as the Risen One has overcome the limit of historical existence, can impart himself when and where he wishes."[127]

Signs, Signification, and the Persistence of Bread and Wine

We have demonstrated, it is hoped, that, in his debate with the Swiss about Christ's presence with the Eucharist, Luther staked out positions on the relationship between faith and reason and on the meaning and possibility of real presence that are compatible with Thomas Aquinas's articulation of transubstantiation, if in a different philosophic register. The final issue between Luther and the Swiss, that of the role of signs and signification in the Eucharist, is, however, more complicated. Luther's affirmation of the continued presence of the (substances of) bread and wine made it, ironically, more difficult for him to affirm their legitimate significatory role in the Eucharist.[128] Faced with the Swiss insistence that the bread and wine were mere signs, Luther awkwardly responded that they were not signs at all![129] We have already seen that Luther's articulations of real presence were sometimes difficult to distinguish from circumscriptive presence. Had he been able to refute the Swiss view of the elements as mere signs without rejecting their value as signs altogether, Luther would have been less often misunderstood on this count. Furthermore, clarity about signs and signification could have helped resolve the christological impasse. By maintaining the significatory role of the bread and wine, Thomas

from an unwillingness to [admit] any objective efficacy at all in the words of consecration," and cites *The Mysteries of Christianity*, 476. That Scheeben is mistaken is good news for ecumenical dialogue. Omnipresence isn't to be opposed to change at the consecration but is, rather, the ground of possibility for such change.

126. Benedict XVI, "Problem of Transubstantiation," 240.

127. Benedict XVI, "Problem of Transubstantiation," 239.

128. On this, see Colwell, *Promise and Presence*, 166: "Moreover, this maintaining of the terminology of 'substance,' while rigorously avoiding the Aristotelian distinction between 'substance' and 'accidents,' only serves to confuse that which the doctrine of transubstantiation was seeking to clarify. Luther's formula not only affirms that both Christ's body and the bread are substantially present at the Supper, it also inadvertently admits the possibility that Christ's body, like the bread, is 'accidentally' present—in other words, it reintroduces the possibility of an all too 'sensualistic' and 'physical' presence of Christ along with the 'physical' presence of bread and wine." Recall that Thomas had rejected the persistence of the bread and wine precisely because it would lead to unsacramental views of presence. See above, pp. 93–94.

129. Davis, *This Is My Body*, 49. Luther seemed to have a better sense of signification in the sacrament before his encounter with the Swiss and their novel use of sign. See Gerrish, "Discerning the Body," 70–71.

had been able to affirm a realistic understanding of both Christ's eucharistic presence and of the ascension.[130] Signification is the key to a sacramental understanding of presence in which Christ can be as genuinely present on the altar as in heaven, but in a different, and therefore noncompetitive, mode.

The Swiss, as we have seen, took the "is" in "This is my body" to mean "signifies": "This bread and wine signify, or are signs of, my body and blood." In this they appealed, above all, to Augustine, who had no qualms about referring to the sacrament as a sign of Christ's body.[131] But, in the patristic period, for something to be called a sign did not imply what it implied for the Swiss—namely, that the signified was absent. Of this Luther was well aware, and he rightly rejected Zwingli's appeals to Augustine to support his view of the Eucharist.[132] But Luther's nominalist background had not prepared him to articulate the role of sign and signified in the Eucharist in a very satisfactory way. Recall that the nominalists, dissatisfied with the realism of the sacramental (i.e., predicated on the logic of sign) presence articulated by transubstantiation, opted for a theory that would make Christ present even according to his "natural mode," thereby making the category of sign superfluous.[133] While Luther himself did not naïvely understand Christ's presence as local or dimensive, his nominalist categories made it difficult for him to consistently convey a sacramental understanding, even though we have seen that he did not intend a natural understanding. As we have already seen, nominalism had obscured the traditional Augustinian (and, building on Augustine, Thomist) language about sign and signified with the conclusion that the earthly leading to the heavenly—the basic presupposition of patristic theology of the Eucharist, reasserted in a new context by Aquinas—was a matter of *deception*.[134]

All of this left Luther ill-equipped to respond to Zwingli's theories of signification with a more adequate theory. Instead, Luther's focus on the words of Christ, entirely legitimate in itself, was expressed in a one-sided way that did not give due appreciation to the signification of the bread and wine. To put it in Thomistic language, Luther focused on the form of the sacrament (Christ's words) so intently that he overlooked the value of its matter (the bread and wine). According to Brian Gerrish, "Luther is not interested in defending the real presence with a more authentically Augustinian view of signs: his single-minded purpose is to exclude sign talk from the interpretation

---

130. See Hunsinger, *Eucharist and Ecumenism*, 47; cf. Gerrish, "Discerning the Body," 74.
131. Gerrish, "Discerning the Body," 61.
132. Gerrish, "Luther and the Reformed Eucharist," 12; Gerrish, "Discerning the Body," 62.
133. See above, pp. 50–52.
134. See above, pp. 50–51.

of the words of institution and to stake everything on the sheer power of the words of institution themselves."[135]

For Augustine, the sign and the signified, the *signum* and the *res*, were, respectively, bread and wine and Christ's body and blood. This schema is elaborated further in the work of the Scholastics. For Thomas and the other Schoolmen, as we have seen, there is not only *sacramentum* (*tantum*) and *res* (*tantum*), but there is also an intermediate category called the *res et sacramentum*.[136] This allowed the Scholastics to incorporate the ecclesial goal of the Eucharist into their treatment of the relationship between sign and signified, something to which Augustine could hardly have objected as it followed the whole thrust of his own theology of the Eucharist. In Thomas's schema, the (accidents of the) bread and wine are the *sacramentum tantum*, the sign. They signify Christ's body and blood, really present under them. But, because Christ's body and blood signify something further, they are not only *res*, but *res et sacramentum*. The final end of the Eucharist signified by Christ's body and blood, the *res tantum*, is the communion of the Church, head and members.

In *The Eucharist in the West*, Edward Kilmartin suggests that, in his preference for the persistence of the bread and wine, Luther "does not recognize that the ontological relation between sign and signified speaks in favor of transubstantiation."[137] The work was posthumously edited, so it is possible that Kilmartin intended to explain this claim in more detail. It stands in Kilmartin's book, however, as an unsupported assertion. What could he have meant by this?

Despite the fact that transubstantiation is often misunderstood as an annihilation of the bread and wine, in Thomas's articulation the accidents, the physical properties of bread and wine, have a very important role. Without their persistence, there would be no signification and, therefore, no sacrament.[138] The nominalists whom Luther followed in preferring consubstantiation (though, as we have noted, he does not use the term)[139] were unconcerned with the sacramental role of the bread and wine, provided that the body and blood of Christ was really, even naturally, present. For them, the bread and wine were more like disguises than signs. Furthermore, by holding that the

135. Gerrish, "Luther and the Reformed Eucharist," 12. Cf. Gerrish, "Discerning the Body," 60, 63.

136. See above, pp. 130–33.

137. Kilmartin, *Eucharist in the West*, 158.

138. See above, pp. 95–96.

139. Stephenson (*Lord's Supper*, 109) calls "consubstantiation" a parody of orthodox Lutheran belief.

bread and wine continue to exist *in the same way* (i.e., substantially) as the body and blood of Christ have come to exist, they effectively collapsed sign and signified. This is quite evident, for example, in Luther's German terms for the elements after consecration, *fleischbrot und blutwein* (fleshbread and bloodwine).[140] (Note the similarity to the patristic term for the incarnation: God-man.)

When faced with the Swiss claim that the bread and wine were mere signs of something absent, Luther rightly balked. But instead of saying that they were rather signs of something truly present, he skipped over them entirely. Luther ostensibly returned to an Augustinian bipartite schema of sign and signified, but what Luther identified as the sign in the Eucharist was not the bread and wine but rather Christ's body and blood present in, with, and under them.[141] The signified had become the sign, and a very odd kind of sign at that: one that is not perceptible to the senses. As Gerrish notes, "Since the presence of the body and blood is not visible, the entire Augustinian notion of a sacrament as a visible sign of an invisible grace is given up: the symbolic relationship of *signum* and *res*, sign and thing signified, is scrambled."[142]

This begs the question, however, "If the body and blood of Christ are the signs, what do they signify?" Here Luther's answer is much more traditional,

---

140. *Confession concerning Christ's Supper* (1528), in *LW* 37:303. Cf. Gerrish, "Discerning the Body," 63.

141. Gerrish, "Luther and the Reformed Eucharist," 12; Gerrish, "Discerning the Body," 62. See *The Babylonian Captivity of the Church* (1520), in *LW* 36:44: "So in the mass also, the foremost promise of all, he adds as a memorial sign of such a great promise his own body and his own blood in the bread and wine when he says 'Do this in remembrance of me.'" Cf. Quere, "Changes and Constants," 70:

> For Luther, however, the sign *is* the body and blood of Christ in and under the bread and wine. This bread-body/wine-blood sign points to the *benefits* of the Sacrament which are forgiveness, life, and salvation. The model may be the same as Augustine's but in Luther it is robbed of its "split-level" structure with the bread on one level and the body of Christ on the next level up in the house of being. Everything in fact is brought down to the ground level—*there*, the body and blood of Christ point to a forgiveness which is also *there*.

142. Gerrish, "Luther and the Reformed Eucharist," 12; cf. Gerrish, "Discerning the Body," 73: In his opposition to Zwingli on the matter of the real presence, he was less concerned to propose an alternative theory of signification than simply to affirm the presence and efficacy of the body and blood. He does so in a way that collapses the symbolic relationship of sign and reality, *sacramentum* and *res*, and moves sacramental causality out of the order of signification. Strictly speaking, the word "sign," when Luther continues to use it in this context, carries an improper sense, since the sign now does what it does, not by meaning, signifying, or symbolizing anything to faith, but purely as an efficient cause. The presence of the body and blood with the elements of bread and wine is indeed a pledge to those who believe it, but it does not, apparently, impart life to their bodies only because they believe; their belief is rather their awareness of what it does anyway. At this point Gerrish cites *That These Words of Christ* (1527), in *LW* 37:93–94.

even if it is not immediately apparent how. While for Thomas, the *res tan-tum*, signified by Christ's body and blood, was the unity of the Church, for Luther, Christ's body and blood signified the forgiveness of sins.[143] These may not look like the same thing, but a moment's reflection shows that they are completely compatible. The whole thrust of Christianity is that human be-ings are separated from God and from one another because of sin and that, in order for that separation to be overcome—that is, in order for communion to be realized—sin must be forgiven. Hence the final stanza of the Apostles' Creed, wherein we profess that the *Holy Spirit* makes the *Church* to be a *com-munion of saints* by the *forgiveness of sins*.[144] In fact, Luther himself did not seem to see forgiveness of sins and the communion of saints as two different ends. While he often emphasized the forgiveness of sins as the fruit of the Eucharist, he also, especially in his early work, talked about communion as the final end of the sacrament. So he writes, in 1519, that "this sacrament, as we shall see, signifies the complete union and the individual fellowship of the saints."[145] It is interesting to note that Luther repreached this sermon in 1528, demonstrating that, while the debate with the Swiss about real presence was occupying his time and energy, he did not repudiate his earlier views about the fruit of the sacrament.[146]

143. Davis, *This Is My Body*, 50.
144. For an exploration of the relationship between forgiveness and communion, see Brett Salkeld, "A Catholic Perspective on Salvation," *One in Christ* 46, no. 1 (2012): 73–75. See also Benedict XVI, *Called to Communion: Understanding the Church Today*, trans. Adrian Walker (San Francisco: Ignatius, 1996), 64: "This seems to me to be a cardinal point: at the inmost core of the new commission, which robs the forces of destruction of their power, is the grace of forgiveness. It constitutes the Church. The Church is founded upon forgiveness." Cf. Lehmann and Pannenberg (*Condemnations of the Reformation Era*, 111–12), who discuss the Council of Trent's condemnation of the notion that "the special fruit of the Eucharist is the forgiveness of sins" (111). They conclude, "Where a narrow interpretation of the forgiveness of sins was involved (or still is), can. 5 (*DS 1655*)—which itself starts from an incomplete way of speaking— still applies. But where 'forgiveness of sins' is seen as being one with the new fellowship (*com-munio*) with God conferred through grace, the canon is null and void" (112).
145. *The Blessed Sacrament of the Holy and True Body of Christ, and the Brotherhoods* (1519), in *LW* 35:50.
146. Davis, *This Is My Body*, 57. Indeed, Luther mentions that "the Supper must indeed prefigure and signify something, viz. the unity of Christians in one spiritual body of Christ through one spirit, faith, love, and the cross, etc." in passing in his 1528 *Great Confession* (*LW* 37:275). Quere suggests that "the emphasis of the Zwinglians on the ecclesiastical presence probably prompted Luther to reintroduce this theme which was prominent in his own earlier writings of 1519 and especially in the Eucharistic theology of the earlier centuries" ("Changes and Constants," 67). Indeed, the context demonstrates that Luther is saying to the Swiss, in effect, "Of course, everyone knows that the Eucharist signifies (in the sense that it signifies com-munion). But you're still wrong about Christ's presence in the elements being merely figurative." Cf. Gerrish ("Discerning the Body," 71), who suggests that Luther avoids any ecclesial emphasis

With this in mind, then, we can see that, while Luther agrees with Thomas about what Thomas called the *res tantum*,[147] even while it must be admitted that Luther approached the *res tantum* from a new angle, what Thomas had understood to be the *sacramentum tantum* and the *res et sacramentum* have been collapsed in Luther's articulation. Or, more precisely, the first has been absorbed by the second. Commentators often remark that Luther rejected the idea of the bread and wine as signs.[148] In my own reading on the topic, at least, they fail to note that Luther's identification of the body and blood of Christ as signs follows Thomas's articulation, even while his denial that the bread and wine are signs does not.[149] Transubstantiation kept the bread and wine and Christ's body and blood at different levels of being and, consequently, different levels of signification.[150] But an articulation that allows the bread and wine to exist at the same level of being as Christ's body and blood ends up putting them at the same level in terms of signification. This is how, through his conviction that the bread and wine remained, Luther ended up with the strange notion that the only signs in the Eucharist were the imperceptible ones.[151] He was very much in line with Thomas when he affirmed that Christ's body and blood were a sign of something more, what Thomas called *res et sacramentum*, but he lost his grip on the sacramental nature of the Eucharist when he ignored the significatory value of the bread and the wine.[152]

---

in his later writing because of "his anxiety that an ecclesial emphasis, in combination with the new symbolic theories, might actually displace belief in the real presence."

147. Cf. Grislis, "Eucharistic Presence of Christ," 15.

148. Davis, *This Is My Body*, 49.

149. The closest I have seen is Quere, who writes, "Medieval theology's *sacramentum tantum* for Luther would include the body and blood and the *res tantum* would be the benefit of forgiveness. Luther has no *res et sacramentum* as such and technically holds a bipartite view as does Augustine. But the content of Luther's parts is radically different from that of his sometime master Augustine" ("Changes and Constants," 53). In a sense Quere is right. Luther has no intermediate term that is explicitly both sign and signified. On the other hand, one could also say that what Luther is missing is the *sacramentum tantum*. He has the *res et sacramentum* in that what he identifies as the sign is not perceptible. And what he calls the sign, Christ's body and blood, is what the Scholastics call the *res et sacramentum*.

150. Cf. Quere, "Changes and Constants," 70, quoted above, 174n141. Zwingli, however, felt that both Luther and Roman Catholics collapsed *signum* into *res*. His reaction to this perception was "to isolate the two and thereby neglect any serious reflection on how signs participate in the reality signified" (Jones, *Christ's Eucharistic Presence*, 124).

151. This is not to say that anyone affirming the persistence of the bread and wine will necessarily end up denying their significatory value. Rather, as we have seen, it was Luther's unique constellation of personal circumstance and education that led from one to the other. As long as one is careful to separate the earthly and the heavenly, to use patristic language, this pitfall can be avoided.

152. As Liam Walsh notes, however, at the time of the Reformation, Catholics were also losing their sense of the significatory value of the eucharistic elements, and for reasons similar to Luther's:

This is certainly a deficiency in Luther's articulation. While some Protestants have insisted that the bread and wine must remain in order for the Eucharist to be properly sacramental (this is the implication behind the Anglican Thirty-Nine Articles' charge that transubstantiation "overthroweth the nature of the sacrament," for instance), and thereby rejected transubstantiation, Luther's preference that the (substance of the) bread and wine remain is rooted rather in a metaphysical preference taken over from late medieval nominalism. But our condemnation of Luther on this count cannot be wholesale. Indeed, it will be tempered when we note the following three considerations.

First of all, Luther is never dogmatic on this point. He is willing to let others hold to the view that (the substances of) the bread and the wine do not remain. He reiterated this view several times throughout his career. It makes its first appearance in *The Babylonian Captivity*, where he writes that, though

> I at last found rest for my conscience in the above view, namely, that it is real bread and real wine, in which Christ's real flesh and real blood are present in no other way and to no less a degree than the others assert them to be under their accidents. . . . I permit every man to hold either of these opinions as he chooses. My one concern at present is to remove all scruples of conscience, so that no one may fear being called a heretic if he believes that real bread and real wine are present on the altar, and that every one may feel at liberty to ponder, hold, and believe either one view or the other without endangering his salvation.[153]

Eight years later, in his *Confession concerning Christ's Supper*, he writes, "I have taught in the past and still teach that this controversy is unnecessary, and that it is of no great consequence whether the bread remains or not,"[154]

At the Reformation, Protestant theologians were happy to say sacraments were signs somewhat in this sense: they served as signs of saving faith in what is done only in and by the cross of Christ. This made Catholic theologians [and Luther!] think they were denying all that the tradition of faith had said about the divine reality that was not just indicated by, but was really present within sacraments—all that made them be mysteries. They became coy about saying sacraments are signs, and the Council of Trent rarely if ever uses the terms. Counter-Reformation Catholic theology became much more intent on affirming and explaining how sacraments were *causes* rather than signs of grace. Students of Thomas kept the idea [of sacraments as signs] alive and it became important again in some currents of neo-scholasticism, although often being given an excessively cognitive sense. (*Sacraments of Initiation*, 73)
Cf. Gerrish, "Discerning the Body," 73: "Strictly speaking, the word 'sign,' when Luther continues to use it in this context, carries an improper sense, since the sign now does what it does, not by meaning, signifying, or symbolizing anything to faith, but purely as an efficient cause."
153. *The Babylonian Captivity of the Church* (1520), in *LW* 36:29–30. Cf. *The Adoration of the Sacrament* (1523), in *LW* 36:287–88.
154. *Confession concerning Christ's Supper* (1528), in *LW* 37:296.

and that "I have often enough asserted that I do not argue whether the wine remains or not. It is enough for me that Christ's blood is present; let it be with the wine as God wills. Sooner than have wine with the fanatics, I would agree with the pope that there is only blood."[155]

Second, in his teaching that the substance of the bread and wine does not remain, Luther is using the term "substance" in a different way than Thomas used it. To Luther, substance cannot be separated from quantity.[156] Accordingly, what Luther was really affirming was the continuation of the physical reality of bread and wine, something Thomas himself affirmed. (Indeed, Thomas affirmed it *by* saying that the quantity remained.) That is why Ratzinger can write, as we have already seen, that an understanding of the different ways in which "substance" was used by Aquinas and by the late nominalists, and, with them, Luther, makes it "clear that 'transubstantiation' forms no antithesis at all to 'consubstantiation,' if the latter is simply supposed to mean that bread and wine as physical-chemical entities continue to exist unchanged."[157]

Finally, while Luther did not feel the need to highlight the sacramental value of the bread and wine (the matter of the sacrament), his emphasis on Christ's words (the form of the sacrament) functioned to point out the imperceptible signs of Christ's body and blood.[158] And words are signs too! So, in a sense, there *was* a perceptible (i.e., audible) sign that led to the imperceptible signs of Christ's body and blood for Luther. Here is how Luther explained the relationship between the word and the sign in *The Babylonian Captivity* (written, *nota bene*, before his controversy with the Swiss—i.e., before he got nervous about the language of signification indicating Christ's absence):

> We may learn from this that in every promise of God two things are presented to us, the word and the sign, so that we are to understand the word to be the

155. *Confession concerning Christ's Supper* (1528), in *LW* 37:317.

156. *The Babylonian Captivity of the Church* (1520), in *LW* 36:32: "Out of this has arisen a Babel of a philosophy of a constant quantity distinct from the substance, until it has come to pass that they themselves no longer know what are accidents and what is substance." Cf. Benedict XVI, "Problem of Transubstantiation," 227–28, 232–38.

157. Benedict XVI, "Problem of Transubstantiation," 237.

158. See Davis, *This Is My Body*, 50:
  In Luther's understanding, the body and blood are truly present by the Word. That is why the Word is powerful: it effects what it says. And it is only this power, Luther thought, that protected what is dependent on it: the forgiveness of sins. The Christian knows that the Word is powerful because it effects Christ's true presence. And here is where sign came in for Luther. Even though the bread and wine cannot be reduced to signs of Christ's absent body and blood, the body and blood themselves—because of the power that guarantees their presence—serve as signs that the promise of forgiveness is true and unalterable.
See also Gerrish, "Discerning the Body," 60.

testament, but the sign to be the sacrament. Thus, in the mass, the word of Christ is the testament, and the bread and wine are the sacrament. And, as there is greater power in the word than in the sign, so there is greater power in the testament than in the sacrament; for a man can have and use the word or testament apart from the sign or sacrament.[159]

In other words, his collapse of the *sacramentum tantum* with the *res et sacramentum* was not complete. The *sacramentum tantum* is not merely the elements of the bread and wine, but those elements precisely once they have been *informed* by the Word.

For Catholics as well, the bread and wine do not signify apart from Christ's words of institution, which both indicate that Christ's body and blood are now present and make them to be so present. As Karl Rahner puts it, "The Eucharist is and remains the presence of the Lord through and under the efficacious word, which has two components: the purely material one, indeterminate in itself and needing to be determined, of the physical species of the bread and wine, and the more spiritual one, formal, determinative, clear, clarifying and declaratory, that of the explanatory words of the Lord."[160] While it is unfortunate that Luther did not respond to Zwingli with a more coherent theory of signs and signification, his own articulation is not totally unsacramental. Luther's focus on the word of Christ, though it suffered by ignoring the signification of the elements, ensured that some level of signification, in fact, the most important and determinative level, was maintained. The great Lutheran scholar Paul Althaus has described the chain of signification in Luther this way: "The words, as the first step, bring with them the bread and the cup for the sacrament; the bread and the cup bring with them the body and blood of Christ; the body and blood of Christ bring with them the New Testament; the New Testament brings with it the forgiveness of sins; the forgiveness of

---

159. *The Babylonian Captivity of the Church* (1520), in *LW* 36:44. Note that it was earlier on this same page that Luther identified the body and blood of Christ as the sign. Here he calls bread and wine the sacrament and also the sign the sacrament, strongly implying that the bread and wine are the sign. In the face of Luther's inconsistency, we do well to follow the advice of Karl Rahner, noted earlier, that "the explanation should be brought into line with what is to be explained, and not vice versa." See above, p. 168.

160. Karl Rahner, SJ, "The Word and the Eucharist," in *Theological Investigations IV: More Recent Writings* (Baltimore: Helicon, 1966), 285. See also p. 266:

Further: we are accustomed when speaking of the sacraments to distinguish between the word and the element, or in hylomorphic terms, between matter and form. But this distinction, correct though it may be in itself, ought not to obscure the fact that both elements, the word and the sacramental action, participate in the symbolic character of the sacrament and hence in its quality of being *word*. The sacramental action too has the character of a word. It designates something, it expresses something, it reveals something that is of itself hidden. To put it briefly, it too is a word.

sins brings with it eternal life and salvation."[161] In his emphasis on the word of Christ, Luther could have only heartily seconded Thomas Aquinas's justly famous office for the Feast of Corpus Christi where Thomas wrote, in the *Adoro te Devote*:

> *Visus, tactus, gustus in te fallitur,*
> *Sed auditu solo tuto creditur:*
> *Credo quidquid dixit Dei Filius,*
> *Nil hoc verbo Veritatis verius.*[162]

The Incarnational Pattern and the Persistence of the Bread and Wine

The reader will recall that Luther's rejection of transubstantiation rested on two pillars.[163] First of all, it struck him as an unwarranted imposition of pagan philosophy onto Christian theology. We have already dealt with this question in detail.[164] Second, however, he believed that transubstantiation did not follow the pattern of the incarnation. As he wrote in *The Babylonian Captivity*,

> Thus, what is true in regard to Christ is also true in regard to the sacrament. In order for the divine nature to dwell in him bodily [Col. 2:9], it is not necessary for the human nature to be transubstantiated and the divine nature contained under the accidents of human nature. Both natures are simply there in their entirety, and it is truly said: "This man is God; this God is man." Even though philosophy cannot grasp this, faith grasps it nonetheless. And the authority of God's Word is greater than the capacity of our intellect to grasp it. In like manner, it is not necessary in the sacrament that the bread and wine be transubstantiated and that Christ be contained under their accidents in order that the real body and real blood may be present. But both remain there at the same time, and it is truly said: "This bread is my body; this wine is my blood," and vice versa.[165]

Indeed, the Catholic suggestion that the bread and wine do not remain is one of the most perplexing aspects of the doctrine of transubstantiation to

161. Quoted in Nagel, "The Incarnation and the Lord's Supper in Luther," 47–48.

162. See, e.g., Stephenson, *Lord's Supper*, 99–100. While he has problems with transubstantiation, Stephenson praises Thomas's hymnody. The most renowned English translation is that of Gerard Manley Hopkins: "Seeing, touching, tasting are in thee deceived: How says trusty hearing? that shall be believed; What God's Son has told me, take for truth I do; Truth Himself speaks truly or there's nothing true." The choice of "deceived" is, however, unfortunate, given Thomas's insistence that there is no deception in the sacrament.

163. See above, pp. 2–3.

164. See above, pp. 78–85.

165. *The Babylonian Captivity of the Church* (1520), in *LW* 36:35.

Protestants. As Luther asks, is such a thing impossible for God? Especially for the God who has become incarnate in Jesus Christ without prejudice to his humanity?

This question is an important one for Catholics to address for several reasons. First of all, the Fathers of the Church, Protestants rightly note, seem to have had no qualms about referring to the sacramental species as bread and wine, and neither did St. Paul.[166] Second, Catholic sacramental theology itself operates on the idea that the Eucharist should follow the pattern of the incarnation.[167] Indeed, one of the most significant developments in sacramental theology in the last one hundred years has been the explicit recognition that the sacraments of the Church, and the Church itself as "universal sacrament of salvation,"[168] are utterly dependent on Jesus as the "primordial" sacrament.[169] And the simple fact that both the Eucharist and the Church are called Christ's *body* makes the link with the incarnation obvious. Finally, the most important ecumenical proposal concerning the Eucharist in recent years, George Hunsinger's *The Eucharist and Ecumenism*, specifically invokes the incarnational analogy with the Eucharist as a means for overcoming the Church's division on the question of eucharistic presence.[170]

It is a matter of historical fact that, for the first millennium of the Church's history, theology had very little problem talking about bread and wine after

166. Karl Rahner argues that "there is no reason why St Paul should not have called the Eucharist bread, either by reason of the species or by reason of its character as 'heavenly' food, whether there was transubstantiation or not" ("The Presence of Christ in the Sacrament of the Lord's Supper," 306). Cf. Stephenson, *Lord's Supper*, 104; Calvin, *Inst.* 4.17:1384 (20).

167. See, e.g., the profound treatment by Robert Sokolowski in "Eucharist and Transubstantiation," 106–11. Of course, neither Catholics nor Luther argue for a strict adherence to this pattern. A too-close rendering of the relationship between the incarnation and eucharistic presence that ignores the essential differences between the terms in the analogy (e.g., God is not the same kind of "thing" as a body, a human person is a free, rational creature while bread is not, etc.) leads to the heresy of impanation. Christ is not hypostatically united to the bread. On these issues see Hunsinger, *Eucharist and Ecumenism*, 77; Hunsinger, "Widening the Circle of Acceptable Diversity: A Reply to My Ecumenical Friends," *Pro Ecclesia* 19, no. 3 (Summer 2010): 280–82; Martelet, *The Risen Christ and the Eucharistic World*, 143; Lehmann and Pannenberg, *Condemnations of the Reformation Era*, 97; Rahner, "Presence of Christ in the Sacrament of the Lord's Supper," 305; Mark A. McIntosh, "Christ the Word Who Makes Us: Eucharist and Creation," *Pro Ecclesia* 19, no. 3 (Summer 2010): 258–59; Kereszty, *Wedding Feast of the Lamb*, 215–20, 223–24n10.

168. *Lumen Gentium*, art. 48. See http://www.vatican.va/archive/hist_councils/ii_vatican _council/documents/vat-ii_const_19641121_lumen-gentium_en.html.

169. The classic expression of this theme can be found in Edward Schillebeeckx, *Christ the Sacrament of the Encounter with God* (London: Sheed & Ward, 1987); see also Karl Rahner, SJ, *The Church and the Sacraments*, trans. W. J. O'Hara, new ed. (London: Burns & Oates, 1974).

170. Hunsinger, *Eucharist and Ecumenism*, 23 (cf. 40, 68, 75).

the consecration.[171] St. Paul and Augustine are the most important figures here, at least in the West, but they do not stand out from the rest of the tradition. It is only at the time of the Berengarian crisis that the practice of denying the persistence of the bread and wine emerges. At that time it became impossible to speak of the persistence of the bread and wine without appearing to reject Christ's real presence in the Eucharist. Connecting this with later developments, Edward Kilmartin explains,

> In the late medieval period, the theory of consubstantiation was clearly rejected by Church authority. Nevertheless, there was very little mention of the main objection against this explanation, namely: If bread and wine are unchanged, it stands to reason that they are not bearers of Christ's presence. They constitute only an occasion of meeting with Christ in faith. However, in the light of the developments in the Western theology of the Eucharist since the eleventh century, it was not possible to speak of the bread and wine remaining untouched by the somatic presence of Christ.[172]

In the worldview that had replaced Platonism, it had become impossible to use the same language as before to affirm the Church's traditional faith. Whereas, for the earlier Platonist Christians, an affirmation of the presence of the bread and wine did not at all impinge upon the real presence of Christ, to affirm their persistence now amounted to a denial of Christ's presence. Within the flattened metaphysics that led to the false dichotomy between Berengarius and his opponents, where the earthly no longer symbolically represents the heavenly, but rather exists alongside it on the same plane, Christ's body and blood are in competition with the bread and wine. If one of the two is *really* present, the other is less so. In such a context, transubstantiation introduces some texture into the metaphysical realm and speaks about two layers of reality that need not be in competition. The bread and wine can be present accidentally, while the body and blood of Christ are present substantially. This solution makes the body and blood of Christ the primary and determining reality without denying the existence of the other reality.[173]

Indeed, it is important to note that the Church, in its acceptance of transubstantiation, did not simply say, "The bread and wine cease to exist. Full stop." Rather, the Church said that the *substances of the bread and wine*

171. The major exception to this being related to the iconoclastic controversy in the East. See Hunsinger, *Eucharist and Ecumenism*, 61–62.

172. Kilmartin, *Eucharist in the West*, 156.

173. Cf. Sokolowski, "Eucharist and Transubstantiation," 107: "The accidents and natural characteristics of the bread are truly there; we should not think of the species of bread and wine as merely images in our minds." Also, see *ST* III, 75.5 ad 2, and p. 106 above.

do not remain. As Liam Walsh notes, someone affirming that the bread and wine remain does not run afoul of Church teaching if such a one does not put the question in terms of substance,[174] or, perhaps we can add, if someone is using the word "substance" in a different sense than it was used by Aquinas and Trent. Furthermore, Thomas's rejection of the idea of annihilation as an explanation gives further precision to what Roman Catholics mean when they deny that the substances of the bread and wine remain.[175]

In other words, the Catholic rejection of the persistence of the bread and wine is both historically conditioned and theologically nuanced. This does not mean it is false! What it means is that we will not be able to discern the truth contained by this way of speaking apart from these historical and theological considerations. The first thing to note is that, in a worldview where *real* presence is no longer easily intelligible according to the basic underlying metaphysics of the broader culture, the circumlocutions that are introduced to avoid speaking about bread and wine (e.g., the *elements* of bread and wine, the *sacramental* bread and wine, or the eucharistic *species*) have a pedagogical function. They are a subtle, but forceful, affirmation of Christ's presence to those without the theological training to carefully parse out the issues involved.[176]

174. Walsh, "Ecumenical Reading of Aquinas on the Eucharist," 237. Cf. Rahner, "Presence of Christ in the Sacrament of the Lord's Supper," 299:

> If one said that what Christ gives his Apostles is bread and is body, understanding by bread, in a sort of positivist empiricism, the experimental reality strictly as such and nothing else, one would have said nothing contrary to Catholic dogma. At the most, one would not have covered it entirely. It is only when one says that the "substance" of bread is there along with the substance of the body of Christ that one would be in formal contradiction to the Catholic dogma. But one would also have said something about which experience gives no information, and on which the words of Christ give no instruction, but rather say the contrary.

See also Stephenson, *Lord's Supper*, 104. Stephenson argues that since "substance" is not required to speak of the Eucharist, Rome should have no problem with Lutheran "sacramental union," especially considering St. Paul himself had no problem in speaking of bread and wine and that transubstantiation does not intend to say anything about the "physical matter of the bread and wine." (On this he is quoting Ratzinger's former colleague Johann Auer's *The Mystery of the Eucharist*, 23.1.)

175. See above, pp. 95–96.

176. In this, they function in much the same way as the practice of eucharistic adoration, which emerges around the same time and for the same basic reason. While the question of adoration and other acts of eucharistic piety are beyond the scope of the present book, two things can be noted in passing. First of all, like transubstantiation and its attendant language, adoration emerges at a time when real presence is being questioned. Thomas Aquinas, who wrote the most important work on transubstantiation, also wrote the office for Corpus Christi, the highpoint for eucharistic piety on the Church's calendar. Eucharistic piety is a liturgical response to the same problem to which transubstantiation is a theological response. Most Catholics will never

The next thing to note is that, since transubstantiation makes a very specific claim about the bread and wine—that is, that they are not annihilated or replaced, that their accidents remain, not as an illusion or disguise but as a sign, and that their substance is precisely what *becomes* the substance of Christ's body and blood—not every claim that the bread and wine remain will necessarily contradict Catholic faith. Rather, each such claim will have to be investigated on its own merits to determine whether what the claimant holds is, in fact, compatible with Catholic faith.[177] To wit, Catholics have no problem with St. Paul's use of the terms "bread" and "wine" to talk about the elements, nor with St. Augustine's. And, as many Protestant ecumenists wryly note, Catholics do not seem to have a problem when contemporary Orthodox theologians speak in this way.[178]

---

read the *Summa* but, for hundreds of years, everyone heard the *Pange Lingua, Lauda Sion,* and *Adoro Te Devote.* And, after a brief eclipse, they are reemerging in Catholic piety.

Second, the Protestant rejection of adoration was intimately linked to the infrequency with which Catholics in the sixteenth century received the Eucharist. Adoration was condemned not primarily because it had no scriptural warrant, though that certainly gave some heft to the Protestant argument, but because it was seen to have overwhelmed the biblical command to take and eat. Furthermore, the general Protestant rejection (mitigated in Luther; see Edward F. Peters, "Luther and the Principle: Outside of the Use There Is No Sacrament," *Concordia Theological Monthly* 42, no. 10 [November 1971]: 643–52) of the permanence of Christ's presence in the bread and wine was entirely caught up in this dynamic. The Reformers were completely justified in their charge that Catholics had allowed looking at the Eucharist to virtually replace eating it. But the question may be asked whether they threw the baby out with the bathwater in rejecting not only eucharistic piety but also, and along with it, permanent presence. If the Catholic practice of careful circumlocution about the eucharistic species and liturgical acts like adoration is pedagogical in nature, so is the rejection of such practices. Consider the pedagogical difference between knowing that leftovers are destined for a gold box (or at least reverent consumption), on the one hand, or a garbage can, on the other. One should not casually dismiss the possibility that the reason Zwingli still reigns in most Protestant Churches, despite the best efforts of Protestant faculties of theology and many clergy, is that Protestantism did away with the means by which Catholicism brought the theology of real presence from the libraries to the pews. In fact, Zwingli made serious inroads into the Catholic Church precisely when Catholics abandoned these practices.

177. See, e.g., the conclusion of the German bishops' study that argues that
when the Council of Trent condemns the view that "in the sacred and holy sacrament of the Eucharist there remains the substance of bread and wine" (can. 2: DS 1652; NR* 578), this condemnation has to be judged in the light of the Lutheran doctrine of the Lord's Supper outlined above (a doctrine which people have sometimes tried to explain by the term "consubstantiation"). This rejection too fails to apply to the Lutheran position, since [and here the study quotes from Ratzinger] "'transubstantiation' does not signify an antithesis to 'consubstantiation,' if the latter is simply intended to mean that the bread and wine continue to exist unaltered, as physical and chemical entities." (Lehmann and Pannenberg, *Condemnations of the Reformation Era*, 99)

178. Indeed, Hunsinger proposes the Orthodox idea of transelementation to his Protestant colleagues precisely because it is both amenable to many Protestant concerns, having a significant Reformation pedigree (in the works of Vermigli, Cranmer, and Bucer), and because Orthodox eucharistic theology is seen as unproblematic by Rome (Hunsinger, *Eucharist and Ecumenism*, 71–72, 91; cf. 180–81).

Why, they wonder, does the Catholic Church seem to demand so much more from Protestants on such questions than from the Orthodox? Without insisting that there are no other considerations involved, I would suggest that one significant reason the Catholic Church is much more careful with Protestant articulations is that the Protestant heritage contains explicit rejections of Catholic teaching on questions such as transubstantiation. Acknowledging the legitimacy of different ways of speaking is much easier when those ways of speaking have not been used in mutually exclusive ways in the past. Given, however, that Protestant affirmations of the persistence of the bread and wine *have* often been made precisely as a denial of transubstantiation, a more careful analysis is required.[179]

But we have seen that Luther's denial of transubstantiation was not a denial of what Thomas had argued. Furthermore, his affirmation of the persistence of the substances of bread and wine was using the term "substance" in a different way than it had been used by Thomas. Finally, Luther's concerns that transubstantiation led to unnecessary philosophical problems were predicated on this, nominalist, view of transubstantiation.[180] If we combine all this with the fact that Luther himself explicitly and repeatedly argues that it is not important to him whether the bread and wine remain,[181] we are surely safe to conclude that Luther's affirmation of the persistence of bread and wine should not be interpreted as a rejection of what Thomas, and the Catholic Church today, means by transubstantiation.

Finally, Luther did not believe in impanation—that is, he did not believe that Christ was hypostatically united to the bread.[182] Luther knew that the analogy between the incarnation and the Eucharist could not be a perfect one. It is obvious to most theologians that the analogy is imperfect because the leading terms in each case (divinity and Christ's body and blood) are not congruent in an essential way—namely, that divinity is a completely different kind of thing than Christ's (*created*) body and blood. In fact, divinity is not a "thing" at all and is therefore not in competition with the second term in the incarnation—Christ's humanity.[183] Transubstantiation follows this logic by positing two realities that, because they exist on different levels, are not in direct competition with one another.

We must now consider an important difference between the final terms in each proportion—humanity and bread and wine. The essential difference

179. Cf. pp. 23–25 above.
180. See above, pp. 146–50, 177–78. See also pp. 52–55.
181. See above, pp. 177–78.
182. Lehmann and Pannenberg, *Condemnations of the Reformation Era*, 97.
183. See, e.g., Hunsinger, "Widening the Circle of Acceptable Diversity," 280.

here can best be seen teleologically and eschatologically. Human beings are eternal sorts of things. In a Christian anthropology, each and every human being will exist forever. The goal of a human person is an eternal one, to be with God and the rest of redeemed creation forever in heaven. For Christianity, unlike certain other religious conceptions, heaven does not destroy or absorb the individual but rather perfects her or him precisely as the person they were created to be. There may be a sense of theosis, of becoming divine—"We will be like him, for we will see him as he is" (1 John 3:2)—but not in a way that removes our unique human identity.

Bread and wine, on the other hand, are not eternal realities. They do, however, have a clear telos, a clear end. They are to be consumed by humans. The goal of bread, in other words, is to become a body. In achieving this goal, bread, unlike humans in heaven, does lose its identity, just as wheat and grapes lose their identity in becoming bread and wine, and sunshine, water, and soil lose their identity in becoming wheat and grapes. In all of material creation, human beings are the only things that keep their concrete, unique identity forever. This is what Christianity asserts by the idea of the unique human soul. Bread, not having any soul, has no principle of continuity. It is meant to become something else. It is meant to become human. The capital-B bread mentioned in the liturgy is eschatologically realized bread, bread that has become what bread was always meant to become, bread that has become body.[184] Transubstantiation, then, in its affirmation that the bread has changed, does not transgress the logic of the incarnation, but rather carefully accounts for the subtle differences between the incarnation and Christ's presence in the Eucharist.

In any case, the denial of the existence of the bread and wine is not an absolute in the Catholic tradition. Rather, it must be understood according to what it is meant to affirm—namely, that there is a genuine change in the elements. Moreover, change specifically in the elements is necessary in order to affirm that what is happening here is God's work. A change in our own minds is insufficient. Historically speaking, the Church begins to be nervous about talking about bread and wine precisely at the time when real presence is threatened. As long as real presence is not threatened, the Church can afford a much more serene attitude toward the language surrounding the elements. If Lutherans need not insist that transubstantiation offends the doctrine of the incarnation, Catholics need not insist that Lutheran affirmation of the persistence of bread and wine compromises real presence.

184. Cf. Durrwell, *Eucharist*, 34–35.

4

John Calvin

If we can see in the development of Martin Luther's thought on the Eucharist a microcosm of the development in the whole Western Church on the same question, in John Calvin we can see something more strictly analogous to the position of Thomas Aquinas himself. Aquinas, as we saw, wrote his treatises on the Eucharist after a great upheaval. Berengarius and his opponents had thrown the whole Western Church into confusion concerning the nature of Christ's eucharistic presence, and the language of "substance" (and, in its train, of "transubstantiation") emerged as a way of affirming both the reality of Christ's presence and the sacramental nature of that reality. Thomas's work was the crowning achievement in this development. Calvin's work on the Eucharist also followed a great upheaval in eucharistic theology. As a second-generation Reformer, Calvin came upon the scene after the earlier debates of Luther and Zwingli had rent the unity of the Reformed movement precisely on the question of Christ's eucharistic presence. And, while we should not imagine that the details of their teaching were the same in every respect, it is fair to note the parallels between Zwingli and Berengarius, on the one hand, and Luther and Humbert, on the other. Certainly Zwingli saw Luther, with his crass language and unqualified insistence on Christ's bodily presence, as a new Humbert; and Luther saw Zwingli, with his vacuous language and unqualified insistence on the symbolic nature of the bread and wine, as a new Berengarius.

Calvin's attempts to unify the Reformed movement on the question of eucharistic presence were not, therefore, unlike Thomas's articulation of transubstantiation. In both cases—as we have seen in the case of Aquinas, and as we shall see in the case of Calvin—there is an attempt to affirm both sign and reality when different parties in the Church were emphasizing one to the neglect of the other. While it is essential to highlight this parallel, we must also guard against pressing it too far. It is also important to note the differences between the contexts of Aquinas and Calvin. Aquinas was writing several generations after the controversy was at its peak. The solution had already been reached in principle, and Thomas's job was one of clarifying and deepening that solution.

Calvin, on the other hand, was writing in the heat of controversy. The previous combatants were still alive and active in his early career and, later on, the theological descendants of Luther and Zwingli continued to pursue the question. Calvin was not unaffected by this.[1] Though he himself preferred Luther to Zwingli,[2] at one point denouncing Zwingli's theology as "profane,"[3] he was able to come to an agreement, known since the nineteenth century as the *Consensus Tigurinus*, or Zurich Consensus,[4] with Zwingli's successor in Zurich, Heinrich Bullinger.[5] Bullinger had nudged Zurich toward Calvin and away from Zwingli, though not unambiguously.[6] This agreement, and Calvin's

1. For a careful exploration of the development of Calvin's eucharistic thought in light of his interactions with the Swiss and the Lutherans, see Wim Janse, "Calvin's Eucharistic Theology: Three Dogma-Historical Observations," in *Calvinus Sacrarum Literarum Interpres* (Göttingen: Vandenhoeck & Ruprecht, 2008), 37–69.

2. Calvin famously declined reading Zwingli and Oecolampadius because of Luther's assessment of them (Janse, "Calvin's Eucharistic Theology," 52). See also Brian A. Gerrish, *Grace and Gratitude: The Eucharistic Theology of John Calvin* (Minneapolis: Fortress, 1993), 139–45; Gerrish, "Sign and Reality: The Lord's Supper in the Reformed Confessions," in *The Old Protestantism and the New: Essays on the Reformation Heritage* (Chicago: University of Chicago Press, 1982), 122–23; Gerrish, "Luther and the Reformed Eucharist," 12–13; Heron, *Table and Tradition*, 126.

3. Gerrish, "Luther and the Reformed Eucharist," 13.

4. For more on the *Consensus Tigurinus*, see Timothy George, "John Calvin and the Agreement of Zurich (1549)," in *John Calvin and the Church* (Louisville: Westminster John Knox, 1990), 42–58; and Paul Rorem, "The Consensus Tigurinus (1549): Did Calvin Compromise?," in *Calvinus Sacrae Scripturae Professor*, ed. Wilhelm H. Neuser (Grand Rapids: Eerdmans, 1994), 72–90.

5. Bullinger was an important theologian in his own right, and no mere mimic of Zwingli. He had already developed a substantial and independent theology of the Eucharist before succeeding Zwingli in Zurich. It was Bullinger's theology, rather than Zwingli's, that Calvin was able to accommodate. See Rorem, "The Consensus Tigurinus," esp. 75–78.

6. Brian Gerrish has proposed a widely accepted distinction between three strands of Reformed eucharistic theology: Bullinger's "symbolic parallelism" is understood as a third way somewhere between the "symbolic memorialism" of Zwingli and the "symbolic instrumentalism" of Calvin. For Zwingli, signs merely commemorate a distant reality. For Calvin, signs are instruments that God uses to bring about the reality of the sacrament. For Bullinger, God brings about the reality of the sacrament alongside the signs of bread and wine. Bullinger, wary of tying God's grace too tightly to the material realm, is allergic to the idea that the sacramental

public defense of it[7] (even while he acknowledged its imperfections privately),[8] ended any chance of accord with the Lutherans, and Calvin engaged in a long polemical exchange with Joachim Westphal, an energetic gnesio-Lutheran pastor at Hamburg, largely defending himself from charges of being a closet Zwinglian.[9] These debates, which stretched on for hundreds of pages, are tedious reading, but they have had an important impact on how Calvin has been read down the centuries. The section on the Lord's Supper (4.18) in the final version (1559) of Calvin's magisterial *Institutes of the Christian Religion* contains much material derived from his debates with Westphal.[10] The 1559 version has, for obvious reasons, come to be read as definitive, and only serious Calvin scholars tend to read the earlier versions.[11]

While Thomas wrote within a still unified Church, over a hundred years removed from the precipitating debate, Calvin wrote in a fractured and fracturing Church where the question was very much a live one, and his most enduring work was significantly shaped by that reality. Thomas, therefore, could write with a serenity and a consistency that was not possible for someone in Calvin's position. But, despite these differences, it remains true that Thomas's and Calvin's projects are remarkably similar. An awareness of the similarities and differences in their respective contexts will make it easier to see just how much these two seminal thinkers have in common as we move forward.

---

symbols function as instruments, but he still wants to affirm a real presence. See Gerrish, "Sign and Reality," esp. 128; cf. Gerrish, *Grace and Gratitude*, 167.

7. Paul Rorem writes that Calvin "put the best construction on it and defended it tirelessly" ("Consensus Tigurinus," 89).

8. In a letter to Bucer, who shared with Calvin a more robust sense of Christ's eucharistic presence and had expressed his reservations about the agreement with Zurich, Calvin wrote, "You piously and prudently desire that the effect of the sacraments and what the Lord confers on us through them be explicated more clearly and more fully than many allow. Indeed it was not my fault that these items were not fuller. Let us therefore bear with a sigh that which cannot be corrected." Quoted in George, "John Calvin and the Agreement of Zurich (1549)," 54–55.

9. On the exchanges with Westphal, see Joseph N. Tylenda, "The Calvin-Westphal Exchange: The Genesis of Calvin's Treatises against Westphal," *Calvin Theological Journal* 9, no. 2 (November 1974): 182–209; and Esther Chung-Kim, "Use of the Fathers in the Eucharistic Debates between John Calvin and Joachim Westphal," *Reformation* 14 (2009): 101–25. On why Calvin could be mistaken for a Zwinglian, see Gerrish, *Grace and Gratitude*, 163–69.

10. Ford Lewis Battles's classic translation of the *Institutes* (1559) notes that "Calvin has in mind through secs. 20–34 the controversial writings of Joachim Westphal, of Hamburg, his most active Lutheran critic." Calvin, *Inst.* 4.17:1383 (20), n. 67. Cf. Janse, "Calvin's Eucharistic Theology," 68; Gerrish, *Grace and Gratitude*, 142.

11. The Canadian Calvin scholar Richard Topping has expressed to me his opinion that the influence of Westphal in the 1559 edition actually makes the penultimate edition of Calvin's *Institutes* (1550) a better text on this question.

A Surprising Trend

The reader who has been given to believe that Aquinas and Calvin represent something like opposite poles in Protestant-Catholic debate about real presence (not to mention other issues)[12] may be surprised to discover that these two thinkers are, in fact, remarkably close to one another on many central features of their eucharistic theology.[13] Indeed, it is a remarkable feature of the secondary literature that more and more scholars note significant agreement between Calvin and Aquinas on real presence. In his lucid and provocative study *Promise and Presence: An Exploration of Sacramental Theology*, the British Baptist theologian John Colwell tells us that he is "increasingly more impressed by the similarities than by the dissimilarities of their thought."[14] The Lutheran Robert Jenson writes in his *Dogmatics* that "it is more remarkable that Calvinist Reformed sacramentology, seemingly so removed from Catholicism, is structurally very close to it. The traditional boundary conditions are unchallenged, even emphasized."[15] And the Dominican Christopher Kiesling—who, it is probably worth noting for the sake of context, is an eager and capable proponent of transubstantiation—writes in a response to the Reformed theologian Ross MacKenzie, "A growing conviction of mine has been that, if Roman Catholics did not have their particular conceptual tools for expounding Christian faith, they would speak very much like John Calvin when they attempt to convey to others their belief in the real presence of Christ in the Eucharist."[16]

Indeed, even in the negative, Thomas and Calvin are grouped together. John Stephenson, a Canadian confessing Lutheran theologian who does not find Thomas "realistic" enough on this question, approvingly quotes Hermann Sasse's assessment that "Yes, Thomas Aquinas was a Semi-Calvinist. He

12. The standard work on Aquinas and Calvin more broadly speaking is Arvin Vos, *Aquinas, Calvin, and Contemporary Protestant Thought: A Critique of Protestant Views on the Thought of Thomas Aquinas* (Grand Rapids: Eerdmans, 1985).

13. Jeffrey Gros notes that "certainly most Catholics are surprised at the seriousness with which Calvin in particular takes the biblical teaching of Paul on Christ's presence in the Supper" (Gros, "A Roman Catholic Response," in *The Lord's Supper: Five Views*, ed. Gordon T. Smith (Downers Grove, IL: IVP Academic, 2008), 83. Many Protestants are equally surprised at just how sacramental, as opposed to magical or carnal, is the eucharistic theology of Thomas Aquinas.

14. Colwell, *Promise and Presence*, 9. He continues, "Both crucially maintain this distinction between the efficient and the instrumental. Both crucially maintain the distinction between the immediate and the mediate. Both acknowledge God's freedom as the freedom of his covenant love. Both therefore can affirm an assurance of faith without this degenerating into an arrogant presumption" (9–10; cf. 60).

15. Jenson, "Tenth Locus," 357.

16. MacKenzie, "Reformed and Roman Catholic Understandings of the Eucharist," 76.

anticipated the ideas of the Swiss reformers which in time totally destroyed the Sacrament."[17] And those Protestants who find Calvin's (or his interpreters') eucharistic doctrine too "realistic" do not fail to note his resemblance to Aquinas and transubstantiation. Ralph Cunnington defends Calvin (unconvincingly in my view) from William Cunningham's charge that "the phraseology of Calvin's doctrine approximates somewhat to the Romish position" by pointing to "his vehement and lengthy attacks upon transubstantiation."[18] And Peter Leithart notes that Robert Dabney "complained that Calvin's doctrine is as offensive to reason as transubstantiation."[19] Mark Karlberg, in his rather unsympathetic review of Keith Mathison's *Given for You: Reclaiming Calvin's Doctrine of the Lord's Supper*, asks (and answers), "Despite terminological and conceptual differences, how does Mathison's *suprasubstantiation*, in the final analysis, differ from Rome's doctrine of *transubstantiation*? I see little, if any substantive difference between the two views."[20] This last group has a venerable heritage. In 1548, Bullinger himself had replied to the twenty-four propositions on the sacraments that Calvin had sent to Zurich that "I do not see how your doctrine differs from the doctrine of the papists."[21]

And the list goes on. Douglas Farrow opines that "the simple fact of the matter is that Calvin's view is not unlike that of Aquinas."[22] Eric Puosi considers that Calvin's "sacramental theology constitutes one of the strongest cases for ecumenical dialogue between Calvinism and Catholicism."[23] And Brian Gerrish, perhaps the doyen of scholars of Calvin's eucharistic theology, explicitly labels Calvin's understanding of the relationship between signs and reality in the Eucharist "Thomistic."[24]

What would Calvin himself have made of these comparisons? Calvin never, to my knowledge, references Aquinas directly, as he does with Peter Lombard,

---

17. Stephenson, *Lord's Supper*, 101.

18. Ralph Cunnington, "Calvin's Doctrine of the Lord's Supper: A Blot upon His Labors as a Public Instructor?," *Westminster Theological Journal* 73, no. 2 (Fall 2011): 224. Whether or not Calvin vehemently attacked transubstantiation—and he did—is rather irrelevant to the question of whether his phraseology approaches the Catholic view. As we shall see, Calvin's attacks deliberately abstracted from the arguments of those he called "the sounder schoolmen" and were more interested in what was being conveyed to the person in the pews.

19. Leithart, "What's Wrong with Transubstantiation?," 323.

20. Mark W. Karlberg, review of *Given for You: Reclaiming Calvin's Doctrine of the Lord's Supper*, by Keith A. Mathison, *Journal of the Evangelical Theological Society* 48, no. 1 (March 2005): 177.

21. Quoted in Gerrish, "Luther and the Reformed Eucharist," 14.

22. Farrow, "Between the Rock and a Hard Place," 178.

23. Eric Puosi, "Ecclesiastical Communion: In Dialogue with Calvinism," in *Ecumenism Today: The Universal Church in the 21st Century*, ed. Francesca Aran Murphy and Christopher Asprey (Aldershot, UK: Ashgate, 2008), 190.

24. Gerrish, "Sign and Reality," 128–29; see also Gerrish, *Grace and Gratitude*, 166–68.

for instance.[25] Nevertheless, there occur throughout the *Institutes* several references to the "sounder schoolmen," whom Calvin acknowledges as having more defensible positions than what he takes to be the standard Catholic view,[26] despite their "syllable snatching."[27] On eucharistic presence in particular, these Schoolmen, "having a horror of such barbarous impiety, speak more modestly."[28] At least some of these references could be taken to indicate familiarity with Thomas's work, though it is impossible to say definitively.[29] Calvin notes that the Schoolmen "grant that Christ is not there contained in any circumscriptive or bodily fashion"[30] and say, "Christ is so contained in the Sacrament that he remains in heaven; and we maintain no other presence than that of a relationship."[31] The Latin here is *habitudinis*, the term used by Aquinas in this context, as we have seen above.[32]

Unfortunately for contemporary ecumenical dialogue, Calvin made the methodological decision not to engage such Schoolmen. Typically he either notes that he has no argument with them, but rather with the mistaken popular ideas of the Christian people, or he dismisses them out of hand. "On the beginning of justification there is no quarrel between us and the sounder Schoolmen."[33] But on the question of eucharistic presence he insists that, even in their modesty, "they do nothing but indulge in deceitful subtleties . . . [devising] a mode which they neither understand themselves nor can explain to others."[34] Because of this,

> one can see in what great superstition not only the common folk but also the leaders themselves have been held for some centuries and today are held in papists' churches. They are little concerned about true faith by which alone we

25. Calvin, *Inst.* 4.17:1373 (12). Here Calvin discerns that Lombard, even in his attempt to explain away the absurdities in the first *Ego Berengarius*, "inclines rather more to a divergent opinion." In this, Calvin anticipates the conclusion of Macy's "Theological Fate of Berengar's Oath," 20–35, by a good four centuries. See above, 70n79.
26. See, e.g., Gerrish, *Grace and Gratitude*, 97. Cf. Calvin, *Inst.* (1559) 3.14:11. Cf. Colwell, *Promise and Presence*, 9n26, 170.
27. Calvin, *Inst.* 4.17:1376 (14). The Latin original is *syllabarum aucupiis*.
28. Calvin, *Inst.* 4.17:1373. Later, in an obvious allusion to Westphal, Calvin writes, "I am not speaking of the papists, whose doctrine is more tolerable, or at least more modest" (*Inst.* 4.17:1402).
29. John Colwell, following Brian Gerrish, wonders aloud "whether Thomas ought to be included amongst the 'older writers' whose interpretations Calvin admits" (Colwell, *Promise and Presence*, 170; cf. Gerrish, *Grace and Gratitude*, 97, 168).
30. Calvin, *Inst.* 4.17:1373 (13); cf. n. 38.
31. Calvin, *Inst.* 4.17:1374.
32. Calvin, *Inst.* 4.17:1374, n. 39. See above, p. 111; *ST* III, 76.6 corpus.
33. Quoted in Gerrish, *Grace and Gratitude*, 97.
34. Calvin, *Inst.* 4.17:1373–74 (13).

attain fellowship with Christ and cleave to him. Provided they have a physical presence of him, which they have fabricated apart from God's Word, they think that they have presence enough. Briefly, then, we see how through this ingenious subtlety bread came to be taken for God.[35]

While we can easily sympathize with Calvin's pastoral instinct to attend to the views of the people in the pews, it is certainly unfortunate that he did not feel the need to engage someone like Aquinas in a more serious and reflective way. It is probably the case, however, that Calvin did not live in a context where he could have read Thomas sympathetically. It had to be left to later generations to discern the affinity between these two great theologians. I myself am convinced, and I appear not to be alone in this, that if Calvin were able to read Thomas sympathetically, he would have found his theology of the Eucharist very congenial. I believe a close look at Calvin's own theology of the Eucharist will demonstrate this clearly.

Sign and Reality

The first edition of Calvin's *Institutes* was published in 1536. He is already keenly aware of those "frightful contentions" that "even within our own memory have miserably troubled the Church."[36] Calvin's diagnosis of the problem is not unlike that of the contemporary ecumenical movement: the warring factions have spent too much time and energy pursuing overly subtle questions and seeking to define just how Christ's body is present in the Eucharist:

> Some men, to prove themselves subtle, added to the simplicity of Scripture: that he is "really" or "substantially" present. Still others even went farther: they said he had the same dimensions in which he hung on the cross. Others devised a wondrous transubstantiation. Others said that the bread itself was the body. Others, that it was the bread. Others that only a sign and figure of the body was set forth.[37]

35. Calvin, *Inst.* 4.17:1374; see also John Calvin, "Short Treatise on the Supper of Our Lord," 2:186–87: "Although the old doctors of Sorbonne dispute more subtilely how the body and blood are conjoined with the signs, still it cannot be denied that this opinion has been received by great and small in the Popish Church, and that it is cruelly maintained in the present day by fire and sword, that Jesus Christ is contained under these signs, and that there we must seek him."
36. Quoted in Joseph N. Tylenda, "The Ecumenical Intention of Calvin's Early Eucharistic Teaching," in *Reformatio Perennis: Essays on Calvin and the Reformation in Honor of Ford Lewis Battles*, ed. Brian A. Gerrish (Pittsburgh: Pickwick, 1981), 29.
37. Quoted in Tylenda, "Ecumenical Intention," 30.

It is not difficult to identify Catholics, Lutherans, and Zwinglians in the above description. Calvin thinks they have all got it wrong, not merely because of poor reasoning or bad faith, but because they are asking the wrong question. To Calvin, the important question is not "How is the body devoured by us?" over which many in the Church are disputing, but rather "how Christ's body, as it was given for us, became ours; how his blood, as it was shed for us, became ours. But that means to possess the whole Christ crucified, and to become a participant in all his benefits."[38] In the language of the Schoolmen, we could say that Calvin is asking the disputants not to lose sight of the *res tantum* because of confusion over the *res et sacramentum*.[39]

Calvin was convinced that this was all that would be required for the Reformers to move beyond the current impasse. And he was quite confident in his early writings that he had found the necessary solution.[40] Scripture did not engage in questions about the nature of Christ's eucharistic presence, but merely assured us of it and, importantly, its benefits to us. If everyone would leave aside idle curiosity and return to the simple word of Scripture, the issue would be settled.[41] This should, of course, sound familiar. It neatly parallels Luther's earlier views on the same topic.[42] Of course, Luther found that Pandora's box could not be shut again; and Calvin too would learn that, once the question of intelligibility has been posed, Christ's eucharistic presence could no longer be asserted on the basis of Scripture alone. In order for the scriptural witness to be heard, it must first be demonstrated that its ostensibly straightforward claim can be meaningfully understood. This is not to say that Calvin was entirely wrong to chastise those who pursued these questions so fervently. It is certainly possible to overanalyze the issue, thereby creating false problems or stripping it of mystery; and no one should lose sight of the reason for Christ's presence while fighting over the mode of it. Nevertheless, in his later writings, as we shall see, Calvin too was forced to demonstrate the intelligibility of the claim that he, like Thomas and Luther before him, found in the Scriptures.

While the 1536 *Institutes* are clearly aware of the disputes, and the contending parties are easily identifiable in Calvin's descriptions, it was not the goal of that work to mediate between Luther and the Swiss on the question of the Lord's Supper. It was, rather, a summary of the whole Reformed faith written for the French people, and it treated the Lord's Supper within that

38. Quoted in Tylenda, "Ecumenical Intention," 30.
39. See above, pp. 130–33.
40. Tylenda, "Ecumenical Intention," 28, 39.
41. Tylenda, "Ecumenical Intention," 32.
42. See above, p. 143.

framework.[43] Calvin's next important work on the Lord's Supper, however, had a clearly ecumenical intention. His "Short Treatise on the Supper of Our Lord" was published in Geneva in 1541, almost immediately after Calvin's return from exile in Strasbourg, where he had been busy with ecumenical activities alongside Bucer, having met and agreed with Melanchthon about eucharistic presence and having heard rumors of Luther's approval of him.[44] In it, he follows his earlier instinct by carefully articulating a Reformed view of the Eucharist (devoting the whole fourth section to forceful denunciations of Roman Catholic views and practices),[45] before explicitly engaging, in the fifth and final section, with the views of Zwingli and Luther on the question of presence. In its very structure, then, this treatise tries to contextualize the disputed question of presence within a broader agreement about the soteriological nature of the Eucharist and, we can add, shared disagreement with Rome.

While the Catholic positions are loudly denounced, Calvin is much more forbearing with the errors he discerns in his fellow Reformers. Luther, while condemning transubstantiation, did not do enough to dispel the idea that he imagined a local presence "as the Papists dream," and, moreover, often spoke immoderately, leaving himself open to misinterpretation. Zwingli (along with Oecolampadius), on the other hand, labored so valiantly to rid the world of superstition and teach the truth of the ascension, and its implications for the Eucharist, that he "forgot to show what presence of Jesus Christ ought to be believed in the Supper, and what communion of his body and blood is there received."[46] While Calvin obviously hoped this gentle chiding would be well taken by those on the receiving end, it is hard to imagine either party being convinced that Calvin had really understood their concerns about the opposing position. Indeed, the Swiss suggested that perhaps Calvin didn't know just how crudely Luther had written about the Eucharist, given his inability to read German! And one wonders what Luther would have had to say about the idea that Zwingli simply "forgot" to teach about Christ's eucharistic presence.[47] This is the danger inherent in the role of mediator.

43. Tylenda, "Ecumenical Intention," 32.
44. Tylenda, "Ecumenical Intention," 34–37.
45. Calvin, "Short Treatise on the Supper of Our Lord," 182–93.
46. Calvin, "Short Treatise on the Supper of Our Lord," 195. On the importance of the ascension for Zwingli's denial of real presence, see above, pp. 157–60.
47. There is a story, difficult to substantiate, that Luther himself read the work and found it pleasing, reportedly saying, "Certainly a learned and pious man. . . . If Zwingli and Oecolampadius had expressed themselves thus at the beginning, we could have come to an agreement." See Heron, *Table and Tradition*, 133. Conservative Lutherans, at least, consider the story apocryphal. See Stephenson, *Lord's Supper*, 72–73.

But Calvin's irenic tone was not merely window dressing. He genuinely believed that the dispute was resolvable in principle, and his "Short Treatise" actually does contain significant theological insights with the potential to move the question forward. The fundamental issue between Luther and Zwingli, as it had been for Berengarius and his opponents before them, was really the nature of signs and their relationship to reality.[48] In the "Short Treatise," Calvin set out his ideas about the relationship between sign and reality in the Supper that he would robustly maintain throughout his career.[49] The parallels with Thomas should be obvious.

> Now, it if be asked whether the bread is the body of Christ and the wine his blood, we answer, that the bread and the wine are visible signs, which represent to us the body and blood, but that this name and title of body and blood is given to them because they are as it were instruments by which the Lord distributes them to us. This form and manner of speaking is very appropriate.[50]

Calvin then furnishes us with a biblical example. We are told in John's Gospel that John the Baptist saw the Holy Spirit, descending like a dove.[51] But, of course, the Holy Spirit is invisible. Nevertheless, having seen the dove and recognized it as a true sign of the Holy Spirit, it is quite legitimate to say that, by seeing the dove, one has seen the Holy Spirit. Elsewhere Calvin calls this principle of giving the name of the thing signified to the outward sign "metonymy."[52]

Compare this with the comments of the Catholic theologian Roch Kereszty on transubstantiation: "In the divine act of symbolic self-communication, the symbolized and the symbol become fundamentally identical while remaining distinct on the empirical level: Christ is not the empirical reality of the bread and wine."[53] The Reformed author Laura Smit offers a helpful phrase in this respect when she notes that, for Calvin, "the bread is genuinely exhibiting the body of Christ, *without being univocal with the body*."[54] And the Catholic circumlocutions about "the eucharistic species" are meant to convey the same

48. For a helpful treatment of this issue, see Gerrish, "Discerning the Body."
49. Rorem, "Consensus Tigurinus," 74.
50. Calvin, "Short Treatise on the Supper of Our Lord," 171.
51. Luther had used the same example. See *Confession concerning Christ's Supper* (1528), in *LW* 37:301.
52. See, e.g., Calvin, *Inst.* 4.17:1385 (21); see also David C. Steinmetz, "Calvin and His Lutheran Critics," in *Calvin in Context* (Oxford: Oxford University Press, 1995), 187.
53. Kereszty, *Wedding Feast of the Lamb*, 216.
54. Laura Smit, "'The Depth behind Things': Toward a Calvinist Sacramental Theology," in *Radical Orthodoxy and the Reformed Tradition*, ed. James K. A. Smith and James H. Olthuis (Grand Rapids: Baker Academic, 2005), 222 (emphasis added).

thing that Calvin is highlighting here: in the Eucharist, sign and reality are distinct without being separate.[55] And for Thomas, while the default terminology is that of "body," it can also be legitimate to call the species "bread."[56] Though coming at the issue from precisely the opposite direction, Thomas's intention is clearly the same as Calvin's: both "body" and "bread" can be accurate terms when referring to the Eucharist, because each speaks about a different aspect of the reality at hand.[57] Colwell notes this similarity as well: "Notwithstanding Calvin's rantings against a doctrine of transubstantiation, one must ask whether his affirmation that the Supper 'consists of two parts, the earthly and the heavenly' [*Inst.* 4.17:14], radically differs in significance from Thomas's affirmation of the 'substance' of Christ's body and blood and the 'accidents' of bread and wine."[58] The "Short Treatise" continues:

> Thus it is with the communion which we have in the body and blood of the Lord Jesus. It is a spiritual mystery which can neither be seen by the eye nor comprehended by the human understanding.[59] It is therefore figured to us by visible signs, according as our weakness requires,[60] in such manner, nevertheless,

---

55. Hunsinger notes that Calvin's use of this Chalcedonian formula hints at the incarnational analogy preferred by Luther and developed by Calvin's Reformed colleague Peter Martyr Vermigli (*Eucharist and Ecumenism*, 38–46).

56. *ST* III, 75.8 corpus; 77.6 ad 1.

57. As Wim Janse points out, Calvin's decision to speak of "bread" primarily and "body" derivatively (the opposite of Thomas, who speaks of "body" primarily, but justifies the use of "bread" derivatively), i.e., rejecting a "literal" interpretation of "This is my body," was circumspect and restrained. Janse quotes Calvin's commentary on 1 Corinthians, in which Calvin writes, "If any are of a different opinion, they will forgive me; it appears to me contentious to dispute pertinaciously on this point. I find then, that there is here a sacramental form of expression, in which the Lord has given to the sign the name of the thing signified" (Janse, "Calvin's Eucharistic Theology," 53). Compare this to the Thomist Colman O'Neill, who notes that, from Berengarius on, "the only way in which mainline theology could preserve the full mystery of the Eucharist was to make two classes of complementary statements about it, the first symbolic and the second realistic, with each in some way modifying the other. This has created for subsequent theology the constantly recurring problem of how to preserve a balance between the two" (O'Neill, *Sacramental Realism*, 99). Are we not justified in reading Calvin's comments as an acknowledgment of this very fact?

58. Colwell, *Promise and Presence*, 170; cf. Pelikan, *Christian Tradition*, 4:197–98. Pelikan notes that, at the time of the Reformation, "Roman Catholics cited as 'clear testimony for transubstantiation' the ambiguous formula of Irenaeus, that 'the Eucharist . . . consists of two realities, earthly and heavenly.'"

59. Cf. *ST* III, 75.1: "We could never know by our senses that the real body of Christ and his blood are in this sacrament, but only by our faith which is based on the authority of God."

60. Cf. *ST* III, 60.4: "Now it is connatural to man to arrive at a knowledge of intelligible realities through sensible ones, and a sign is something through which a person arrives at knowledge of some further thing beyond itself. Moreover the sacred realities signified by the sacraments are certain spiritual and intelligible goods by which man is sanctified. And the consequence of this fact is that the function of the sacrament as signifying is implemented by some sensible realities."

that it is not a bare figure but is combined with the reality and substance.[61] It is with good reason then that the bread is called the body, since it not only represents but also presents it to us.[62] Hence we indeed infer that the name of the body of Jesus Christ is transferred to the bread, inasmuch as it is the sacrament and figure of it. But we can likewise add, that the sacraments of the Lord should not and cannot be at all separated from their reality and substance. To distinguish, in order to guard against confounding them is not only good and reasonable, but altogether necessary; but to divide them, so as to make the one exist without the other, is absurd.[63]

And, a little later,

We must confess, then, that if the representation which God gives us in the Supper is true, the internal substance of the sacrament is conjoined with the visible signs; and as the bread is distributed to us by the hand, so the body of Christ is communicated to us in order that we may be partakers of it. Though there should be nothing more, we have good cause to be satisfied, when we understand that Jesus Christ gives us in the Supper the proper substance of his body and blood, in order that we may possess it fully, and possessing it have part in all his blessings.[64]

It should now be clearer why Brian Gerrish felt justified in describing Calvin's views of sign and reality as "Thomistic." Like Thomas, Calvin insists on both the necessity of signs in the sacrament and on the reality conveyed through those signs by the power of God. While Calvin could emphasize either the value of the signs or the presence of the reality, depending on whom he was engaging, he maintained this Chalcedonian balance, distinguishing sign from reality without separating the two, throughout his career.[65] Here is how he puts the matter in the 1559 *Institutes*:

61. Cf. *ST* III, 75.1: "When [Augustine] adds, *I have entrusted a mystery to you. If you take it in a spiritual way it will bring you life*, he does not mean that the body of Christ is in this sacrament only as in a mystical symbol; it is said to be there spiritually, that is, invisibly and by the power of the spirit;" and "we do not mean that Christ is only symbolically there, although it is true that every sacrament is a sign, but we understand that Christ's body is there, as we have said, in a way that is proper to this sacrament."
    62. Cf. *ST* III, 62.1, where Thomas rejects any interpretation of the sacraments that "does not attribute any further force to them beyond that of a sign."
    63. Calvin, "Short Treatise on the Supper of Our Lord," 171–72.
    64. Calvin, "Short Treatise on the Supper of Our Lord," 172–73.
    65. Rorem, "Consensus Tigurinus," 73; cf. Hunsinger, *Eucharist and Ecumenism*, 38–39; Heron, *Table and Tradition*, 126; Gerrish, *Grace and Gratitude*, 137. Gerrish notes that, from Calvin's perspective, transubstantiation collapses sign and signified. On this issue, see above, pp. 114–15, 173–74.

There is no reason for anyone to object that this is a figurative expression by which the name of the thing signified is given to the sign. I indeed admit that the breaking of the bread is a symbol; it is not the thing itself.[66] But, having admitted this, we shall nevertheless duly infer that by the showing of the symbol the thing itself is also shown. For unless a man means to call God a deceiver, he would never dare assert that an empty symbol is set forth by him. Therefore, if the Lord truly represents the participation in his body through the breaking of the bread, there ought not be the least doubt that he truly presents and shows his body. And the godly ought by all means to keep this rule: whenever they see the symbols appointed by the Lord, to think and be persuaded that the truth of the thing signified is surely present there. For why should the Lord put in your hand the symbol of his body, except to assure you of a true participation in it? But if it is true that a visible sign is given to us to seal the gift of a thing invisible, when we have received the symbol of the body, let us no less surely trust that the body itself is given to us.[67]

Not Real Enough

If this kind of articulation truly is "Thomistic," as Gerrish asserts, what is the Catholic reader to make of Calvin's forceful attacks against transubstantiation? Here it is important to recall two things. First of all, Calvin has explicitly told us that his concern with transubstantiation is with its effect on the views of the general population, including the hierarchy of the Church.[68] The second thing is to recall that transubstantiation had more or less stopped functioning as a careful articulation balancing sign and reality and had slid ever closer to being merely a cipher for a crudely physical, nonsacramental presence.[69] Calvin's attacks, then, are not on Thomas's careful articulation (even as he seems aware that some of the Schoolmen are less offensive than the popular ideas), but on what has become of transubstantiation (though he could not have been aware of the radical philosophical shift underlying this transformation) and its impact on the popular understanding of Christ's eucharistic presence. Catholic theologians too have sought to remedy the view that transubstantiation implies that "a physical presence [is] presence enough." Is Calvin's point any different from that of Joseph Ratzinger in the following quote? "Jesus is not there like a piece of meat, not in the realm that can be measured and quantified. Anyone who conceives of reality as being

---

66. Cf. *ST* III, 77.7 ad 3, where Thomas demonstrates how Berengarius's profession of faith is to be understood. See above, pp. 121–22.

67. Calvin, *Inst.* 4.17:1370–71 (10).

68. See above, pp. 192–93.

69. See above, pp. 51–53. See esp. Benedict XVI, "Problem of Transubstantiation," 233.

like that is deceiving himself about it and about himself. He is living his life all wrong."[70]

In fact, Calvin's concern is not that such a "physical" presence is too real, but rather that it is not real enough. Calvin insisted on the distinction of the signs and the reality without their separation against two fronts. First of all, against the Zwinglians, he insisted against the separation because that would strip the sacrament of its content, leaving only bare symbols that could function as nothing more than mnemonic devices. Second, against the Lutherans and Roman Catholics, he insisted on the distinction because of his belief that both the Lutheran view and transubstantiation ended up collapsing sign and reality. But if the sign is overwhelmed by the reality, the presence is no longer sacramental.[71] And, if it is not sacramental, if it does not lead beyond itself, it is no longer beneficial.[72]

Thomas Aquinas could have only agreed, of course. As we have seen, an essential consideration in the Catholic rejection of consubstantiation, going back to Aquinas, is the concern that collapsing sign and signified renders eucharistic presence unsacramental, leaving only an unsatisfactory physical presence. This is not to suggest that Calvin was completely wrong to identify this problem with at least the popular notion of transubstantiation. Especially in the nominalist context of the late Middle Ages, it presented the accidents of bread and wine as mere disguises rather than signs. But it does not necessarily follow, as Calvin supposes, that Catholic language about the transformation of the bread and wine into Christ's body and blood necessarily leads to an unsacramental view of Christ's presence.[73] As Christopher Kiesling points out, "the language of the Schoolmen and Roman Catholic documents is very precise: they do not speak of the change of the bread and wine into the body and blood of Christ but the change of the *substance* of the former into the *substance* of the latter."[74] This is important because, for Thomas Aquinas, "the appearances which remain in this sacrament . . . are enough to bring out what the sacrament signifies [because] it is actually through the accidents that the nature of any substance is discerned."[75] While, for Calvin, the substances of

70. Benedict XVI, *God Is Near Us*, 85; cf. Rahner, "Presence of Christ in the Sacrament of the Lord's Supper," 305–6.

71. Jones, *Christ's Eucharistic Presence*, 142–43; cf. Keith A. Mathison, *Given for You: Reclaiming Calvin's Doctrine of the Lord's Supper* (Phillipsburg, NJ: P&R, 2002), 22.

72. Cf. Smit, "Depth behind Things," 211.

73. Indeed, Calvin himself does not reject the language of "conversion" outright. See Calvin, *Inst.* 4.17:1375 (14).

74. Kiesling, "Roman Catholic and Reformed Understandings of the Eucharist (with Reformed Response by Ross MacKenzie)," 81–82; see also Walsh, *Sacraments of Initiation*, 307–8.

75. *ST* III, 75.2.

bread and wine are necessary to bring out the sacramental signification, for Thomas, the accidents are sufficient. "Transubstantiation," Kiesling notes, "does not confuse sign precisely as sign or signification and the thing signified. Signs precisely as such are in the realm of the sensible, the phenomenal order, the domain of appearances."[76] David Willis explains that for Calvin, on the other hand,

> it is because the sign and the reality are not arbitrarily connected by our imaginations or customs, that Calvin insists on the substance of the bread and wine remaining after the consecration of the elements. His point is that Christ takes the signs which he himself designates for that purpose and makes them the means by which we participate in their reality. And Calvin's point is stronger yet: namely, that if we do anything to violate the reality of the sign, we thereby detract from the sacred conjunction which Christ himself effects by his Word and Spirit. Hence the Reformer's insistence on the substance of the bread remaining and the substance of the wine remaining: *so that* the Real Presence is not minimized. Insisting on the continuing substance of the elements is the only way of sticking to the basis of the Real Presence through the bread and wine.[77]

It is important to remember, in seeking to resolve this difference, that "substance" did not mean for Calvin what it had meant for Thomas. Indeed, Calvin's use of "substance" was inconsistent and elusive.[78] In any case, it did not denote, as it did for Thomas, precisely that which was not apprehensible by the senses. Calvin is not, therefore, arguing with Thomas's suggestion that what is apprehensible to the senses is enough to account for the significative role of the bread and wine. Indeed, it is hard to see how he could disagree

---

76. MacKenzie, "Reformed Theology and Roman Catholic Doctrine of the Eucharist as Sacrifice (with Response by Christopher Kiesling)," 439; cf. Kiesling, "Roman Catholic and Reformed Understandings of the Eucharist (with Reformed Response by Ross MacKenzie)," 82–83:
> But are things such as bread and wine signs in virtue of their appearances or their radical identity, their "substance," or is such a distinction invalid? To answer either question, as Calvin did explicitly or implicitly, is metaphysical speculation. If Roman Catholic doctrine about the real presence of Christ under the appearances of bread and wine and about the change of substance of the elements into the substance of Christ's body is conditioned by philosophical theory, the same must be said about Reformed doctrine. Neither Roman Catholics nor Reformed Christians can boast of being in possession of pure faith undiluted by metaphysical presuppositions.

77. David Willis, "Calvin's Use of Substantia," in *Calvinus Ecclesiae Genevensis Custos*, ed. Wilhelm H. Neuser (Frankfurt am Main: Peter Lang, 1984), 296. This passage also occurs, with minor stylistic changes, in David Willis, "A Reformed Doctrine of the Eucharist and Ministry and Its Implications for Roman Catholic Dialogues," *Journal of Ecumenical Studies* 21, no. 2 (Spring 1984): 301.

78. Willis, "Calvin's Use of Substantia"; Crockett, *Eucharist*, 158; Gerrish, *Grace and Gratitude*, 178–80.

with that. Rather, Calvin's concern is that the "accidents" are not generally understood as signs at all, but as disguises and shadows that degrade the reality of the bread and wine.[79] Recall that, while Thomas had insisted that there was no deception in the sacrament because the accidents that are perceived are really there, Scotus considered the Eucharist an exception to the rule that there should be no deception in the sacraments.[80]

This widespread attitude, rather than Thomas's view, is Calvin's concern in his insistence that the substance of the bread and wine remain. Indeed, his intention is to recapture the precisely significative role for the bread and wine that Thomas had carefully spelled out centuries earlier. Furthermore, though Thomas himself was not so explicit, Calvin could not but approve of the contemporary Catholic theologians, such as Ratzinger and Durrwell,[81] who see in transubstantiation a transformation of the gifts that is the result of a lifting up to a higher plane of existence, not their degradation.[82] As we have seen, this follows from Thomas's insistence that transubstantiation does not entail the annihilation of the bread and wine, but precisely their conversion.[83] But Calvin, like many at the time of the Reformation, believed that transubstantiation *did* entail the annihilation of the bread and wine. As he writes in the *Institutes*, "They therefore had to take refuge in the fiction that a conversion of the bread and body takes place; not that the body is properly made from the bread, but because Christ, to hide himself under the figure, annihilates its substance."[84] But Thomas had rejected precisely this interpretation! And for reasons of which Calvin would certainly approve, notably that it degrades creation and strips the Eucharist of its eschatological dynamism.

So we can see how, underneath a veneer of disagreement about the persistence of the substances of bread and wine, lies a deeper agreement about the relationship between sign and signified, with ramifications even for creation and eschatology and therefore the broader context of salvation history in which the Eucharist is necessarily understood. Both Thomas and Calvin, in

79. Such a degradation has implications for both a doctrine of creation and for eschatology. See, e.g., Willis, "Calvin's Use of Substantia," 296, 300; Willis, "Reformed Doctrine of the Eucharist and Ministry," 300; Smit, "Depth behind Things," 222.

80. See above, pp. 50–51.

81. See above, pp. 95–96, 117–19.

82. George Hunsinger has noted the ecumenical promise of these articulations as well (*Eucharist and Ecumenism*, 79). Cf. MacKenzie, "Reformed and Roman Catholic Understandings of the Eucharist," 77.

83. See above, pp. 95–96.

84. Calvin, *Inst.* 4.17:1374 (14). The editor of this edition notes that this idea of transubstantiation is from Ockham and Biel, not Aquinas, n. 42. Cf. Calvin, *Inst.* 4.17:1375; Calvin, "Short Treatise on the Supper of Our Lord," 185.

their own philosophical and historical contexts, sought to uphold the sacramental nature of Christ's eucharistic presence by holding tightly to both symbol and reality in their theologies of the Eucharist. And, if Brian Gerrish is correct that "it is not too much to say that Calvin's entire sacramental theology lies implicit in his doctrine of sacramental signs (which, of course, he borrowed from St. Augustine),"[85] then we should be able to work outward from this central instance of agreement with Thomas toward ecumenical understanding on the other important features of Calvin's theology of the Eucharist.

Res Tantum *in Calvin*

We have already hinted at another important aspect of Calvin's theology of the Eucharist that is not typically observed to align him with Thomas. But when the early Calvin eschewed debate on the nature of Christ's presence and insisted that what really matters is "to possess the whole Christ crucified, and to become a participant in all his benefits,"[86] he was in at least partial continuity, perhaps unwittingly, with the medieval insistence that the eucharistic body and blood of Christ were only the *res et sacramentum*, but that there is a deeper, more ultimate goal, a *res tantum*, of the Eucharist.[87] This was typically understood by medieval theologians as the unity of the Church, but we have already seen, in our investigation of Luther, that this is, in fact, quite complementary to the idea that the goal of the Eucharist is the forgiveness of sins,[88] and we can now add, from Calvin, *all* Christ's benefits. For surely Christ's benefits include the forgiveness of sins, the unity of the Church, and eternal salvation, for these things all imply one another. Throughout his corpus, Calvin regularly employs a twofold phraseology along the lines of "Christ and his benefits" to describe what is given in the sacraments.[89]

85. Brian A. Gerrish, "Gospel and Eucharist: John Calvin on the Lord's Supper," in *The Old Protestantism and the New: Essays on the Reformation Heritage* (Chicago: University of Chicago Press, 1982), 111. Of course, Thomas's work is also heavily dependent on Augustine.

86. Quoted in Tylenda, "Ecumenical Intention," 30.

87. Colwell also notes this dynamic, though with reference to Calvin's emphasis on the role of the Holy Spirit in the Supper (*Promise and Presence*, 10n28).

88. See above, p. 175.

89. Davis, *This Is My Body*, 132. E.g., Calvin, "Short Treatise on the Supper of Our Lord," 169: "Hence we conclude that two things are presented to us in the Supper, viz., Jesus Christ as the source and substance of all good; and secondly, the fruit and efficacy of his death and passion." See also Calvin, "The Best Method of Obtaining Concord: Provided the Truth Be Sought without Contention," in *Tracts and Treatises on the Reformation of the Church*, trans. Henry Beveridge (Grand Rapids: Eerdmans, 1958), 2:578: "For certainly the reality and substance of the sacrament is not only the application of the benefits of Christ, but Christ himself with his death and resurrection." Calvin is here reversing his typical order to make the point,

The basic motivation is, I believe, clear. Calvin was concerned that medieval piety (rooted in transubstantiation) had misrepresented the importance of the Eucharist by insisting on the reception of Christ's body without reference to the reason for that reception (e.g., "They are little concerned about true faith by which alone we attain fellowship with Christ and cleave to him. Provided they have a physical presence of him . . . they think that they have presence enough").[90] For Calvin, transubstantiation had not merely collapsed the sign into the signified; it had eclipsed the finality of the sacrament.[91] And so he emphasizes, "It is not, therefore, the chief function of the Sacrament simply and without higher consideration to extend to us the body of Christ. Rather, it is to seal and confirm that promise by which he testifies that his flesh is food indeed and his blood is drink, which feeds us unto eternal life."[92]

What is remarkable is how close, in his attempt to remedy this situation, Calvin gets to Thomas and the medieval idea of *sacramentum tantum*, *res et sacramentum*, and *res tantum*.[93] He writes,

> The sacred mystery of the supper consists in two things: physical signs, which, thrust before our eyes, represent to us, according to our feeble capacity, things invisible; and spiritual truth, which is at the same time represented and displayed through the symbols themselves.
>
> When I wish to show the nature of this truth in familiar terms, I usually set down three things: the signification, the matter that depends upon it, and the power or effect that follows from both. The signification is contained in the promises, which are, so to speak, implicit in the sign. I call Christ with his death and resurrection the matter, or substance. But by effect I understand redemption, righteousness, sanctification, and eternal life, and all the other benefits Christ gives to us.[94]

---

against Zwingli, that one cannot get the benefits without the person. See Herman Bavinck, "Calvin's Doctrine of the Lord's Supper," trans. Nelson D. Kloosterman, *Mid-America Journal of Theology* 19 (2008): 137. See also John R. Meyer, "*Mysterium Fidei* and the Later Calvin," *Scottish Journal of Theology* 25, no. 4 (November 1972): 403.

90. Calvin, *Inst.* 4.17:1374 (13).

91. MacKenzie, "Reformed and Roman Catholic Understandings of the Eucharist," 74; cf. Kiesling, "Roman Catholic and Reformed Understandings of the Eucharist (with Reformed Response by Ross MacKenzie)," 80. Colwell notes Thomas's and Calvin's agreement on the "ultimate goal of the Supper," citing *ST* III, 79 and *Inst.* 4.17:2–3 (*Promise and Presence*, 175n66).

92. Calvin, *Inst.* 4.17:1363 (4). As Tylenda notes, "To overemphasize eucharistic presence to the detriment of eucharistic finality, i.e., spiritual nourishment, is to obscure, even to do away with the Supper's true meaning" ("Ecumenical Intention," 30). Cf. Rahner, "Presence of Christ in the Sacrament of the Lord's Supper," 310–11.

93. See above, pp. 130–33.

94. Calvin, *Inst.* 4.17:1371–72 (11). Calvin goes on to note, "Now, even though all these things have to do with faith, I leave no place for the sophistry that what I mean when I say Christ is received by faith is that he is received only by understanding and imagination."

This tripartite scheme replicates the earlier Scholastic categories almost without remainder.[95] This is more obvious when we note that Calvin is not unaware of the ecclesial reality of the sacrament, at one point quoting Augustine, from whom the medievals too would have learned this insight, that the Eucharist is the sacrament "of the unity of the Lord's body."[96] And with reference to St. Paul's First Letter to the Corinthians, and the ancient metaphor of the one loaf from many grains (also invoked by Thomas), he writes,

> For the Lord so communicates his body to us there that he is made completely one with us and we with him. Now, since he has only one body, of which he makes us all partakers, it is necessary that all of us also be made one body by such participation. The bread shown in the Sacrament represents this unity. As it is made of many grains so mixed together that one cannot be distinguished from another, so it is fitting that in the same way we should be joined and bound together by such great agreement of minds that no sort of disagreement or division may intrude.[97]

Furthermore, this "eucharistic sustenance is," as Owen Cummings notes, "eschatologically oriented."[98] And he goes on to quote from the *Institutes* (4.17:33): "It is 'a help by which we may be ingrafted into the body of Christ, or, already ingrafted, may be more and more united to him, until the union is complete in heaven.'"[99]

Zwinglian or Thomist?

But, even with such remarkable agreement between Calvin and Thomas on signs and signified in the Eucharist, it remains the case that many Catholics suspect that Calvin taught a merely symbolic presence.[100] As we have seen, this

95. We will have to revisit below Robert Jenson's claim that, for Calvin, "Christ's body and blood are *res* only and not also sign. There is, by the Calvinist account, nothing in the supper that is both *res* and sign" ("Tenth Locus," 358).

96. Calvin, *Inst*. 4.17:1423 (45). See also Nathan Kerr, "*Corpus Verum*: On the Ecclesial Recovery of Real Presence in John Calvin's Doctrine of the Eucharist," in *Radical Orthodoxy and the Reformed Tradition*, ed. James K. A. Smith and James H. Olthuis (Grand Rapids: Baker Academic, 2005), esp. 236–37, 240–41; Gerrish, *Grace and Gratitude*, 189–90; Mathison, *Given for You*, 41–42.

97. Calvin, *Inst*. 4.17:1414–15 (38).

98. Owen F. Cummings, "The Reformers and Eucharistic Ecclesiology," *One in Christ* 33, no. 1 (1997): 54.

99. Cummings, "Reformers and Eucharistic Ecclesiology," 54.

100. E.g., the popular Catholic evangelist Bishop Robert Barron, in an otherwise quite commendable video on the Eucharist, lumps Calvin in with Zwingli as an heir of Berengarius

was already the case at the time of Calvin's polemics with Westphal. Why is Calvin, despite all his protests to the contrary, so often understood as merely a "subtle sacramentarian"?[101] There are, first of all, contextual considerations. Calvin managed to reach agreement with Zurich rather than Wittenberg. The simple fact that his heirs have been in communion with those of Zwingli (and that Zwingli's legacy seems to dominate) makes it counterintuitive that Calvin was much closer to Luther on eucharistic presence than to Zwingli, even though that is the opinion of the overwhelming majority of Calvin scholars on the question. Second, as Brian Gerrish notes, it was precisely Calvin's theology of signs, so close to that of Thomas Aquinas, that engendered suspicion among the Lutherans. Luther, as we have seen in his debates with the Swiss, ends up abandoning much talk of sign in the Eucharist for fear of downplaying the reality. When Calvin came along articulating the role of signs in the Eucharist, "it was a matter of guilt by association: the Lutherans heard Calvin saying things that Zwingli had said about signs and symbols, and they assumed that he meant what Zwingli had meant. In actual fact, Calvin held a totally different theory of signification from Zwingli's, even though it equally clearly separates him from Luther."[102]

And Calvin did not just *appear* to agree with Zwingli about signs; he actually *did* agree with Zwingli, against Luther and the Lutheran ideas about ubiquity, about the ascension and its importance for understanding eucharistic presence: Christ's risen body really is in only one place—heaven—and any articulation of his presence in the Supper must not obscure that central fact. On this, of course, Calvin (and Zwingli too!)[103] follows Aquinas rather precisely.[104] And, like Thomas, he fully acknowledges the reality of both the ascension and Christ's presence in the Supper, here parting ways with Zwingli who, like Luther, understood these two claims as mutually exclusive.[105] Because most of Calvin's reputation as a theologian who denies real presence was

---

(*Eucharist* [West Milton, OH: Message Shop, 2009]). This video is based on Barron's book of the same title, *Eucharist*. He does not make this charge against Calvin in the book. Someone like Brian Gerrish might point out that this results from the fact that, even in officially Calvinist churches, "Zwingli . . . reigns by default in the pews" (Gerrish, "Luther and the Reformed Eucharist," 18).

101. "Sacramentarian" was a pejorative term with which the Lutheran party tarred the Swiss who denied real presence. Calvin was a "subtle sacramentarian" because, according to his opponents, he asserted a belief in Christ's eucharistic presence, but then qualified it away.

102. Gerrish, *Grace and Gratitude*, 163.

103. Grislis, "Eucharistic Presence of Christ," 25: "St Thomas, of course, had refuted the argument that on account of his ascension Christ cannot be eucharistically present; . . . Zwingli, by contrast, fully accepted the refuted suggestion."

104. Cf. *ST* III, 75.2 corpus.

105. See above, p. 159.

formed during his debates with the Lutherans, his disagreement with them on the ascension has contributed to this reputation even among Catholics, his agreement with Thomas on this point notwithstanding.

Seeing Through the Mirage

How ironic, then. Calvin's reputation as a Zwinglian is based largely on his theology of signs and his affirmation of the ascension, two points on which he is in strict agreement with Aquinas! We can see now the deeper logic behind the Lutheran Sasse's claim that Aquinas was a semi-Calvinist. But Calvin's ostensible agreement with Zwingli is largely a mirage. While he forthrightly acknowledges that the Eucharist is a sign, he does not agree with Zwingli about the implications of that claim. And while he forcefully affirms the importance of the ascension for understanding the nature of Christ's eucharistic presence, he completely rejects Zwingli's conclusion that it rules out such presence altogether. We shall take the two issues in turn.

We can first mention that it is possible, due in part to his writing in differing circumstances and against different opponents over the years, to find in places in Calvin's corpus a too-sharp distinction between sign and reality. "Then the signs could *appear* to be what he vigorously insisted they were not—'naked and bare signs,' rather than concrete vehicles of the promise which Jesus Christ himself is. Certainly, such an interpretation of him does not do justice to his intentions or indeed to his own statements."[106] And it is not simply that Calvin made statements that sounded like Zwingli and didn't always take care to append the appropriate qualifications. It is rather that Calvin could make statements like Zwingli but mean the very opposite because he had a completely different view of symbols in the sacraments. As Gerrish puts is, "Because the nature of the symbolical is . . . the total determinant of sacramental theology, it follows that even the verbal agreements of Zwingli and Calvin are totally qualified and may conceal actual disagreement."[107] While both men insisted on distinguishing between sign and signified over against what they perceived as the collapse of the two for the Lutherans and Catholics, "for Zwingli, symbolism is what enables him to use realistic language

---

106. Heron, *Table and Tradition*, 132. Cf. Benedict XVI, "Problem of Transubstantiation," 222–23: "Certainly one should not make too much of these statements; other assurances of real sacramental faith contrast with them, but neither should one underestimate them: the completely and utterly pneumatic-dynamic understanding of worship necessarily produces such thoughts, and while they do not negate a certain form of Eucharistic Real Presence, they tend nevertheless to make it synonymous with the general presence found in faith."

107. Gerrish, "Sign and Reality," 122.

without meaning it realistically. For Calvin [again, like Thomas!], symbolism is what assures him that he receives the body of Christ without believing in a localized presence of the body in the elements."[108]

The fundamental idea that puts Calvin in Thomas's camp and opposes him to Zwingli is that of the sacramental signs as instruments. One of Calvin's primary theological themes is the sovereignty of God. He believed that transubstantiation tied God to the sacraments, at least in practice, making them causes in their own right and putting grace at human disposal. This was simply anathema to Calvin,[109] and in this he agreed with Zwingli and Bullinger. "But it is an intolerable blasphemy to declare literally of an ephemeral and corruptible element that it is Christ."[110] Nevertheless, Calvin was able to affirm what neither Zwingli nor Bullinger dared—namely, that the sacraments are not signs of an absent reality (Zwingli), nor even simply signs of a present reality given independently and alongside of them (Bullinger), but rather signs through which the present reality is manifested, or, to use Calvin's favored term, exhibited.[111] Because it is precisely through the signs, and not simply alongside of them, that Christ's body and blood are present, they are appropriately called instruments.[112]

Brian Gerrish has made the widely cited distinction within the Reformed tradition of "three conceptions of sacramental signs: symbolic memorialism, symbolic parallelism, and symbolic instrumentalism,"[113] with reference to Zwingli, Bullinger, and Calvin, respectively. It is in this context that he refers to Calvin's view as "Thomistic."

> Ever since Zwingli . . . one could no longer be as trustful as the medieval Christian that in handling symbols one of course touched reality. Calvin and Bullinger struggled with this modern predicament, but the theories they came up with . . . actually mirrored the old medieval division between Thomists and Franciscans. Whereas for Thomas a sacrament was an instrumental cause by which God,

108. Gerrish, "Sign and Reality," 122. Cf. pp. 110–11 above.
109. Crockett, *Eucharist*, 150–51.
110. Calvin, *Inst.* 4.17:1384 (20).
111. On Calvin's use of *exhibere*, see Tylenda, "Ecumenical Intention," 31–32; George, "John Calvin and the Agreement of Zurich (1549)," 49; Richard A. Muller, "From Zürich or from Wittenberg? An Examination of Calvin's Early Eucharistic Thought," *Calvin Theological Journal* 45, no. 2 (November 2010): 249–52; Michael Allen, "Sacraments in the Reformed and Anglican Reformation," in *The Oxford Handbook of Sacramental Theology*, ed. Hans Boersma and Matthew Levering (Oxford: Oxford University Press, 2015), 292.
112. It is precisely on this issue that Paul Rorem concludes that the Consensus Tigurinus was a compromise document. Calvin had insisted on the idea of sacraments as instruments, and Bullinger rejected this interpretation ("Consensus Tigurinus," esp. 79–83).
113. Gerrish, *Grace and Gratitude*, 167; cf. Gerrish, "Sign and Reality."

the principal cause or agent, imparted grace to the soul, Scotus could only understand a sacrament as a sure sign that, by a concomitant divine act, grace was simultaneously being imparted.[114]

It is almost certainly due to Calvin's insistence that sacraments not infringe upon God's freedom and sovereignty that his sacramental instrumentalism is not a constant, but rather a developing, feature of his theology of the sacraments. In the 1536 edition of the *Institutes*, he had explicitly rejected the idea that sacraments were instruments.[115] Over the course of his career, however, he came to believe that one could affirm sacraments as instruments without impugning God's sole agency. As he wrote to Bullinger in the lead-up to the Zurich Consensus during which Calvin's instrumentalism was the most contentious issue, "What is your argument, that God acts alone, therefore all instruments cease?"[116] Colwell notes that the Aristotelian scheme, used by Thomas, that distinguishes efficient from material causality, was later used by Calvin to the same end,[117] so that "what we have, then, at the root of both the Catholic and the Reformed tradition, is an understanding of a sacrament, not as an empty sign, but as a sign through and in which God freely accomplished that which is signified, not in a manner that can be presumed upon or manipulated, but in a manner that is truly gracious."[118]

Already in the "Short Treatise on the Supper of Our Lord," written five years after the 1536 *Institutes*, instrumental language and ideas are present. The bread and wine can be called Christ's body and blood "because they are as it were instruments by which the Lord distributes them to us."[119] It is not improbable that, as Calvin sought to express a real presence without abandoning the reality of the signs—something required to resolve the differences between Luther and Zwingli—he found the category of instrument more and more necessary. It at once safeguarded the reality of the sacrament and insisted on its symbolic nature. Randall Zachman has even suggested that

114. Gerrish, *Grace and Gratitude*, 167–68. Egil Grislis also sees a connection between Calvin's view and Thomas's on this issue ("Eucharistic Presence of Christ," 19). Thomas rejects Bullinger's argument in *ST* III, 62.1, "Do the sacraments of the New Law cause grace?"
115. Thomas J. Davis, *The Clearest Promises of God: The Development of Calvin's Eucharistic Teaching* (New York: AMS Press, 1995), 7–8, 212.
116. Quoted in Rorem, "Consensus Tigurinus," 83.
117. Colwell, *Promise and Presence*, 7–8.
118. Colwell, *Promise and Presence*, 11.
119. Calvin, "Short Treatise on the Supper of Our Lord," 171. Cf. Leanne Van Dyk, "The Reformed View," in *The Lord's Supper: Five Views*, ed. Gordon T. Smith (Downers Grove, IL: IVP Academic, 2008), 75.

Calvin's development on this question might be related to his encounters with Roman Catholic thought.[120] But this development should not be taken to indicate that Calvin ever gave ground on God's sovereignty. He did not understand his deployment of instrumental language as a compromise on this point and always held "that the hand of God must not be tied down to the instrument. He may of himself accomplish salvation."[121] And Gerrish notes that this insistence is not a qualification of Calvin's "Thomistic" view, but an expression of it: "Moreover, quite unlike Zwingli, [Calvin] had no difficulty with the notion that God works through instruments or means. To be sure he insisted that the primary agency is God's. (Thomas Aquinas had said the same.)[122] But that, Calvin held, does not prevent God from freely using creaturely instruments as he pleases."[123] John Colwell offers the following assessment of what Calvin and Thomas together teach about sacraments as instruments:

> That which is mediated sacramentally is the presence and action of this one who loves in freedom; it is gratuitous; it is grace. It is not a "something" at our disposal; it is not a "something" we can manipulate—such notions do not merely misunderstand sacramentality, they misunderstand and offend a doctrine of God. It is God's presence and action that is communicated sacramentally and God cannot be manipulated; he is never at our disposal; he is not capricious, but neither is he subject to necessity; a sacrament may be the means of his presence, but it is never his prison; he is freely and graciously here, but he is not confined or controllable here or anywhere else. If grace might rightly be used with reference to a gift then this one who loves in freedom remains the free Lord of the being-givenness of that gift; God may give himself but he never gives himself away; he never becomes our possession or property—as Thomas Aquinas rightly maintains, God and God alone is the efficient cause of grace in a sacrament.[124]

---

120. Randall C. Zachman, "Revising the Reform: What Calvin Learned from Dialogue with the Roman Catholics," in *John Calvin and Roman Catholicism: Critique and Engagement, Then and Now* (Grand Rapids: Baker Academic, 2008), 165–91. Zachman looks at many areas of Calvin's sacramental thought in this light, including baptism and ordination. The section on the Lord's Supper can be found on pp. 173–79. He concludes (191), "It is hoped that these reflections might show that his dialogue with his Roman opponents had a more positive influence on Calvin than might otherwise be discernable in light of his continual polemic against them, and that he actually took the point of many of their criticisms of his earlier theological positions and changed his teaching accordingly, sometimes quite dramatically."

121. Quoted in Zachman, "Revising the Reform," 172; cf. Colwell, *Promise and Presence*, 29n32.

122. Gerrish here references *ST* III, q. 62, a. 1.

123. Gerrish, *Grace and Gratitude*, 165–66.

124. Colwell, *Promise and Presence*, 29. Cf. 60:
    All too easily we confuse instrumentality and agency. All too easily we confuse the sacramental sign with the reality signified. All too easily we assume an unmediated

The evident agreement between Thomas and Calvin on the instrumental-
ity of the sacraments is not unrelated to their agreement on the ascension.
It is precisely because Christ is no longer of this world that his presence, if it
is to be granted at all, must be granted through things that still are of it. It
is important here to note a difference in the contexts of Thomas and Calvin,
however. While, for Thomas, a literal reading of the ascension was simply
assumed, for Calvin, it was a matter of serious intra-Protestant polemic.[125]
Thomas can calmly state that "it is clear that the body of Christ does not
begin to exist in this sacrament by being brought in locally . . . because it
would thereby cease to be in heaven,"[126] and that because "the body of Christ
in heaven is at rest . . . it is not in movement in this sacrament."[127] Calvin,
on the other hand, feels the need to assert Christ's local presence in heaven
against Lutheran denials of the same:

> Do not the Evangelists clearly relate that he was received into heaven? These
> clever Sophists reply that he was taken away from their sight in a cloud in order
> that believers might learn that he would not be visible thereafter in the world.
> . . . But when he is borne high into the air, and by the cloud beneath him, teaches
> us that he is no longer to be sought on earth, we safely infer that his abode is
> now in heaven—just as Paul also declares, and bids us look for him in heaven.[128]

But, as John Colwell notes, Calvin seems not to have been aware that, in his assertions of the doctrine of the ascension against Lutheran ideas about ubiquity,
he was restating an important aspect of Thomas's teaching on the Eucharist.[129]

---

immediacy and lose sight of the mediate. That which Thomas Aquinas and John Calvin
have in common is a recognition of the mediateness of sacramentality: a sacrament is
a "means" of grace; only God is the efficient cause of grace within a sacrament. It was
perhaps the loss of this stress on the mediate in the years intervening between Thomas
and Calvin that provided a basis for the sacramental presumption against which the
Reformation was a protest.

125. Benedict XVI, "Problem of Transubstantiation," 221: "Since Calvin obviously learned
about the Real Presence primarily in its Lutheran form as a doctrine about the ubiquity of the
man Jesus, he felt obligated just by his stance on the humanity of Jesus to reject this doctrine:
Christ is seated at the right hand of the Father and *not* on our altars."

126. *ST* III, 75.2 corpus.

127. *ST* III, 76.6 sc.

128. Calvin, *Inst.* 4.17:1394–95 (27). Cf. *Inst.* 4.17:1373 (12): "For as we do not doubt that
Christ's body is limited by the general characteristics common to all human bodies, and is contained in heaven (where it was once for all received) until Christ return in judgment [Acts 3:21],
so we deem it utterly unlawful to draw it back under these corruptible elements or to imagine
it to be present everywhere." See also *Inst.* 4.17:1401: "Christ's body was circumscribed by the
measure of a human body. Again by his ascension into heaven he made it plain that it is not in
all places, but when it passes into one, it leaves the previous one."

129. Colwell, *Promise and Presence*, 168.

Calvin's concern for the doctrine of the ascension and its implications for eucharistic theology were twofold. First of all, he rejected any theological construction that evaporated Christ's bodiliness. A body, by its very nature as body, must be in a place. Second, the doctrine of the ascension tells us that that place is heaven, and it is necessary for our salvation that he really has ascended thence. These two concerns are evident in Calvin's famous boundary conditions for articulations of real presence:

> Let us never (I say) allow these two limitations to be taken away from us: (1) Let nothing be withdrawn from Christ's heavenly glory—as happens when he is brought under the corruptible elements of this world or bound to any earthly creature. (2) Let nothing inappropriate to human nature be ascribed to his body, as happens when it is said either to be infinite or to be put in a number of places at once.[130]

He continues:

> But when these absurdities have been set aside, I freely accept whatever can be made to express the true and substantial partaking of the body and blood of the Lord, which is shown to believers under the sacred symbols of the Supper—and so to express it that they may be understood not to receive it solely by imagination or understanding of mind but to enjoy the thing itself as nourishment of eternal life.[131]

One wonders whether Thomas's articulation would have satisfied Calvin in these terms. Thomas certainly affirmed that Christ remained in his heavenly glory in his own real body, the same one that was born of the Virgin Mary and that died and rose again for our salvation. In a nonpolemical context, would Thomas's affirmations that Christ is not moved when the host is moved precisely because he is in heaven or that a mouse eating a consecrated host does not access Christ's substance be enough to preserve him from the charge of bringing Christ under corruptible elements or binding Christ to any earthly creature? It seems clear, at least, that this was Thomas's intention with such careful qualifications.

Ascension and Real Presence

In any case, it is necessary to consider Calvin's insistence on the impact of the ascension on eucharistic theology more deeply. David Steinmetz writes that

130. Calvin, *Inst*. 4.17:1381–82 (19).
131. Calvin, *Inst*. 4.17:1382 (19).

"Calvin's problem is to explain how the humanity of Christ, though absent from the bread in one sense, is nevertheless present in another."[132] In a way, this is not just Calvin's problem, but *the* problem of anyone who wants to affirm real presence. Nevertheless, it is true that Calvin feels the problem in a particularly acute fashion since he follows on a debate where both parties assumed that real presence and a literal ascension were incompatible.[133] Like Thomas, Calvin believes that the two are not incompatible.[134] As he wrote to Bullinger, "Although the flesh of Christ is in heaven, . . . I see no absurdity in saying that we truly and in all reality receive the flesh and blood of Christ, and that he is substantially our food so long as it is admitted that Christ comes down to us not only by means of external symbols but also by the secret workings of his Spirit, so that we through faith may rise up to him."[135] Nevertheless, Calvin's context made it much more difficult, and more important, to indicate just why not.

As in our discussion of transubstantiation, we must guard against thinking about this issue as a kind of logic problem without reference to theological considerations. The ascension, whatever it may mean in terms of physics or biology, is first and foremost a theological claim, and its importance for understanding eucharistic presence must be approached from this direction. What, then, were some of the theological implications for eucharistic presence that Calvin saw implicit in the doctrine of the ascension?

First of all, we can agree with Peter Leithart that "Calvin's basic concern was to emphasize that there has been real progress in redemptive history."[136] That Christ is now glorified and seated at the right hand of the Father in heaven means that humanity's relationship to God is now determined by Christ's victory over death. To bring Christ down from heaven is to deny Christ's victory and glorification and to undo the means of our salvation. In this way, our salvation actually depends on Christ's absence from earth,[137] or perhaps better, on his bodily presence in heaven. For, if Christ's body is not risen, what hope is there for our own bodies?[138]

But it is not merely that progress has been made in redemptive history. It is also the case that that history is still ongoing. "Calvin is suspicious of over-realized eschatologies that announce Christ's return in the flesh prior to

132. Steinmetz, "Calvin and His Lutheran Critics," 187.
133. Cf. Van Dyk, "Reformed View," 78.
134. Hunsinger, *Eucharist and Ecumenism*, 35.
135. Quoted in Jones, *Christ's Eucharistic Presence*, 141.
136. Leithart, "What's Wrong with Transubstantiation?," 319.
137. Davis, *This Is My Body*, 130.
138. Jones, *Christ's Eucharistic Presence*, 141; N. Kerr, "*Corpus Verum*," 234.

his second coming and he is especially emphatic in maintaining the reality of Christ's humanity in his post-resurrection glory."[139] The ascension points to what Douglas Farrow calls "the eschatological dialectic of the departure and return of Jesus."[140] Christ has gone away and he will return. But he has not yet done so. Calvin writes, "When Scripture speaks of the ascension of Christ, it declares, at the same time, that he will come again. If he now occupies the whole world in respect of his body, what else was his ascension, and what will his descent be, but a fallacious and empty show."[141] This is obviously written with an eye to the Lutherans, but it is safe to say that Calvin feels there is a danger, not merely in the ubiquity doctrine, but in any articulation of real presence that renders the second coming superfluous by ignoring Christ's current location in heaven.

Joseph Ratzinger highlights this stance as one of the two things in Calvin's articulation "deserving a positive evaluation," writing that

> one could speak about a dialectic between a theology of the Incarnation of the Lord, who gives himself completely into our hands, and a theology of the Ascension of the Lord, who nonetheless remains the completely-Other in his superior power, which nothing and no one can bind or obligate. The mysterious "simultaneity" of Christ's "being here" and "not being here," of his being a servant and being Lord, becomes visible in this dialectic in an astonishing way.[142]

Ratzinger here hints at a further implication of Calvin's emphasis on the ascension for eucharistic theology. While maintaining that we are existing in the time of the Church, the time between Christ's first and second comings, it also says something about Christ's relationship to the Church—namely, that he is its risen Lord. The Reformers were gravely concerned that the Catholic view of the sacraments had granted sacramental agency, not to Christ, but to the Roman Catholic priesthood. Language of "descent" surrounding the consecration gave the impression of priests pulling Christ down from heaven,

---

139. Michael Scott Horton, "Union and Communion: Calvin's Theology of Word and Sacrament," *International Journal of Systematic Theology* 11, no. 4 (October 2009): 410.

140. Farrow, "Between the Rock and a Hard Place," 172; See also N. Kerr, "*Corpus Verum*," 233–34: "This emphasis on the ascended body of Christ highlights an irreducibly eschatological dimension to Calvin's account of eucharistic presence. Eucharist takes places within the interval of Christ's ascension and second coming ([*Inst.*] 4.17.27), which is to say that our partaking occurs within a time of eschatological hope. That Christ's body has indeed actually ascended into heaven suggests to us that our bodies too must be resurrected in the same way if our participation in Christ is to be fulfilled as *koinonia* with the *totus Christus*."

141. *Tracts and Treatises* 2:286, quoted in Farrow, "Between the Rock and a Hard Place," 178. See also the quote from *Inst.* 4.17:1373 (12) above (211n128).

142. Benedict XVI, "Problem of Transubstantiation," 222.

and therefore of having power over him. Calvin's insistence that Christ remains in heaven reinforces his insistence that Christ, through the Holy Spirit, and not the priest, is the agent of the sacrament.[143]

If transubstantiation, linked with the words of consecration, gave the impression of descent and of the agency of the priest, Calvin highlighted another part of the liturgy as an antidote. Because of his focus on Christ's presence in heaven, for Calvin the *sursum corda* ("Lift up your hearts") provided the key to understanding the direction of the sacramental action.[144] But the temptation to make the sacraments a function of human agency cannot be skirted so easily. While the temptation of transubstantiation may be an overemphasis on the role of the priest, the temptation of the *sursum corda* is to imagine that we worshipers pull ourselves up to heaven by our own efforts. In order to combat this temptation, Calvin also had recourse to the language of "descent." It is only because Christ descends to us in symbol and Spirit that we are able to lift our hearts on high.[145] His opponents "do not understand the manner of descent by which he lifts us up to himself."[146] For Calvin, descent and ascent are not opposed. It is in order to raise us up to heaven that Christ comes down to us and accommodates himself to our weakness.[147] It is worth noting that this sounds remarkably like Thomas's justification for the necessity of sacraments in the first place.[148] Furthermore, in line with the eschatological emphases of Ratzinger and Durrwell, Kiesling notes an upward dynamic in the distinction between impanation and transubstantiation:

> Significantly, Roman Catholic doctrine speaks of the conversion of the substance of the elements into the substance of the body and blood of Christ, *not the other way around*. Christ does not change. Christ is present, not because he comes down, but because the bread and wine are raised up to him, so that *we* may be raised up to him in his glorious humanity to be nourished by it—all of course, by the power and action of the Holy Spirit.[149]

It is important to recognize that none of this rather spatial language should be understood in a naïve way. Calvin is using spatial language because it is all

---

143. Puosi, "Ecclesiastical Communion," 192.
144. Zachman, "Revising the Reform," 180.
145. Heron, *Table and Tradition*, 131; see also Grislis, "Eucharistic Presence of Christ," 21. Note this dynamic also in the letter to Bullinger quoted above, p. 213.
146. Calvin, *Inst.* 4.17:1379 (16).
147. Davis, *Clearest Promises of God*, 211.
148. See *ST* III, 61.1.
149. Response to MacKenzie, "Reformed and Roman Catholic Understandings of the Eucharist," 77 (emphasis added).

that is available to us, but he does not understand either the *sursum corda*,[150] or the various images of descent and ascent in the Supper, or even the ascension itself in terms of physical operations. When it is insisted that Calvin (and Thomas) believed in a "literal" ascension, this indicates their belief that Christ's physical absence needs to be accounted for in their theology of real presence. It does not mean that they imagine Christ literally seated at some remote physical locality a great distance from earth. As Calvin insists, "'Departing' and 'ascending' do not signify giving the appearance of one ascending and departing, but actually doing what the words state. Shall we therefore, some will say, assign to Christ a definite region of heaven? But I reply with Augustine that this is a very prying and superfluous question; for us it is enough to believe that he is in heaven."[151]

Nevertheless, Catholic commentators have sometimes concluded that Calvin's theology of eucharistic presence is weakened by his emphasis on the ascension understood in too local a way.[152] This may be a function of reading the 1559 *Institutes* to the exclusion of other sources.[153] As we have seen, the final edition of the *Institutes* was heavily influenced by Calvin's polemic battles with Westphal, and this opponent, with his doctrine of ubiquity, not to mention his infuriating persistence, would have drawn from Calvin his less nuanced assertions about the ascension. Thomas Davis has argued, however, that, while "it is easy to come to divergent conclusions,"[154] Calvin's commentaries on Scripture provide the key for resolving the ambiguities present in the *Institutes* because it is in his commentaries that "Calvin remarked most clearly on the figurative nature of speech when talking about the ascension of Christ."[155]

---

150. Bavinck, "Calvin's Doctrine of the Lord's Supper," 138: Calvin does not mean "a magical rising or relocations of believers into heaven, effected by the Holy Spirit," but rather "that each one must remember that this is a spiritual mystery, one that according to the nature of the kingdom of Christ must be distinguished from all earthly activities."

151. Calvin, *Inst.* 4.17:1394 (26).

152. See, e.g., Benedict XVI, "Problem of Transubstantiation," 221: "Calvin's starting point is a strong emphasis on the real humanity of Jesus that manifests itself in his writings as a *theology of the Ascension* understood very emphatically and quite essentially in a local sense as well. Christ sits at the right hand of the Father and nowhere else; because he is true man he cannot be everywhere at the same time." See also Kilian McDonnell: "There is in [Calvin's] Eucharistic doctrine . . . an unmistakable local sense. . . . For Calvin, the Ascension experience has to do with body, space, movement from an earthly here to a heavenly there. . . . One cannot interpret Calvin's Eucharistic doctrine without this strong spatial element." Quoted in Davis, *This Is My Body*, 129.

153. Davis, *This Is My Body*, 131n10.

154. Davis, *This Is My Body*, 129.

155. Davis, *This Is My Body*, 132–33. Cf. Cunnington ("Calvin's Doctrine of the Lord's Supper," 230), who suggests that Calvin's best explanation of his ascent/descent dynamic can be

In his illuminating chapter "'He Is Outwith the World . . . That He May Fill All Things': Calvin's Exegesis of the Ascension and Its Relation to the Eucharist," Davis presents two theses:

> Thesis one: Calvin believed that it is absolutely essential for the ascension to be understood as the removal of Christ's body from earth to heaven so that it is corporeally absent from believers. Calvin's understanding of salvation depended on this.
>
> Thesis two: Calvin thought it absolutely essential that believers have access to the body of Christ in heaven so that it is corporeally present to them. Calvin's understanding of salvation depended on this.[156]

In order to resolve these seemingly exclusive claims, Davis highlights how Calvin, in his commentaries, indicates that "heaven has to do with something more than space: reality. Heaven . . . is not a place above the spheres but a different order of reality, or as Calvin put it, something 'set over against the fabric of the world.'"[157] He concludes that, for Calvin,

> separation from Christ is not a function of distance; rather, distance is a metaphor for separation. In other words, separation from Christ is not a function of physical removal, but it is that language of physical removal that best conveys to the human mind the reality of separation. To put it yet another way, the notion of distance was Calvin's way of speaking about the radical divide that separates the heavenly from the earthly, the divine from the human.[158]

And Laura Smit concurs, suggesting that, regarding heaven, Calvin insists on two simple things: "(1) Heaven is not here, in the world of our everyday experience, which means that we must in some way experience Christ as absent from us, but (2) heaven *is* our final destination and being with Christ is our ultimate purpose."[159]

This demythologization of Calvin's views about heaven and the ascension is important because it highlights, again, the precisely *theological* import of doctrine. Calvin's insistence on Christ's physical absence is not intended "to inform us of the exact location of the body (a question he dismisses), but to show that the mode of its presence cannot be what it was in the days of

---

found in his commentary on Genesis: "It is Christ alone who joins heaven to earth. He alone is Mediator. He it is through whom the fullness of all heavenly gifts flows down to us and through whom we on our part may ascend to God."

156. Davis, *This Is My Body*, 130.
157. Davis, *This Is My Body*, 133. See also Davis, *Clearest Promises of God*, 20.
158. Davis, *This Is My Body*, 136.
159. Smit, "Depth behind Things," 212.

Christ's earthly life."[160] But the ascension does not only show that Christ's eucharistic presence must be different from his earthly presence; for Calvin it is also the ground of possibility for that presence.

Mode of Presence

In his debates with the Lutherans, Calvin had always insisted that his concern was not with the fact of Christ's presence, but rather with the *mode* of that presence.[161] Calvin was concerned with any articulation that did not clearly distinguish between the mode of presence Christ had during his earthly ministry and that which he has in the Eucharist. As we have already seen, Luther's ubiquity doctrine has often been misread as indicating a rather naturalistic presence (in part because his own philosophical background led him in that direction and in part because he was willing, in polemical situations, to make rather bald statements). On the other hand, we have seen that such readings are not fair to Luther's own intentions and that he did, in fact, make other statements that indicate a more sacramental understanding. Calvin, on the other hand, has been misread as indicating a rather naturalistic ascension (and therefore absence). But we have also seen that his insistence on the ascension is a primarily theological affirmation, the intention of which is to insist that the kind of presence available to us in the Eucharist must be different from that of either the first or second coming. It would seem then that, in the attempt to articulate Christ's eucharistic presence, Luther and Calvin start on opposite sides of the presence/absence dialectic, but are both straining toward a more balanced position. Both men significantly qualify their statements precisely in the direction (if not necessarily to the degree) that the other would have desired.

This takes place in a rather striking way in Calvin's articulation of how the ascension makes eucharistic presence possible. While for Luther the movement of the eucharistic action is above all downward and incarnational—in at least one place he attributes Christ's omnipresence to the incarnation rather than, as is often suggested, the resurrection[162]—for Calvin it is primarily upward. Nevertheless, it is important to recognize that, while ascent is undeniably dominant in Calvin,[163] he attempts to balance it with language of "descent," as

160. Gerrish, *Grace and Gratitude*, 183.
161. Gerrish, *Grace and Gratitude*, 144; Calvin, "Best Method," 574–75.
162. *This Is My Body* (1527), in *LW* 37:66. See also Stephenson, *Lord's Supper*, 253n32; cf. Calvin, *Inst.* 4.17:1379 (16), n. 54: "Luther had taught the ubiquity of Christ's *postresurrection* body" (emphasis added).
163. Cunnington, "Calvin's Doctrine of the Lord's Supper," 230; cf. Benedict XVI, "Problem of Transubstantiation," 222. Ratzinger expresses concern that it "has won a one-sided victory"

we have already seen. But even if Calvin's dialectical approach—which "traces a movement downward *and* upward: condescension *and* elevation, incarnation *and* resurrection/ascension, and so stresses the distinction between the 'earthly' and the 'heavenly'"[164]—is the cause of Lutheran mistrust, as Alasdair Heron notes, it is also the case that his view of the ascension is what allows Calvin to affirm Christ's descent to us by the signs of the Eucharist.

The ascension, for Calvin, does not only insist on Christ's bodily absence, though it certainly does that, but it also grants to Christ a share in God's omnipresence and so makes possible a presence that does not transgress upon his bodily ascension.[165] As Calvin puts it in the 1559 *Institutes,*

> For though he has taken his flesh away from us, and in the body has ascended into heaven, yet he sits at the right hand of the Father—that is, he reigns in the Father's power and majesty and glory. This Kingdom is neither bounded by location in space nor circumscribed by any limits. Thus Christ is not prevented from exerting his power wherever he pleases, in heaven and on earth. He shows his presence in power and strength, is always among his own people, and breathes his life upon them, and lives in them, sustaining them, strengthening, quickening, keeping them unharmed, as if he were present with his own body. In short, he feeds his people with his own body, the communion of which he bestows upon them by the power of his Spirit.[166]

The metaphor Calvin prefers to express this dynamic is that of the sun, which communicates its life-giving rays to the earth without leaving the sky.[167]

The affinity of this understanding with the Lutheran view, while incomplete, should not go unremarked. In fact, when Calvin responded to Tileman Heshusius's attack on his doctrine of the Lord's Supper, which included an argument that "by the communication of properties (the *communicatio idiomatum*) ubiquity is ascribed *in concreto* to the whole person of Christ, the answer may have surprised him: Calvin replied that this was his own doctrine

---

so that "in the dialectical interplay of 'being here' and 'not being here,' the 'being here' runs the risk of being abolished in practice." We will revisit this issue below.

164. Heron, *Table and Tradition,* 132–33; see also Horton, "Union and Communion," 409.

165. Richard Muller and Joseph Tylenda both highlight that Calvin's conception of the ascension is necessary for understanding his preference for the term *exhibere* to indicate how Christ is present in the Eucharist. *Exhibere* presupposes a Christ who is not bound spatially and who can truly hold himself forth to believers. Muller notes that this verb indicates a distancing from Zwingli. Muller, "From Zürich or from Wittenberg?," 249, 252; Tylenda, "Ecumenical Intention," 31–32.

166. Calvin, *Inst.* 4.17:1381 (18). Cf. Gerrish, *Grace and Gratitude,* 177. Gerrish notes that the final sentence quoted here was added in 1539. This is consistent with what we have seen in terms of Calvin's growing affirmations of eucharistic realism at this time in his career.

167. Gerrish, *Grace and Gratitude,* 177–78.

exactly."[168] Of course, the implications for Calvin were not the same as they were for the Lutherans.[169] And Calvin was concerned that the Lutheran idea of ubiquity erased the distinction between Christ's presence in heaven and his presence in the Eucharist by bringing Christ down from heaven. For him, on the other hand, Christ's participation in God's ubiquity is what allowed Christians to experience his presence, even while he remained in heaven. What is interesting is that, in responding to the Lutherans on this question, Calvin appeals to the Scholastics:

> There is a commonplace distinction of the schools to which I am not ashamed to refer: although the whole Christ is everywhere, still the whole of that which is in him is not everywhere. And would that the Schoolmen themselves had honestly weighed the force of this statement. For thus would the absurd fiction of Christ's carnal presence have been obviated. Therefore, since the whole Christ is everywhere, our Mediator is ever present with his own people, and in the Supper reveals himself in a special way, yet in such a way that the whole Christ is present, but not in his wholeness. For, as has been said, in his flesh he is contained in heaven until he appears in judgment.[170]

If it is true that Thomas actually did weigh the force of this statement and therefore actually did preserve the distinction between Christ's presence in heaven and in the sacrament, and if it is also the case that the Lutherans, despite their polemic emphases against the Swiss and Calvin, did not intend to affirm a presence that is indistinguishable from Christ's first or second coming, have we not here a significant ecumenical convergence? Let us pursue the matter a little more closely.

Eschatology, Again

In his article "Between the Rock and a Hard Place: In Support of (Something like) a Reformed View of the Eucharist," Douglas Farrow argues that the weakness of Calvin's articulation, that which leaves it open to being understood as a purely subjective view, is Calvin's failure to radicalize the eschatological dynamism inherent in his dialectic.[171] For Farrow, "Calvin handled the dialectic of presence and absence almost exclusively in spatial terms, and to that extent in

---

168. Gerrish, "Luther and the Reformed Eucharist," 17.

169. Cf. Steinmetz, "Calvin and His Lutheran Critics," 183.

170. Calvin, *Inst.* 4.17:1403 (30). See also Steinmetz, "Calvin and His Lutheran Critics," 187; Willis, "Reformed Doctrine of the Eucharist and Ministry," 301–2: "Moreover, while Calvin rejects the doctrine of *bodily* ubiquity, he obviously always teaches that Christ is ubiquitous according to his divinity which was and is hypostatically united to the flesh but not restricted to it."

171. Farrow, "Between the Rock and a Hard Place," 181.

a *non*-eschatological fashion."[172] Something understood spatially is either present or it is not and, within such a framework, Calvin would have to be read as
professing Christ's absence. Eschatology, with its already-but-not-yet dynamism,
allows for a more nuanced relationship between presence and absence. But we
have already seen Thomas Davis's conclusion that Calvin's use of spatial terminology was analogical, though we have also seen that Davis himself needed to
go to Calvin's commentaries to demonstrate this point. In the *Institutes*, which
is what most people read, this dynamic is less clear. But if Davis is right, then
Farrow's suggestion—that Calvin's insistence on the presence/absence dialectic
becomes more ecumenically helpful when understood in a radically eschatological way—is a suggestion that Calvin himself would seem quite comfortable with.
In such a case, "the ubiquity confessed would be that for which Irenaeus looks
on the far side of the resurrection, where in the kingdom of God the creation
itself will be reconfigured for the sake of true communion, and the savior shall
be seen everywhere 'according as they who see him shall be worthy.'"[173]

It is fascinating that this proposal by Farrow finds echoes in both Davis's
and Ratzinger's assessments of Calvin. Davis writes that, for Calvin,

> heaven is the place of God's rule, which is no place at all but fills all places
> without being contained thereby. Christ in power and majesty and as God also
> rules in heaven in this omnipresent manner, and Calvin admitted that Christ is
> present with believers in this manner. But he also asserted that Christ's body
> cannot be presumed to be present locally because of this doctrine of divine
> ubiquity; . . . Bodies must be in a place because that is their nature; Christ's
> body as body is an instrument of salvation and thus must remain human and
> therefore must be contained as in a place. Calvin declared that that place is
> heaven; but though Calvin did say that, he almost always added, when pressed
> to explain, that heaven, as such, is not a place.[174]

For his part, Ratzinger supplements this eschatological theme with an appeal
to the personal order, which also admits of a presence/absence dialectic,[175] to
make the same point. Because God is not present locally, but personally, the
same must apply to the risen (i.e., eschatological) Christ,

> who has burst the confines of the "sarx," of historical delimitations, and has
> the power to impart himself in all places, to be really present with his complete

---

172. Farrow, "Between the Rock and a Hard Place," 182.
173. Farrow, "Between the Rock and a Hard Place," 185. The internal quote is from Irenaeus,
Against the Heretics 5.36.1.
174. Davis, *This Is My Body*, 134; see also Horton, "Union and Communion," 411.
175. See, e.g., Benedict XVI, "Problem of Transubstantiation," 239.

fullness for the Thou of mankind: precisely this openness of self-giving beyond all places is the essence of his Resurrection existence that has now passed through death. Through his Resurrection, Christ has entered into the freedom that allows him to grant his Thou where he wishes; and he imparts himself in and through the thanksgiving prayer of the Church gathered together in his name.[176]

Ratzinger goes on to conclude that

we can preserve the element that correctly kept [Calvin] from a simple agreement with Luther's ubiquity doctrine. So we will now say that certainly no natural ubiquity is to be attributed to Christ, and on this point Calvin is right as opposed to Luther. But no local limitation to an imaginary heavenly place should be attributed to him, either. Nowhere does the Risen One have a physically restricted place that can be designated. As the Risen One he has entered into a new mode of existence and participates in God's might, by virtue of which he can give himself to his own whenever and wherever he wishes.[177]

Now, it must be frankly acknowledged that Ratzinger has not taken full account of the nuances in the positions of Luther and Calvin. Though it is not difficult to find supporting quotes to buttress the contention that they had naïvely local views of ubiquity or ascension respectively, we have seen that to attribute these views to them is to fail to adequately represent their thought. This does not mean that their articulations did not suffer from ambiguities and deficiencies in precisely these directions. They did, as we have already seen. But those deficiencies are best interpreted as failures by either Reformer to do full justice to his own position and, often enough, as the products of a polemical age in which rhetorical force could sometimes take precedence over doctrinal precision.[178] What seems likely, given a more careful investigation of their thoughts on the matter, is that both Luther and Calvin would agree with Ratzinger that there is no "physically restricted place" in which the risen Christ could be located[179] and that Christ's capacity to be present in the Eucharist is a function of

176. Benedict XVI, "Problem of Transubstantiation," 239. For more on Ratzinger's views on the resurrection of the body, see Benedict XVI, *Introduction to Christianity*, trans. J. R. Foster (San Francisco: Ignatius, 2004), 356–59; *Eschatology: Death and Eternal Life*, ed. Aidan Nichols, trans. Michael Waldstein, 2nd ed. (Washington, DC: Catholic University of America Press, 2007), 191–94.

177. Benedict XVI, "Problem of Transubstantiation," 240.

178. For an example of a polemical exchange in which the atmosphere becomes so poisonous that one is certain the two combatants simply do not *want* to agree, see Tylenda, "Calvin-Westphal Exchange."

179. Davis, *This Is My Body*, 132: "No more than Luther did Calvin think, when Scripture spoke of Christ ascending to the right hand of the Father, that that phrase in itself meant a specific location."

his participation in God's power (even if Ratzinger grounds that participation in the resurrection, Luther in the incarnation, and Calvin in the ascension).

It seems that the fundamental difficulty is that of using physical, spatial language to address a problem that is not in its essence a physical problem. What that means is that the theological intention behind the spatial affirmations can easily get lost in the polemic so that compatible theologies are expressed through incompatible metaphors.[180] In the worst instances, the metaphors themselves can start to control the theologies and theological systems can choke out mystery. Insights like those of Farrow and Ratzinger that bring other, less spatial, categories to bear on the problem are very helpful in such a context. What we can note here, however, is that Calvin himself had had recourse to just such a category in his own articulation. In fact, Calvin appealed to something that no one denied, though many neglected, in the history of the debates about real presence. Or, rather, he appealed to someone.[181] Through his introduction of the agency of the Holy Spirit into the problem of eucharistic presence, Calvin too was introducing the personal as a category for understanding eucharistic presence.[182]

The Holy Spirit

The classic text in this regard is:

> But greatly mistaken are those who conceive no presence of flesh in the Supper unless it lies in the bread. For thus they leave nothing to the secret working of the Spirit, which unites Christ himself to us. To them Christ does not seem present unless he comes down to us. As though, if he should lift us to himself, we should not just as much enjoy his presence! The question is therefore only of the manner, for they place Christ in the bread, while we do not think it lawful for us to drag him from heaven.[183]

While it may at first appear that Calvin's appeal to the Spirit in this context is little more than an example of *deus ex machina*,[184] such an assessment fails to

180. Cf. Lehmann and Pannenberg, *Condemnations of the Reformation Era*, 98: "The concern and fundamental intention of the other position in each given case can be better understood in retrospect. All three doctrinal forms [Catholic, Lutheran, and Calvinist] were trying to express the mystery of Christ's presence in the Eucharist, but by way of different theoretical approaches which were apparently irreconcilable under the conditions of the sixteenth century."

181. Colwell, *Promise and Presence*, 171.

182. Colwell, *Promise and Presence*, 9; Power, *Eucharistic Mystery*, 253; Puosi, "Ecclesiastical Communion," 192.

183. Calvin, *Inst.* 4.17:1403 (31).

184. Cf. Farrow, "Between the Rock and a Hard Place," 171.

appreciate the theological import of this move. But Calvin's spatial imagery could give the wrong impression, as it seems to have given Gustave Martelet. Martelet praises Calvin for reintroducing the Holy Spirit into Western eucharistic theology but is not satisfied with Calvin's understanding. "The Holy Spirit," Martelet admonishes,

> is far from being a happily chosen device that enables us to cross a spatial gulf opened up between Christ and ourselves by a deceptively representational imagery. There is, indeed, a gap between Christ and ourselves, but it does not belong to the order of space: it lies in the order of parousia and freedom. Similarly the function of the Holy Spirit in the Eucharistic mystery has a depth other than that of filling a completely imaginary void.[185]

I want to suggest that Calvin would agree with Martelet. While Calvin's physical language (e.g., "The Spirit truly unites things separated in space")[186] does leave him open to the charge brought against him by Martelet and others, his invocation of the Holy Spirit is actually a perfect theological complement to his focus on the ascension. "Surely," Calvin argues, "the coming of the Spirit and the ascent of Christ are antithetical; consequently, Christ cannot dwell with us according to the flesh in the same way that he sends his Spirit."[187] Christ had declared that he must go in order that he might send the Spirit. The time of the Church, the time between the ascension and the second coming, is, then, the time in which Christ is mediated to us by the Spirit.[188] That is why the Church belongs in the third stanza of the creed. The role of the Spirit in the Eucharist is not, accordingly, mere post hoc explanation. Rather, it is ecclesiological and eschatological. If we are to experience the risen Christ in this phase of salvation history, these last days, it can only be through the mediation of the Holy Spirit.

On the other hand we can note that, even while the role given to the Holy Spirit by Calvin is completely justified, even essential, it was not present in Calvin's earliest works on the Eucharist.[189] Like Luther and like the whole Catholic tradition before transubstantiation, Calvin's early work on the Eu-

---

185. Martelet, *The Risen Christ and the Eucharistic World*, 146.

186. Calvin, *Inst.* 4.17:1370 (10).

187. Calvin, *Inst.* 4.17:1393 (26); see also Jones, *Christ's Eucharistic Presence*, 144. Cf. *ST* III, 75.1 obj. 4, ad 4.

188. Cf. Horton, "Union and Communion," 411: "Instead of saying that because Christ is Lord over time and space and therefore does not conform to the rules of ordinary bodies, we should say that because Christ is Lord over time and space *in the power of the Spirit*, the past of his work in the flesh for our salvation and the future consummation converge in a semi-realized manner at the Lord's Table."

189. Muller, "From Zürich or from Wittenberg?," 252–54.

charist did not include any attempt to demonstrate the coherence of the claim of real presence. But when Calvin's opponents doubted whether he actually did teach Christ's presence in the Eucharist, especially given his insistence on Christ's physical presence in heaven, he invoked the ministry of the Holy Spirit in his defense.[190] Given this, those observers are correct who point out that the Holy Spirit plays the same role for Calvin that ubiquity (though we should add ubiquity plus nominalist distinctions about different kinds of presence) has for Luther and that transubstantiation has for the Catholic tradition.[191] In each case, faith in the real presence is seeking understanding.[192]

Furthermore, while it is the case that Calvin's invocation of the Holy Spirit was seen by him to obviate the need for ubiquity or transubstantiation, both of which were seen to "drag Christ down from heaven," closer investigation shows that these doctrines are not as antithetical as they were understood to be in the sixteenth century. We have already seen the "agreement" of Heshusius and Calvin on ubiquity, something affirmed in its intention by Ratzinger. The Holy Spirit need not be an alternative to ubiquity thus understood, but can easily be seen as complementary to, or even as the medium of, it. Indeed, the other aspect of Calvin's eucharistic theology that Ratzinger highlights is that "the pneumatological character of Christian worship and of the eucharistic celebration is again seen clearly in Calvin's writings. Christian worship is something that happens in the Holy Spirit. The Holy Spirit is the space in which Christian worship of God is enacted."[193] Even while Ratzinger criticizes Calvin's "local" view of the ascension, he acknowledges here that Calvin is not merely using the Holy Spirit as a convenient bridge over some imagined space. Rather, the Spirit itself is the "space" in which encountering the Lord in the Eucharist is possible.

Substantial(ly)? Or Spiritual(ly)?

How then does this relate to Thomas and transubstantiation? As we have already seen, Thomas had no intention of "dragging Christ down from

190. This conclusion seems justified given the language we have already seen quoted above—namely, that "greatly mistaken are those who conceive no presence of flesh in the Supper unless it lies in the bread. For thus they leave nothing to the secret working of the Spirit." Calvin, *Inst.* 4.17:1403 (31).
191. Lehmann and Pannenberg, *Condemnations of the Reformation Era*, 98; Willis, "Reformed Doctrine of the Eucharist and Ministry," 300; cf. Colwell, *Promise and Presence*, 169; Hunsinger, *Eucharist and Ecumenism*, 35.
192. Willis, "Reformed Doctrine of the Eucharist and Ministry," 300; cf. Lehmann and Pannenberg, *Condemnations of the Reformation Era*, 101.
193. Benedict XVI, "Problem of Transubstantiation," 221–22.

heaven," and referred explicitly to Christ's presence at the right hand of the Father in order to clarify several points for understanding eucharistic presence. We have also seen that Thomas himself had recourse to the ministry of the Holy Spirit in his discussion of sacraments and their efficacy. As Thomas quotes St. John Damascene: "It is only by the power of the Holy Ghost that the change of the bread into the body of Christ takes place."[194] Thomas himself would never deny Calvin's invocation of the Spirit in this context. But, beyond these initial observations, one wonders, with John Colwell,

> whether Calvin's language of spiritual rather than bodily presence fulfills a similar function to Thomas's distinction (following Aristotle) between substance and accidents: to affirm that the substance of the elements (notwithstanding their continuing accidents) is determined by the Word of God, corresponds to the affirmation that Christ is spiritually (rather than bodily) present under these physical signs; i.e., that which is "spiritual" is that which is "substantial," that which is "physical" is "accidental."[195]

The problem Calvin faced, that of affirming Christ's eucharistic presence despite his literal understanding of the ascension, was precisely that faced by Aquinas, even if Aquinas did not have to deal with it in a polemic context. It should not be surprising, therefore, that their answers would end up structurally very similar. Both men needed to affirm that there was a way for Christ to be present in the Eucharist even while his physical body was and remained elsewhere. Furthermore, both men affirmed the physical reality of the bread and wine. The parallel that we have already seen between Aquinas and Calvin on the relationship between sign and signified, then, shows up again in the context of Calvin's teaching on the role of the Holy Spirit, and consequent use of the term "spiritually," in the Lord's Supper.[196]

194. *ST* III, 78.4 obj. 1. Thomas further explains that "when we say that it is by the power of the Holy Ghost and by it alone that the bread is changed into the body of Christ, we do not rule out the presence of an instrumental power in the form of this sacrament; just like when we say that it is only the craftsman who makes the knife, we do not exclude all power of the hammer" (78.4 ad 1). Cf. Gerrish, *Grace and Gratitude*, 138: "It follows that the sacraments are strictly the Spirit's means or instruments: where the Spirit is absent, the sacraments achieve no more than the sun shining on blind eyes or a voice sounding in deaf ears." See also Gerrish, "Luther and the Reformed Eucharist," 14.

195. John Colwell, *Living the Christian Story: The Distinctiveness of Christian Ethics* (Edinburgh: T&T Clark, 2001), 158n26; cf. Colwell, *Promise and Presence*, 170–71.

196. Cf. Gordon E. Pruett, "Protestant Doctrine of the Eucharistic Presence," *Calvin Theological Journal* 10, no. 2 (November 1975): 157. Pruett also notes the connection between the role of the Holy Spirit and Calvin's understanding of sign and signified, though he opposes it, awkwardly and without explanation, to transubstantiation.

One reason this parallel, which seems obvious once stated, has been so often overlooked is that language has confused the issue.[197] While the adjectives "substantial" and "spiritual" meant very similar things for Thomas and Calvin respectively, many have understood "substantial" to mean precisely "physical," and "spiritual" to mean precisely "subjective." The two terms, then, end up being seen as opposite ends of a materialistic view of the Eucharist that each, in its own context, is trying to subvert. Both terms were meant to assert an objective, though nonphysical, reality.

Calvin himself was forced to repeatedly explain his use of the adverb "spiritually." As he notes in his "Best Method of Obtaining Concord," "many are averse" to the term "*spiritually* . . . because they think that something vain or imaginary is denoted."[198] His opponents also suspected that Calvin taught that Christ was present only in spirit and, therefore, not in body. But he denied both of these interpretations repeatedly, insisting that the term "spiritually" indicated that Christ's body was present by the work of the Spirit.[199] And, as David Willis notes, Calvin "almost always (this is even a cautious statement) uses the adverb 'spiritually' rather than the adjective 'spiritual' to modify 'Presence' when referring to the whole Christ. The whole Christ is spiritually present—which is more than saying that the Reformer's position taught a spiritual presence of Christ in the eucharist."[200] Such usage reinforces Calvin's insistence that what was in question was not *what* was present—all agreed that Christ's body and blood, indeed the whole Christ,[201] was present—but merely the mode of that presence. As Michael Horton puts it, for Calvin, "it is not the *substance* of the Supper that is spiritual, but the *medium*—namely, the Holy Spirit."[202]

This emphasis on the medium was intended to guard against—in the same way that the category of "substance" had for Thomas—the idea "that the very substance of Christ is transfused into us *in the same way* as bread is eaten."[203] As Keith Mathison bluntly puts it, "According to Calvin, we do not partake

197. Indeed, "spiritual" and "substantial" were not the only controverted terms. Calvin often rejected the term "real" because it was the language his Lutheran opponents used to describe what Calvin understood to be a carnal presence. He preferred the term "true." Joseph N. Tylenda, "Calvin and Christ's Presence in the Supper—True or Real," *Scottish Journal of Theology* 27, no. 1 (February 1974): esp. 70–72.
198. Calvin, "Best Method," 577–78.
199. Gerrish, *Grace and Gratitude*, 137–38; Mathison, *Given for You*, 31–32; see, e.g., Calvin, "Best Method," 577–78; Calvin, *Inst.* 4.17:1370 (10); Calvin, "Short Treatise on the Supper of Our Lord," 197–98.
200. Willis, "Calvin's Use of Substantia," 294–95.
201. See, for Calvin, *Inst.* 4.17:1381 (18).
202. Horton, "Union and Communion," 409.
203. Calvin, "Best Method," 578 (emphasis added).

of Christ by means of the human digestive system."[204] Nevertheless, Calvin affirms that "Jesus Christ gives us in the Supper the proper substance of his body and his blood, in order that we may possess it fully, and possessing it have part in all his blessings."[205] For Calvin "spiritual" and "substance" are not mutually exclusive terms. Neither, of course, are they synonymous. For Calvin, "substance" could be used to describe *what* was present, but by his time it could not describe the mode. Thomas's *per modum substantiae*, in the mode of substance, captures what Calvin means by spiritually present, but Calvin himself could not have used Thomas's term. For him it would have indicated the very opposite of what it meant for Thomas.[206] Rather, intending what Thomas intended when he said that Christ's *body* was present *in the mode of substance*, Calvin said the *substance of Christ's body* was present *spiritually*. Furthermore, David Willis echoes Thomas's claim that God could make Christ present *per modum substantiae* because, as Creator, it is within his power to determine things at the core of their being: "To describe the Spirit's work [the way Calvin does] is not a substitute for an ontology of Christ's real presence. It is rather to say that there is no stronger ontology than that of the being and activity of the Spirit, who is not just the agent of personal sanctification but is no less Creator Spirit."[207]

Finally, we have seen how "substance" functioned for Thomas, not only as a way to mitigate carnal or physical interpretations of eucharistic presence, but also to guarantee the objectivity and reality of that presence; this is also true of

204. Mathison, *Given for You*, 32; see also Pruett, "Protestant Doctrine of the Eucharistic Presence," 157: "Participation in Christ is not a matter of swallowing Christ's flesh."

205. Calvin, "Short Treatise on the Supper of Our Lord," 172–73; see also Mathison, *Given for You*, 35–36. On p. 35, Mathison quotes Calvin's response to Heshusius's suggestion that Calvin denies that Christians partake of Christ's substance: "But it is declared in my writings more than a hundred times, that so far am I from rejecting the term substance, that I ingenuously [i.e., candidly] and readily declare, that by the incomprehensible agency of the Spirit, spiritual life is infused into us from the substance of the flesh of Christ. I also constantly admit that we are substantially fed on the flesh and blood of Christ." Calvin had rejected "substantial presence" in the first edition (1536) of the *Institutes*, but that was dropped in subsequent editions. See also Muller, "From Zürich or from Wittenberg?," 252–53.

206. Crockett highlights three different ways that Calvin uses the term "substance," and concludes, "By denying that the 'substance' of Christ's body is present in the eucharist in the first meaning of the term [i.e., Christ's natural body] Calvin intends to exclude any local or physical presence of Christ in the Supper. Calvin sees no opposition, however, between the second [i.e., Christ himself] and the third meaning [i.e., Christ's life, benefits, and power] of the term 'substance,' between the assertion that we receive the very body of Christ in the Supper and the assertion that 'a life-giving power from the flesh of Christ is poured into us through the medium of the Spirit'" (*Eucharist*, 158). For more on Calvin's use of the term "substance," see Willis, "Calvin's Use of Substantia." Willis concludes that Calvin's "aim is to teach Christ's real presence in the eucharist" (301).

207. Willis, "Reformed Doctrine of the Eucharist and Ministry," 300.

Calvin's understanding of the role of the Spirit. The particular difficulty in Calvin's case is that, since he believed that Christ's presence could not be received without faith, it risks being understood as dependent on faith and therefore upon something subjective within the individual believer.[208] In response to this dilemma, Calvin argued for a "double agency of the Holy Spirit": "The Holy Spirit is both the agent of the presence of Christ and the one who gives the gift of faith by which it is received. Faith itself, therefore, is the effect of the divine action of the Holy Spirit. The Holy Spirit provides the objective bond between the presence of Christ in the eucharist and the subjective response in the believer in faith."[209] The Holy Spirit, therefore, provides not only the objective content of the Supper, communion with Christ's body, but also the subjective faith in the recipient needed to truly receive the objective content.[210] This twofold agency is connected to the ascent/descent dynamic as well. Christ descends in symbol and Spirit so that we can ascend to him in faith.[211]

An Obstacle and a Way Forward

While no one would want to deny the necessity of faith for the proper reception of the Eucharist, it is difficult not to conclude that this is the one place where Calvin's critics have a legitimate concern that his articulation does not actually safeguard real presence. Can Calvin, after all, truly ground the objective nature of the Supper by grounding the subjective faith of the believer in the objective work of the Spirit? Several conclusions that follow from this affirmation of his seem to indicate not.[212] We shall look at three in particular: (1) that the Lord's Supper does not contain anything more than the sacrifices of the old law, (2) that the Lord's Supper contains no more than what is available to faith without it, and (3) that the one who receives the Lord's Supper without faith receives nothing but mere bread and mere wine.

Something More?

According to Thomas Aquinas, one reason that we must profess that Christ is "really and truly in this sacrament" is because "it was only right that the

208. Crockett, *Eucharist*, 158.
209. Crockett, *Eucharist*, 159; see also Heron, *Table and Tradition*, 140; Pruett, "Protestant Doctrine of the Eucharistic Presence," 142, 157, 167.
210. Smit, "Depth behind Things," 220.
211. Pruett, "Protestant Doctrine of the Eucharistic Presence," 168.
212. See Jenson, "Tenth Locus," 358. According to Jenson, Calvin's account, while plausible, "does, however, have consequences."

sacrifice of the New Law instituted by Christ should have something more, that it should contain Christ himself who suffered for us, and contain him, not merely as by a sign or figure, but in actual reality as well."[213] That the sacrifices of the old law contained Christ "only in a figurative way" seems supported, thinks Thomas, by the Letter to the Hebrews, which calls them "a shadow of the good things to come instead of the true form of these realities" (Heb. 10:1). Calvin, on the other hand, considers that

> the ancient sacraments had the same end in view as our own—viz. to direct and almost to lead us by the hand to Christ. . . . There is only this difference, that while the former shadowed forth the promised Christ while he was still expected, the latter bear testimony to him as already come and manifested. . . . The scholastic dogma . . . by which . . . the difference is made so great that the former did nothing but shadow forth the grace of God while the latter actually confer it, must be altogether exploded.[214]

While the difference here can look quite radical at first glance, it is important to note that Thomas's position is not that the sacrifices of the temple do not confer the grace of God, as Calvin interprets the Scholastics, but that they do not contain Christ *himself* in the same way as Christ's own sacrifice, presented in the Supper. Thomas does not deny that the grace of Christ's cross was available to those under the old law.[215] And Calvin does affirm that Christ was "shadowed forth."

Indeed when challenged on this point by Westphal, Calvin sounds much more like Thomas than his criticisms of Scholasticism seem to allow. In his *Second Defense*, Calvin writes that "there is a difference in the Christian eating the flesh of Christ and the father [*sic*] of the Old Covenant. The former eat in a substantial mode and the latter ate in a limited anticipatory mode. Yet all are common partakers but in different degrees."[216] The difference, then, is not as radical as it might appear, but it is still significant. Both Thomas and Calvin acknowledge that grace is available under the old law because of Christ's sacrifice, and both acknowledge that the sacrament of the new law, the Lord's Supper, contains something more. But for Thomas this something more seems to be what we might call qualitative, while for Calvin it seems merely quantitative.[217]

213. *ST* III, 75.1.
214. Quoted in Heron, *Table and Tradition*, 139.
215. *ST* III, 61.3 ad 2.
216. Quoted in Meyer, "*Mysterium Fidei* and the Later Calvin," 406.
217. As an aside, we can note that there seems to be a tension here between Calvin's insistence on the progress in salvation history that we witnessed in his theology of the ascension and his suggestion that the difference between the sacrifices of the old law and the Lord's Supper is only one of degrees. See above, pp. 213–14.

I suggest that the root of this difference lies in Calvin's refusal to separate receiving Christ from receiving his benefits.[218] If the fathers under the old covenant receive the grace of Christ—and Thomas and Calvin agree that they do—then, for Calvin, they must receive Christ himself as well. In fact, as Calvin argues in his commentary on 1 Corinthians, Old Testament believers "received [Christ's flesh] by the secret power of the Holy Spirit, 'who was active in such a way that the flesh of Christ, even if it was not yet created, might be efficacious in them.'"[219] This stance of Calvin's makes it difficult for him to clearly assert something new in the Lord's Supper without seeming to deny the grace of Christ to believers under the old law. What is new can only be a matter of form, not content.[220]

This same dynamic is at play in Calvin's teaching that the Lord's Supper does not contain anything more than what is available to faith in general. As Davis points out, in both cases—the difference between the Old and New Testaments and the difference between what is available simply through faith and what is available in the Supper—Calvin sees a "difference in degree."[221] Calvin's teaching on this issue makes it difficult for Gerrish to discern whether "the Sacrament actually offers us something or only confirms that we possess it already."[222] It is not, concludes Gerrish, that the Supper "brings about a communion with Christ, or a reception of his body, that is not available anywhere else, but rather that it graphically represents and presents to believers a communion they enjoy, or can enjoy, all the time."[223] This is Calvin's theme when expounding the specific and irreplaceable role of the Supper, that it shows us, weak and halting as we are, "the substance of his promises, to confirm and fortify us by delivering us from all doubt and uncertainty."[224] What "is done through the gospel" is done "more clearly through the Supper, where he offers himself with all his benefits to us, and we receive him by faith."[225]

Whether this amounts to something more, a sacramental "plus," as Gerrish calls it,[226] is not an easy question to answer. Melvin Tinker suggests that

---

218. Davis, *This Is My Body*, 132: "Indeed, one must have Christ bodily, Calvin repeatedly asserted, if one is to have his benefits."

219. Cunnington, "Calvin's Doctrine of the Lord's Supper," 228.

220. Cf. Calvin, *Inst.* 4.18:1440 (12).

221. Davis, *Clearest Promises of God*, 217.

222. Gerrish, *Grace and Gratitude*, 127.

223. Gerrish, *Grace and Gratitude*, 133; cf. Gerrish, "Gospel and Eucharist," 110: "On the other hand, if sacraments confer no more than the Word, it is equally clear to Calvin that they confer no less. The sacraments have the *same* function as the Word of God: to offer and present to us Jesus Christ."

224. Calvin, "Short Treatise on the Supper of Our Lord," 166.

225. Calvin, *Inst.* 4.17:1364 (5).

226. Gerrish, *Grace and Gratitude*, 162.

contemporary studies in the philosophy of language and ritual studies could "provide the explanatory framework for which Calvin was striving,"[227] in his articulations of the specific role of the sacraments in a way that would allow him to affirm "something more."[228] And Paul Jones puts the matter in an interesting way when he writes that, for Calvin, "the eucharist, with no unique content, has a specific function,"[229] that of interpreting "more precisely and more concretely that union we have with Christ."[230]

In both cases, that of the relationship of the old and the new laws and of the relationship between what is received in faith generally and in the Supper, Calvin seems conflicted.[231] He wants to affirm something stronger for the new law vis-à-vis the old and for the Supper vis-à-vis faith generally, but he cannot affirm any specific content in the Supper that is not available elsewhere. Lutheran and Catholic advocates of real presence wonder, then, just how real the real presence Calvin professes is. Ratzinger, for instance, notes the tension in Calvin between statements that seem to deny any distinctiveness to the Eucharist and others that affirm a more robust sacramental faith and concludes that, even taking the latter statements into account, the former statements, "while they do not negate a certain form of eucharistic Real Presence, they tend nevertheless to make it synonymous with the general real presence found in the faith."[232] And the Lutheran Robert Jenson writes that Calvin's

> surely is a plausible account of real presence. It does, however, have consequences. Whereas the existence of the believing church can be thought to guarantee the presence of Christ's body independently of the faith or unfaith of the communing individual, the individual's faith obviously cannot make that guarantee. Therefore the classic Reformed theologians taught that for the unbelieving communicant Christ is simply absent.[233]

227. Melvin Tinker, "Language, Symbols and Sacraments: Was Calvin's View of the Lord's Supper Right?," *Churchman* 112, no. 2 (1998): 147.

228. Tinker, "Language, Symbols and Sacraments," 146.

229. Jones, *Christ's Eucharistic Presence*, 139; cf. Gerrish, *Grace and Gratitude*, 163. Gerrish concludes that "there is not a different gift, only a different manner of giving insofar as a sacrament recruits all the five senses, not hearing only, and so presents the one and only gift still more effectively—that is, more forcefully and clearly."

230. Jones, *Christ's Eucharistic Presence*, 139. Jones is here quoting Kilian McDonnell's classic study.

231. Cf. Gerrish, *Grace and Gratitude*, 176: "Calvin appears to have let himself become caught in a logical bind."

232. Benedict XVI, "Problem of Transubstantiation," 223.

233. Jenson, "Tenth Locus," 358. Cf. Ratzinger's conclusion that "despite all the important initial steps, the *sacramentum ecclesia* has finally slipped from his grasp after all along with the *ecclesia*" ("Problem of Transubstantiation," 224).

On the other hand, it is important to recognize that Lutherans and Catholics too do not strictly dichotomize between the gift of Christ's body and blood in the Supper and that which is available outside of it. As Gerrish reminds us, "Luther, too, could say that Christ was present in faith itself."[234] And Catholics are aware, especially through the practice known as spiritual communion, recommended to those who, for whatever reason, cannot receive the Eucharist, that the grace of Christ is not tied exclusively to the sacrament.[235] This is particularly evident in Thomas's affirmation that the Eucharist is not necessary for salvation. What is necessary for salvation, says Thomas, is the *rem sacramenti*, the thing signified—namely, the unity of the mystical body of Christ (also known as the *res tantum*). But, since that is available even without the *ipsum sacramentum*, the sign itself (or the *sacramentum tantum*), the grace of salvation is available even without sacramental reception of the Eucharist.[236]

The difference, though real, is not as large as it first appears. While Lutherans and Catholics would desire a clearer articulation from Calvin about the unique character of the gift of Christ's body and blood in the Eucharist, they too acknowledge the legitimate concerns that keep Calvin from that kind of affirmation in their own theology and practice. And Calvin himself strives mightily to speak as strongly about the eucharistic presence as his system will let him, but he is aware that, within his own construction, to say anything too explicit about the unique character of eucharistic presence is to deny grace to those who do not receive it. This is why Ratzinger highlights the "airtight logical consistency" of Calvin's system when he registers his concern that, for Calvin, "ultimately the Eucharist no longer has anything proper or distinctive vis-à-vis other ways of encountering the glorified Lord."[237] Christ must never be severed from his benefits, and since Christ's benefits are fully available outside the Eucharist, it becomes nearly impossible to articulate what is unique about his presence in it.

Manducatio Infidelium

But even if, on these first two questions, there is a kind of straining within different systems toward common ground, on the third question—that is, what is received by an unworthy communicant—the gulf seems much greater. This,

234. Gerrish, "Luther and the Reformed Eucharist," 19.
235. On Trent's attitude to this practice, see Walsh, *Sacraments of Initiation*, 327–28.
236. *ST* III, 73.3 corpus. See also *ST* III, 64.7 corpus: "God did not cause his power to be restricted to the sacraments in such a way that he could not bestow the effect of the sacraments without the sacraments themselves"; and *ST* III, 68.2 on the necessity of baptism. Cf. Levering, *Sacrifice and Community*, 110–11.
237. Benedict XVI, "Problem of Transubstantiation," 224.

in fact, is the issue that convinced the Lutherans that Calvin was, despite all his protests to the contrary, no more than a "subtle sacramentarian," for he felt it necessary to assert repeatedly that what the unworthy receive is simply nothing.[238] Since they obviously do not receive Christ's benefits, there can be no way by which to say that they receive anything at all, beyond the simple elements of bread and wine.

While it may at first appear that, in this, Catholics would have to simply side with the Lutherans, I want to suggest that it is in fact here, at the point of sharpest disagreement between Calvin and Luther's descendants, that the Catholic tradition, and particularly the articulation of Aquinas, might offer a way to mutual understanding. We can begin by noting that Calvin did not accept the Lutheran conclusion that because an unbeliever received nothing, real presence was thereby reduced or eliminated.[239] According to Calvin,

> And this is the wholeness of the Sacrament, which the whole world cannot violate: that the flesh and blood of Christ are no less truly given to the unworthy than to God's elect believers. At the same time, it is true, however, that, just as rain falling upon a hard rock flows off because no entrance opens in the stone, the wicked by their hardness so repel God's grace that it does not reach them.[240]

What we see here, again, is the intimate connection between receiving Christ and receiving his benefits. Because Christ's benefits are not attained, neither can his flesh and blood be, no matter how truly proffered.

But what, wonders the critic, of eating and drinking one's condemnation, as St. Paul warns against? To such critics, says Calvin, "I reply that they are not condemned because they have eaten, but only for having profaned the mystery by trampling underfoot the pledge of sacred union with God, which they ought reverently to have received."[241] As Richard Muller puts it, "The 'godless' do not, in Calvin's view, bring condemnation on themselves because they receive Christ unworthily, but because they reject him."[242] This argument had no purchase with the Lutherans. To them, "affirmation of the *manducatio infidelium*, participation in the body of Christ by unbelievers, is . . . an unavoidable conclusion from the doctrine of the eucharistic real presence of Christ. Unless the body of Christ is really present for both, for unbelievers as well as believers, it is really

---

238. See, e.g., Steinmetz, "Calvin and His Lutheran Critics," 184–85.

239. Steinmetz, "Calvin and His Lutheran Critics," 187.

240. Calvin, *Inst.* 4.17:1407 (30).

241. Calvin, *Inst.* 4:17:1408 (33); cf. 4.17:1417 (40) for a fuller and more nuanced account.

242. Richard A. Muller, "Calvin on Sacramental Presence, in the Shadow of Marburg and Zurich," *Lutheran Quarterly* 23, no. 2 (Summer 2009): 161.

present for neither."[243] Furthermore, the *manducatio infidelium* (or, sometimes, *impiorum*) was seen as the logical conclusion of the *manducatio oralis*, that Christ was taken and eaten, not simply by faith, but by the mouth. In order to avoid the Zwinglian conclusion that the eating intended in the Lord's Supper was simply a metaphor for faith, and so ground the objective reality of Christ's gift, Lutherans insisted that Christ was taken by the mouth. Calvin did not agree with Zwingli that eating was simply faith, but insisted that eating was *by* faith. To the Lutherans this was a distinction without a difference, but for Calvin it guarded the reality of Christ's gift. He was not interested in guarding that reality in a way that implicated Christ in human digestion.

But here, perhaps, we see the limitations of this seemingly intractable dichotomy. For is there anyone on any side of the divide who actually wants to affirm that Christ is consumed in the same way as ordinary food? Surely, here, our limited ways of speaking about the mystery have backed us into an unnecessary corner. Can we not affirm with the Lutherans that the presence is real enough that the unbeliever in some way, if not in the same way as the believer, receives it? And can we not affirm with Calvin that the end of the sacrament is its proper reception and not simply Christ's presence in the elements themselves? Thomas Aquinas certainly thinks so.[244]

The test question of *manducatio infidelium* did not exist for Thomas per se, but it is possible, I suggest, to ascertain how he would respond to it, given several things he did say. In responding to the question "Can only the upright receive Christ sacramentally?," Thomas says that sinners also receive sacramentally, and he references the Pauline admonition about eating and drinking judgment.[245] In expounding his answer, Thomas makes two important distinctions. First of all he notes that the sinner does not receive spiritually—that is, sinners do not receive the grace of the sacrament, the *res tantum*. On this all are agreed. Second, Thomas reasons,

> Should an unbeliever receive the sacramental species he would receive Christ's body under the sacrament, and so would eat Christ sacramentally, if the term

243. Steinmetz, "Calvin and His Lutheran Critics," 184.

244. Thomas is not alone in this. The Leuenberg Concord, between Lutheran and Reformed Churches, agrees that "in the Lord's Supper the risen Jesus Christ imparts himself in his body and blood, given up for all, through his word of promise with bread and wine. He thus gives himself unreservedly to all who receive the bread and wine; faith received the Lord's Supper for salvation, unfaith for judgement." The German trilateral study on the condemnations of the sixteenth century observes that "this formulation clearly goes beyond Calvin, but at the same time tries to preserve his concern" (Lehmann and Pannenberg, *Condemnations of the Reformation Era*, 91).

245. *ST* III, 80.3 sc.

"sacramentally" qualifies the verb as to what is eaten. However, if it qualifies as to the eater, then properly speaking an unbeliever does not eat sacramentally, because he uses what he takes as simple food, not as a sacrament.[246]

The important distinction, one that is important to Calvin himself, is that between subjective and objective. Objectively speaking, the elements convey the body and blood of Christ and so, with respect to them, Christ is received sacramentally. Subjectively speaking, however, Thomas affirms Calvin's conclusion: the sinner "uses what he takes as simple food."

But it is not simply that Thomas thought up a clever distinction that was later forgotten. Rather his theology of real presence, and particularly of the relationship between sign and signified in the Eucharist, gave him the tools to make this distinction in a way that was not possible for Luther or Calvin. Recall that arguably the weakest point of Luther's theology of the Eucharist was that it sometimes lost its hold of the distinctly sacramental nature of Christ's presence, especially as he downplayed the role of the bread and wine as signs in his response to Zwingli. Recall also that Calvin, on the other hand, came remarkably close to Thomas on the relationship of sign and signified, to the point, even, of highlighting a three-part schema of (a) bread and wine, (b) Christ's body and blood, and (c) Christ's benefits; which, at first glance, neatly paralleled Thomas's (a) *sacramentum tantum*, (b) *res et sacramentum*, and (c) *res tantum*. Yet, as close as Calvin comes to Aquinas here, there is a subtle but important difference in their understandings at this point. While they are agreed on the role and value of the bread and wine as signs, Calvin rejects the idea of any sign value in the second term. He writes (with respect to Lombard, note well, not Thomas),

> I agree with his distinction between the flesh of Christ and the effective nourishment which inheres in it, but his pretending it to be a sacrament, and even one contained under the bread, is an error not to be endured.
>
> Hence arises their false interpretation of the sacramental eating. For they suppose that even the impious and the wicked eat Christ's body, however estranged from him they may be.[247]

In other words, if Luther collapsed the first and second terms of the tripartite Scholastic structure, Calvin collapsed the second and third terms. Christ cannot, after all, be separated from his benefits. But does this difference not account for the false dichotomy at the root of the split between Calvin and

246. *ST* III, 80.3 ad 2.
247. Calvin, *Inst.* 4.17:1406 (33).

the Lutherans? What made Calvin nervous about the Lutheran articulation was that it seemed unable to distinguish clearly between receiving Christ's body and blood and receiving the signs of bread and wine. Indeed, Calvin felt the Lutherans strongly implied that Christ was consumed just like normal food. His strong reactions against the *manducatio oralis* were, more or less, rejections of cannibalism. Of course, no Lutheran intended such eating, but their system made it difficult for them to articulate a clear difference.

And what made the Lutherans nervous about Calvin's articulation was that his teaching that the unbeliever did not receive Christ's benefits, on which all were agreed, could not avoid the conclusion that there was no way to say that Christ's body and blood were received by them at all. In Calvin's system, a denial of the third term entailed a denial of the second as well. But to the Lutherans this was indistinguishable from the idea that the presence was, in practice, if not in theory, completely dependent on the faith of the recipient and, therefore, not real after all, despite Calvin's protests to the contrary. This was not, it should be obvious, Calvin's intent, but his system made it difficult for him to articulate a clear difference.

Thomas Aquinas, on the other hand, could distinguish between what was received objectively and subjectively because for him, Christ's body and blood were both sign *and* thing. As sign, it is received, objectively, sacramentally, regardless of the faith of the recipient.[248] As thing, however, it is only accessible to one who has first read and believed the sign. The unique nature of the middle term as both sign and signified allows Thomas to avoid the impasse that later split the Reformation while, at the same time, honoring the key concerns of both the Lutheran and Reformed parties.

Are we too bold, however, to propose as a way forward something about which Calvin was aware and which he explicitly rejected? Perhaps. But let us press on just a little further.

In his lucid little piece "The Best Method of Obtaining Concord," appended to Calvin's last polemic foray against Heshusius, Calvin proposes, "Let it be agreed, then, in regard to this article, that the body of Christ is eaten by the wicked sacramentally, not truly or in reality, but in so far as it is a sign."[249] On the one hand, this looks remarkably like Thomas, even referring to the body of Christ as a sign! On the other hand, it would be too much to imagine that Calvin has here changed his mind and openly adopted the Scholastic distinction, for he still rejects what he calls "a sacramental eating, which they insist

---

248. Reception by an animal or an ignorant person, Thomas notes, is a different kind of thing, in which Christ is only received "accidentally" (*ST* III, 80.3). See above, pp. 133–35.
249. Calvin, "Best Method," 578.

to be an eating of the substance of the flesh without grace or effect."[250] Nevertheless, there is an opening here. For when Calvin rejects such eating, he has in mind a crude and carnal eating that he imagined his Lutheran (and Catholic) opponents were advocating. As Richard Muller points out, when Calvin rejects such a presence for the unworthy recipient, he is rejecting something that he also rejects for the worthy one![251]

This conclusion is affirmed if we look at the section of the *Institutes* in which Calvin rejects the idea that Christ's flesh is also a sign. Two short paragraphs later he declares, "However, I should like to know from them how long they retain it when they have eaten it. Here, in my judgment, they will find no way out."[252] But this is an attack against a carnal view of presence, not a sacramental one. Considered physically, this question is very embarrassing, but considered sacramentally, it is fairly simply resolved: the presence lasts as long as the symbol.[253]

Is it possible, then, that transubstantiation, properly understood as a careful articulation of a precisely sacramental presence, opens the door to an articulation of sign and signified in the Lord's Supper that could resolve the differences between Lutheran and Reformed Christians? Would it allow the Lutherans to make a clearer distinction between the physical elements of bread and wine and Christ's body and blood so as to alleviate Reformed concerns? Would it allow the Reformed to acknowledge a sacramental reception of Christ even by unworthy recipients that does not make eucharistic presence into a crudely physical idea?

And, if it could help Protestant Christians to better understand one another and acknowledge each other's legitimate concerns, does it not go without saying that it need no longer be a stumbling block to unity between Protestants and Catholics?

250. Calvin, "Best Method," 578.
251. Muller, "From Zürich or from Wittenberg?," 251.
252. Calvin, *Inst*. 4.17:1406 (33).
253. *ST* III, 76.6 ad 3. See above, p. 110.

Conclusion

In her very positive response to George Hunsinger's *The Eucharist and Ecumenism*, Margaret O'Gara ends with a few "mild admonitions." "Since Hunsinger has asked Roman Catholics for a charitable view of his Eucharistic proposal," she notes,

> I would like to ask him for the same in his thinking about transubstantiation. Aquinas developed this earlier idea in response to popular practices and views of his day that misunderstood the change in the Eucharist as a material change. To counter this, Aquinas emphasized its mysterious, even miraculous, nature: this change was not visible, not material, and yet it was real. Is this idea—an exciting example of inculturation of the gospel in the thirteenth century—really so unworthy of the attention of Reformed thinkers today? If its intention, its apologetic purpose, and its cultural context could be recovered, transubstantiation might be heard more sympathetically by those outside the Roman Catholic tradition.[1]

In the ecumenical search for common understanding on Christ's real presence in the Eucharist, transubstantiation has been a major stumbling block. It is often simply assumed that the idea could not be countenanced by Protestants and that agreement requires that Catholics somehow move past it. This attitude has led to the term's marginalization in ecumenical dialogue. But, as we have seen, the Christian people find the resulting agreements ambiguous. Catholics worry that their faith in real presence has been abandoned due to transubstantiation's absence, and Protestants worry that the "realistic"

---

1. Margaret O'Gara, "Toward the Day When We Will Keep the Feast Together," *Pro Ecclesia* 19, no. 3 (Summer 2010): 265.

language of the agreements indicates a hidden—horror of horrors—theology of transubstantiation.

But O'Gara is right. Transubstantiation is considered "unworthy" primarily because its original context (both historical and theological) and intention have been lost. Transubstantiation was not (and is not) an endorsement of a materialistic view of eucharistic presence and change, but a defense against just such a misunderstanding. Transubstantiation was not (and is not) an attempt to fully explicate the mystery of the Eucharist, but rather an attempt to locate and carefully protect that mystery by ruling out inadequate conceptions of it.

The transubstantiation (rightly!) rejected at the time of the Reformation was not the teaching of Thomas Aquinas, nor is it the teaching of the Church of today. The Council of Trent, the most authoritative voice on the matter for Catholics, in its positive teaching (i.e., not in its anathemas) declared only that "by the consecration of bread and wine, there takes place the change of the whole substance of the bread into the substance of the body of Christ our lord, and of the whole substance of the wine into the substance of his blood. And the holy catholic church has suitably and properly called this change transubstantiation."[2] Such a declaration manifestly does not teach a materialistic or rationalistic version of transubstantiation since it does little more than repeat language that was derived precisely to combat such an understanding. And this remains the case despite the fact that it would have inevitably been understood to do so by the Reformers at the time, even as Trent would have understood, for instance, Luther's belief in the persistence of the substances of the bread and wine as a denial of genuine change in the Eucharist.

But if the teachings of Trent and Aquinas are not what has been rejected under the name of transubstantiation, must the notion continue to divide Christians? Transubstantiation, we have seen, manages to do very effectively a few things that any ecumenically satisfactory articulation of real presence must do. It carefully distinguishes sign and signified in a way that gives the bread and the wine a genuine role without denying the primacy of Christ's body and blood in the sacrament. It is thereby able to acknowledge the essentially symbolic character of the sacrament without reducing Christ's presence to something that happens only in the minds of the community. And this also makes it able to describe a realism with regard to Christ's presence that is neither crude nor naïve. It is able to hold, at the same time, that Christ is genuinely, bodily ascended and also able to give himself to us bodily in the sacrament. It is able to tie Christ's promise of presence intimately to the

2. *Decrees of the Ecumenical Councils*, 2:695.

elements of bread and wine (those elements are what Jesus took in his hands before announcing them as his body and blood, after all), without restricting it to them or making them ends in themselves. It opens Christ's eucharistic presence outward to the ecclesiological and eschatological themes that Scripture and tradition demand for the Lord's Supper. And it is helped to do all this because it witnesses to a worldview in which God is the transcendent ground of all being, where God makes things to be what they are at their deepest level by the power of his creative Word, a worldview in which it is not absurd to believe that God has really pitched his tent with us. Surely all of this recommends the doctrine to the ecumenical community.

Indeed where Protestant communities have rejected any of the above, it is only because a given item on the list was seen as incompatible with one of the other items. And this was largely because of the polemical situation between Protestants at the time of the Reformation. That is to say, Protestants who have rejected these assertions of transubstantiation have done so *because they were believed to be incompatible with other of its assertions held by other Protestants.* Because Thomas himself was not writing in a polemical context, the serenity and balance of his theology of the Eucharist could help those traditions whose eucharistic theology occasionally fell off balance—precisely because it was conceived in polemic—to agree not only with Catholics, but with one another.

On the other hand, it is essential to remember that the theology of transubstantiation is only that—theology. It is not the article of faith itself. Its function is merely to make coherent the article of faith and defend it against misinterpretation. As such, it cannot be demanded of non-Catholic Christians as a prerequisite of Christian unity. Consensus about transubstantiation is necessary only to demonstrate that what we hold about real presence is truly the same faith. Consensus, then, does not mean that everyone signs a document agreeing to adopt a theology of transubstantiation. It only requires that Protestants acknowledge that transubstantiation is not contrary to the faith of the Church and agree to allow it as an articulation of real presence. From the Catholic point of view, other articulations are certainly permissible, provided that they do not deny what transubstantiation affirms.[3] Our

3. Cf. ARCIC II, "Clarifications of Certain Aspects of the Agreed Statements on Eucharist and Ministry," 302; cf. *Mysterium Fidei*, #25. As Michael Root notes in the foreword to this book, "But the council [Trent] insists, as a matter of binding teaching, that the term 'transubstantiation' rightly represents the faith, even if there might be other ways, linked to other conceptual schemes or forms of theological discourse, that also get at the reality described. That the language of official Catholic teaching rightly represents what occurs is thus here explicitly made a matter of official Catholic teaching. Joining together in the Eucharist does not require

Conclusion

investigations of Luther and Calvin make it clear that Protestants need not make such denials. George Hunsinger's suggestion that the Reformed tradition could come closer to its ecumenical partners by retrieving an articulation from its own heritage, that of transelementation,[4] does precisely this and has been favorably received by Catholics.[5]

And indeed there are reasons why such other articulations are ecumenically desirable. In the first place, the weight of history and identity is an essential consideration for ecumenism. Forcing Protestants to accept a theology that is not traditional for them when the faith of the Church manifestly does not require it (as demonstrated by the lack of transubstantiation in the patristic Church and in Eastern Christianity) would be vain and foolhardy. In this light, it is encouraging to note that Hunsinger finds not only that transelementation has patristic and Eastern pedigrees but also that early Reformed theologians (he is especially interested in Peter Martyr Vermigli) made effective use of it in their own theologies of the Eucharist.[6]

Second, there is one weakness of transubstantiation that cannot withstand the critiques of the Reformers: its propensity for being misunderstood. It is simply undeniable that transubstantiation is widely and seriously misunderstood. This is especially the case since the fundamental categories that transubstantiation had exploited to defend the Church's faith in real presence against Berengarius and his opponents were altered prior to the Reformation. Nevertheless, as people who live not only after Berengarius but also after Descartes, and even after Dawkins and company, we must acknowledge that any articulation of real presence that successfully captures the Church's faith is going to be open to this same charge. In such a context, transelementation will fare no better than transubstantiation. On the other hand, if ecumenical theology can show that different articulations are complementary rather than contradictory, the propensity of certain articulations to be misunderstood in certain directions can be countered by the knowledge that we do not hold other articulations, which may be more likely to be misunderstood in another direction, in suspicion.

A concrete example might be helpful here: Catholics who know that the Vatican accepts the Liturgy of Addai and Mari as valid even though it does

---

that all adopt this language, but it does require that this language not be rejected as misrepresenting what is going on" (pp. viii–ix above). See also pp. 18–25 above.

4. Hunsinger, *Eucharist and Ecumenism*, 71–81.

5. See, e.g., O'Gara, "Toward the Day When We Will Keep the Feast Together," 263; John F. Baldovin, "Liturgy and Reunion," *Commonweal* 136, no. 6 (March 27, 2009): 15.

6. Hunsinger, *Eucharist and Ecumenism*, 39–46. Hunsinger also highlights Cranmer and Bucer.

not include the words of institution are far less likely to artificially isolate the words of institution from the rest of the liturgy in their own understanding of eucharistic presence. The Vatican's judgment on transignification was much the same: as long as it is not taken to deny transubstantiation, it can exist as a healthy qualifier against poor interpretations of it. (And, of course, the Vatican was keen to insist that transubstantiation is necessary for a proper understanding of transignification.) There is no reason why intra-Christian examples cannot function the same way as these intra-Catholic examples. If other articulations are understood to complement, explain, or balance transubstantiation, rather than contradict, debunk, or correct it, there should be no reason they cannot coexist in an ecumenical Church.

When, in the late Middle Ages, substance became just one more accident and thereby turned the accidents of bread and wine from signs into disguises, transubstantiation itself stopped being a sign of the Church's genuine eucharistic faith and became a disguise for it. Of course, this nominalist version of transubstantiation was rejected at the Reformation, along with all kinds of distortions that nominalism had brought into theology that disguised the true claims of Christianity. Catholics and Protestants agree in their rejection of nominalism, which invited first fideism, then skepticism. The worldview that it eventually engendered made the Christian notions of God, creation, and incarnation incoherent. But if transubstantiation was disguised by nominalism, it is hoped that this work of showing what transubstantiation really signifies can be an important step in the ecumenical project of moving beyond the distortions of nominalism that led to the Reformation in the first place. My task here has been to show the connection between the "accidents" of the doctrine of transubstantiation and its genuine "substance" and to clarify where those accidents have become disguises. I have tried to add clarifying "form" when the "matter" has become indistinct.

If I have been successful, I hope for three things. First, I hope that the Christian people may be reassured that the eucharistic agreements of the ecumenical movement, while incomplete, are not a fudge. Thomas Aquinas, Martin Luther, and John Calvin all genuinely believed and sought to teach Christ's real presence in the Eucharist and came much closer to one another than it may first appear. No tradition has abandoned its best lights in signing agreements about eucharistic presence: Catholics have not abandoned transubstantiation; Protestants have not abandoned the Reformation. The two are not mutually exclusive. Second, I hope that ecumenists may be emboldened to treat the question of transubstantiation head-on and make their agreements more complete by the recognition that transubstantiation need not be an ecumenical stumbling block. And I hope that my own work will give them a resource for just such a project. Third and finally, I hope that clarity and consensus about an issue as contentious as transubstantiation spurs on ecumenical hope. Transubstantiation is not unconnected with other doctrines that currently divide the Church. Questions of eucharistic sacrifice and holy orders would seem the most intimately connected with this project. But if disagreement about transubstantiation is rooted in nominalist distortions, then the doctrine has connections with a whole Christian worldview that Protestant and Catholic theologians together are trying to rearticulate for the Christian people in the contemporary world. Transubstantiation, properly understood, highlights and reinforces our agreements about God, creation, Christ, the Church, and the destiny of the world—a world Christ is drawing to himself, bread first.

Bibliography

Primary Sources

Anglican–Roman Catholic International Commission. "An Agreed Statement on Eucharistic Doctrine." In *Modern Eucharistic Agreement*, 23–31. London: SPCK, 1973.

———. "Eucharistic Doctrine (1971)." In *The Final Report*, 12–16. Washington, DC: US Catholic Conference, 1982.

———. "Eucharistic Doctrine: Elucidation (1979)." In *The Final Report*, 17–25. Washington, DC: US Catholic Conference, 1982.

ARCIC II. "Clarifications of Certain Aspects of the Agreed Statements on Eucharist and Ministry." *Origins* 24 (October 6, 1994): 301–4.

Calvin, John. "The Best Method of Obtaining Concord: Provided the Truth Be Sought without Contention." In *Tracts and Treatises on the Reformation of the Church*, translated by Henry Beveridge, 2:573–79. Grand Rapids: Eerdmans, 1958.

———. *Institutes of the Christian Religion.* Edited by John T. McNeill. Translated by Ford Lewis Battles. Library of Christian Classics. Philadelphia: Westminster, 1960.

———. "Short Treatise on the Supper of Our Lord." In *Tracts and Treatises on the Reformation of the Church*, translated by Henry Beveridge, 2:163–98. Grand Rapids: Eerdmans, 1958.

Carey, George. "Comments of the Archbishop of Canterbury on the Response of ARCIC-I." *One in Christ* 28 (1992): 47–48.

Cassidy, Cardinal Edward. "Letter to the Co-chairs of ARCIC-II (March 11, 1994)." *Origins* 24 (October 6, 1994): 299–300.

Congregation for the Doctrine of the Faith and Pontifical Council for Promoting Christian Unity. "Observations on the ARCIC Final Report." *Origins* 11 (May 6, 1982): 752–56.

———. "The Official Response of the Roman Catholic Church to ARCIC I." *One in Christ* 28 (1992): 38–46.

The Council of Trent. "Trent." In *Decrees of the Ecumenical Councils*. Vol. 2, *Trent to Vatican II*. Edited by Norman P. Tanner, 657–799. Washington, DC: Georgetown University Press, 1990.

Denzinger, Henry. *The Sources of Catholic Dogma*. Translated by Roy J. Deferrari. Fitzwilliam, NH: Loreto, 2002.

Disciples of Christ–Roman Catholic International Commission for Dialogue. "The Presence of Christ in the Church, with Special Reference to the Eucharist: Fourth Agreed Statement of the Disciples of Christ–Roman Catholic International Commission for Dialogue, 2003–2009." *Call to Unity* (October 2012): 58–74.

Faith and Order Commission of the World Council of Churches. "The Eucharist in Ecumenical Thought." In *Modern Eucharistic Agreement*, 79–89. London: SPCK, 1973.

Group of Les Dombes. "Towards a Common Eucharistic Faith?" In *Modern Eucharistic Agreement*, 51–78. London: SPCK, 1973.

Luther, Martin. *The Adoration of the Sacrament*. In *Luther's Works* 36:269–305. Translated by Abdel Ross Wentz. Philadelphia: Fortress, 1959.

———. *The Babylonian Captivity of the Church*. In *Luther's Works* 36:3–126. Translated by A. T. W Steinhäuser and revised by Frederick C. Ahrens and Abdel Ross Wentz. Philadelphia: Fortress, 1959.

———. *The Blessed Sacrament of the Holy and True Body of Christ, and the Brotherhoods*. In *Luther's Works* 35:45–73. Translated by Jeremiah J. Schindel and revised by E. Theodore Bachmann. Philadelphia: Fortress, 1960.

———. *Brief Confession concerning the Holy Sacrament*. In *Luther's Works* 38:279–319. Translated by Martin E. Lehmann. Philadelphia: Fortress, 1971.

———. *Confession concerning Christ's Supper*. In *Luther's Works* 37:151–372. Translated by Robert H. Fischer. Philadelphia: Fortress, 1961.

———. *The Sacrament of the Body and Blood of Christ—Against the Fanatics*. In *Luther's Works* 36:329–61. Translated by Frederick C. Ahrens. Philadelphia: Fortress, 1959.

———. *That These Words of Christ, "This Is My Body," etc., Still Stand Firm against the Fanatics*. In *Luther's Works* 37:3–150. Translated by Robert H. Fischer. Philadelphia: Fortress, 1961.

A Lutheran–Roman Catholic Statement. "The Eucharist as Sacrifice." In *Modern Eucharistic Agreement*, 33–49. London: SPCK, 1973.

Paul VI. *Mysterium Fidei: Encyclical of Pope Paul VI on the Holy Eucharist*. September 3, 1965. http://www.vatican.va/holy_father/paul_vi/encyclicals/documents/hf _p-vi_enc_03091965_mysterium_en.html.

Thomas Aquinas. *Summa contra Gentiles, Book Four: Salvation.* Edited and translated by Charles J. O'Neill. Garden City, NY: Image, 1957.

————. *Summa Theologiae.* Vol. 56, *The Sacraments (3a. 60–65).* Edited and translated by David Bourke. London: Blackfriars in conjunction with Eyre & Spottiswoode, 1975.

————. *Summa Theologiae.* Vol. 57, *Baptism and Confirmation (3a. 66–72).* Edited and translated by James J. Cunningham. London: Blackfriars in conjunction with Eyre & Spottiswoode, 1975.

————. *Summa Theologiae.* Vol. 58, *The Eucharistic Presence (3a. 73–78).* Edited and translated by William Barden, OP. London: Blackfriars in conjunction with Eyre & Spottiswoode, 1965.

————. *Summa Theologiae.* Vol. 59, *Holy Communion (3a. 79–83).* Edited and translated by Thomas Gilby, OP. London: Blackfriars in conjunction with Eyre & Spottiswoode, 1975.

Vatican II. "Dogmatic Constitution on the Church: Lumen Gentium." Solemnly Promulgated by His Holiness Pope Paul VI on November 21, 1964. http://www.vatican.va/archive/hist_councils/ii_vatican_council/documents/vat-ii_const_19641121_lumen-gentium_en.html.

World Council of Churches. *Baptism, Eucharist, and Ministry.* Geneva: World Council of Churches, 1982.

————. *Churches Respond to BEM.* Vols. 1–6. Geneva: World Council of Churches, 1986.

Zwingli, Huldrych. *Huldreich Zwinglis sämtliche Werke. Bd. IV, Werke April 1525–März 1526.* Edited by Emil Egli, Georg Finsler, Walther Köhler, and Oskar Farner. Corpus Reformatorum 91. Leipzig: Heinsius, 1915–27.

Secondary Sources

Allen, Michael. "Sacraments in the Reformed and Anglican Reformation." In Boersma and Levering, *Oxford Handbook of Sacramental Theology,* 283–97.

Anscombe, G. E. M. "On Transubstantiation." In *Ethics, Religion, and Politics,* 107–12. The Collected Philosophical Papers of G. E. M. Anscombe 3. Oxford: Blackwell, 1981.

Baldovin, John F. "Liturgy and Reunion." *Commonweal* 136, no. 6 (March 27, 2009): 15.

Barr, Stephen. "Does Quantum Physics Render Transubstantiation Meaningless?" *First Thoughts* (blog). *First Things,* May 25, 2010. https://www.firstthings.com/blogs/firstthoughts/2010/05/does-quantum-physics-render-transubstantiation-meaningless.

Barron, Robert E. "The Christian Humanism of Karol Wojtyla and Thomas Aquinas." In *Bridging the Great Divide: Musings of a Post-liberal, Post-conservative, Evangelical Catholic,* 107–23. Toronto: Rowman & Littlefield, 2004.

———. "Creation, Transubstantiation, and the Grain of the Universe: A Contribution to Stanley Hauerwas's Ekklesia Project." In *Bridging the Great Divide: Musings of a Post-liberal, Post-conservative, Evangelical Catholic*, 214–19. Toronto: Rowman & Littlefield, 2004.

———. *Eucharist*. Maryknoll, NY: Orbis, 2008.

———. *Eucharist* (video). [West Milton, Ohio]: Message Shop, 2009.

———. *The Priority of Christ: Toward a Postliberal Catholicism*. Grand Rapids: Brazos, 2007.

———. "Thomas Aquinas: Postmodern." In *Sacramental Presence in a Postmodern Context*, edited by Lieven Boeve and Lambert Leijssen, 265–78. Leuven: Peeters, 2001.

———. "Thomas Aquinas's Christological Reading of God and the Creature." In *Bridging the Great Divide: Musings of a Post-liberal, Post-conservative, Evangelical Catholic*, 87–106. Toronto: Rowman & Littlefield, 2004.

Bauerschmidt, Frederick Christian. *Holy Teaching: Introducing the* Summa Theologiae *of St. Thomas Aquinas*. Grand Rapids: Brazos, 2005.

Bavinck, Herman. "Calvin's Doctrine of the Lord's Supper." Translated by Nelson D. Kloosterman. *Mid-America Journal of Theology* 19 (2008): 127–42.

Benedict XVI. "Address of His Holiness Benedict XVI." Presented at the Ecumenical Meeting, Crypt of St. Mary's Cathedral in Sydney, July 18, 2008. http://www.vati can.va/holy_father/benedict_xvi/speeches/2008/july/documents/hf_ben-xvi_spe _20080718_ecumenism_en.html.

———. *Called to Communion: Understanding the Church Today*. Translated by Adrian Walker. San Francisco: Ignatius, 1996.

———. *Eschatology: Death and Eternal Life*. Edited by Aidan Nichols. Translated by Michael Waldstein. 2nd ed. Washington, DC: Catholic University of America Press, 2007.

———. *God Is Near Us: The Eucharist, the Heart of Life*. Edited by Stephan Otto Horn and Vinzenz Pfnür. Translated by Henry Taylor. San Francisco: Ignatius, 2003.

———. *Introduction to Christianity*. Translated by J. R. Foster. San Francisco: Ignatius, 2004.

———. "The Problem of Transubstantiation and the Question about the Meaning of the Eucharist." In *Collected Works of Joseph Ratzinger*, edited by Michael J. Miller, translated by John Saward, Kenneth Baker, Henry Taylor, et al., 11:218–42. San Francisco: Ignatius, 2013.

Boersma, Hans. *Heavenly Participation: The Weaving of a Sacramental Tapestry*. Grand Rapids: Eerdmans, 2010.

Boersma, Hans, and Matthew Levering, eds. *The Oxford Handbook of Sacramental Theology*. Oxford: Oxford University Press, 2015.

Broadie, Alexander. "Duns Scotus and William Ockham." In *The Medieval Theologians: An Introduction to Theology in the Medieval Period*, edited by G. R. Evans, 250–65. Malden, MA: Blackwell, 2001.

Brock, Stephen L. "St. Thomas and the Eucharistic Conversion." *The Thomist* 65 (2001): 529–65.

Brown, David. "The Response to ARCIC-I: The Big Questions." *One in Christ* 28 (1992): 148–54.

Burke, Archbishop Raymond. Foreword to Classen, *Meat and Potatoes Catholicism*, 11–15.

Burrell, David B. *Freedom and Creation in Three Traditions*. Notre Dame, IN: University of Notre Dame Press, 1993.

Chadwick, Henry. "Ego Berengarius." *Journal of Theological Studies* 40, no. 2 (October 1989): 415–45.

Chung-Kim, Esther. "Use of the Fathers in the Eucharistic Debates between John Calvin and Joachim Westphal." *Reformation* 14 (2009): 101–25.

Cipolla, Richard G. "Selvaggi Revisited: Transubstantiation and Contemporary Science." *Theological Studies* 35, no. 4 (1974): 667–91.

Clark, J. T., SJ. "Physics, Philosophy, Transubstantiation, Theology." *Theological Studies* 12 (1951): 24–51.

Classen, Joseph F. *Meat and Potatoes Catholicism*. Huntington, IN: Our Sunday Visitor, 2008.

Colwell, John. *Living the Christian Story: The Distinctiveness of Christian Ethics*. Edinburgh: T&T Clark, 2001.

———. *Promise and Presence: An Exploration of Sacramental Theology*. Milton Keynes, UK: Paternoster, 2005.

Connell, Richard J. "Substance and Transubstantiation." *Angelicum* 69 (1992): 3–37.

Coolman, Boyd Taylor. "The Christo-Pneumatic-Ecclesial Character of Twelfth-Century Sacramental Theology." In Boersma and Levering, *Oxford Handbook of Sacramental Theology*, 201–17.

Craycraft, Kenneth R. "Sign and Word: Martin Luther's Theology of the Sacraments." *Restoration Quarterly* 32, no. 3 (1990): 143–64.

Crockett, William R. *Eucharist: Symbol of Transformation*. New York: Pueblo, 1989.

Cross, Richard. "Catholic, Calvinist, and Lutheran Doctrines of Eucharistic Presence: A Brief Note towards a Rapprochement." *International Journal of Systematic Theology* 4, no. 3 (2003): 301–18.

Cummings, Owen F. "The Reformers and Eucharistic Ecclesiology." *One in Christ* 33, no. 1 (1997): 47–54.

Cunnington, Ralph. "Calvin's Doctrine of the Lord's Supper: A Blot upon His Labors as a Public Instructor?" *Westminster Theological Journal* 73, no. 2 (Fall 2011): 215–36.

Davies, Horton. *Bread of Life and Cup of Joy: Newer Ecumenical Perspectives on the Eucharist.* Grand Rapids: Eerdmans, 1993.

Davis, Thomas J. *The Clearest Promises of God: The Development of Calvin's Eucharistic Teaching.* New York: AMS Press, 1995.

———. *This Is My Body: The Presence of Christ in Reformation Thought.* Grand Rapids: Baker Academic, 2008.

de Lubac, Henri. *Corpus Mysticum: The Eucharist and the Church in the Middle Ages.* Edited by Laurence Paul Hemming and Susan Frank Parsons. Translated by Gemma Simmonds with Richard Price and Christopher Stephens. Notre Dame, IN: University of Notre Dame Press, 2007.

Dupré, Louis K. *Passage to Modernity: An Essay in the Hermeneutics of Nature and Culture.* New Haven: Yale University Press, 1993.

Durrwell, F.-X. *The Eucharist: Presence of Christ.* Denville, NJ: Dimension, 1974.

Egner, G. "Some Thoughts on the Eucharistic Presence." In *God Matters,* by Herbert McCabe, 130–45. London: Continuum, 2005.

Emery, Gilles, OP. "The Ecclesial Fruit of the Eucharist in St. Thomas Aquinas." *Nova et Vetera* 2, no. 1 (2004): 43–60.

Evans, Gillian R. "Rome's Response to ARCIC and the Problem of Confessional Identity." *One in Christ* 28 (1992): 155–67.

Fagerberg, David W. "Translating Transubstantiation." *Antiphon* 6, no. 3 (2001): 9–13.

Farrow, Douglas. "Between the Rock and a Hard Place: In Support of (Something like) a Reformed View of the Eucharist." *International Journal of Systematic Theology* 3, no. 2 (July 2001): 167–86.

———. *Theological Negotiations: Proposals in Soteriology and Anthropology.* Grand Rapids: Baker Academic, 2018.

Feingold, Lawrence. *The Eucharist: Mystery of Presence, Sacrifice, and Communion.* Steubenville, OH: Emmaus Academic, 2018.

FitzPatrick, P. J. *In Breaking of Bread: The Eucharist and Ritual.* New York: Cambridge University Press, 1993.

George, Timothy. "John Calvin and the Agreement of Zurich (1549)." In *John Calvin and the Church,* 42–58. Louisville: Westminster/John Knox, 1990.

Gerrish, Brian A. "Discerning the Body: Sign and Reality in Luther's Controversy with the Swiss." In *Continuing the Reformation: Essays on Modern Religious Thought,* 57–75. Chicago: University of Chicago Press, 1993.

———. "Gospel and Eucharist: John Calvin on the Lord's Supper." In *The Old Protestantism and the New: Essays on the Reformation Heritage,* 106–17. Chicago: University of Chicago Press, 1982.

———. *Grace and Gratitude: The Eucharistic Theology of John Calvin.* Minneapolis: Fortress, 1993.

———. "Luther and the Reformed Eucharist: What Luther Said, or Might Have Said, about Calvin." *Seminary Ridge Review* 10, no. 2 (Spring 2008): 5–19.

———. "Sign and Reality: The Lord's Supper in the Reformed Confessions." In *The Old Protestantism and the New: Essays on the Reformation Heritage*, 118–30. Chicago: University of Chicago Press, 1982.

Gibson, Margaret. "The Case of Berengar of Tours." *Studies in Church History* 7 (1971): 61–68.

Grisez, Germain. "An Alternative Theology of Jesus' Substantial Presence in the Eucharist." *Irish Theological Quarterly* 65, no. 2 (2000): 111–31.

Grislis, Egil. "Eucharistic Convergence in Ecumenical Debate: An Intimation of the Future of Christianity?" *Toronto Journal of Theology* 6, no. 2 (1990): 247–65.

———. "The Eucharistic Presence of Christ: Losses and Gains of the Insights of St. Thomas Aquinas in the Age of the Reformation." *Consensus* 18, no. 1 (1992): 9–31.

———. "The Manner of Christ's Eucharistic Presence according to Martin Luther." *Consensus* 7, no. 1 (January 1981): 3–14.

Gros, Brother Jeffrey, FSC. "A Roman Catholic Response." In *The Lord's Supper: Five Views*, edited by Gordon T. Smith, 83–84. Downers Grove, IL: IVP Academic, 2008.

———. "The Roman Catholic View." In *The Lord's Supper: Five Views*, edited by Gordon T. Smith, 13–31. Downers Grove, IL: IVP Academic, 2008.

Haldane, John. "A Thomist Metaphysics." In *Reasonable Faith*, 18–36. London: Routledge, 2010.

Hanson, R. P. C. "Eucharistic Agreement: An Ecumenical and Theological Consensus." In *A Critique of Eucharistic Agreement*, 25–36. London: SPCK, 1975.

Hemming, Laurence Paul. "After Heidegger: Transubstantiation." *Heythrop Journal* 41 (2000): 170–86.

Hendel, Kurt K. "Finitum Capax Infiniti: Luther's Radical Incarnational Perspective." *Currents in Theology and Mission* 35, no. 6 (December 2008): 420–33.

Heron, Alasdair. *Table and Tradition: Towards an Ecumenical Understanding of the Eucharist*. Edinburgh: Handsel Press, 1983.

Hinlicky, Paul R. "Christ's Bodily Presence in the Holy Supper—Real or Symbolic?" *Lutheran Forum* 33, no. 3 (Fall 1999): 24–28.

Horton, Michael Scott. "Union and Communion: Calvin's Theology of Word and Sacrament." *International Journal of Systematic Theology* 11, no. 4 (October 2009): 398–414.

Hunsinger, George. *The Eucharist and Ecumenism: Let Us Keep the Feast*. Cambridge: Cambridge University Press, 2008.

———. "Widening the Circle of Acceptable Diversity: A Reply to My Ecumenical Friends." *Pro Ecclesia* 19, no. 3 (Summer 2010): 273–84.

Hütter, Reinhard. "Transubstantiation Revisited: Sacra Doctrina, Dogma, and Metaphysics." In *Ressourcement Thomism: Sacred Doctrine, the Sacraments, and the Moral Life*, edited by Reinhard Hütter and Matthew Levering, 21–79. Washington, DC: Catholic University of America Press, 2010.

Janse, Wim. "Calvin's Eucharistic Theology: Three Dogma-Historical Observations." In *Calvinus Sacrarum Literarum Interpres: Papers of the International Congress on Calvin Research*, edited by Herman J. Selderhuis, 37–69. Göttingen: Vandenhoeck & Ruprecht, 2008.

Jenson, Robert W. "Tenth Locus: The Means of Grace, Part Two: The Sacraments." In *Christian Dogmatics*, edited by Robert W. Jenson and Carl E. Braaten, 289–389. Philadelphia: Fortress, 1984.

———. *Unbaptized God: The Basic Flaw in Ecumenical Theology*. Minneapolis: Fortress, 1992.

Jones, Paul H. *Christ's Eucharistic Presence: A History of the Doctrine*. New York: Peter Lang, 1994.

Jordan, Mark D. "Theology and Philosophy." In *The Cambridge Companion to Aquinas*, edited by Norman Kretzmann and Eleonore Stump, 232–51. Cambridge: Cambridge University Press, 1993.

Karlberg, Mark W. Review of *Given for You: Reclaiming Calvin's Doctrine of the Lord's Supper*, by Keith A. Mathison. *Journal of the Evangelical Theological Society* 48, no. 1 (March 2005): 174–78.

Kasper, Walter. *Harvesting the Fruits: Basic Aspects of Christian Faith in Ecumenical Dialogue*. London: Continuum, 2009.

Kelly, Gerard. "The Eucharistic Doctrine of Transubstantiation." In *The Eucharist: Faith and Worship*, edited by Margaret Press, 56–74. Homebush, Australia: St. Pauls, 2001.

Kereszty, Roch A., OCist. "On the Eucharistic Presence: Response to Germain Grisez." *Irish Theological Quarterly* 65, no. 4 (2000): 347–52.

———. *Wedding Feast of the Lamb: Eucharistic Theology from a Historical, Biblical, and Systematic Perspective*. Chicago: Hillenbrand, 2004.

Kerr, Fergus, OP. "Transubstantiation after Wittgenstein." *Modern Theology* 15, no. 2 (April 1999): 115–30.

Kerr, Nathan. "*Corpus Verum*: On the Ecclesial Recovery of Real Presence in John Calvin's Doctrine of the Eucharist." In *Radical Orthodoxy and the Reformed Tradition*, edited by James K. A. Smith and James H. Olthuis, 229–42. Grand Rapids: Baker Academic, 2005.

Kiesling, Christopher, OP. "Roman Catholic and Reformed Understandings of the Eucharist (with Reformed Response by Ross MacKenzie)." In *The Eucharist in Ecumenical Dialogue*, edited by Leonard Swidler, 78–86. New York: Paulist Press, 1976.

Kilmartin, Edward J. *The Eucharist in the West: History and Theology*. Collegeville, MN: Liturgical Press, 1998.

Kimel, Alvin F. "Eating Christ: Recovering the Language of Real Identification." *Pro Ecclesia* 13, no. 1 (Winter 2004): 82–100.

Lefler, Nathan. "Sign, Cause, and Person in St. Thomas's Sacramental Theology: Further Considerations." *Nova et Vetera* 4, no. 2 (2006): 381–404.

Lehmann, Karl, and Wolfhart Pannenberg, eds. *The Condemnations of the Reformation Era: Do They Still Divide?* Minneapolis: Fortress, 1990.

Leithart, Peter J. "What's Wrong with Transubstantiation? An Evaluation of Theological Models." *Westminster Theological Journal* 53 (1991): 295–324.

Levering, Matthew. *Sacrifice and Community: Jewish Offering and Christian Eucharist.* Malden, MA: Blackwell, 2005.

Levy, Ian Christopher. "The Eucharist in the Fourteenth and Fifteenth Centuries." In Boersma and Levering, *Oxford Handbook of Sacramental Theology,* 235–48.

———. *John Wyclif: Sacramental Logic, Real Presence, and the Parameters of Orthodoxy.* Marquette Studies in Theology 36. Milwaukee: Marquette University Press, 2003.

Lewis, C. S. *Letters to Malcolm: Chiefly on Prayer.* London: G. Bles, 1964.

MacKenzie, Ross. "Reformed and Roman Catholic Understandings of the Eucharist (with Roman Catholic Response by Christopher Kiesling)." In *The Eucharist in Ecumenical Dialogue,* edited by Leonard Swidler, 70–77. New York: Paulist Press, 1976.

———. "Reformed Theology and Roman Catholic Doctrine of the Eucharist as Sacrifice (with Response by Christopher Kiesling)." *Journal of Ecumenical Studies* 15, no. 3 (Summer 1978): 429–40.

Macy, Gary. *The Banquet's Wisdom: A Short History of the Theologies of the Lord's Supper.* 2nd ed. Akron: OSL Publications, 2005.

———. "The Theological Fate of Berengar's Oath of 1059: Interpreting a Blunder Become Tradition." In *Treasures from the Storeroom: Medieval Religion and the Eucharist,* 20–35. Collegeville, MN: Liturgical Press, 1999.

———. *The Theologies of the Eucharist in the Early Scholastic Period: A Study of the Salvific Function of the Sacrament according to the Theologians, c. 1080–c. 1220.* New York: Clarendon, 1984.

Marshall, Bruce D. "The Eucharistic Presence of Christ." In *What Does It Mean to "Do This"? Supper, Mass, Eucharist,* edited by Michael Root and James J. Buckley, 47–73. Eugene, OR: Cascade, 2014.

———. "What Is the Eucharist? A Dogmatic Outline." In Boersma and Levering, *Oxford Handbook of Sacramental Theology,* 500–516.

———. "The Whole Mystery of Our Salvation: Saint Thomas Aquinas on the Eucharist as Sacrifice." In *Rediscovering Aquinas and the Sacraments,* edited by Matthew Levering and Michael Dauphinais, 39–64. Chicago: Hillenbrand, 2009.

Martelet, Gustave. *The Risen Christ and the Eucharistic World*. New York: Seabury, 1976.

Mascall, E. L. "Egner on the Eucharistic Presence." *New Blackfriars* 53, no. 631 (December 1972): 539–46.

Mathison, Keith A. *Given for You: Reclaiming Calvin's Doctrine of the Lord's Supper*. Phillipsburg, NJ: P&R, 2002.

Mattox, Mickey L. "Sacraments in the Lutheran Reformation." In Boersma and Levering, *Oxford Handbook of Sacramental Theology*, 269–82.

McAdoo, H. R. "Introduction: Documents on Modern Eucharistic Agreement." In *Modern Eucharistic Agreement*, 1–21. London: SPCK, 1973.

McCabe, Herbert, OP. "The Eucharist as Language." In *God Still Matters*, 123–35. London: Continuum, 2005.

———. "Eucharistic Change." In *God Still Matters*, 115–22. London: Continuum, 2005.

———. "Sacramental Language." In *God Matters*, 165–79. London: Continuum, 2005.

———. "Transubstantiation." In *God Matters*, 146–54. London: Continuum, 2005.

———. "Transubstantiation and the Real Presence." In *God Matters*, 116–29. London: Continuum, 2005.

McCue, James F. "The Doctrine of Transubstantiation from Berengar through Trent: The Point at Issue." *Harvard Theological Review* 61, no. 3 (July 1968): 385–430.

———. "Luther and Roman Catholicism on the Mass as Sacrifice." *Journal of Ecumenical Studies* 2, no. 2 (Spring 1965): 205–33.

McIntosh, Mark A. "Christ the Word Who Makes Us: Eucharist and Creation." *Pro Ecclesia* 19, no. 3 (Summer 2010): 255–59.

McKenna, John H. *Become What You Receive: A Systematic Study of the Eucharist*. Chicago: Hillenbrand, 2011.

McPartlan, Paul. "*Ut Unum Sint*: Eucharist and Ecumenism." In *The Mystery of Faith: Reflections on the Encyclical* Ecclesia de Eucharistia, edited by James McEvoy and Maurice Hogan, 341–55. Dublin: Columba Press, 2005.

Meyer, John R. "*Mysterium Fidei* and the Later Calvin." *Scottish Journal of Theology* 25, no. 4 (November 1972): 392–411.

Milbank, John, and Catherine Pickstock. *Truth in Aquinas*. London: Routledge, 2001.

Mitchell, Nathan. *Cult and Controversy: The Worship of the Eucharist outside Mass*. New York: Pueblo, 1982.

Morerod, Charles. *Ecumenism and Philosophy: Philosophical Questions for a Renewal of Dialogue*. Ann Arbor, MI: Sapientia Press of Ave Maria University, 2006.

Muller, Richard A. "Calvin on Sacramental Presence, in the Shadow of Marburg and Zurich." *Lutheran Quarterly* 23, no. 2 (Summer 2009): 147–67.

———. "From Zürich or from Wittenberg? An Examination of Calvin's Early Eucharistic Thought." *Calvin Theological Journal* 45, no. 2 (November 2010): 243–55.

Nagel, Norman E. "The Incarnation and the Lord's Supper in Luther." *Concordia Theological Monthly* 24, no. 9 (September 1953): 625–52.

Nichols, Aidan, OP. *The Holy Eucharist: From the New Testament to Pope John Paul II.* Dublin: Veritas, 1991.

Nichols, Terence. "Transubstantiation and Eucharistic Presence." *Pro Ecclesia* 11, no. 1 (Winter 2002): 57–75.

Oberman, Heiko. *The Harvest of Medieval Theology: Gabriel Biel and Late Medieval Nominalism.* 2nd ed. Grand Rapids: Eerdmans, 1967.

O'Connor, James T. *The Hidden Manna: A Theology of the Eucharist.* San Francisco: Ignatius, 2005.

O'Gara, Margaret. "Toward the Day When We Will Keep the Feast Together." *Pro Ecclesia* 19, no. 3 (Summer 2010): 260–66.

O'Neill, Colman E., OP. *Sacramental Realism: A General Theory of the Sacraments.* Wilmington, DE: Michael Glazier, 1983.

Osborne, Thomas. "Faith, Philosophy, and the Nominalist Background to Luther's Defense of the Real Presence." *Journal of the History of Ideas* 63, no. 1 (2002): 63–82.

Pelikan, Jaroslav. *The Christian Tradition: A History of the Development of Doctrine.* Vol. 4, *Reformation of Church and Dogma (1300–1700).* Chicago: University of Chicago Press, 1984.

Pesch, Otto Hermann. *Theologie der Rechtfertigung bei Martin Luther und Thomas von Aquin: Versuch eines systematisch-theologischen Dialogs.* Mainz: Matthias Grünewald, 1967.

Peters, Edward F. "Luther and the Principle: Outside of the Use There Is No Sacrament." *Concordia Theological Monthly* 42, no. 10 (November 1971): 643–52.

Power, David N., OMI. *The Eucharistic Mystery: Revitalizing the Tradition.* New York: Crossroad, 1993.

Pruett, Gordon E. "Protestant Doctrine of the Eucharistic Presence." *Calvin Theological Journal* 10, no. 2 (November 1975): 142–74.

Puosi, Eric. "Ecclesiastical Communion: In Dialogue with Calvinism." In *Ecumenism Today: The Universal Church in the 21st Century*, edited by Francesca Aran Murphy and Christopher Asprey, 183–200. Aldershot, UK: Ashgate, 2008.

Quere, Ralph W. "Changes and Constants: Structure in Luther's Understanding of the Real Presence in the 1520's." *Sixteenth Century Journal* 16, no. 1 (Spring 1985): 45–78.

Rahner, Karl, SJ. *The Church and the Sacraments.* Translated by W. J. O'Hara. New edition. London: Burns & Oates, 1974.

———. "On the Duration of the Presence of Christ after Communion." In *Theological Investigations IV: More Recent Writings*, 312–20. Baltimore: Helicon, 1966.

———. "The Presence of Christ in the Sacrament of the Lord's Supper." In *Theological Investigations IV: More Recent Writings*, 287–311. Baltimore: Helicon, 1966.

———. "The Word and the Eucharist." In *Theological Investigations IV: More Recent Writings*, 253–86. Baltimore: Helicon, 1966.

Rorem, Paul. "The Consensus Tigurinus (1549): Did Calvin Compromise?" In *Calvinus Sacrae Scripturae Professor*, edited by Wilhelm H. Neuser, 72–90. Grand Rapids: Eerdmans, 1994.

Salkeld, Brett. "A Catholic Perspective on Salvation." *One in Christ* 46, no. 1 (2012): 72–78.

Sasse, Hermann. *This Is My Body: Luther's Contention for the Real Presence in the Sacrament of the Altar*. Minneapolis: Augsburg, 1959.

Scampini, Jorge A. "The Sacraments in Ecumenical Dialogue." In Boersma and Levering, *Oxford Handbook of Sacramental Theology*, 675–91.

Scheeben, Matthias Joseph. *The Mysteries of Christianity*. Translated by Cyril O. Vollert. St. Louis: Herder, 1946.

Schillebeeckx, Edward, OP. *Christ the Sacrament of the Encounter with God*. London: Sheed & Ward, 1987.

———. *The Eucharist*. London: Sheed & Ward, 1968.

———. "Transubstantiation, Transfinalization, Transfiguration." *Worship* 40, no. 6 (1966): 324–38.

Schmemann, Alexander. *The Eucharist: Sacrament of the Kingdom*. Crestwood, NY: St. Vladimir's Seminary Press, 1987.

Selvaggi, Filippo, SJ. "Il concetto di sostanza nel dogma eucaristico in relazione alla fisica moderna." *Gregorianum* 30 (1949): 17–45.

Sheed, Frank. *Theology and Sanity*. Reprint. San Francisco: Ignatius, 1993.

Smit, Laura. "'The Depth behind Things': Toward a Calvinist Sacramental Theology." In *Radical Orthodoxy and the Reformed Tradition*, edited by James K. A. Smith and James H. Olthuis, 205–27. Grand Rapids: Baker Academic, 2005.

Smith, James K. A. *Introducing Radical Orthodoxy: Mapping a Post-secular Theology*. Grand Rapids: Baker Academic, 2004.

Sokolowski, Robert. "The Eucharist and Transubstantiation." In *Christian Faith and Human Understanding: Studies on the Eucharist, Trinity, and the Human Person*. Washington, DC: Catholic University of America Press, 2006.

———. *Eucharistic Presence: A Study in the Theology of Disclosure*. Washington, DC: Catholic University of America Press, 1994.

Steinmetz, David C. "Calvin and His Lutheran Critics." In *Calvin in Context*, 179–94. Oxford: Oxford University Press, 1995.

———. "The Catholic Luther: A Critical Reappraisal." *Theology Today* 61 (2004): 187–201.

———. "Luther among the Anti-Thomists." In *Luther in Context*, 47–58. Grand Rapids: Baker, 1995.

———. "Scripture and the Lord's Supper in Luther's Theology." *Interpretation* 37, no. 3 (July 1983): 253–65.

Stephenson, John R. *The Lord's Supper.* Confessional Lutheran Dogmatics XII. St. Louis: The Luther Academy, 2003.

Sullivan, Francis A. "The Vatican Response to ARCIC-I." *One in Christ* 28 (1992): 223–31.

Tabbernee, William. "BEM and the Eucharist: A Case Study in Ecumenical Hermeneutics." In *Interpreting Together: Essays in Hermeneutics*, edited by Peter Bouteneff and Dagmar Heller, 19–46. Geneva: WCC Publications, 2001.

Thompson, Mark D. "Claritas Scripturae in the Eucharistic Writings of Martin Luther." *Westminster Theological Journal* 60, no. 1 (Spring 1998): 23–41.

Tillard, J. M. R., OP. "The Eucharist as the Bread and Sign of Brotherhood, Part 3." *Emmanuel* 81, no. 5 (1975): 204–12.

———. "Reflections on the Real Presence and Encountering the Lord in the Eucharist, Part 1." *Emmanuel* 81, no. 3 (1975): 106–13.

———. "Reflections on the Real Presence and Encountering the Lord in the Eucharist, Part 2." *Emmanuel* 81, no. 4 (1975): 156–63.

———. "Roman Catholics and Anglicans: The Eucharist." *One in Christ* 9, no. 2 (1973): 131–93.

Tinker, Melvin. "Language, Symbols and Sacraments: Was Calvin's View of the Lord's Supper Right?" *Churchman* 112, no. 2 (1998): 131–49.

Tylenda, Joseph N. "Calvin and Christ's Presence in the Supper—True or Real." *Scottish Journal of Theology* 27, no. 1 (February 1974): 65–75.

———. "The Calvin-Westphal Exchange: The Genesis of Calvin's Treatises against Westphal." *Calvin Theological Journal* 9, no. 2 (November 1974): 182–209.

———. "The Ecumenical Intention of Calvin's Early Eucharistic Teaching." In *Reformatio Perennis: Essays on Calvin and the Reformation in Honor of Ford Lewis Battles*, edited by Brian A. Gerrish, 27–47. Pittsburgh: Pickwick, 1981.

Vaillancourt, Mark G. "Sacramental Theology from Gottschalk to Lanfranc." In Boersma and Levering, *Oxford Handbook of Sacramental Theology*, 187–200.

Van Dyk, Leanne. "The Reformed View." In *The Lord's Supper: Five Views*, edited by Gordon T. Smith, 67–82. Downers Grove, IL: IVP Academic, 2008.

VanderWilt, Jeffrey T. *A Church without Borders: The Eucharist and the Church in Ecumenical Perspective.* Collegeville, MN: Liturgical Press, 1998.

Vollert, Cyril. "The Eucharist: Controversy on Transubstantiation." *Theological Studies* 22, no. 3 (1961): 391–425.

Vos, Arvin. *Aquinas, Calvin, and Contemporary Protestant Thought: A Critique of Protestant Views on the Thought of Thomas Aquinas*. Grand Rapids: Eerdmans, 1985.

Wainwright, Geoffrey. "The Eucharist in the Churches' Responses to the Lima Text." *One in Christ* 25, no. 1 (1989): 53–74.

Walsh, Liam G., OP. "The Divine and the Human in St. Thomas's Theology of Sacraments." In *Ordo Sapientiae et Amoris: Image et Message de Saint Thomas d'Aquin à Travers les Récentes Études Historiques, Herméneutiques et Doctrinales*, 321–52. Fribourg: Éditions Universitaires Fribourg Suisse, 1993.

————. "An Ecumenical Reading of Aquinas on the Eucharist." In *Liturgia et Unitas*, edited by M. Klöckener and A. Join-Lambert, 226–40. Freiburg: Universitätsverlag Freiburg Schweiz, 2001.

————. *Sacraments of Initiation: A Theology of Life, Word, and Rite*. 2nd ed. Chicago: Hillenbrand, 2011.

————. *The Sacraments of Initiation: Baptism, Confirmation, Eucharist*. London: Chapman, 1988.

Wawrykow, Joseph. "Luther and the Spirituality of Thomas Aquinas." *Consensus* 19, no. 1 (1993): 77–107.

————. "The Sacraments in Thirteenth-Century Theology." In Boersma and Levering, *Oxford Handbook of Sacramental Theology*, 218–34.

Williams, R. R. "Agreements: Their Sources and Frontiers." In *A Critique of Eucharistic Agreement*, 9–23. London: SPCK, 1975.

Willis, David. "Calvin's Use of Substantia." In *Calvinus Ecclesiae Genevensis Custos*, edited by Wilhelm H. Neuser, 289–301. Frankfurt am Main: Peter Lang, 1984.

————. "A Reformed Doctrine of the Eucharist and Ministry and Its Implications for Roman Catholic Dialogues." *Journal of Ecumenical Studies* 21, no. 2 (Spring 1984): 295–309.

Zachman, Randall C. "Revising the Reform: What Calvin Learned from Dialogue with the Roman Catholics." In *John Calvin and Roman Catholicism: Critique and Engagement, Then and Now*, 165–91. Grand Rapids: Baker Academic, 2008.

Author Index

Subject Index

accidents
  and Aristotle, 79, 81, 83
  and bread and wine, 111, 182, 184, 243
  and Calvin, 200, 202
  and change, 34n110, 113
  and Luther, 2–3, 146–47, 149
  and Thomas, 48, 50, 52, 84, 87, 93n177, 94,
    104–6, 114, 115–16, 118–20, 134, 173, 201
  See also substance
Agreed Statement on Eucharistic Doctrine, 19
agreement. *See* ecumenism: and agreement
Alger of Liège, 69
Ambrose, 59, 126
analogia entis, 41–43
anamnesis, 10, 12–14, 16, 23, 27
Anglican–Roman Catholic International Commission (ARCIC), 8, 18–19, 22, 25, 28. *See
  also listing in author index*
Aristotle/Aristotelianism, 42, 48, 67, 78–85, 93,
  96, 99, 115–17, 147
articles of faith, 2, 76, 145nn17–18, 241
Augustine, 41n137, 59, 60, 62, 63, 66n57, 72,
  91n169, 95, 129, 132n311, 141, 152, 172–73,
  174n141, 176n149, 182, 184, 198n61, 203,
  203n85, 205, 216

Babylonian Captivity of the Church, The (Luther), xii, 1, 143, 145, 147, 177, 178, 180
Bandinelli, Roland, 70
baptism, 88, 132
Baptism, Eucharist, and Ministry (BEM), 8–10,
  12–13, 16, 18, 26–30
becoming, 18–21

being, 40–41, 44–45, 117
Berengarius, 36, 48, 49, 62–74, 121, 122, 140,
  143, 182, 187
"Best Method of Obtaining Concord, The"
  (Calvin), 203n89, 227, 237
*Blessed Sacrament of the Holy and True Body
  of Christ, and the Brotherhoods* (Luther),
  141
bread, 96–98, 110, 111, 116, 185–86
Bullinger, Heinrich, 188, 188nn5–6, 191, 208–9,
  208n112, 209n114, 213, 215n145

Calvin, John
  and accidents, 202
  and annihilation, 202
  and ascension, 206–7, 211–14, 216–19
  and benefits of Christ, 231, 233, 234, 237
  and Bullinger, 209
  and Christ, 203–7, 211–20, 231, 233, 234, 238
  and Church Fathers, 4
  and controversy, 188–89
  and descent of Christ, 214–16, 218–19
  and elements, 4–5
  and eschatology, 220–21
  and Eucharist, 193, 195, 224–25
  and God, 208–10
  heaven, 211–13, 215, 217
  and Holy Spirit, 223–27, 229
  and instruments, sacraments as, 208–11
  and law, 230, 231
  and Lord's Supper, 197, 231
  and Luther, 188, 194, 195, 206, 218, 226–27

Printed and bound by CPI Group (UK) Ltd, Croydon, CR0 4YY

13/04/2025

14656461-0001